The
Night
Sky

The Night Sky

RICHARD GROSSINGER

Sierra
Club
Books
San Francisco

THE SIERRA CLUB, founded in 1892 by John Muir, has devoted itself to the study and protection of the earth's scenic and ecological resources—mountains, wetlands, woodlands, wild shores and rivers, deserts and plains. The publishing program of the Sierra Club offers books to the public as a nonprofit educational service in the hope that they may enlarge the public's understanding of the Club's basic concerns. The point of view expressed in each book, however, does not necessarily represent that of the Club. The Sierra Club has some fifty chapters coast to coast, in Canada, Hawaii, and Alaska. For information about how you may participate in its programs to preserve wilderness and the quality of life, please address inquiries to Sierra Club, 530 Bush Street, San Francisco, CA 94108.

Library of Congress Cataloging in Publication Data

Grossinger, Richard, 1944-
    The night sky.

    Bibliography: p. 449
    Includes index.
    1. Astronomy—Popular works.   I. Title.
QB44.2.G765   520   81-5293
ISBN 0-87156-288-X   AACR2

Jacket design by Fred Marcellino
Book design by Wolfgang Lederer
Printed in the United States of America
10 9 8 7 6 5 4 3 2 1

For Richard Crowne, Roy Whong,
Ginny Stangeland Johnson,
Abdisalam Y Mohammed, and those
other shadows who lie behind
this book; and for Robin and Miranda
in the year 2000.

Acknowledgments

Grateful acknowledgment is made to the following poets for permission to reprint selections from their work:

James Bogan: from "Rhapsody for McCoy Tyner," quoted from manuscript.

Edward Dorn: "This is the way I hear the Momentum," copyright © 1969.

Robert Duncan: from the dream of April 24, 1963, in *The H.D. Book,* Part 2/Chapter 3, quoted from manuscript.

Robert Kelly: from "The Alchemist," copyright © 1961, and "Re: The Occult," copyright © 1964.

Gary Snyder: from "The Manicheans," copyright © 1960.

Contents

But our present earth may have been repeated a billion times. Why, it's become extinct, been frozen; cracked, broken to bits, disintegrated into its elements, again "the water above the firmament," then again a comet, again a sun, again from the sun it becomes earth—and the same sequence may have been repeated endlessly and exactly the same to every detail . . . . .

FYODOR DOSTOEVSKY, *The Brothers Karamazov*,
translated by Constance Garnett

Because we cannot penetrate directly to lower worlds, we do not guess what blinding disintegration, explosion and ecstatic fusion the oxygen of our breath brings to the molecules of blood. But for ourselves we realize that this shock which separates the end of one life from the beginning of the next, which severs essence from the corpse and launches it back into the seed, is the most tremendous which a human being is called upon to face. In fact, it is too strong for ordinary man, who has *no choice* but to forget and fall asleep.

RODNEY COLLIN, *The Theory of Celestial Influence*

Above us, only sky.   JOHN LENNON, *Imagine*

Preface

THE NIGHT SKY is a book about the stars, the planets, and the creation—that is, about the attempt of our species to locate itself in the vast universe in which it has arisen. It is an account of the various myths, sciences, and other systems that have developed over the several million nights of our brief sojourn in this physical cosmos.

Each creature experiences itself as alive and perceives the abundant nature all around it. Existence has no implicit meaning and no explanation. Meaning comes into being only through living animals themselves and as part of the mystery of their life. It is as originless and boundaryless as the universe; in fact, it is coterminous with the universe. The night sky is an irrevocable statement of this condition. It gathers infinity into a radiant field and envelops the Earth. It is at once the most blatant clue to the origin of all this and the shroud which negates any possible resolution and leads every trail into wilderness. The night sky expresses the order and cohesiveness of the creation, but also its chaos and arbitrariness. The constellations were one of our species' first attempts to impose its own order and meaning onto the impinging randomness of nature. All astronomical systems repeat the desperation and peril of this initial act.

We are beings who require a context for each little thing we do but have no context for the whole big thing. This is the primary disturbance within human society and the force that drives us through structures and symbols in search of an impossible resolution. We are a process in coming to terms with the night sky and its implications. We may ignore it consciously, but this does not change the fact. When we stare into it, we feel the chilling brevity and smallness of life, but we also feel the something else that feels that. It is this second thing that makes all the rest possible and to which this book speaks.

The modern universe may be random and disordered, but it is also exquisitely interrelated and connected down to the minutest layer. Astral mythology and magic reflected this symbolically and sympathetically; later astrophysics has shown that all matter obeys the same laws—that the stars appear where they do for the reason that the wind blows, the grasses sprout, and cells divide. These laws are more than inviolable. They are the basis for a physical universe whose manifestation then falls into their only domain. In criticizing modern astrophysics for its moral and spiritual emptiness, we must not forget that it also gives us a magical sense of how humble and obscure animals arose, magnificently and unexpectedly, from the bare primal complexities of raw atoms to stand presently among the stars in a condition of consciousness and observation. This, in many ways, is more spiritual than the various dead theological versions of creation by an external deity or force.

This is an astronomy book not because the structure of stars and planets or the physics and geography of the heavens are its main subjects but because they stand both functionally and symbolically for its actual subject: the creation. Although everything we know and experience is the creation, the stars come closest to providing a context for all the rest. They are the eternal perceptible manifestation of unity and infinity in concordance. The venous patterns on a maple leaf, the thousands of insect larvae in a cocoon, the interstices of frost on glass or limestone in a cave, the webs of Spinoza, the flashes of Proust, the harmonies of Johann Bach, the dreams of Sun Chief all stand in correspondence to star-stuff, and all ostensibly originate from it in the fine rare pulp of the planets.

This book does not favor the night sky above these other replicas, but it does set its unity, amplitude, and originary qualities as yardsticks for the rest. In a black sea of discrete incandescent entities and luminous dust, we were born. Or this is how we come to comprehend it.

Earth and sky are inseparable. In ancient myth and cosmogony, their single body cleaved and differentiated. In modern science and astrophysics, there is no world outside of night; the starry field is a two-dimensional illusion. We now know that the tides, the winds, and the glaciers are star effects. Flowers, worms, and honeybees also reflect the night. All share its texture, light, and gravitational unity.

Deep within matter, the shape of the sky is repeated. There is a void sparsely filled with tiny nuclei and their orbital systems. These are stars, and the atomic microcosm is their night. Nuclear forces incorporate stellar gravitational fields while providing their substance in minute packets of which there are enough for a physical universe. Matter differentiates from and also builds upon itself in a network from the minute to the massive. No part of it is ever out of touch with the rest of it. Furthermore, infinity may have once been contained in a subatomic space from which it continues to propel outward across all dimensions. The night sky thus stretches from a microcosm to eternity. We see but one "night." We contain others, and still others pile up beyond our range.

Poetry, philosophy, government, and industry are all stellar phenomena. Our bodies and minds are star fabric material, and they occur in the phenomenological context of starfields. That we know the stars *is* the stars. Somewhere in that paradox and mystery is our destiny.

What makes this book larger in scope than most astronomy books is that it expresses the fundamental dichotomy of the creation (or universe) and the incarnation (or our existence in and of that universe). In any true astronomy, these are the same phenomenon and must be understood in terms of each other.

Science unwittingly misleads us. We can certainly explore the stars and the planets with instruments. We can know the physics of materials on Earth and can study elements, molecules, atoms, and subatomic particles with a high degree of refinement. We can understand the mechanism by which life propagates and the laws by which diverse living systems come into being. Embryology and astrophysics are subtle, complex, and progressive self-critical systems. So are psychology, anthropology, and linguistics.

We know a great deal about what is around us, what we are, how we interact, and how we perceive, cognize, and express the nature of things. But for all this, we cannot know and express the creationary event. We can only manifest it.

As important as astronomy and physics are in our knowledge of the creation, they must finally be satisfied with limited territories, any grasping outside of which distorts them. They are most distorted when they pretend to get to the bottom of things. The great physicists, like Newton and Einstein, laughed at the delusion that such was even possible. They were delighted to know anything at all.

To find the stars outside of stellar science, we must explore ancient myth, theogony, ethnoastronomy, astrogeny, interior astronomy, astromancy, and astrology. These systems are not scientific by contemporary standards, but we do not ask of them a description of the scientific universe. In cross-cultural anthropology we can use their structural and historic relationship to our own science to define hidden elements of it. And we can take them on their own terms as expressions of the creation by creatures within it.

We have images of galaxies, electrons, and atomic nuclei. Prior to them, we had other images, which led us to develop instruments by which we see these new and present ones. Non-Western and tribal peoples have had their own images: of spirit forces, gods and goddesses, divine energies, totem stars, astral realms, karma, stellar sentience, and star-incarnated shapes. Their explanations for how we got here are expressed in totemic and mythological codes and enacted and reexperienced in ceremonies, vision-quests, and meditation. The pre-Columbian American Indians did not know about quasars, atoms, or embryonic meiosis, but that does not mean that they did not experience the universe from within and come to some unique and accurate conception of its nature. Science may give us facts about the interactions of physical systems, facts crucial to an overall knowledge of the night sky, but ethnoastronomy and astrology give us facts about the riddles of creation and incarnation, facts which are not only inaccessible to science as it is currently practiced but which are contained in other forms within its fundamental structure because of our history and phylogeny.

So astronomy is born of the occult and requires it to make conscious its own language and instrumentation. We ourselves are born of unknown forces that we explore intuitively every day. The creation encompasses all of these modes, and the incarnation literally incarnates them, in our species and in the long evolutionary chain of plant and animal life.

What this book is about, since it cannot be about the creationary event, is the means we have of imaging the wholeness and complexity and mystery of what we are. It is a history, an anthropology, and an epistemology of stellar systems. The images we have of the formation of the universe determine the types of values we have, the societies we develop, and the moralities and aesthetics by which we live. How we think we came into being is who we think we are. And this was never in deeper crisis than in the present—when we know, it seems, too much, and knowledge itself has become fragmented and debased. We can criticize the ignorance of our ancestors, but we have covered ourselves in a new ignorance.

Clearly we know something that we call "the stars" and "the creation." But then there is something we do not know and cannot know. If we did, there would already be millions of books on it, or books on it would be totally unnecessary, and probably *we* would be unnecessary too. Because we don't know it and because we don't face it squarely and unblinkingly through the increasing layers of bigness that are imagistically provided out of our present knowing of something, there are no books on it. This is a primitive attempt at such a book—a book about our struggle to know something which is unknowable, using the stars as our measure and guide. That struggle shapes our lives and our society. But what is the thing that gets described instead of the creation, and by what distortion?

This book shifts from one system of creationary events to another. None of them can be wholly right, but none of them is wrong either, for all are part of the universe and reflect it from within. What makes a particular system or image more or less interesting is how it engages us in understanding our own coming to be in this pool of light, how it somehow parts time to give us a glimpse of the beginning which our being contains. From these single images and their interaction, we can regain the bigness and the unity which modern astronomy has stolen from us, and we can use the fruits of modern astronomy as crucial antidotes to its own poison. In fact, we *must* use them, for we have brought them into being, and if we do not swallow and transform them, they will surely swallow and transform us.

Throughout this narrative, I have tried to encompass and beat back the infinity and to work against the nihilism it proposes. The modern materialist universe has no place for us, and we would be fools to try to survive in it. We must assault it in its own terms, and not from any false idealistic ground. Eventually it will crumble anyway; but unless we are active in making a new universe, it will leave us only with ravaged fields. We must stare down the shafts of infinity; we must enter the violence and the emptiness, experience them in ourselves, and transform them into something livable. I have tried to prove, in some small way, that this is possible, that it is a human thing and not one of *their* things. Coming to terms with it is coming to terms with ourselves as much as with the seeming physical fact of the universe.

To this point, the astronomical and spiritual universes have both failed us. It does little good anymore to accept uncritically a vitalist universe in which spirit is always present in matter. The conviction of spirit must still be reconciled with the constancy and intricacy of the physical manifestation. The ambiguities of quantum theory and the resulting taos of astronomy merely pose a limited and idealized view of the dilemma. To claim a cosmic dance on false or apostate grounds is to remove us even further from the possibility of such a dance. In writing this book, I found the crisis of faith almost unbearable. It was certainly more than I had counted on. Not only was there no easy way in which to confront the spiritual/material dichotomy, but the very posing of such a dichotomy seemed to be an evasion of some more fundamental truth, some other unknown pattern hidden in the material.

At first, the imposition of a vital force behind the physical agency of creation seems to provide a spiritual alternative to a purely mechanical evolution. On closer inspection, however, vital forces come to look like fictitious mechanical devices, and they cannot be naively slipped into creation without betraying spiritualism too. Linguistic philosophers, conceptual artists, and grammatologists all provide models that locate the true complexity in ourselves. The models are not particularly starry or creationary, but this tells us that the universe lies closer to our disjunctures and paradoxes, especially in symbolic processes, than to our cybernetic replicas of remote galaxies. The formal elegance, however, betrays our emotional and psychic connection to the universe, and our need to make things conscious and visible. It is brilliant, but in the face of the great danger and crisis of incarnation, it comes to feel like pretense and dilettantish dabbling. Finally, it was very difficult to find a mode of astronomical analysis that satisfied even the conflicting positions in myself. Again and again I saw, across the surface fabric of my work, nothing but mind games and intellectual pieties, and it hardly mattered whether these were physical or spiritual in their bias. I had to transcend these without submerging the book in a lyrical muddiness.

Against the simple universe of the narrative of this text, with all its spiritual and physical variants, another universe breaches, shadowy and incomplete, and through it, another, fragmentary and illogical. These universes engage with the problem of language itself, and they must be allowed to distort the righteousness of the text. The occult sky and the physical sky must interfere with each other and create the rough edges of an unknown cosmology. Otherwise I must side with either the eternal archetypes of the astrologers and star magicians or the progressive scientism of the professional astronomers, or pretend to syncretize them in New Age jive.

In the end, I am probably guilty of exactly such a rapprochement. Astrology, science fiction, ethnoastronomy, astrophysics, linguistics, and New Age thought all merge in this book, for I hope to speak to the practitioners of each of these arts. But I also intend to propose an unknown direction, a direction unknown even to myself. Astrology and astronomy both cast falsely confident smiles over the great unknown soul of being, but they are modes that we can use en route to new systems of thought for which our age is the true midwife.

A good portion of this book is simply a history of Western astronomy from the time of Copernicus to the present, with an emphasis on overall philosophical and civilizational issues. Other chapters explore occult astronomy, the astral sky, star myth, ethnoastronomy, ancient astronomy, astrology, flying saucers, extraterrestrial life, and science fiction themes. There are also sections on viewing the night sky, the politics and sociology of stellar images, star dreams, the space program, the cognitive and linguistic issues of night sky systemization, and star themes in popular American culture.

In the way that Herman Melville "violated" the structure of the nineteenth-century novel to say everything there was to say about whales (while still writing a novel), I have redefined the format of the twentieth-century science/anthropology book to show the many contexts, both objective and subjective, in which stars occur in our culture—from the broad exterior heavens to the myriad internalized skies and asterisms. It is a sixteenth-century view of the universe reconceived in terms of twentieth-century structural anthropology, Freudian linguistics, and Oriental metaphysics. As the French historian Michel Foucault said in writing of the naturalist Aldrovandi and his contemporaries:

> When one has the story of an animal to tell, it is useless and impossible to choose between the role of a naturalist and that of an anthologist: in one and the same form of knowledge must be gathered all that has been *seen* and *heard,* all that has been related by nature or by men in the language of the world, of tradition, or of poets. To know a beast, or a plant, or anything from the earth is to collect the whole thick layer of signs that have been deposited in them or on them; it is to recover all the constellations of forms when they take on the characteristic of emblems.[1]

Aldrovandi's list of topics for a chapter on serpents in his natural history is the forerunner of my own table of contents on stars:

Equivocation (the different senses in which the word *ser-pent* can be used), synonyms and etymologies, differences, form and description, anatomy, character and habitats, temperament, sex and reproduction, voice, movements, places, food, physiognomy, antipathy, sympathy, ways to catch, death and wounds by the serpent, methods and signs of poisoning, remedies, epithets, designations, marvels and omens, monsters, mythology, gods to which he is consecrated, fables, allegories and mysteries, hieroglyphics, emblems and symbols, adages, coins, miracles, enigmas, devices, heraldic signs, deeds, dreams, reproductions and statues, uses as food, uses in medicine, diverse uses.[2]

Foucault concludes that "nature, itself, is a seamless fabric of words and marks, of stories and letters, of discourses and forms. . . . There can be no commentary unless beneath the text that one reads and explicates, runs the sovereignty of an original Text."[3]

As we have attempted to move deeper into the heavens, we have gone back through our own historical and linguistic conceptions of star terminology—so that the origin of time and space at the quasar disintegrates into the origin of star terminology and the human mystery in the Old Stone Age.

This is the second book in a series currently planned as three. Each book stands alone and contains no specific references to the others, but the series, as it is assembled, contains a second subject matter beneath the surface, which develops as the overall themes and meanings change. The first book, *Planet Medicine: From Stone-Age Shamanism to Post-Industrial Healing* (Doubleday Anchor, 1980), dealt with the history and anthropology of healing, including ancient medicine, non-Western therapeutics, and the origins of contemporary holistic health. Insofar as it was explicitly an exploration of medicine and the second book is a history of star-viewing and astronomical images, there is no connection. However, on the deeper level, *Planet Medicine* asks the following questions: What is mind? What is body? How are they joined? What is health? What is disease? How does a cure work? How do the definitions and meanings of health, disease, and cure change historically and from culture to culture?

Planet Medicine is based on the perception that ancient medical systems and healing methods from other cultures can never be recovered. They can only be invented anew—by anthropologists, who give us their partial and external versions of internal systems as they perceive them, and by radical healers, who rediscover ancient principles in the open context of their own work.

In *The Night Sky,* the opening questions are: What is matter? What is the universe? How does life come to be? And who are we?

These touch upon unasked questions in *Planet Medicine:* How do we have such histories, bodies, and minds? And what is the cosmic source of the life-energy that lies behind all vitalistic healing systems, Western, Oriental, and tribal? *Planet Medicine* must necessarily define the cure and life in human terms. *The Night Sky* redefines life in the universe at large within the limits that the universe places on human meaning and development.

It is a mistake, though, to think that *The Night Sky* provides an external context for *Planet Medicine* and is bigger and more cosmic. If the titles were switched, each book would reveal a new aspect of the conceit under which the other was written.

Both of these are pieces of writing, books. One is not a disease or a medicine, and the other is not itself the sky. Insofar as they belong to the same period of American literature and come from the same author, they share territories, themes, and meanings, and are interwoven with each other. Neither one can have a bigger territory.

To the unknown malaise that confronts us, both are medicines. The first is a medicine that discusses healing; the second is a medicine that discusses our imaging of the night sky and the stars. The actual disease is beyond both books, and each is written as an act of healing—self-healing and community healing. They ask the reader to be active, to reach to the same levels of paradox and disquiet in himself or herself, and to work with the text in making a curative act of vision.

Modern science has concluded that we are the minutest fleck of scum within an expanding atom, and that the "vastness" of the night sky is simply the innards of that atom strewn through hollow and warped space-time and composed in centers of gravity. We are dust motes upon eternity, specks of chemical texture in a puddle, held to a large molten stone which itself is a dot in the pool of debris. No wonder we are also the poor specimen in whom modern medicine diagnoses and discovers discrete diseases from mere random somatic interference. Even so-called genetic illness is external, for it comes from arbitrary disorder in the genes and not from within the organism's personal process. In such a universe, diseases must be as meteors, and the only cure for them is physical and mechanical manipulation. No one denies that all is internal to the cosmos, but it is now a barren internality of subsurfaces. The old medicines are discarded with the old systems of astronomy, and the New Age holistic sciences are vilified as fantasies and deceptions. In either case, the universe is dead, and its sprat are minute robots.

While *Planet Medicine* precedes *The Night Sky* in my own development of these themes, I actually began exploring astronomy far earlier in my life. It was a childhood interest, and I did more writing on stars, planets, flying saucers, and science fiction than on medicine right up to my research and writing for *Planet Medicine.*

The underlying medicinal theme of both books explains the order of their writing: unconsciously, I perceived the need for curative activity and radical personal change before continued exploration of cosmic issues. The culture also requires inner transformation, or all space exploration will be sterile and disappointing. The universe presented to us by NASA scientists and "image teams" and self-aggrandizing media astronomers is simply not satisfactory. There is nothing wrong with their data, but the universe they promote is a symptom of our cultural disease. Their superstar demands are no different from those of baseball players or politicians or Las Vegas performers; the only additional problem is that they mislead themselves into thinking that the neutrality of science protects them. But it does not. We are sold their unexamined social images, including macho and capitalist roles, along with outer space and the stars. We still await a creative public astronomy.

My own order was to confront the starry abstraction first within my own being: as a deeper breathing, an ability to move through conscious pain, and a dream within dreaming. Then it was necessary to test this medicinal insight against the vastness of the stars. In our dilemma, a commitment to healing must precede and then engulf the night sky. We must literally flood it with homeopathic remedies and *chi* flow, with color therapy and chanting. It is alone the power of the infinitesimal, the microdose, projected into infinity, that can cure the expanding universe, or heal us of its plague.

For a time, I did not realize this, and I was planning to do only a series of medicine books. In fact, for months I had been planning a second book on medicine called *The New Healers* when I realized that the true sequel to *Planet Medicine* was a book of a wholly different order. This book must then stand for the "New Healers" in their place.

The change came and *The Night Sky* began on March 5, 1979, with the transmission of photographs from the planet Jupiter and its moon Io by Voyager I. My own relationship to Io the moon goes back to 1964, when I named a journal after it based on the sense of remoteness and mystery of that planetary body. Prior to that, it had been my favorite moon name in childhood; and as a teenager, I had used it in stories and poems. *Io* (the journal) explored mythical, anthropological, literary, and scientific themes, and became known in Whole Earth circles during the late 1960s and early 1970s, though few people understood that it was named after the moon rather than the goddess. A pictograph of Io and Jupiter appeared on the cover of the very first issue, but that was long out of print by the time the journal became popular.

In 1968, I was preparing an ethnoastronomy issue in Ann Arbor, Michigan, and was seeking a source for information on quasars, pulsars, and the planets. An archaeologist led me to a radio astronomer named Fred Haddock, but he was interested in writing an article only when he thought I was the editor of a scientific publication. When he realized that it was a journal of literature and myth, he declined. Out of politeness, though, he asked me the name of the journal, and when I told him, he was visibly startled. Io the moon was the body in the Solar System that interested him the most as a radio astronomer because of its effect in intensifying radio emissions from Jupiter. Not only was he responsive, but he provided great amounts of previously unpublished material on Io, and sent copies of the issue to astronomers all over the world.

At the time of its publication, the issue went virtually unread locally; but many years later, after I moved to northern New England, the journal picked up a following in Ann Arbor, and countercultural emissaries went to find this unsung hero of a back issue and eventually convinced him to teach an astronomy course in the experimental branch of the University of Michigan.

Many years later, I returned to Ann Arbor and found Dr. Haddock a new man. His lifestyle had changed, and by 1980 he was a bearded sage talking about interior visioning of archetypes and building a solar-heated house outside town. He might have been transformed anyway, but in some synchronous sense Io moved him.

When I saw those pictures from the real Io flashed across the TV screen, I felt the prophetic mystery and awe of that unknown world. Twenty years earlier, I had written poems about it, not expecting that it would be photographed in my lifetime. Fifteen years earlier, I had named a journal after it and seen the name fulfilled in one major synchronicity and several minor ones with either the goddess or the moth. Now it was on the front page of the *New York Times,* and in the following months it appeared on the cover of *Time, Newsweek,* and many scientific journals. It was the moon of the year, if not the century. I understood almost immediately that the stars had come before radical medicine, and that they now had to be reclaimed; and that afternoon, while doing deep-breath Lomi work with Polly Gamble (to whom *Planet Medicine* was dedicated), I began *The Night Sky* in my mind. Or it began there despite her directive to empty my mind of thoughts. As I did, it was waiting.

I began the outline that evening and worked on it for a month and then again in the summer. From an outline and rough draft, the book itself was written from November 1979 through September 1980, with some rewriting in December 1980 and January 1981.

I did not plan on a series of books when I began *Planet Medicine,* nor did I think *The Night Sky* would open further territory. In fact, the scope of this book seems to defy the possibility of going on. However, each book also expresses one pole of an unknown polarity, and through the writing of the book, the other pole becomes visible. The nature of the hidden shape behind this process is so complex that it will continue to generate poles, no matter how complete the text appears at any point. My hope now is to contain this shape in a trilogy and to bend the loose ends back into the circle of three books.

The stars and galaxies lie at our external limits. At the opposite pole, billions of creatures (among them, ourselves) struggle into being to experience lives their bodies and minds create. In the next book, I will explore the plants and animals of the Earth—not in the singular context of the cosmos but in the existential mystery of their own unsummoned shapes. The material of this book will include: the oceans and the beginning of life; the genetic code and embryology; sexuality and the nature of man and woman; and then the entire realm of unconscious thought, especially symbols, the origin of language, and dreams. The unexplored infinity without will give rise to an equally fundamental infinity from within.

Richard Grossinger

Richmond, California

October 1980–March 1981

My special thanks to John Brockman and Daniel Moses for making possible not only this book but the best book possible under the circumstances; to Charles Stein for twenty years of star dialogue that informs so much of this writing; to Robert Kelly for teaching me about the planets; to Jule Eisenbud for asking hard questions about stars, years before this book was begun; to William Lonsdale for his insight into the zodiac; to Geoff Young for the enthusiasm of his star visions in the desert; to Marty Bickman for his help on science fiction; to Willie Riser for playing the star jazz; to Leon Salanave for his scientific criticism; to Ken Wilson of the Morrison Planetarium in San Francisco for his astronomical information and corrections; to Paul Weisser for his thorough and astute editing of the manuscript; to Bob Callahan and Michael Palmer for hearing out the arguments of this book and giving me new language and feedback; and to Abdul Ahad for the closing image in the book.

The
Night
Sky

I

The Night Sky

SPRING IMAGINE YOURSELF on a road leading
out of the village. It is a clear moonless night. The land is a
mixture of blindness and shadows with a few smudges of man-
made light. Against your skin the breeze awakens memories
brighter than daylight.

> *This is not the start of a mystery novel.*
> *But it is.*
> *The mystery is eternal and goes on generation after gen-*
> *eration unsolved. Hundreds of detectives lie in cemeteries*
> *on a planet in a system of planets. Newborn frogs appear*
> *on the margin of the pond, in the fresh weed. They are*
> *suspects too. And they are agents . . . spies.*
> *Who brought these creatures here to enact this episode?*
> *Do they know how moist and dark it feels inside?*

You stand alone and solitary, against the bigness of time, the
bigness of space. The sky is more than a visible plane. It is a
black translucent sea on whose edge you hang upside down—
filled with stars beyond number and beyond comprehension.
The Pleiades dance in a flecked cluster. The Dipper and the
horns of the Bull emerge; the Hyades sit above Taurus, bearing
the sigil of Aldebaran. The large reddish marker is Mars, and it
will wander from night to night in an ancient path. Bright Sirius
glows near the horizon in the treetops, casting a faint light on
the blossoms. Through the clearing, Regulus sits at the heart of
a Lion, dozens of fainter stars in his fur and on his paws. Cassiopeia rests in her cradle, tipping across another plane, overlooking this wildness from the dome. On the old Great Lakes,

1

the Indians saw an eagle, a snake, and three deer; in Brazilian jungle clearings, the same stars became a jaguar and a pig, as the Amazon rushed from one eternity to another.[1] These fragments do not diminish the immensity or challenge the mystery. Our knowledge of the sky, in its complication and bigness of proposition, can never replace the actual bigness.

When we stand beneath the night sky, we stand beneath the history of the whole of creation. It is a miracle that so much of it is perceptible—a miracle we might appreciate more if it had not occurred and we did not have senses to discern it.

The stars alone, scattered in a black pool, speak both for and against the lifeless corpse. The young woman in the morgue, the old man in his bed, the warriors bloody on the hillside: these too in their stillness are the night sky.

When the dead leave us their bodies, where do they go? Do they vanish, and does their being dissipate? What, if anything, exists beyond the skull and the mask?

The stars do not answer the question, but they alone stand for a possible answer, for the hope that there even is a question. However remote and enigmatic they seem, random in their design, they are all we have now, all we've ever had.

To look at the sky is to look at your own death. This is as true for the Pawnee priest for whom the stars are spirits whose glyphs are emblazoned on buffalo hide as it is for the late American village-dweller for whom they are the leftover light of objects which continue to burn elsewhere or which burned out millennia ago.[2]

But the sky is also the truth, and it has the power to draw us beyond our petty concerns and compulsions and temporary goals. We see what we are and what all this is, and we are stunned and exhilarated. It is, perhaps, a terrible truth, but the feelings respond to it, the heart opens.

Man under the night sky is man alone with his destiny. The stars inspire him to create the biggest things of which he is capable: gods, odes, number systems, and the temples and observatories that house them. It is not a matter of the absolute bigness of these things, for nothing man does is physically big before the stars. It is a matter of the internal bigness he feels, which his experience of the night reaches to. The stars expose something deep and true. Scientists and lovers know this each in their own ways. The unconscious shock of a flaming infinity without enables a tangent space within to break free.

This is different from and yet suggests the objective truth that we contain galactic-like clusters set in darkened distances through whose collective electricity we feel anything at all. It is different from and also suggests the astrological intimation that our destiny is written in and by the stars.

It is closer to the perception of Immanuel Kant that the creation has a dual form. "Two things fill the mind with ever new and increasing admiration and awe," he wrote, ". . . the starry heavens above and the moral law within."[3]

SUMMER HERE ON THE DESERT, the hot air escapes and the sand turns into heaps and shadows. Daylight is gone and we stand on the beachhead of the universe. A few stars appear, and then a billion of them—far more than we expected. The simple group of Pleiades explodes into hundreds of densely clustered stars. Arid zones are filled with unfamiliar clusters and wisps of Galactic haze. Even without the Moon, they light the desert—forming shadows of creation itself.

The Galaxy is so thick its far robes sweep about the mountains. Sage dew sweetens the air. All about, meteors race through the stars, then return to darkness.[4]

The monuments of Hohokam peoples stand against the eternity they thought once to measure. They are now ruins, but the Sun and Moon and some of the planets still return—in the numerical order of the heavens—to the windows and grindstones the pre-Papago star-priests cut into their observatories. How many other temples and measuring devices sit on the deserts entangled in the second-growth shrubs of other planets, having outlived their makers, continuing to measure the local cycles against the backdrop of all of time? The universe passes from muteness to knowledge into hieroglyphic again and again, even as stars are born and die.

Now the desert sky is as full of stars as the densest field of white blossoms. It is an overwhelming perspective dashed down upon mortality. See them as sound, see them as light, see them as harmony, see them as discordance: it doesn't matter, for one sees something that is more than any of those things and more than all of them. They are light, but they are primary spectral white light, as no other thing is. They are sound, but their silence is deafening. Heard on a radio telescope, they are eerie and alien, like the intelligence of the dolphin and whale whose sounds bypass us. We are left out, but, in another sense, the thing we are left out of is the thing we *are* and cannot know.

We both fear and desire an infinite universe. Now we know that beyond every galactic center, every climax forest of stars, lies another. Millions of miles from the center of a stellar empire, the simple inhabitants see it as a star. But what empire: ours, theirs, or another? And do they know that the star is an empire, or is it simply part of a giant bird of an unknown species or some other creature alien to us and to the emperor's people but not to them? In the outlands beyond these imaginary observers, there are those who cannot even see the empire, or another empire lies out in a different direction, another star. All the people on planets around other stars in this Galaxy, to say nothing of people in other galaxies, come into being, live and die, and cease being without knowing of us and without our knowing of them. This is the question in terms of which our own life/death is posed. And if there is no other universe, we must move anyway into another universe, for our minds cannot withstand or comprehend eternal sameness either. The egg is so rich that maybe the white stuff does pour out forever, stars and snows and thoughts and campfires of pygmies in Africas beyond Africas and through the systems of Antares, of Sirius, one eternity bright and fiery upon the heels of another. Continuous. Simultaneous.

The night sky is a photograph of eternity. The thousands of lights, standing for billions of billions of lights, that we look out upon at the moment they stand there for us, they are the creation. We cannot expand it; we can only add to its richness. Each single breath of ours, filling our mind, is matched by a counter-breath within the absolute of space and time. What joy is there, but what sorrow too, what infinite sorrow.

We read in science fiction books that Antares was once the center of a great empire of star cities. Could this be true?

Undoubtedly it is not. Already it lies in our own past and we move on to new imaginary planets and beings. We weep for the cities of Antares as we do for the Minoans and Picts; we weep for our own loss, that we were there, and now we are here. We weep for how deep in our own body we feel what it is we know. Not what we want. Nor what we desire. It's what we know. What we know we know. To set it square, right; to come out of this undiminished.[5]

We appreciate that it is mainly still a mystery because there is not enough here to explain all of this or our place in it. We are born into daylight, but we are also born into darkness; and the darkness of the night sky confirms and reflects our suspicions of the darkness of our origins.

Where *do* we come from?

Who is behind this?

Who are we in it?

We are like the figures in a deck of cards shuffled for an instant in the tinder of light. We see by a lantern that is already being extinguished, which we breathe into being by vision itself that passes from our lungs into our chests up the thin passage-ways into cranium, nose, and eyes.

We have moved north to the Bay of Fundy, in the last stand of coniferous forests before the Earth vanishes from history into that other timelessness of glaciers, beyond the habitations of men.

We float in the sky, but in something more than the sky. The solid Earth does seem almost like a rustling in infinity, and the trees stir in the wind, unconnected to the stars but as a further state of cosmic night. Darkness lies in those collective leaves— the same darkness filled with light-bearers that bridges the gap above us.

Lightning bugs swim in the altered air. Their lives are short, a few weeks; but all lives, the great books tell us, are of the same length. In the quick successions of images that flash in their sensoria, they see everything, they know all there is to know.

They are not alienated from their creation, though we stand outside their zone and watch them as if a tragedy, disappearing and reappearing in broken pulsation.

Where do we float? Whence came we to this clime?

By our consciousness, that other night sky—cupped as a lightning bug its light—we suffer the riddle imposed in thought. We are the gods whom those in darkness have set against the darkness. They may bear the candelabra through halls of pure nectar, but we cannot see them or know them or be so assured. They perhaps cannot see us. They are vanishing into oblivion. They perhaps never existed.

They are our fathers.

Our only fathers.

The agony they pose for us is not to stumble blankly back. When we signal them from this bare turf under the complete cosmological sky, their answer is the obvious one: terror is a luxury too; behind our panic is a witch who will not take us no matter how we submit to her. But then we are all afraid of the same thing—that we will not be afraid in time.

There is no other life, not only for us to live but to refuse to live. Better to plunge in that dark pool with its bright rays, to risk being pulled up out of it like a rat on the end of a cyanide pole.

It is all held together on a thread, great suns as well as lightning bugs, each one, where they are, across our system as galaxies across the bands of telescopic haze, haze caused only by our limited senses and the limits too of thought. The Milky Way twists around behind us, and out across the sky, the center of our Galaxy seen across the plane of its own tail. It is so far away, and yet it penetrates us. The Galaxy is umbilical. It touches us gently on the forehead, between the eyes; it touches us as our belly button, because we are made of it, as it ascends, curls, and vanishes into infinity, its main branch an ancient river revealed each night by night itself, as if that were meant to teach us something, as if being instructive were the first order of being present.

The fierce edge of creation cuts the hierarchical arrangement of existences. Yes, there are messages, sent between incommensurate locales, but they are no different from the rest. The things happening are the messages—lightning bugs, memory, stars—their staccato and rhythmic order is all that meaning can be.[6]

That which exists through itself is meaning, the magus said.[7]

We come here once, and it all happens, from the birth of cosmos to the rebirth in fire, in water, in the ellixis alleghensis of light. It is a primary transformation that joins us to Sun, as two chunks of embryonic scum in the same contaminated pool.

Look back at us in the Martian night sky. Through the oceans and conifer forests of the north, the blue-green of old Earth shows, a singular glow among astral birthstones: plankton aura, mist in solar wind—bioluminescent. All creatures are whelped in it, joined to their material line by murky matter, strewn as sour milk in a black sea. Strands cling to their prior strands like worms in a heap: the red fox limping through the morning, the giant crow picking at the woodchuck corpse, the clams breathing in their caves of muffled gravity, the minnows in flurries of light flesh. The Moon's body rolls in the Bay without touching it.[8]

This is all the initiation we will have. We are no different from firebugs; at times of being brought into creation, we lie in an eternity untouched. As carriers of the light, this far from homeland, we stand in darkness.

AUTUMN   DEATH ALONE, they say, gives life its meaning.[9] And it must be true, for each of us exists briefly inside an eternity of nonexistence about which we can know nothing because knowing ends too. There are hundreds of explanations and reprieves, but they belong to life, not death. Perhaps our karma follows us, perhaps some aspect of the mind (not memory), perhaps the spirit remembers this in a way which explains why *it* is the spirit—though not to us, not while we are alive. Perhaps life is eternal, and death a mirage, so we live this same life over a billion billion times, each time experiencing different parts of it, like this one, until consciousness is entire and there are no boundaries.

All this may do us some good someday, but we are tiny, fragile, hungry, and afraid of the unknown, afraid of not living. We resist the smaller changes; how could we not resist the change of everything we hope and know? The animals teach us that life does not die easily, even if it dies willingly. Or perhaps we do not live easily either, and death is the only resolution. We complicate our lives until they are hopeless. Then we say, "at least we will not live forever, so there is no need to straighten all this out." Death allows us our waste, our cruelty, our agony of disappointment in who we are, for it will eventually swallow them, and then all the people who are alive at this time, and then all the people and races on this planet, and then all the graveyards and even the planet itself. So why do we care? Why do we even try to set it right? As bad a mess as we have made of things (or so some claim), we have also created an order of things, a way of being, and even an honor, in a transitory country in an unknown place. Within life, we have made nations and languages and laws; and though none of these will survive, we have made them as well as they can be made here. We have somehow served that renegade within night who arranged for our brief flash of consciousness, and we have left him with something else, as final as death, for his pains.

Our complication resembles the complication of the stars in the original formation, however that is theorized. New layers keep getting laid down on what's already very complicated. All these things were complicated from the beginning—and then they begin to accumulate our memories and references and glosses of early attempts to solve them onto later attempts, as our life moves on also. By the middle years, we realize that we cannot resolve everything, we can only complicate it. There are some people we will never see again, though we do not know who they are; there are some languages we will not speak, some places we will not ever visit: we always assume there will be another chance, for everything. Our memory interferes with the present, and the present interferes with itself. We think we can make more time for ourselves to get these things cleared up, but the attempt to make more time, and the time in which we do it, makes less time, and complicates them still more. So it requires infinite time. This is the way it was in the primal nebula, which might have expressed itself by now, except that it made galaxies of light and expanded them through a prior void. They might have resolved light and time, only they brought new light and time, new properties of matter and shape into being. And then stars and worlds arose, and on them the chemicals carried even more complicated meanings into being, meanings which could no more recover the beginning and explain it than they could attain eternity or than the beginning could regain its priority and omneity. So we are born into life in the middle of things that are in the middle of things, in the middle of ourselves, in a continuum of memory and desire.

We cannot get out of this. And the sky, even if it were a sky of frogs and lily pads, spreads itself out as the widest ramification of conditions. Clearly, this is it.

The idea that the Sun was created for man is ridiculous, but so is the idea that it just sits there randomly in exactly the right place to give us heat and light. Twentieth-century cosmology has given the Sun and us inherence in the same cloud. It has passed the real question on to the time before the cloud, and the cloud before that. So we sit in our solar paradise, allowed to be by an accident of stellar evolution we also do not believe.

"What is life like?" the lawman asks the rustler in *The Missouri Breaks*.[10]

"It's like nothing else I've ever seen."

"Against his will he dieth that hath not learned to die. Learn to die and thou shalt learn to live, for there shall none learn to live that hath not learned to die." So says *The Book of the Craft of Dying* in the English translation of the *Tibetan Book of the Dead*.[11]

It is the unlived in us that cries out to the Creator for its chance to come into the world, even as the unborn, in our imagination of them, must cry to be born. Or else why would they risk so much for so little when in the end they must be worse than unborn, they will be dead?

On the eve of his execution, the outlaw sings: "I wouldn't mind the dying, but the laying in the grave so long, poor boy. I've been all around this world."[12]

"One sticks a finger into the sand to see what country one is in," said Søren Kierkegaard. "I stick my finger into existence and feel nothing. How came I here? Why was I not consulted?"[13]

We come into being in a way we cannot account for. Memory does not follow us back to the first words, and then before them to the precipice. Language is more complicated than that, right from the beginning. By the time we know anything, it too goes back to the beginning. We forget not knowing.

Life is shaped from within as Einstein shaped the universe we now inhabit, a flux of energies creating their own boundaries outside of which nothing can exist, not even war. Come to any point on the wall and it will very articulately throw you back to a space inside that wall, whether in the language of your own breathing, the precise equations of physics, or the dialects of some ancient people. Push English to the limits of consciousness, and Old English will gradually replace it, or French, or German; push it far enough back to the melting of the glaciers and the last solstices of the Ice Age, and it could even be Tibetan or Apache, Cro Magnon. But it will keep on talking about the formation of all these things, and its own formation, from within itself within earlier languages within protean speech.

We cannot go beyond thought, though we precede thought in every way.

When we die, all this will change. The blue vellum of the sky, the green parchment, the trees and fields will be peeled away. The night of stars and galaxies, though it is as undiminished and hollow as death, will be peeled away also.

Death does not allow an easy way out. We may think: "This is the nature of things. I did not ask to be born, and yet I am here. I do not ask to die, but that is the destiny of all living things." We can offer ourselves to death by our reason, but we contain far too much energy to make peace with death. All those eggs within eggs and languages within languages are no pretension. The memories and memoryless tissue formed within us are a thirsty lattice. When we lean over the drinking fountain and put our lips and gums and tongue into the water and cannot drink fast enough and want to drink forever, filling ourselves, whose thirst do we think we are? Whose thirst do we feel through the cells also longing to be filled? We may crumble in the grace of old age or yield to some other death agony, but *they* are not quenched. Something does not die—this hungry thing which embraces the animal. Something lives forever or not at all.

Shore up the fort as we may, at odd times we must know it— deep in daytime naps or beyond passion—there is an ocean dashing on the rocks below; it goes on until it meets the night. We are a hurricane of light and nerves and space. Water rushes through us, more than the whole ocean, more than the oceanic mass of planets, so ripe that meaning itself rings and aches. There are terrible storms in the universe, light years long, light years thick. There are equally violent storms inside the universe, long in consciousness, thick in consciousness. We are those. Such storms cannot be snuffed out by the end of life as simply as an ant seems to be crushed and is forgotten. Those in the storm must swallow it in and take it to eternity, with them if they go on, and to eternity anyway if life is the end.

After all, none of these kingdoms could exist without us, not as they do now. Death likewise.

It is only our purpose that is at odds with mortality. All this has another purpose too.

WINTER "THE SKY over a modern city is oc-culted by smoke & industrial throwaway, its proper atmosphere," writes the poet Robert Kelly.[14] But the cities are also celestial replicas, as any night view from an airplane reveals. The streets and stray glows of New York look like the nervous system of a great beast still being born or the dense center of a galaxy. Man has constructed something nerve by nerve and star by star from within that is not what he experiences, and it engulfs him.

For a child growing up in the city, the land of the stars is the Planetarium. In a room surrounded by silhouettes of the local skyline at dusk, a computer resembling an alien vehicle flashes the full heavens onto the ceiling to a haunting timeless music. Suddenly the buildings are gone and the disk is full of antique stars, as when the land was wilderness and Indians lived by the river.

Outside the star room is a night sky museum, with hunks of meteoric rock; scales for taking one's weight on the Sun and the Moon and the other planets; and epic kodachromes of the deep galaxies showing the vastness of space—the exploding nebulae with their reds and blues and aboriginal white light in shapes and figurements as exotic and primal as the fish and sea-plants in the nearby aquarium. It is dizzying to leave such a building and return to the city streets. Once, all human events occurred within the brightness of the night sky. That was the original cinema we attended each day as the Sun set.

"Countrymen are unlikely to forget," writes Kelly, "how after a quarrel with the wife and a quick getaway, they came out to see the Pleiades flirting in & out of sight at the top of a cold sky. Or 'Orion blazing.' "[15]

The man fights, then bursts out into a bigger world of himself, a world of fires, a world of origins.

In D. H. Lawrence's *The Rainbow,* Tom Brangwen falls in love with a Polish woman whose remote beauty he cannot penetrate, even in passion:

> Such intimacy of embrace, and such utter foreignness of contact! It was unbearable. He could not bear to be near her, and know the utter foreignness between them, know how entirely they were strangers to each other. He went out into the wind. Big holes were blown into the sky, the moonlight blew about. Sometimes a high moon, liquid-brilliant, scudded across a hollow space and took cover under electric, brown-iridescent cloud-edges. Then there was a blot of cloud, and shadow. Then somewhere in the night a radiance again, like a vapour. And all the sky was teeming and tearing along, a vast disorder of flying shapes and darkness and ragged fumes of light and a great brown circling

halo, then the terror of a moon running liquid-brilliant into the open for a moment, hurting the eyes before she plunged under cover of cloud again.[16]

All the woman's strangeness and distance is set off against the strangeness and distance of the night. But the night is also familiar and reachable in a burst of solitude. The greater strangeness lies within us, Lawrence is saying. The distance of the sky is flat and illusory compared to the foreignness in our own souls and between two of us. It is in ourselves that we feel the vastness and passion of creation for which the night sky is the externalized image.

Orion is the single most sentient-looking object in the sky, with its two rows of three stars set angularly toward each other within a triangle of three bright stars.[17] Rigel, Bellatrix, and Betelgeuse form the torso. At the edge of the glittering Sword is a swab of haze indicating an enormous luminous cloud, the Great Nebula in Orion. The Belt is made of three almost evenly-spaced stars of equivalent brightness. The upper one, Mintaka, is brilliant white; the middle one, Alnilam, is of flatter hue and named for a string of pearls; the bottom star, Alnitak, the girdle, is yellow and purplish, and actually a triple star.

In India the Belt was an arrow. In Greenland these same stars were seal-hunters lost in the ocean. The Australian aborigines believed that the stars of the Belt were young men, cavorting with the young women of the Pleiades.

It is the set of the Belt in the sky, with the Sword falling beneath it, all within the seeming bounds of Rigel and company, that gives Orion its singularity. It is not a matter of complex aesthetics. Orion is raw creation in the semblance of a hieroglyph. Its name most likely comes from the Akkadian Uru-anna, who was not a hunter but "Light of Heaven," a chief of unknown lineage and sorcery. Only in Roman times did Orion become a warrior or a figure engaged in the hunt. For the Egyptians, it was Horus, in a boat surrounded by stars, and bright Sirius beneath was a Cow, also traveling in a boat. In the *Egyptian Book of the Dead* it is named: "I see the motion of the holy constellation Sahu."

In Hindu myth, Orion was part of the superconstellation Pra-
ja-pati; he was a stag called Mriga, who chased his daughter
Rohini, a red deer we know as Aldebaran. Mintaka, Alnilam,
and Alnitak are arrows stuck in him by the hunter we call Sirius.

In China, Orion was a White Tiger.

In Ireland, he was an Armed King.

Flammarion, strangely, called it "California of the sky."
Whether he meant that it was like the coastal border of the West
on the great Eastern sea we do not know.

The seventeenth-century writer William Derham, in his *As-
tro-Theology*, described the pale light in Orion as the one spot in
the night sky where the empyreal heavens shone through. The
luminosity did not belong to Orion itself, but came through an
invisible crack in the higher astronomical spheres.[18]

The ginseng hunters of Asia seek an almost transparent,
gnarled wild root, shaped like a man with head and limbs, a root
which squeals when pulled from the ground and which has a
universal curative power lost in the cultivated varieties. This rare
medicinal plant they know by the local names for the constellation Orion.[19]

In matters of this star-group, one is struck by a simultaneous
obscurity and intelligibility. Orion most forcibly expresses the
mystery that all stars do, which is the mystery of creation itself.
It strikes to the heart and goes through us like a knife. The
mystery of our flesh.

In a sky where wonder is everywhere, Orion is the closest
thing to a feasible object, a clue. But, of course, it is no such
thing astrophysically. It is a random set of events associated by
the accidental plane of our Solar System in the Galaxy. It is a
radio disturbance of jewels. It is a bag of glowing gas hung on
a Sword. And yet, is anything up there, in here, random or
accidental?

If there were a message from a higher intelligence—not even
to us—Orion is it. From a higher intelligence to another higher
intelligence. From before history until beyond our history. Ours
is the privilege only. Because it is utterly lucid. More lucid than
we are. But we can see it. We are inside it. We alone create the
glyph.

On cold winter nights, when the winds blow to 100 degrees below zero and mice are born in the pipe straw, Orion is a heat, a priorness, a omneity that balances it. When summer settles in these parts, Orion is gone.

Lyra is the answer. A silence in three essential notes. Without reprieve.

Another singular object is the great Andromeda Galaxy. It is the furthest thing we can see with our naked eye, two million light-years away.[20] Through field glasses, its galactic spiral is obvious. Look down from Cassiopeia toward Pisces, go between the bright star of Aries, Hamal, and the bright star of Pegasus, Alpheratz. The eye is stopped by a smudge or blur in the sky.

We are not just looking at another world or a big star. We are looking through a hole in our own galaxy of billions of stars at an object which is the combined light of billions of other stars. Everything that happens in those stars is a unity in visible Andromeda, which is no doubt called by more names than it has stars within.

It is our absolutely straight-on view of an island universe. That we can see so far with comprehension is incredible. If only a fraction of the stars in that galaxy have planets, and only a fraction of those have life, we are still looking at the single beacon of millions of inhabited worlds, hundreds of thousands of civilizations, virtually as remote from each other as they are from us, and which see us as a single obscure object out a hole in their galaxy—and not even us, just the hazy oval of which we and all the rest of the Milky Way are part.

2

The Creation

PRIMITIVE MAN and modern Western man share the intuition that we come from the heavens. To primitive man we are the incarnation of fiery spirits in the sky. To modern man we are the formation of life in space debris. Either way, the night sky is the one big hole through which we look back toward the beginning.

Early man was ten times the devotee of the heavens that even our best scientists are. To him they were necessity, not a job or a conundrum he could escape from. He observed their lights and motions and changes. He experienced the warmth-giving Sun and the brilliant sparkle of the night sky, and he came to the conclusion most suggested by the appearances and his experience of his own insides—that he was looking into the radiant world of the gods, the place from which either he himself came or the instruction for his creation came. Instead of pushing the stars away by his intellect, he took them into his bloody taste of the universe. Our skyfield is flat and disconnected, essentially arbitrary. His was alive and vibrating; it pressed down on him aflame with messages, beyond wisdom.

Since the time of Galileo, Western man has "known" that those things out there are neither spirits nor gems, but stones, pebbles and dirt. Some of them are frozen; most of them are molten. The display itself is created by the gargantuan sizes of the objects, the distances between them, and the primary forces that govern their arrangement. If we could look inside a flower or a bug or our own flesh and blood on an equally long focal plane, we would see a similar display. The microscope gives us such vision. We see that we contain replicas of the night sky; in

16

fact, all matter, animate or not, is filled with skies. These might be more than replicas; they might be the same thing.

The paradox of being suggests the heavens. There is no mystery greater than our own experiencing of mind and existence from within. Either we come from the sky or we are manifested in correspondence to it as in the hermetic law: "As above, so below." The two main aboriginal sources of omens are the sky and dreams, for both of them are substantially rootless. That one comes from within and the other from without is a meaningless distinction so long as the degree to which we ourselves are inside or outside phenomena is unknown.

Dreams are the sky in other senses. Entering them, we pass into discrete worlds, completed and inhabited.

Science has tracked the sky down to a complex field of exploding objects that contain the basic stuff of matter, then to the single fireball of the first explosion. It has tracked dreams to the chemico-electrical makeup of the brain tissue and nervous system which contains all conscious images and thoughts in an unconscious matrix. This brain tissue, these quasars and nebulas, mark the furthest we know that nature has gone in the two directions possible: unlimited extension and manifestation of prime energy in time-space, and crystallization of consciousness and meaning in the microtexture of space. Insofar as these two paths join in a paradox, current physics mirrors it. Those objects which are either too big and faraway or too small and quick for us to describe and know are subject at the same time to the bias of the cognitive structures created in the brain, a brain made of star debris. So the further we go into the sky and matter, the deeper we go into the riddle of consciousness.

It is not enough to look into the night with the confidence of scientific knowledge. We are wrapped in a fire-filled abyss. It is not an abstraction, a postulate, or a model. It is our experience. Just as our experience of being born is unalleviated by our knowledge of genetics and embryology, so our experience of the creation is direct and intimate in a way that astronomy cannot lessen.

According to modern scientific cosmology, the universe ostensibly manifested itself in an all-engulfing explosion, an explosion we still sense in the background radiation of space. The "Big Bang," as it is called, occurred on such a grandiose scale that we are bare cosmic seconds into the pop. In our own time, fifteen billion years later, its nearly spent blast can be heard as a murmur.

The idea of space or location or even time in such an event is meaningless. It was everywhere and everything. Material, thrown in all directions, created space. There was no space otherwise for this explosion to expand into. But if it created space, then out of what? We have no answer. "Nothing" does not explain it because, for us, it is a hole. But there was nothing for there to be a hole in.

Where did this explosion get its matter and energy from? The frightening answer is either that we do not know or that it is debris from the last creation.

What was the last creation like?

As long as it obeyed the ultimate laws of substance, it could have been anything. It could have contained planets, babies, painted pots, chipmunks, lichen, electricity, and gravity, just like this one. Or it could have contained different things.

If we ask: was there life on Earth in those times?, we must answer: what Earth?, what time? A different explosion would have led to a different creation, another space, a time before time itself, a unique outlay of planets, galaxies, and stars, if even there were such things.

If somehow we were to enter this last creation, we would not be able to tell where we were in it, what "where" meant, or how it fell in any hypothetical sequences of universes coming before or after. There could have been billions of such universes, or more, each within their own parameters of space and formation in cosmic time, endlessly created and destroyed, forever unto eternity.

The destruction implied by this is in no way partial. The obliteration of planets or whole galaxies does not rival it. In the "Big Bang" at the end and beginning of time, all things are destroyed. Suns and planets of course are destroyed; people are destroyed; their artifacts are destroyed; the memory that there ever were people is destroyed; continuity ceases; philosophy ends; every clue even to the implication of our existence is wiped out. All are ground into atoms and subatomic particles and stored in a single inclusive mass as if they had never existed. They are scrubbed clean. And then they burst into the milky fleece of new stars and worlds. Creation starts over again: reference points, matter, meaning, life. Then it ends.

The Big Bang Theory is currently popular, for it apparently solves many puzzles: Why are the galaxies rushing away from each other? How came to be the loosely distributed stars of the night sky? Of what origin is the background of radio noise in the universe? How does time begin and end? Perhaps it is not so surprising that the papacy gave its approval to the Big Bang Theory because it seemed also to be a confirmation of a single divine origin of the universe.

As long as there is an expanding universe to explain, alternatives to the Big Bang are few. In fact, there is only one basic alternative, the Steady State Theory, in which the matter of the universe is seen as continually created, either uniformly or in certain hot spots, with old matter continuing to move into space or beginning to dissipate and collapse. This theory does not require a cataclysm, and it allows the present universe to be as old as time itself, to retain its basic archaeological integrity. This that we see *is* the creation, instead of just one in a series of "creations."

Where does the matter come from in Steady State? What was the initial creation?

According to one of its propounders, Fred Hoyle: "It does not come from anywhere. Material simply appears—it is created. At one time the various atoms composing the material do not exist, and at a later time they do."[1]

If we were to suggest that this is difficult to accept, he might well point out that Big Bang doesn't solve the problem of original matter either; it just gives the impression that it does. Either we have new matter emerging from an explosion, or we have it dribbling into space at a few remote points—not very many, but then not very many are needed in a big universe. To answer any further question, we must go back, which is impossible, to before the creation.

Hoyle suggests that if a film were made from any point in the universe, galaxies would be seen emerging from the background material. Though galaxies would also be "blowing" away into the hindmost zones of space, the film would not show much change because new galaxies would replace these. "How long would our film go on?" Hoyle asks himself. "It would go on forever" is his answer.[2]

Steady State Theory makes the universe homogenous in time as well as in space. If galaxies are moving away from each other, new ones *must* be formed to take their places; otherwise the universe would eventually thin out. Once a galaxy reaches a place where its light can no longer overcome the speed of its recession from us, then we cannot know its existence. It will have been lost to the expansion of space. But new galaxies are being formed, which could not happen without the spontaneous creation of matter in space.

Of course, all of these explanations come to the ultimate problem: how did the universe begin? does the universe have a beginning? an end?

Either way we are in trouble. If it does not have an end (or a beginning), then truly we dwell in an incomprehensible eternity. If it does have an end, if it did begin once upon a time, then what lies beyond it? Nothing? Gods?

It is even possible to imagine that this entire universe is one atom in a "ladybug" in another universe, which is an atom in a meteor in another universe, and so on. Likewise, deep within the subatomic particles of this universe, which number in the trillions of trillions, there may be countless other universes. And these may all be part of a larger universe. It is impossible to know.

The temporal origin of the universe is much more difficult to comprehend than the spatial dimension (though these are, finally, the same). Time is a theological, mythological, or epistemological question. No matter how many beginnings and ends scientists define, there will always be the question: and what before that? Before the universe, what? Why did it come into existence? Did it happen right away? Was there a delay? What stalled it? How did it move from nonbeing into being?

Of course, the other form of this same question is: Where were we before we were here? Where shall we be after we have finished our allotment? What delayed us from coming into being at the beginning of things?

Science will never answer these questions satisfactorily, for it will always give secondary causes in place of first ones, or its so-called first causes will suggest even prior causes.

The spatial question is not insoluble in the same way. If we assume, for instance, that matter creates the space (or the illusion of space) which it occupies, then we can also suggest that the universe is everywhere; and if it is growing bigger, the space into which it is growing is literally the extension and complexification of its own fabric.

Einstein tried to do away with the problem of inside space and outside space when he mapped space itself as a kind of hyperspace such that all which is outside is also back inside. Not only can we not get outside this space, we cannot even touch the outside from the inside. It is a space that continues to emerge from its own properties only. It has as an outside barrier the speed of light, which is threaded through its inside, and the bending of space-time, which is probably an illusion. This universe can have no inside or outside, and its original point is everywhere; hence the microwave background in space.

But the universe did not stay completely closed. Einstein left a theoretical hole in it, a tunnel whereby matter could jump from one realm of space to another. In the second half of the twentieth century, astrophysicists began to explore hypothetical events in which concrete things seem to get outside space-time itself. What happens to matter supposedly crushed to zero volume in a black hole? It must leave the universe. But it cannot leave the universe. So it must appear elsewhere *in* the universe. The laws of nature require it. It cannot be obliterated. It can only be changed into some other thing. California Institute of Technology astronomer Kip Thorne gave us an unexpectedly memorable image when he said that it might come bubbling up, like spring water in the mountains, in another region of this universe or in some other universe. Even so, that "other" universe must still be part of the creation.[3]

The Big Bang Theory tells us about a creationary explosion from which matter came into being and continued to expand and dissipate—a fireball racing outward in all directions at incredible speeds. At first it wasn't even matter; it was pure radiation, energy, in which matter formed as a contamination in the way that ice will suffocate a pond in a severe winter. Summer ended for the original farmlands and vineyards of light, and in almost all areas of the cosmos they withered and died. But their seeds became the loom of a new cosmos. Intrinsic forces—gravitation, and within that, electromagnetism, and within that, intraatomic nuclear forces—combined, and still combine, giving shape to a present order of things we call the universe.

As the primeval nebula swirled tumbling through space, its fabric tore apart, radiated, and condensed anew. Tatters collected around cores, and from the cores gravitation reached out; whirlpools of starry tincture swept up the matter from space around them until they were all that was left, fiery beacons in a cold winter desert, only the thinnest of radioactive veils to settle over the rest of time and space. That veil is all the thinner now.

Big Bang tells us that the pure and original universe is fire, fire of a nature to make the fires of the suns themselves seem cold, fire in which matter cannot form. The stars are then the ice in this cooling pond, and the nebulae a flowing white field of cosmological hydrogen. They are cauls. Cauls hot enough to form suns. But these too are dissipating. Unless there is some unknown spring supplying fresh water to the cosmos.

The forces of matter are universal: gravity and its handmaidens work in the universe at large as they do in the minutest sphere. A galactic dust storm, giving birth to star systems, is obedient to the same ancient law as the fog off the ocean or the north wind carrying dust. Matter goes where it is compelled and where there is least resistance, be it silt, water, or hydrogen fire. The various spiral and ring shapes suggest the underlying turbulence, composition, and attractions. We have never seen a universe before this one, but we see the results of its having been.

Within the hydrogen whirlpools that contain all the heat left from the age of light (as it continues to escape), smaller eddies form. The big whirlpools are mostly empty space, with the centers of essence knotted throughout them: the single stars. Rotating clouds of hydrogen dust contract into dense massive objects, hundreds of times denser than water in their cores and with millions of degrees of temperature. Of course, these are our flimsy millions, formed on the cold side of light. No doubt the savants of the original golden universe would consider the star centers the last almost burned-out embers of a moderate heat, almost too faint to measure. The planets are the ashes of those stars—the bits of matter left when solar gravity has claimed all the rest. They ride through space on tracks that it took the beings on this world millions of years to perceive in their raw simplicity.

The single stars are given motion from the Explosion (or the fireball was given motion by some other protean activating force), and the planets take their motion from what remains of that primordial system. From galaxy to star to planet, matter cools, striates, develops characteristics, and differentiates. This was not a simple hierarchy in time and space. Stages of creation went backward and forward, enveloping each other and then spitting out new levels. The first monstrous protogalaxies were torn apart, and billions upon billions of stars were formed in second-generation galaxies. The present universe is a relit one.

The primordial nebula was at least 99.999 percent pure hydrogen and helium. The galaxies formed in a brief time about a million years after the Big Bang, when matter was dense enough to overcome dispersive radiation. The other elements were built in the nuclear furnaces of the stars, where intra-atomic rearrangements took place and new atoms were formed. Although they no doubt take their character from the unknown particles that lie within them, they contain *the* original structures for us. Our entire world is built upon the properties arising from the numerical relationships inside these atoms. The shininess of metal, the bright flare of phosphorus, the cool miscibility of oxygen, the deep mimelike life-chains of our grandfather carbon atom are all the result of intra-atomic shuffling, like the shifting of beads in a moiré pattern. The elemental properties show up in flower shapes, animal behavior, and human thought. The "meaning" of the elements that stand within them is beyond us; it is of such a pure algebra that we can read it only as numbers set against other numbers, things we have come to call "color" and "charm" and "strangeness" because of their seeming resemblance in their mathematical behavior to secondary qualities and images of our own lavish microcosm. Since these characteristics come into being in the first thousandth of a second of the Explosion, when nothing can mean anything, scientists have compensated for the void by giving them garish and familiar images.

The interstellar gas would have remained hydrogen and helium if it were not for the supernova explosions that enriched it with the heavier elements for planets of water, stones, and flesh. In the primordial cloud, matter is young and simple. In the stars, it becomes complex *on an atomic level.* On the planets, atoms form molecules, and then characteristics that were absolutely hidden on the stars burst into being, laying the basis for a world long before we inherit it.

In the stars, each more complicated element is built upon a simpler one. The transmutation of hydrogen into helium is the heartbeat of the stars, and it gives off the photons which fill the night sky. The starry heaven is not corporeal suns but their elemental transformation. We see the white light of a unity twaining—not by the splitting of a whole star but by the continuous fusion of its individual atoms. This is the source of our day as well as our night. Without the stars to transmute the primal hydrogen, there would be no planets, no stone, no water, and no life. Hydrogen alone is not capable of these things; but in the star centers, hydrogen provides the basis for a whole elemental hierarchy. Later stars, formed of the debris of ancient stars, contained the enriched matter at their births.

From helium we get carbon and oxygen, sulphur and silicon. There are ninety-two naturally produced elements, including hydrogen; but iron, the twenty-sixth, is about as complicated as the stars' interiors get before the building of elements consumes too much energy and leads to the deterioration of the stars from the weak nuclear force. Elements heavier than iron, such as gold, lead, and so on up to uranium (the heaviest one that occurs naturally), could only have been formed in an even greater explosion.

The material of the galaxies and stars collects gravitationally around centers; the stars ignite and then burn out. But their deaths are not simple; both gravity and the nuclear force must collect their due. Some massive stars become supernovae, burning their own ash, collapsing from gravity, imploding, and then exploding again suddenly and violently. During the explosive phase, heavy nuclei capture neutrons and build elements above iron on the periodic scale. The elemental material splattered with heavier atoms is then broadcast to the universe in cosmic rays. We inherit our silver and gold and our radium and uranium from the second-generation stars of an earlier universe. We also inherit the oxygen and carbon in our bodies and the iron and tin in the Earth's crust from a crumbling dynasty of original and secondary stars. The death of kings provides the primal stuff of a new world-age. Our Sun is a third-generation star, made of the slag of dead suns. All except its hydrogen and helium was synthesized in stars far away. The Sun came out of a stellar nursery somewhere in the Milky Way before arriving at its present locale in the System. Its brother suns, formed with it in the nebula, lie unknown to us in other parts of the Milky Way. Chances are we will never know which ones they are, or if we share anything with creatures of our own star cloud.

The raw hydrogen of future stars travels in galactic space. But, to the astonishment of contemporary astronomers, organic molecules also drift in the debris between the stars. Both kinds of alcohol (ethanol and methanol) have been detected by radio astronomers in interstellar gas clouds. Sometimes they are associated with a visible patch, but not always. During the 1960s and 1970s, it seemed that virtually every day a new complex molecule was found floating in space. Some meteorites have incorporated carbon-hydrogen compounds during their formation in nebulae. Clearly, the ingredients for the planets contain the kind of complex material once thought to evolve only after planet-formation. In fact, interstellar space seems to hold build-

ing blocks of life itself. This is still a mysterious phenomenon—
an apparent fact of nature that may or may not have direct consequences in the evolution of living matter on the planets. After
all, astronomers did not require such complexity in the cosmic
gas to derive a plausible sequence of evolution for the Earth or
any other planet.

It was in the ancient rocks of the original Earth, those cooled
lattices of the old fire, that the atoms of carbon, nitrogen, oxygen, sodium, potassium, silver, gold, and so on gained their freedom from fire; they oozed upward, filling the oceans with water,
the air with gases, and providing the variety of substances for
accretion into the terrestrial scenery. The blue of our sky is a
nitrogen hue.

Radioactive elements such as thorium and uranium were included in the original rocks, and they continue to provide a
source of internal geological heat. Such heavy elements are un-
stable because the strong nuclear force in them is only about a
hundred times stronger than the electric force. So electric repulsion between protons tends to decay their nuclei. When the
nuclei split, the fragments rebound, releasing energy and elim-
inating some of the overburdening mass.

The Earth's exact size is an exact balance between the gravity
composing it and the collective electric force in the atoms of all
its materials, from its rare and noble gases to its shifting bedrock
and molten nickel-iron core. The iron is a red-star heritage: a
king's corpse maintained in a sanctum. When we think about
energy these days—fossil fuels, nuclear energy, solar energy, hot
springs, volcanoes, tides, wind—clean energy or dirty energy—
renewable energy or nonrenewable energy—we should realize
that a bank of stellar energy is built into the planet. It is not
some after-the-fact thing we invented, like automobiles or oil
wells; the planet is held together by networks of atomic and
molecular energy, a minute by-product of which we tap.

Once atoms build molecules and molecules enter into chemical compounds, the situation becomes very complex. The
planets are jungles, and any exact lineage is buried in the overall
fertility and boundaryless intimacy of matter and nature. Planets
are woven of elements with a thickness of billions of years and

slow spindling. On the Earth, the ninety-two natural elements interact constantly to form new chains and structures.

Closer to suns, more elements occur as gases and liquids; further from suns, there are more solids. Three-quarters of our world is ocean, but on Venus this ocean would boil into water vapor, and on Mercury other solids would turn to liquid and boil off. On Pluto, not only the water but the air itself would freeze hard.

From our standpoint, the Earth has a rich mixture of all three forms of matter: airy molecules, liquid molecules, and hard substances. They are in constant interaction on both the molecular and chemical levels. Water rushes onto the beaches and sweeps the residue of stones into its solvent; sea creatures are left on the sand to decompose and be ground into stones. Elemental gases, like hydrogen and oxygen, under the proper conditions, can form a liquid, a liquid which becomes a gas at much higher temperatures than its constituents, and one with very different properties from those of either. That compound remains a liquid on Earth, and without it there would be no human life. It gives us the oceans, the puffy clouds, the glacial icebergs, the rain, and the moist sweetness of our flesh.

A sometime solid like calcium can join with another sometime solid, carbon, and with a gas, oxygen, to form rugged limestone and marble. Iron in contact with oxygen—like so many metals—rusts (oxidizes). Gases are not limited to the atmosphere. Rocks decompose, and molecules rush upward from deep underground.

As atoms, molecules, and compounds join in overlapping lattices, fuse and differentiate layer after layer, a complex and delicate geography forms, totally different from anything in the stars and galaxies or suggested by the fireball. Matter is remarkable long before it spawns life or intelligence: it is a surprise and a delight in a universe of such violent and bastard ancestry.

And there is no evading the fact that we are made of this matter. We contain its atoms, its shimmering electrical fields, its violent particles and nuclear forces, its nuclear decay. It is our destiny, and we are its destiny. Anything we are, it must be too; but anything it is, we must share. No wonder Joseph Stalin and

Mao Zedong worried about what science would find inside the atom. The future possibility for a social order of man lies in what man really is. And that lies in the nature of matter. For Mao, quantum theory was a confirmation of a revolutionary and communist social order, and he supported Heisenberg's atom. It is strange to think that the subatomic particles, in their brief mute lives, might spell out the destiny of the peasants of China in a world as far from them as the quasars are from us. But the issue is a real one, and Marxists have kept as close an eye on it as they have on the protean matrilineal and patrilineal configurations of primitive societies, searching for the inevitability of an evolving universe. After all, we come along a single and particular path, and our evolutionary line contains only one set of molecular and genetic potentials at any one point. There is only one family of lizardlike creatures in our ancestry. On the path from star-stuff to consciousness, we incorporate everything we pick up along the way, every cell and every lizard, and any one of them is capable of a revolution or an act of vision in the darkness of a night.

The raw creation seems alien to us. We seem strangers to ourselves. The inner sky is as explosive and terrifying as the outer sky, for they are the same firmament, the same extension of space through the properties of matter to form an anything. We are this, finally and forever. We are other things too, in our thoughts and philosophy, but these other things must also be true to protons, neutrons, electrons, and their component charges, or to those things to which we have given such names. We look upon the sky in its vast openness, its ceaseless depth, but the sky is simply a field of opacity. Stones are also opaque fields, so are molecules, and so are we. A shell *is* infinitesimal compared to a star, but they are continuations of the same tubular space. Not only are they continuations of extent, but they are each a discrete and equivalent manifestation of its internal properties, with distinct boundaries nested upon symmetries. Mental images are continuations of space, even as they are images of space. We have minds which are different from the mental images that infest them. Our integrity and the very fact of our existence depend on our not being pure matter so much as a building up of fields within a very old and tightly sustained organization. Life seeps out of unruly electrical and molecular fields, but it tames them. In fact, it has tamed them layer by layer over billions of years, so the flowers and the flesh hardly show their fiery atomic makeup. Where in a kiss are the molecules? They have "disappeared" entirely into the structure; yet they have built for aeons for such a moment. Where is hydrogen in a gull? Yet without hydrogen the gull would not exist. The sheer rigor of assembling and nesting these fields over time, assimilating matter through them and reproducing them hierarchically through themselves alone, gives a semblance of decency and philosophy to this realm. How else could the violent nuclear universe hold the delicate embryo, the soft robin's egg, in its ogre arms?

If we look back over creation, it seems an unlikely thing. The planets are built of the materials of the stars, and the stars are simply the hot ash of the original explosion. What causes anything to happen, except for secondary explosions and gross distribution of matter, is the intrinsic capability of atomic substance to form texture and structure. Cooled off and organized on small spheroids, matter arranges itself in intricate patterns and generates materials that are inconceivable in terms of the separate stars or the vastness of space. These materials are everything we know and understand. They are not only what we make things out of and what we are made out of; they are the possibility that anything can be made at all in this swift violent storm. The planets provide zones in which the properties of the elements manifest, and in which, ultimately (since this tale is being told), the animalcules of this creation gather.

These creatures mark the opposite pole to the fireball and the galactic vastness. Without them there would be only an unknown turmoil traveling blind and senseless in a void. With them there is a wondrous sky filled with sparks that they either have no name for or they call gods or hydrogen fires or anything else they choose. Without creatures, a rough simple universe roars, an unabated cataclysm. With them there are senses to reflect the inside of this cataclysm, words to describe it and build other

systems out of it, including temples which contain representations of the paths of heavenly bodies, and radio telescopes which
record the background noise of outer space. Without creatures
there would be no universe. With them the universe bursts into
light from within. Light is comprehended by light. Outside is
comprehended by inside. Inside is comprehended by outside.
Consciousness roars through the paths it forges from unconsciousness, creating mind from darkness even as matter differentiates itself once and eternally out of an original homogeneity.
Everything the macrocosm contains, the microcosm reinvents
symbolically, since it is the microcosm to exactly that macrocosm. This is why moral law and the field of stars are one. This
is why we embrace the heavens as everything we are and know
we are and everything we are and don't know we are. This unity
holds when the stars are spirits, gods, or beasts in a zodiac. And
it holds when they are flaming plasma balls and suns.

It is the physiology of the eye that locates the night sky, not
the contingent relationship of that sky to this world. The eye is
created in darkness to receive light. Layers and layers of cells
multiply in the optic cup. Fibers transmit the electrical disturbance of light to a field of brain tissue where these currents of
electrical potentials, which do not contain corresponding depth
and space, are translated into shapes and directions. Space is
created in a forest of nerve lines. The night sky is literally and
embryonically made out of albumen, salt, and water.

And the sky is everywhere. It is the embryo, layer of cells by
layer of cells, each of which is a sky to the infant bursting from
the cocoon imposed by some previous cell, some previous sky.
It is paramecia pouring into the lens like stars. It is the elemental
rock of the planet, each individual gem of which cracks open to
show another gem, inside of which is yet another heavens. All
of this rock was resplendent galactic fire to the hypothetical
inhabitants of another region at a far earlier time. It is inside the
bud and the fruit of the flower. And it is also inside the mind of
man, inside him so many times that he no longer knows whether
he is coming or going but seems somehow to walk straight down
the hallway of an invisible house in an unknown city. He en-
graves it as substitute skies in star temples, and planetaria, and

ephemerides, on vases, and globes, and maps, and in his most sacred texts. When men drill through the Arctic snowcap and ice into the ocean beneath, and go in diving suits and swim in that cold sky, they find living mites in the freshwater ice-crystals that have burst into the ocean edge. These creatures spend their whole existence in these fragile crystals. For them the night sky is simply their being; they look out through the cellularity of their bodies at the infinite.

"This pendant world," mused John Milton, "in bigness as a Starr."[4] And he hung it there vulnerable to Satan and the other angels and devils. Whatever man will make of his lot, he will also live. And although it is death to us finally, we inhabit it now against the backdrop of gems.

It is no idle conceit that our Earth is a mirror of the heavens and we are made of the stars. Magical law says: "Every man and every woman is a star."[5] Science says this in its own way. We are so, first, in the Big Bang; second, as we are made of materials either directly from the body of the Sun or from the same hot cloud that the Sun came from; and third, as the Earth is showered with atomic materials from throughout the universe. Our hair and eyes and flesh and freckles contain atoms from remote stars, atoms that have been in suns, in Antares, Betelgeuse, Sirius, and Vega. But these are our names, not theirs. Not only do the stars provide the materials, but their radiation reaches the structures made of those materials, which respond mutagenically to transform themselves. Or, to stay accurate to Darwinian neutrality, they are transformed, and the result is the variety of living species through the histories of all the planets of the cosmos. The radiation of the stars, including the individual suns to which planets are bound, also propels major climatic changes on those worlds. Thus, stars provide the old material, the new materials, the mutagenic material around which genetic memory forms, and the vibrations which spawn glaciers as big as planets and decade-long thunderstorms. As the ice moved in across the Earth, through what were previously temperate zones, those primitive men who lived there found survival more difficult. Mutations leading to higher intelligence were occurring along with other kinds of mutations, but intelligent man made fire and tools and clans and strategies, and he came out of the Ice Age in tribes and communities, counting the phases of the Moon and speaking the original languages.

The mechanism of our becoming flesh is a chain going back to the beginning of living matter—and before that, to the beginning of the universe. This chain seems to have folded in on itself again and again, turning inside out at critical moments, deriving from its own interstices shapes that were not there before. How else could molecules be spun from atoms? How else could living tissue evolve from the mineral waters, free itself from the sea, yet contain that briny yolk in a new materiality? By what other wizardry could eggs be fashioned from frogs and lizards, eggs containing yet another embryo, and feathers and blood from those eggs, and mind from the mammal of the forest? How else but as forest crept too from slime atop pools, pools formed in cavities of rock, wind issued from gravity, and gravity from space itself?

A current proceeds from suns and galaxies onto single worlds with eggs and buds and germs, connected only to the beginning of itself, dependent on what it is in order to become what it is not. Somewhere in the chain of life, which goes on beyond us to the end of time, we come into being. We grow to consciousness as life grew once from matter, and the many cells grow and differentiate from the single sperm and egg. Nothing can make us any less discrete or unique, but nothing can bring us into being without requiring the universe to compile the material necessary from its own beginning in something else.

In one of the oldest Greek myths recorded by Hesiod, the sea was born of the earth asexually. She was a clone. She lay for the embrace of the sky, to whom she bore an offspring: "the thing which encloses everything, Okeanos." Eros followed, "flooding the mind and all gods and men into further nature."[6] Night was born from Chaos, and then—in loving union with its sister, the Underworld (Erebus)—spawned the Bright Sky, the Aether, and Day. The Earth bore also the starry Heaven and the high Hills to cover herself.

Chinese cosmology describes a somewhat different quality of the universe: Before the division of empty space into the clear and the turbid, a Vast Prime (*hung yuan*) alone existed. The All-Highest Lord Lao opened the heavens. A raw germinal stuff poured forth, immediately separating into yin and yang, the receptive and active poles of nature. All subsequent form germinated from their polarity. As in Steady State Theory, the Void is no longer a void; it is a loom of potentiality, a warp on which matter forms.[7]

The original stuff of creation was fleecy white like the Milky Way. The name for cosmos, *hun-t'un,* shares a root with *won-ton.* As it drops down into the microcosm, it is a tasty dough indeed. It grows less by expansion and more by polarity, fission, and inversion. The sculpting of a universe from without is imaginary only. Nothing touches it on the outside. It contains, like the embryo, the princple of its own shape, and continues to emerge from itself by divisions more and more complexly.[8] In fact, embryogony and cosmogony may disclose the same beginning.

The Chinese postulate a divine wind feeding creation from the outside. The fertilized egg also draws nourishment from outside its tissue. If we watch an embryo form, we have an illusion of there being an outside edge to it because we are outside it. But the principle is intrinsic. Hemispheres develop, and material passes from region to region. Some regions grow thicker and envelop others. Material duplicates itself; other material "disappears." At certain unpredictable points, the embryo turns inside out, in whole or in part, and then continues to grow and differentiate. Limbs and orifices emerge as though drawn magically out of the interior substance. The creation of the sky was a similar process of turning something inside out again and again while differentiating its parts. The Chinese and the Greek versions intuit this in different ways. Creation is the simultaneous extraversion and internalization of matter. We are summoned up through the abyss, summoned by the same voice that summoned all the creatures. The birth which places each person here and repeats, for each one of them, the creation itself, is no simple matter. It is a subtle bond between cell and sky which seals us into the system. In the sixteenth century, Paracelsus wrote of a quality by which fire was joined to air, a chain which, somehow, without materiality or visibility, held nature together and bound its parts:

> As the chicken is sustained in its egg by its albumen without touching the shell, so chaos sustains the globe and prevents it from tottering. This chaos is invisible, though it appears of a light green tint. It is an intangible albumen, having the power and property of sustaining, so that the earth shall not fall from its position. . . . And as every morsel of flesh lies in its own liquid, or the generating seed in the sperm, so the stars lie in this albumen, and move therein like a bird in flight. . . .[9]

Wilhelm Reich saw in the galaxies embryos continually formed by two sexually charged streams of particles copulating and discharging new star material. This is another way of saying that the sexual throes of orgasm and birth reach to the fundament of creation. Or, from the other side: the nuclear process is the sexual process in its original form. The passion we feel in lovemaking is directly linked to the formation of stars and systems of stars. That is why the feeling is so powerful and why it is functionally associated with passing the cellular blueprint into history. Above, the spiraling galaxies; below, the seed-bearing creatures of the planets—one creation.[10]

A Bushongo Bantu version from the Congo River has the entity Bumba surrounded by water and alone in the darkness:

> One day Bumba was in terrible pain. He retched and strained and vomited up the sun. After that, light spread over everything. The heat of the sun dried up the water until the black edges of the world began to show. Black sandbanks and reefs could be seen. But there were no living things.
>
> Bumba vomited up the moon and then the stars, and after that the night had its own light also.
>
> Still Bumba was in pain. He strained again and nine living creatures came forth: the leopard named Koy Bumba, and Pongo Bumba the crested eagle, the crocodile, Ganda

Bumba, and one little fish named Yo; next, old Kono Bumba, the tortoise, and Tsetse, the lightning, swift, deadly, beautiful like the leopard, then the white heron, Nyanyi Bumba, also one beetle, and the goat named Budi.[11]

In an Eskimo version of creation, the first man decides to burst out of the pod in which he is hanging from a beach-pea. He is astonished at himself, his arms and legs, the open pod on the vine, then this dark object with wings looking at him. It was a Raven who pushed up its beak like a mask and became a man. Then it asked the first man what he was and where he came from. When the man answered, the Raven exclaimed: "Ah! I made that vine, but did not know that anything like you would ever come from it."[12]

Zuni cosmology has the Maker and Container of All, Awonawilona, standing alone: "There was nothing else whatsoever throughout the great space of the ages save everywhere black darkness in it, and everywhere void desolation. In the beginning of the new-made, Awonawilona conceived within himself and thought outward in space, whereby mists of increase, steams potent of growth, were evolved and uplifted." He created himself in person and then caused the Sun "to exist and appear. With his appearance came the brightening of the spaces with light." Mist-clouds formed in the brightness and provided water for the "world-holding sea." Then, taking flesh-substance from his person, he "formed the seed-stuff of twain worlds, impregnating therewith the great waters." After shaping the raw lands, he spread them out with his palm downward "and into all the wrinkles and crevices thereof he set the semblance of shining yellow corn-grains; in the dark of the early world-dawn they gleamed like sparks of fire, and moved as his hand was moved over the bowl, shining up from and also moving in the depths of the water therein." So was the night sky formed and space and time wound together on the wheel.[13]

The Mayan creation myth begins by making the Void as empty as possible: "all was in suspense, all calm, in silence; all motionless, still. . . . There was nothing brought together, nothing which could make a noise, nor anything which might move, or tremble. . . . Tepei and Gucumatz came together in the darkness, in the night." They were "great sages and great thinkers," but they had been "hidden under green and blue feathers," a startling paraphernalia for pre-existence. "They talked then, discussing and deliberating; they agreed, they united their words and their thoughts. . . . While they meditated, it became clear to them that when dawn would break, man must appear."[14]

In the Aranda creation myth from central Australia, the ancestor Karora "was lying asleep in everlasting night. . . . Over him the soil was red with flowers and overgrown with many grasses."

Flowers before flowers? Grasses of the Cosmic Mind from which the prairie grasses flowed?

"And Karora was thinking, and wishes and desires flashed through his mind. Bandicoots began to come out from his navel and from his armpits. They burst through the sod above, and sprang into life."[15]

Creation occurs in primordial Tahiti when Ta'aroa breaks through his egg which "revolved in space in continuous darkness." He stands upon the great broken shell and shouts: "Who is above there? Who is below there?" There is no answer. "Who is in front there? Who is in back there?" He hears only his own voice echoing. Then the first thing he does is to take his broken shell and raise it into a dome for the sky.[16]

The Japanese embryogenesis resembles the Chinese one:

> Of old, Heaven and Earth were not yet separated, and the *In* and *Yo* [feminine and masculine principles] not yet divided. They formed a chaotic mass like an egg which was of obscurely defined limits and contained germs.
>
> The purer and clearer part was thinly drawn out, and formed Heaven, while the heavier and grosser element settled down and became Earth.[17]

In Hebrew Qabalistic tradition, the creation emanates from God's intelligence as a series of primes generating other numbers, the sheaths of subsequent landscapes emerging as dreams within dreams until they manifest far beyond His images and He can no longer touch or alter them. They are subject only to the rule of the original numbers and the derivations from them.[18]

Our own "scientific" myth has elements of these various images because they are inherited or, in any case, unavoidable.

Some eighteenth-century scientists believed in a primeval germ which contained in miniature an image of all of the creation that would follow, so that each succeeding generation was contained in the prior one. The skin would peel off the bud, and a new creature, identical to its ancestor (or subtly different), would arise. When all the material within the germ was expended (the microcosmic germs within germs), that line would come to an end. Ultimately all lines would come to an end.

It was only later that scientists imagined a field which could recreate itself almost forever so long as the blueprint contained in that field was not destroyed and there was nourishment to sustain it. It would take billions of years to form such a blueprint, and its survival was always a delicate matter; but once in existence, it could go on using existing mass and energy indefinitely.

"We are the end of the leeching that produced us," writes the poet Edward Dorn. "A spoonful left at the bottom, very refined, pure stuff, the final dry powder, the dust that lives."[19]

Using the raw materials available on this planetoid in an ingenious fashion, our species has taken the smallest step back into eternity. It is also a big one, as Neil Armstrong intuited when he placed his hind limb, descendant of the phalanges of a frog and the spiny arms of a starfish, on the Moon. In overcoming an immense gravitational wall that held him in for thousands of generations, man has made a statement that would have seemed impossible, impossible forever, for a world of dragonflies and gulls. He has entered another space, however clumsily, however briefly. But this is not the way back into eternity, not the way he came. If he stares into space that way, he sees only a prison. The further he looks, in millions of light-years, the further he is from the center. Already the numbers are incomprehensible. The only way we make sense of them is to feed them into computers in greater and greater lump sums, making new exponential classes.

Our destiny in the sky is behind us and not before us. We and the stars float in the same cradle and are made of the same matter. In myth, we face each other in a concurrence beyond space and time. We are an indispensable part of their riddle, their own destiny. The consequences of walking on the Moon and sending satellites to photograph the outer planets of the Solar System are unknown at this point. But whether or not we adapt to outer space and pass to other planets, or even to another star, we share with the most remote galaxies we know, and those beyond them, a simultaneity on the inside of an unfolding virus. This is why Bumba's crocodile crawls out onto another planet in another galaxy too. This is why Karora's bandicoots flower with the birth gases of the remotest stars. This is why thought in the Mayan temples is akin, somehow, to something like thought in creatures who will never hear of us and whom we will never see. The real science fiction is the shared creation, which will never be known, and yet the intuition of it makes us who we are and gives rise to our images of fantastic beings derived from the same deep unconscious dark within us that atoms sprang from, and from them the earth and sky and protoplasm and genes of all those worlds and microcosms. Bumba's white heron is a white unknown bird flying toward the center of our galaxy, or away from it. His single bug appeared simultaneously throughout the universe, minute and unseen. This is true because there is no other truth to replace it, and any truth which replaces it will be of the same order. Because we cannot know, we must be; and in the unconscious origin of all things, knowing and being are finally the same. This is our oneness with both the Creation and the Void. And the night sky is the clearest statement, despite all that has happened to us in the subsequent turmoil of embryogenesis and local time, of who we are.

3

Occult
Astronomy

THE BIG BANG seals us into a dead universe that is also
dying. We too are extinguished without a ghost or a trace. We
huddle around the random embers of a sun-star, nursing the
faint currents of heat: the hot springs, the electron baths, the
summer grains and flowers, the glows in our bodies, and the
fossil fuels of their antecedents in the DNA blueprint. Not only
does nothing else remain: nothing else ever existed. But this is
the present endpoint of only one line of inquiry into the heavens: external, objective, and, in the modern sense, progressive.
The other is internal, magical or telepathic, and inherently te-
leological. At one pole of the universe, the Big Bang is everything. At the other pole, it is only a perceptible shell, a vivid
externalization, and we are the spawns of a profoundly internal
spiritual force. The Sun may heat the physical universe, and
barely so at that. There is an archetypal Sol which lights the
spiritual universe and will continue to forever, or until there is
no longer a need for this manifestation.

It would be a mistake to call one universe intuitive and the
other empirical: both are intuitive and both are empirical,
though in different ways and in relation to different ostensible
objects. Both are equally subject to psychological and cultural
biases. We can best understand the history of astronomy as a
dialectic of the lineages arising from these poles. Occult and
scientific astronomy inspire each other, they become one another, they mistake the other for themselves. In modern times, they
work not toward a rapprochement but toward a deeper and more

final polarity: on one side, the Big Bang; on the other, the astral universe in which all things endure forever.

The prototypical internal astronomer is the Egyptian priest in his pyramid. As he meditates on star images and decans (the thirty-six gods of the 10-degree divisions of the zodiac), the meanings of the sky come to him in his mind and spirit. The internal astronomer believes he can tell the difference between the images of his own brain and the messages of the stars. His methods are rigorous and certified, having been passed down for generations from the dawn of time. He knows the stars because he trains himself to be on their channels of intelligence, because he is the mirror of their life. His own knowledge is a version only of their cosmic and eternal wisdom.

Internal astronomy is our idea—not theirs. The priests do not think their stars are internal. Those are the real stars, the bright supernaturals in the sky and in magic texts, communicating clairvoyantly as well as visibly. Their messages fall into the bodies of plants, animals, and other entities. Magicians are actually internal astrologers who operate from this astral and planetary residue. Early man drank potions and went on vision-quests to get into the mind of the heavens. He stood outside in the night, night after night, and prayed for admittance and truth. What he learned he considered sky-intelligence. It is this visionary lore, this system of correspondences from a journey, imaginary or not, that sets the basis for internal astronomy with its star charts and sigils.

In one Taoist system of "interior astrology," as the translator renders it in English, the stargazer finds the stars by pressing the tips of his fingers just at the corners of his eyes and wiggling them until "the stars" appear. This is not some other arbitrary sky; for purposes of divination, it is the same sky, and the sage Shih K'uang tells Duke P'ing that he should use it "if the sky is cloudy and the stars are invisible." He goes on to remark that Alcor can still be found as a Helper Star, though no longer next to the Big Dipper.[1]

Duke P'ing is ecstatic at learning this method. "I will have [it] engraved on jade tablets and stored in my treasure chest," he says, "so that I can look at it often."[2]

"If a man's heart is true," Shih K'uang goes on to say, "he can see celestial lights and take their visibility into his heart through his eyes, or he can generate spirit lights and take them in through his breath and nerves. It is the same."[3]

To the external astronomer, this is not the sky at all, and it is not the stars. He observes the actual night sky in order to understand its patterns and cycles—the passage of different star-groups across the dome in the course of a night and the seasonal and millennial changes. Later in history, in the West, he comes to explore, by analysis of the electromagnetic band, the composition of the stars and the shape of the universe as a whole. It is the same activity carried on with new instruments from a cumulative bibliography. The external astronomer is concerned to know what the sky *is* in some absolute sense, just the way a biochemist might want to know what the ocean is. To him, the celestial sphere is imaginary, the constellations are imaginative projections, and the night sky is actually a field of infinite radius upon which the celestial objects appear to be placed. There is not one field but many individual fields, depending on the location of the viewer. The stars travel at speeds ranging from two hundred miles to billions of miles per second, but distance absorbs their motion, casting this temporary "stable" sky.

The internal astronomer is less concerned with the stars as they are in abstract nature and more with what they are in *his* nature. His nature is fused with the whole of the universe; he looks always into one through the other. From the point of view of the external astronomer, the internal astronomer is condemned never to know the actual stars, only the aspects of his own consciousness (and unconsciousness) assigned to the heavens by tradition, mythology, and lore.

Internal astronomy may come first in the history of mankind, but it is a totally hypothetical priority: our awareness of our own existence precedes our awareness of the sky. Internal astronomy is never entirely divorced from external astronomy. It could not be. Man knows the stars only from seeing them. Though the internal sky may have been intuited visionarily at some apocryphal moment before he looked upward, it was not then the sky but a field of unknown composition and shape extending infinitely within, filled with sparks and talismans. A series of insights joined this at once to the night sky, and a ritual methodology sealed the marriage for as long as we are together on this world. The darkness without and the phenomenological field within became the night sky, so now we can barely imagine what preceded a prehistoric system millions of years old. By the time we hear of astronomy, in our voyage backward before it disappears into the mute darkness of our own ancestry, it already includes uncountable varieties of astrology, astromancy, and astral magic.

Stonehenge is the work of priests, but the precision of its architecture leads one to consider it a primitive computer, a "machine" that remembers positions in the sky to allow exact calibration, at the solstices and equinoxes, of moonrise and sunrise, moonset and sunset. In fact, these positions are stones on the heel of which or through the minute openings between which the Sun or Moon appears at appropriate times. The larger temple, including the so-called Aubrey Holes for sticks to be set in, served as a general computer for the prediction of eclipses.[4] If this was 3,500 years ago, as is generally believed, some 20,000 years earlier the ostensible ancestors of these people in France and Spain kept track of the phases of the Moon with tiny notches on antlers, bones, tusks, and pebbles.[5] As Alexander Marshack indicates in his studies of these objects, they correspond so exactly to lunar cycles in their mathematical series that they could hardly, within reason, be anything else—especially, we might add, given the lunar obsessions of later, historically-known peoples or the rich and complex development of lunar symbolism by the time we receive it in written text. The earliest lunar (and solar) imagery is so exquisite in its interpenetrating themes and counterpoints that it is more like the remains of a dying civilization on another planet than the inheritance of the dawn of our race. No doubt this is part of the temptation of various mythographers and other exotic historians to assign this imagery to visitors from other worlds, other times, other galaxies.

The particular crudeness of the scribbles Marshack discovered, such that they had been overlooked by all prior archaeologists, is far outweighed by their mathematicity. The people of the late Stone Age may have had rough tools to record with, but they understood cyclicity and its relationship to stellar events. The sky was the biggest and most obvious text to study, however it got there. It was blazing reality. It contained the basis of time and number in space, concepts so large that they seemed to contain the universe. Ancient man studied this luminous text nightly for generations and learned the whole system, made of it a noetics and a poetics without having to know what the stars were made of; they were made, in a sense, of the numbers they generated, numbers which were also generated by flowers, seasons, rivers, and man's mental and biological rhythms, hence sacred numbers, giving rise to the divine beings who also appeared in dreams and visions. It is not happenstance at all that when the gods of the sky appear in historical times in the early civilizations, they are involved with mathematics, or that early astronomy *is* astrology. And as far as Stonehenge itself is concerned, the twenty thousand years between those ancient counting boards of the Moon and the temple observatories of both the Old World and the New are enough to engulf all of history since many times. They are certainly enough to allow a linear phase-count to be transformed into three-dimensional reflecting pools of stone.

Divination, magic, and the calendar share an origin in this larger system. The association of Sirius with the inundation of the Nile at the summer solstice may be a "scientific observation," but the larger system of which it is part is experienced internally. One school of contemporary ethnoastronomy argues that the origin of writing systems—Egyptian hieroglyphics, Chinese ideograms, and Canaanite-Phoenician syllabic alphabets—long a mystery, must lie in this same ancient astro-philosophy. Specifically, Hugh Moran and David Kelley propose that the twenty-two letters of the Hebrew alphabet and the twenty-eight letters of the Arabic alphabet "are based on the signs of the lunar zodiac, which long antedates the twelve signs of the ecliptic or solar zodiac." The age of this system is demonstrated by global correspondences which suggest a pre-Indo-European, even an Ice Age, origin. It includes Chinese and Hindu lunar mansions,

Jain symbols for the lunar constellations, Aztec day gods and day names, Mayan glyphs and day names, Burmese constellations, and Cambodian lunar animals. Of course, the Greek and Roman alphabets, and our own Romance ones, follow from the Semitic.[6] It is as though the Moon herself, in our magical and mythical devotion to her and her numbers and symbols, gave us the system of recording from which all history radiated. No wonder she has an astrological association with memory, the unconscious, and the duplication of codes.

The traditional Western name for the spiritual sky is the astrum. This astral realm is not organized according to normal linear geometry. Things small in real space (like the planet Pluto) may be astrally equivalent to Saturn, or even the Sun. Physical remoteness of the stars does not change their astral nearness. Those bodies we see distributed in "outer space" are simply three-dimensional footprints of bodies of many dimensions.

Strictly speaking, in order to "see" astral space, one must enter an astral body. In that form a person can travel and visit other worlds while his physical body remains on Earth. The astral realm is a manifestation of the ultimate night sky, so knowledge of correspondences gained on these transphysical journeys is applicable to the visual sky. The astral and the astrological are definitely related: the planets move visibly in the zodiac, but the meaning of this movement is perceptible only in astral form. That is not to say that astrology derives from astral projection. It may well precede it, coming not from that method of "seeing" but from its own long tradition of celestial and terrestrial observation and intuition.

In the astrum, stars and planets show things most inherent to them. They appear with their original colors; they hum their natural sounds.[7] At the same time that they reach upward into a divine and supernal realm, they are imbedded in a physicalizing hierarchy that requires the Earth at its other pole. Sky and stars and gods came into being in the lotus burst of creation. As the petals of this lotus continue to unfold and create the outermost and the profound, its fine roots grow downward through the rich humus of the Void, a fertility associated in hermetic tradition with the number Zero, the Fool of the tarot, and the egg of the Gnosis. When Zero opens, it contains All.

The flower of the heavens reaches down over us and covers us; the elemental life of the world surges up within it as different octaves of occult vibration. The Earth is the sphere of magical operation. It is removed from the center of creation, where magic is natural and influence direct, but it has a direct rhythmic and sympathetic connection to this realm through the astrum. Inasmuch as the physical world was brought into being invocatorily and magically from the Source, it can reach the Source by invocation and magic. The lunar alphabet and calendric number systems are the most important tools.

The trees, the animals, the flowers, the fish all originally had counterparts in the sky, stars or constellations that reflected their essential being, that arose from the same archetypes. To look into the night sky was to look at the different flowers in the fields, to see the fish of the deep. It was also to see the character of mankind, for the different types of human beings, the idiosyncratic nations and occupations, the various clans and totems, were all written in the sky. A particular tree or herb or stone may be associated with a planet or star, such as juniper with Saturn or the lemon-yellow gem apatite with Mercury.[8] The Star of Bethlehem coincided with the advent of Christianity. Some modern astrologers have claimed that the comet Kohoutek deposed numerous heads of state, including Richard Nixon. The birth chart gives another version of Earth-Sky correspondence. A being is, in some primary sense, a replica of the heavens at the moment of his birth. He or she is not absolutely condemned to one linear pattern of action, but the potential contained in that moment of the cosmos is incarnated in a unique life.

Rudolf Steiner, the twentieth-century German mystic scientist, claimed that if we knew how to interpret and read the brain tissue, we could see the constellations of the sky written into the delicate flesh below the skullcap:

> If one photographed the brain of a person at the moment of his birth, and then photographed the sky as well, exactly as it stood over the place of birth, this picture would show quite the same thing as the human brain. . . . Man bears

within him an image of the heavens, and this image is different for every person, depending upon the place and time of his birth. This is an indication that man is born out of the whole universe.[9]

Like the eighteenth-century Swedish theologian and scientist, Emanuel Swedenborg, Rudolf Steiner believed that all the planets and stars are inhabited: Mercury, Venus, Jupiter, Saturn, Uranus, the Sun, Rigel, and the planets of Rigel and Canopus. But, he pointed out, they are not inhabited in this plane.

Johannes Kepler, one of the founders of modern astronomy, was a committed astrologer who conjectured that the geometrical effects of the stars and planets were transmitted to the Earth much in the way that light reaches the senses. This "astral light" is not perceived but translated into concrete effects. It could not be seen in his time; and Kepler believed that it would never be seen. It passed from the souls of the luminaries to the soul of this Earth, and it was comprehensible intuitively by the soul of man.

"The natural soul of man," wrote Kepler, "is not larger in size than a single point, and on this point the form and character of the entire sky is potentially engraved, even if it were a hundred times larger."[10]

"Even if it were a trillion times larger," we might say today, but it is not a matter of quantitative size. It is the perception of the universe as a spiritual whole. Kepler had it by his birth. We must struggle to it, if we want it, through appearances which challenge us and deny the grand harmony every step of the way.

An hermetic description of the Creation appears in *The Divine Pymander*,[11] an Hellenic mediaeval work attributed to a much older Hermes. This contains the background theology for internal astronomy and an explanation for the merging of astrum and night sky: The spoken Word of God touches the creative Mind, and a speech-driven impulse hurtles through an infinite Below. It becomes entangled in the whirlpool of incipient Nature and is spun around and around in circles and circles within circles. There it loses its simple relationship to the origination and is "turned from an indefinite beginning to an interminable end."[12] Seven paths, or vibrations, connect back to the Creator, for there is a Seven within Him that He has imparted to the Creation. He smiles with love upon this maelstrom; then He sees reflected back an "insatiate beauty," the form of Man rippling in the shadow, carried through light and water. So taken is He with this appearance that He "willed to dwell within it" and "begat the irrational form."[13] Nature looks back through this beautiful image of God and longs to embrace the Man. Man also sees himself for the first time in his reflection in the body of Nature and in her desire for him; he is enamored and reaches down through the shells and embraces himself in her. The shells break, and Man and Nature are locked eternally in an embrace. Neither can escape the other.

There is still no sky, only the movement of forces—Mind, shadows and water, the turbulence of disturbed fields. The sky comes into being after and in correspondence with the "beasts, quadrupeds, and reptiles, and aquatics, and winged, and every fruitful seed, and grass and green herb, having the seed of reproduction in themselves."[14] The seed seals the circles and the Seven into the world. The whirlpool becomes the microcosm.

From the beginning, there is another "Sky," the cosmic background against which Creation emerges. As long as there is no starry night, nothing separates time from the eternal. Finally, a thin translucent layer turns the Earth inside the Creation and gives the illusion of geography, space, and time. Later astronomers will see that the illusion is infinite and goes on galaxy upon galaxy, but the infinity is not what removes the Earth from the Creation; it is a secondary effect. What removes the Earth is the mirage of geography and sky, the perceptual trick, or, in Qabalistic lore, the whirling sword which God placed to keep man and woman from returning to Eden, a sword which could now only be the speed of light, as it relates both to the physics of particles and the physiology of the eye. The original Sky is woven through the Earth and reachable in intermediate form as the astrum.

The optic image and the hermetic one fall simultaneously upon man in his intuition that he is inside something that has formed around him not once but many times, and not in one way but in many ways, and so that he cannot tell the difference between the source inside him and the source outside him. The whole geography of future worlds from which we might come before birth and later worlds to which we might go after death hangs in the balance of this unresolved episode in a whirlpool, with the sole significant clue being the number Seven. We talk of spirit and matter, or the divine realm beyond the stars, even the physical realm of galaxies and quasars, and all these things follow from the way in which we believe that the world was imbued with life and meaning in the first place.

After the formation of the night sky, the Seven Circles worked their way up to the top of our sphere. The divine aspects in them took on stellar forms, and the constellations were made. Then the circumference was wrapped around, forming a visible plane in which these original creationary forces shone. The night sky is thus the last vestige of matter where matter becomes more and more permeated with spirit as it moves toward spirit. Some mediaeval and Renaissance occultists believed that the material part dominated and the stars showered the Earth with poisons and destructive influences which man could ward off by amulets and signets. Others saw those same influences as free stellar energy, useful to create medicines, perform magic, and even to escape astrological destiny.

Taoist astronomers believed likewise that the true heavens lay behind the transient visible sky, or within it, as candles in a glass lantern: "Outside the sky the Luminous Ho throws up waves of jade."[15]

We can picture these purple-black waves, like an ocean, washing up against the universe.

Rodney Collin's occult definition of light, fully informed by twentieth-century science, gives a sense of the simultaneous hermetic and astrophysical cosmos:

> If light can diffuse and endure undiminished for half-a-billion years, it can surely do so for ever. This means that all light, from a candle or from a super-sun, sooner or later fills the entire universe. Light is *undiminishable, eternal and omni-present*. In every religion that existed these qualities have been recognized as divine. So that we are forced to the conclusion that light—actual sensible light—is indeed

the direct vehicle of divinity: it is the consciousness of God.[16]

So we can look at the sky as a screen of hydrogen fires, or we can look at the same light as the divine component of creation transmitted eternally. The Sun is the local embodiment of this material, and the Earth is constructed of solar material. When we imagine the primordial seas with their millennial rains and steam, the upheaval of the molten core, the emergence of bare rock, and the clinging life mantle, we can intuit an inside to this process so that the astral is transmitted through the elemental. Then the Sun becomes something more than an incandescent cloud of molten seas and gaseous corona. Beyond its granularity and molecularity is another characteristic. Collin says:

> Go out and stare at the sun in the sky. Why are you blinded? Why are you unable to define or describe what you see? Why is the impression incomparable with anything else you know? It is because you are looking through a hole in our three-dimensional scenery, *out into the six-dimensional world.*
>
> The matter of the Sun, or electronic matter, is beyond form and beyond time. It is even beyond the recurrence of form and the repetition of time. . . .[17]

The Jesuit anthropologist Pierre Teilhard de Chardin has a modern evolutionary version: The mass of the Sun contained a psychic interior which it inherited from the origin of the cosmos and the beginning of time itself. The Earth is an interstellar germ, endowed with a sidereal aspect by the Sun. This aspect emerges through the combination of complex molecules. Cells differentiate from a native hydrosphere, then the organs of larger animals from cells, and still more complex layers of animal life upon these. None of this could have happened, argues Teilhard, if it were not already present at the beginning. Life is an expression of inner substance attempting to return to an original spiritual state. As plants and trees reach up to the sky for light, transforming that light by photosynthesis into the food of creatures from the food of stars, they are reenacting a pure divine form, they are reaching for the Sun. Their "without" projects the patterns of nature; their "within" is archetypal. In one aspect of their being, they penetrate the six-dimensional cosmos; in another aspect, they differentiate, spread, branch, think, and make philosophy, art, and science—to imitate, by intelligence, the pre-intelligent source.[18]

Teilhard calls it "a doubly related involution, the coiling up of the molecule upon itself and the coiling up of the planet upon itself. The initial quantum of consciousness contained in our terrestrial world is not formed merely of an aggregate of particles caught fortuitously in the same net. It represents a correlated mass of infinitesimal centres structurally bound together by the conditions of their origin and development."[19]

These coilings take place simultaneously across the entire planet as a series of waves. First there is chemical activity, then simple cell growth and bacteria teeming across the surface, then animals, then a wave of thought which sweeps the planet first as telecommunications and later as an actual noosphere. At this stage, the Earth merges again with the spiritual cosmos.[20]

We are encouraged to look anew into the night sky, and it is a hive of cells and souls traversed by divine light and the archetypal data of creation. In Gurdjieff's system, light carries information from higher worlds into lower ones, information which can be transformed by physical nourishment and breath back into astral thought. But those beings which do not develop souls from this stellar debris and which are unable to transcend three dimensions at death become light itself. They are damned to return unrequited to the stars and, with their flawed energy, light the cosmos for eternity.[21]

In Ptolemaic astronomy and the systems which it summarized and gave birth to, we find the sense of an enclosure within spheres, with the Earth in the center where the roots of the divine whirlpool hang. In their own time, the hermetic astronomers were moderns, not primitives, for they inherited the astral science of prehistoric times and translated it into a reasonable predictive astronomy and a geometry of movement.

The related science of astral talismans, signets, and decans was based on compelling influence from the appropriate heavenly body—or contrarily, on warding off heavenly influence. Ultimately it developed its own set of images for terrestrial divination. They were celestial only as the sky was imagined through them.

In the fifteenth century, in Ferrara, Italy, the Duke Borso d'Este had a ballroom in his palace covered with the thirty-six hermetic decans, representing the so-called Egyptian gods of time. This group included a tall dark man in white, a woman hiding her missing leg under her skirt, a man holding a circle, etc. Each of these represented a portion of the astral sky, as well as a part of the human body, a color, a musical note, etc.[22] The seventeenth-century astrological geomancy of Henry Cornelius Agrippa continues this tradition, listing the shapes in which the spirits of the different planets appear on Earth. Saturn is a bearded King riding on a Dragon, but also an Old Woman leaning on a staff, a Dragon, an Owl, and a black Garment. Jupiter is a King with a drawn Sword riding on a Stage, a Box-Tree, a Peacock, and a Maid with a Laurel Crown adorned with flowers. Mars's King is armed, riding upon a Wolf, but he is also Wool, a Stage, a He-goat, and a Woman holding a buckler on her thigh. The Sun King holds a Scepter and rides on a Lion, or he is crowned; the Sun Spirit also occurs in a gold color, with the tincture of blood; its invocation moves the person who calls on it to sweat. Venus has Maids which provoke and allure and call to play. The Venusian King rides on a Camel, but Venus is equally a naked Maid, the herb Savine, and a green Garment. Mercury is clear and bright, with movement of silver-colored clouds; its King rides upon a Bear; it is also a Magpie and a Dog. The Moon is swelling and phlegmatic, an Archer-King, a little Doe, a Cow, a Goose, an Arrow, and a Creature with many feet.[23]

The astral correspondences are at once traditionary and visionary. One learns them by perceiving them internally, but first one must saturate oneself in the already existing occult systems. Some uneducated mystics may have a spontaneous insight into correspondences, but most occultists need to study magic, alchemy, astrology, spiritual botany, and the other hermetic texts.

One might object that this prejudices them into supplying traditional images as if they were discovering them anew. Of course, skeptics deny that there is any objective source for this kind of information. It can come only as hand-me-downs because it is nothing more than antique prescientific fantasies of the structure of nature. If mystics were truly left on their own to discover relations, they would make up inconsistent and wildly diverging meanings for all the stars and planets. This misses another point.

The hermetic texts contain the cumulative attempt of Western mystics to discern the hidden correspondences between man and the cosmos—from their own experiences and those transmitted from the non-Western world. The importance of these symbols and correspondences is not that they have been fixed by occult authority, nor that they are ancient. Their significance lies in the fact that they are our only history of the spiritual universe to this point, that they have been found satisfactory on an unconscious psychological level over millennia, and that they represent a collective cultural experience over many aeons and lifetimes: they are our single thread going back to the beginning.

It is not that no other meanings are acceptable, but that these are the training ground for all future researchers. There are other occult and astral systems in Oriental, American Indian, Australian, and African cultures. These are very difficult for Westerners to learn. The association of a certain species of turtle with the Sun or of a wolverine with a constellation has particular meaning only in cultural terms. To understand the association, one must be inside the culture. These different incommensurate systems which share no common yardstick like science could be proof of the arbitrariness of the astral tradition, but they could indicate also that the truth is not on an obvious level and that there are viable local systems for interpreting a paradoxical universe.

The astral and astronomical universes obviously share nothing today, and it is difficult to make a case for a relationship. I had not thought this problem through when, in January of 1972, I stumbled onto it in an interview with the astronomer Carl Sagan.[24] He expressed contempt for the occult arts and indicated that it was far simpler to dream up a planet than actually to go there and see what it was. This seemed an ethnocentric and technocratic point of view, so I challenged it, saying that there was a relationship between the planets in the astrum and the planets in the sky. He laughed and asked me to prove it. My quick response was that the Mars being photographed then by Mariner cameras was only known at all insofar as it had existed in the whole history of our trying to visualize and understand it, and that that history was inextricably interwoven with the photographs even before they were taken. Sagan objected that this was to say the unconscious mind could have some knowledge of astronomy apart from what the conscious mind tells it. He argued that some sort of scientific tests would have to be carried out before data could be considered valid. Otherwise it was just wishful thinking. As we talked longer and longer, it became clear that this was an important issue to him. His sense of personal maturity came from not believing in occult things and from having grasped and taken the one opportunity there was in this age to visit other planets. He had translated a boyhood fantasy into a real adult life, and these other things seemed to him like the indulgences of adults who could not grow up and were probably not good scientists anyway.

"In my mind," he said, "there's a big difference between something I want to be true and therefore pretend inside my head is really true and something that's really true. . . . Suppose you lived your whole life in a very subdued and puritanical and uptight way because that was what you had to do to get to heaven, and then you die and that's it. Well, I think you would have been had."

"You wouldn't know it," I said.

"Nevertheless, it makes a difference to me. The fact that you would have foregone all sorts of satisfactions and pleasures for a supposed infinite reward and then that infinite reward was never delivered."[25]

One would hardly want to deny us the treasures that the space program has brought back from the nearby planets, and in any case Sagan's point of view is the conventional materialistic one and does not engage the astral problem except to dismiss it, which is certainly a legitimate stance. There is, however, another aspect of our experience, and we lose it if we are this quick to do away with the spiritual sky. The stars may be made out of hot gas and atoms, but that is not what they *are*. In fact, we do not know what they are.

The modern astral tradition does not deny scientific information; it feeds off it. As the planets change from animals and luminous bodies to worlds, these worlds have new kinds of astral fields and auras. We live in our internalizations of our images, which themselves change the nature of things. We unknowingly forge new talismans in the lineage of those Egyptian priests who said their charms held the spirits of individual stars. The NASA photographs are among these now; they are syncretized in contemporary astrology and divination, even as bits of European machinery and junk are incorporated as trinkets within sacred Crow Indian medicine bundles without undermining the bundles' sacred power.

Of course, there is only one real universe. There are the two vying impostors of our modern times: the spiritual and the material. Though the law of creation demands that these be absolutely merged at every linear moment, they have become now as two separate systems of belief which divide the world. The difference between capitalism and socialism palls beside this.

To look at the heavens and realize that one is staring into a vast mirror of correspondence and sympathy is very different from looking out into the expanding body of the fireball. We cannot do away with the radio sky or the sky of the Big Bang and its galaxies and cosmic rays and hungry suns. But we can impose those two skies on each other and realize that they are opposite terms in an identity that for us is not resolved—that they are both inevitable, and it is up to us to square them in ourselves. The astral and astrological sky is what we contact as we go back into our own history, our infancy as a species, but also into our moment of identification with the cosmos, which is still inside us in some way. The physical expanding sky is what we contact as we go outward into contemporary physics and astronomy and the dismissal of all unproven synchronisms and correspondences. Both are there in our heritage and both are necessary. They deny each other, but then we deny each other.

They also require each other, and so do we. Without astrology, there never could have been astrophysics. Not only does astrology give birth to astronomy in the minds of Kepler and Newton; it does so again in the minds of us all. And astrology requires an age like this one, or if it did not, it would have to require it, for it has happened, in correspondence perhaps to some Aquarius who has slipped out of the visible sky and stumbled badly from alignment, but not in the astral sky where the Water-Carrier is true.

New Age astrology, which avoids astrophysics and even astronomy like the plague, is out of touch with cosmic astrology, which stays in tune with the changing world aeons and evolving views of the stars. The modern dilemma is reflected decisively in astronomy, not in astral magic or astrology, at least not as we understand them. This is the truth that lies behind Sagan's unexamined bias. Our dilemma may return to a spiritual sky, but only through the present secular heavens. Until then, the sky of astrophysics must be part of the astral and astrological skies, and we will struggle all our lives toward a reconciliation.

If we look into both skies at once, we stare down a strange and chilling tunnel into the thing we are. And the deeper we look into the contradiction, the paradoxes on either half of the contradiction—zodiac symbols and fleeing quasars—the more we can see and the more we realize what it took to get us here.

4

Star Myth

THE SKY was originally a palace and a kingdom, a zone where deities acted out eternal roles. It was also a dark crystal in which the Earth's landscapes reflected authentically and permanently. The alchemists thought of their work as literally capturing part of the sky. The planets and stars moved again in the constituent chemicals and their interactions. The alembic itself enclosed the experiment in a sphere, and a local sky formed, often twinkling with "stars" or arched with a fine rainbow. The sixteenth-century alchemist Edward Kelly called his work "the theatre of terrestrial astronomy," and he raised a golden Sun and a green lion which bit the Sun, causing it to bleed red into the waters.[1] But Earth and sky have been coeval since the dawntime, and every ancient tribe and civilization viewed their marriage as an active account of cosmology smelted in radiant metals.

The River Eridanus, later identified with the Nile, the Po, and the Danube, was a river in the sky, a constellation of hundreds of faint stars flowing out of the heel of Orion toward Cetus, then meandering back toward Lupus. The faintness of the stars was not as important as the existence of the river itself, a river on whose banks gods walked and which carried traffic to the land of the dead. It is in that starry river that the body of Phaëthon lies, and the sparkling waters flow over him on their continuous journey to the other world. The Eridanus is the river whose confluence with another river—not the Nile, Tigris, or Euphrates—marks the birthplace of civilization. That other river is either the zodiac or some faint tributary leading into the Galaxy itself, a torrent of light that the Greeks called a helix and

56

that we still imagine rushing simultaneously over and under us to the center.

On the Earth, things changed swiftly and irregularly—a sudden gust of wind in the trees, a crashing wave, a burst of violence, a passage of birds, a fever. In the sky, things changed slowly and regularly and according to profound cosmic rhythms and numerological codes. With the wobbling of the Earth on its axis and the consequent precession of the equinoxes through the zodiac, the celestial aeons were transformed, one into another. The Sun abandoned its scorched trail in the Milky Way, and the flow of waters to the Underworld was diverted from the Galaxy into the Eridanus. But even if this is not true, it is the way that ancient man had conceived the single frame to which Heaven and Earth adhere. The "modern" destruction of that frame began at least a millennium before the birth of Christ. The cosmic unity was challenged, then disassembled, and the sky against which our species was born became disjointed from the Earth's axis. Some three thousand years later, that sky was set adrift without a single stellar deity, and it settled—infinite, directionless, and outside time.

Homer was probably our last living link with Ice Age cosmology and the mythic heavens. All the rest of our "data" is archaeological and ethnographic. But even Odysseus's voyage was nostalgic—a return to the fading vestiges of an Atlantean kingdom that swept simultaneously once across the Earth and Sky. It is fitting that we know Homer as a voice rather than a man.

Dante spoke the truth for our whole tribe of wandering, faithless Indo-Europeans when he wrote:

> I woke to find myself in a dark wood,
> Where the right road was wholly lost and gone.[2]

That road had been lost long before the Church schisms, and Nazareth was a surprise and premature flash of its connection to all of space and time before and after. Dante's astronomy was more savage than Jesus's, and it invoked a star for which Bethlehem was one cycle of an eternal return.

Dante sent Odysseus on a final voyage into cosmogonic space.

He sailed to the outermost West, beyond Spain and the Pillar of Hercules. Five times Odysseus watched the Moon fill with light and then wane. The known stars failed to rise from the ocean, and new stars filled the sky. Then he and his men reached a mountain surrounded by a whirlpool, a pinnacle rising from the sea to the heavens, Purgatory. His ship was swept up in the current and spun three times around. Then the hollow above it closed, and Odysseus's wanderings were at an end, though ours had barely begun. The whirlpool that swept up Dante's Odysseus was found in the Southern sea only by the displacements of an exiled civilization that no longer saw the gods or knew where they lived. It was originally in the sky, beside Rigel, and it led directly through the sacred Eridanus to the Land of the Dead.[3]

The charisma that attends myth is still, in part, the charisma of the superior lands of the sky. To the Indians of the Plains, the Milky Way was dust kicked up by the Buffalo and the Horse— the original Buffalo and Horse who prefigured the ceaseless herds of the daylight. Imagine the moonlit dust across Dakota, and how it sparkled against its stellar counterpart. The difference between Alexander and Napoleon was that Alexander was the last of the old kings. When he attempted to conquer the world, his image was the Cosmos, the Sky. There was no clear map for such a conquest, but it was intimated in his taking over the temples and texts and priests of the peoples of the world and in the prophecies of the Heavens he sought and summoned as he moved across their terrestrial reflection. Napoleon simply sought lands and territories; his military strategy was secular and without a supernatural element. Both men died with their goal unattained, but Alexander's failure was different from the other. He was already at the dawn of the modern world, when the sky had changed so much that it could no longer hold his deed or those of the Persian kings he supplanted. It was astonishing to him to find that the cosmos could not be conquered. He arrived after the twilight of the gods, when the center had fallen out of the sky and the constellations had shifted from their ancient homes.

In a mythic sense, Alexander's campaign was to restore the

old sky, to bring meaning back through cosmic adventure. He failed, and history washes over him as Eridanus washes over the body of the fallen Galaxy. The oracles, in the words of Plutarch four centuries later, were no longer true; they no longer spoke of the cosmos; the telepathic star-priests heard nothing, and they have heard nothing since, though we have probed the heavens from the electromagnetic to the psychic bands. A pilot at sea during the reign of Tiberius, in the first years of the first century A.D., heard the last cry of the ancient world as his ship drifted near the island of Paxi: "Great Pan is dead!" A voice from nowhere speaking words that were utterly clear. The gods were leaving us, and we would have to follow them into the night.[4]

Alexander and Plato had come too late. Napoleon was a forerunner of the modern darkness and the malignant world wars. By then the sky had descended to the Earth and been divided, and we have come to speak of quantity only, no longer unity and cosmos. Space rockets now mark our promised connection to the golden civilizations of the sky, civilizations in our future whose sources predate the inhabited Earth. We have almost completed a cycle, it seems. Its origins are invisible because they have been buried, and its destiny is invisible because it is yet unborn. We may never recover the star myth, but, at this point, we must go either back in time, into the depths of collective unconsciousness, or out into the undiminishable heavens.

Astronomy has never been a neutral objective science. Once man developed systems for decoding the obscure patterns of the heavens, he was subjected to an ongoing flood of messages and meanings. No one man or woman developed these systems, so all men and women were subject to their collectivity.

The changing shapes of the constellations and the movements in the sky, as an independent feature of nature, have a dynamic effect on the peoples who observe and study them. Generation by generation, the stars are transformed, but so are the species and the planet. Our great battle, after all, has been with meaning, not with nature. The stars do not visibly control destiny or, by strings attached, cause floods and invasions. They do, however, control meaning, and meaning controls these cataclysmic events, for meaning alone can justify and explain them. This is the intimation of planetary motion, solstice, and Moon phase. It is as though the universe were trying to speak to us from the depths of its being, to tell us what it is and what is happening to us. An eclipse or comet seems to scream warning and transition from the mute heavens. Since there was no known script, tribal man made a hieroglyphic alphabet for the stars.

It is not just a matter of primitive society being influenced by sidereal divination. Johannes Kepler's "solution" of the orbit of Mars led, by its algebra, to the industrial revolution. Albert Einstein's resolution of matter and energy led to Hiroshima and Three Mile Island. Star knowledge is literally and always brought down to Earth, where it has a profound effect on the condition of our life. Admittedly, it is our *interpretation* of the stars' behavior that has the impact rather than the stars themselves. But they have a primacy in that, and their natural continuity carries our meanings from aeon to aeon. Were their nature otherwise, our societies would be different too.

We and the night sky are truly indistinguishable partners in cosmology and creation. We give the sky an identity which is, in fact, our own. Each society that has sought pure knowledge of the heavens has imposed on the heavens the meaning of itself, and thus taken back a certain truth about objective nature simultaneous with its self-fulfilling prophecy about what all this is. We are initially embryos in an embryological expansion of matter. And we are internal forms within an internalization of images and forms. We cast against the remote and eternal heavens something from the depths of our unconscious process as well as the conscious bias of our institutions. We do it to all of nature, but the sky is the most remote and mysterious feature of our world, so it takes on the deepest and most unconscious expression of our hidden agenda.

We tend not to question the mythical basis of astronomy when it is applied to the god-inhabited skies of native peoples or to the astral skies of astrologers and theosophists. "Of course, these are projections," we think. "They are the results of prescientific ignorance, and they have nothing to do with the sky itself." Some ultimate court may decide so, but since there is presently no such court nor the likelihood of one, we must accept that divine, astral, and astrological skies remain coexistent with the series of increasingly refined skies discovered by astronomers of the last centuries.

What may be harder to accept, especially for some of these astronomers and their contemporary advocates, is that their own skies are also cultural projections. The Big Bang, the expanding universe, neutron stars, and even gravity are finally ethnic and provincial notions. None of these things really exist. They are approximations—compromises between what nature is and what society is—even as primitive myths are. Both were equivalently brought into being by cosmogenesis and embryogenesis, and each expresses an aspect of that process. The very rapid shift in theory among astronomers, even from decade to decade in our own time, should tell us that none of these present maps is absolute. In a hundred years, they will seem quaint period pieces. In a thousand years, they will be all but forgotten. Another universe may come into being, one that we cannot presently imagine, which will be as different from ours as ours is from the Babylonian.

Alfred North Whitehead spoke of the "background" of civilizations. Any given culture exists in the foreground of its beliefs, its institutions, its mysteries, and even its self-criticisms. These are all the things it knows. There is also a background of which it can never be aware and which will define it.[5] Even as we look back on the Egyptians and know what they could not, the people of a future time may be able to look back and see who we were and in what sort of heavens our cities stood. But they will not know the truth of their own cities and skies. Even if they are only hypothetical, we are still trapped by the fact that our attention must be on our actions and intentions and not on their definition against time.

In both a physical and a mythical sense, the sky is the background to all of civilization—on other worlds: other skies. Ancient myth is originally stellar myth, cosmic philosophy. We have emerged out of it, and its meanings and directives are now un-conscious in us. We carry out aspects of their societies that the Phoenicians and Celts could not know. Much of our hidden background is ancient and archetypal; some of it may lie in fu-ture worlds, but even these, the old stories tell us, are the eternal return of original worlds.

Star myth is virtually as old as consciousness. It originates in the Pleistocene epoch, before the dawn of writing; and by the time it is written down, as *Gilgamesh, Gawain,* and the *Kalevala,* it is already a relic of a million dead peoples.

As historical remnants, myths are attuned to the oldest as-pects of somatic consciousness. Their chthonian affinities and basic impenetrability make them finally transhistorical. The pro-fundity of Pleistocene consciousness, removed from us in linear time, is similar to our cellular codes, from which we are not separated at all in time (since they are inside us) but by the hierarchical branching of tissue in our bodies. And it is this that myth has always tried to remedy. It has tried, by a strangeness and a discontinuity equal to the facts, to recover the impossible treasures: our origin in the time-space of creation and our kin-ship with ancestors whose children we are and whose care and blessing we have by the direct bonds they formed with those to whom they gave birth.

The night sky is the bedrock of myth, and it remains so today, providing us with astrophysical and science fiction myths, "star wars" and "close encounters" to give voice to those things deep inside us that nothing else can pretend to express.

In their epic work on star myth, *Hamlet's Mill,* Giorgio de Santillana and Hertha von Dechend portray cosmic beings which are strung on the stars in the same way that we now string time itself on the speed of light:

> These personages are unmistakably identified, yet elusively fluid in outline. They tell of gigantic figures and superhu-man events which seem to occupy the whole living space between heaven and earth. Those figures often lend their names to historical persons in passing and then vanish. Any attempt to tie them down to history, even to the tradition

of great and catastrophic events, is invariably a sure way to a false trail. Historical happenings will never "explain" mythical events. Plutarch knew as much. Instead, mythical figures have invaded history under counterfeit present-ments, and subtly shaped it to their own ends.[6]

These are the archetypes, and they are virtually our only con-vincing version left of the gods behind history. For the Egyptians and their ancestors, they were true gods, star-beings and crea-tors. Plato saw their elemental geometry and passed it on as number. Galileo Galilei exposed the corporeal robes of the planets, and the gods were driven out of history. We now find their fragments and reflections in psychology and political ritual, where they vary with unconscious process, and in a realm of so-called matter, where they vary still between matter and energy.

"To be sure," write Santillana and von Dechend, "mythical beings are born and pass on, but not quite like mortals. . . . They have been before, or will be again, in other names, under other aspects, even as the sky brings back forever its configurations. . . . If one respects their true nature, they will reveal that nature as *functions*."[7]

Now we are simultaneously in the world of ancient totem beings and topological algebras. Star myth embraces both. In one aeon, it shows its countenance as Osiris and Set; in another aeon, as electromagnetism and radiation.

"Functions of what?" ask the star-myth historians. "Of the general order of things as it could be conceived. These figures express the behavior of that vast complex of variables once called the cosmos. They combine in themselves variety, eternity, and recurrence, for such is the nature of the cosmos itself."[8] The real night sky is revealed not by science or "by the poet's con-scious thinking, but by the power of the lines themselves, so utterly remote, like light coming from a 'quasi-stellar object.'"[9]

We may be deprived of the ancient stars, but we are not deprived of everything. They lie dormant in our geology as much as our astronomy, and in TV soap operas and rock and roll songs. The ballplayers on their arc-lit diamond at night and the flashing stars of the disco palace may be pale reminders of real cosmology and myth without an authentic sky to back them.

But they are given power and beauty by what remains of the old gods. Because these are so far away and we have none as great as they were to replace them, the current sparkle is tinsel before the real night. Unless we get back in touch with the gods, the light will go out altogether, and we will suffer the loss very directly and more than we know.

"Each actual entity," wrote Whitehead, "is itself only describable as an organic process. It repeats in microcosm what the universe is in macrocosm. It is a process proceeding from phase to phase, each phase being the real basis from which its successor proceeds towards the completion of the thing in question. Each actual entity bears in its constitution the 'reasons' why its conditions are what they are."[10]

A survey taken in urban American ghettoes at the time of the first Moon-landing in 1969 showed that a majority of the people interviewed believed it was a hoax.

"Man on the Moon. That's just crazy," said one person.

"The American government and the stuff it makes up. They must think we're pretty dumb to fall for that."

Modern man no longer knows what the sky is, let alone what's possible technologically in the continuum of which his automobiles and heated homes are a part. He has lost a contemporary geography of the stars as thoroughly as he lost the ancient one generations ago.

He does not know the planets or the constellations, and he has been shown so many fireworks and strobes—so much electric gaudiness—in this century that he regards the stars as decorative, or simply as extensions of this exploited world. People are generally busy with other things, or with what they think are other things, and their idle thoughts do not take a cosmic bend. They prefer matters of relationship or finances. The stock market and the Equal Rights Amendment are more burning issues. If they get really cosmic, it is about patriotism, a great comeback in a sporting event, or sex. People do not like the dark hole in reality that nighttime discloses. Neither did the Sioux warriors, but they studied it and they inhabited it within their means.

Native man was privileged in that regard to be able to stand under the full conflagration of the heavens and not know or pretend to know what they were. They were dazzling and superior; they were above him; and they contained enduring meanings and destinies. Their luminosity and mysterious motions suggested intelligence and hidden dimensions of reality. They were a far far greater thing than he could ever hope to be. Yet, in another sense, they were exactly who he was.

Star loss is not a trivial matter, for, in the breaking asunder of cosmic wholeness, there is a severing of psychic unity. We now suffer a "mental" disorder so vast and general that we do not notice it anymore. But every day we are troubled by upsurges of unconscious cosmic material that disrupt our fragile identities. Behind the little anxieties lies the big one of the sky. Behind the fragmented panics is a single human bolt of terror. And the thing we call schizophrenia exists unknown and collectively in mankind. We are disreputable and self-contradicting by nature. We are born at best into a partial reality. Robert Temple diagnoses it in *The Sirius Mystery:*

> Our modern civilization does not ignore the stars only because most of us can no longer see them. There are definitely deeper reasons. For even if we leave the sulphurous vapours of our Gomorrahs to venture into a natural landscape, the stars do not enter into any of our back-to-nature schemes. They simply have no place in our outlook any more. We look at them, our heads flung back in awe and wonder that they can exist in such profusion. But that is as far as it goes, except for the poets. This is simply a "gee whiz" reaction. The rise in interest in astrology today does not result in much actual star-gazing. And as for the space programme's impact on our view of the sky, many people will attentively follow the motions of a visible satellite against a backdrop of stars whose positions are absolutely meaningless to them. The ancient mythological figures sketched in the sky were taught us as children to be quaint "shepherds' fantasies" unworthy of the attention of adult minds. We are interested in the satellite because we made it, but the stars are alien and untouched by human hands—therefore vapid. To such a level has our technological mania, like a bacterial solution in which we have been stewed from birth, reduced us.

... The numbers of people in insane asylums or living at home doped on tranquilizers testifies to our aimless, drifting metaphysic. And to our having forgotten orientation either to seasons (except to turn on the air-conditioning if we sweat or the heating system if we shiver) or to direction (our one token acceptance of cosmic direction being the wearing of sun-glasses because the sun is "over there").

We have debased what was once the integral nature of life channelled by cosmic orientations—a wholeness—to the enervated tepidity of skin sensations and retinal discomfort. . . . We are causing ourselves to become meaningless body machines programmed to what looks, in its isolation, to be an arbitrary set of cycles.[11]

We proclaim, rather haughtily: "It *should* be sunny at this time of year!" without realizing the bigness we could have if we knew and accepted the cycles themselves. Like existential waifs, we never get to the bottom of our psychological mysteries and malaises, and move from incident to incident without real connection. We postpone and buy off the cosmos until death itself.

In the beginning of stargazing, the universe was a flood of sacred matter, set in harmony and regulated by the deep rhythms and cycles of nature. If man was a spirit, the stars were sentience floating in a spiritual medium, a cosmic music beyond time, but carrying time through its eternal return of individual entities and constellations. This movement was grounded in the world itself. If history seemed a series of enfolded cycles, repeating and changing, the sky was the visible and orchestral arrangement of the series. Human cycles were part of larger cosmic cycles. The slipping of the seasons from the precession of the zodiac was understood exactly as a progression in the cosmic order. The oscillation of the Earth on its axis, which caused the precession, became the simple aeonic metric because it changed gradually and irredeemably, while the major cycles (of daily rotation and annual revolution, and the waxing and waning of the Moon) remained the same. Of course, the oscillation gave rise to a cycle too, but it was well beyond the life span of men or civilizations and was recognized only perhaps in the great World Ages of some systems—for instance, in the present Hindu *Kali Yuga,* which comes close to the actual span of the precession cycle we now know as 25,725.6 years. The precession of the equinoxes was a cosmic guarantee that the gods required millennial change on the Earth and a succession of civilizations. And this omen of the Great Year stood against Rome as it had stood against Persia and Egypt, and then Christianity adopted its apocalyptic message within its own set of meanings.

The original sky was a cosmic harmony, unreachable in essence by man, but from which he derived mathematics, music, divination, and law. He had a direct internal experience of the movements of the heavens, an almost telepathic kinship with the things he called the stars or with that essence for which he thought the stars stood. If man suffered under such a sky, he also found redemption in it, for its movements were subject to universal karma. He could hardly complain, for he was spiritually and psychically one with the heavens. That experience, as a collective activity, is gone.

The late Greek philosophers, even from pre-Socratic times, were already intellectualizing the sky; they made a new science of spiritual essence that allowed them to *know* as well as experience the creationary process. Kepler, Newton, and the other early modern astronomers inherited their tradition. Man saw himself as responsible for the evolution of the cosmos; language, philosophy, and science were his tools. Images arising from society replaced those of an unseen star-connected force. It did not happen all at once, and it has not even happened completely yet, nor shall it; but secular law has made the world what it is today, not only in Europe and North America, but in Africa, Asia, and South America too. There may be astrologers, star-priests, astral travelers, and people in the jungles who keep their society's star links and astronomical totems; they are pockets in a world of jet planes, international markets, and computers.

The early scientists did not give up the divine sky all at once, but it came to resemble a mind, a puzzle, a cryptogram, more than a myth. Neither Kepler nor Newton foresaw the implications of the modern linear sky they helped to create. For both of them, the sky remained an otherworldly mystery and a reflection of a more perfect geometry beyond it. Motion and gravity were visible forms of invisible forces. Still, they had dislodged the spiritual underpinning of heavenly movement; they had reduced the cosmic basis to numbers and geometries. Gradually, even the riddle and the mind of God disappeared, even though, well into the twentieth century, astronomy books continue to discuss, almost nostalgically, the place where God might fit into this eternal collection of stars and galaxies. But those first astronomers experienced the last waves, at least in the West, of the sweet astral heavens with their celestial music, and they plotted the night sky with that harmony in their brains: the bounty of astral white marking the past; modern scientific instruments pointing to an equally unknown future.

A City of the Sun was mapped by the revivalist hermetic movement of the sixteenth century but was more fully conceived by the science and astral magic of the following century. Tommaso Campanella, the Italian philosopher, was the transitional figure. He wrote the book *Città del Sole*. If the correct stellar influences could be drawn into the habitat of man by the proper talismanic figures and perfect circles, the celestial order would begin to shine in the houses and streets. The city might itself light automatically by divine sympathy. Angelic light would be drawn numerologically into its lanterns. In such a place, there would be no criminals; laws could not be disobeyed.[12] Fantastic as this may sound, it stands directly prior to Newton in the tradition that gave us electricity. Electricity would have satisfied Campanella too; it was stellar and geometric enough. But he would have been shocked to know that natural forces did not guarantee universal justice, plenty, and eternal brotherhood on Earth. His goal was to rule human society not by the sympathetic and synchronous magic of the heavens, as in astrology and the occult sciences, but by the mathematical and structural laws of the heavens applied to human society. Where else would justice and harmony reside but in the night sky? Where else could we seek the end to the discord of nations and the slaughter of man and beast? Here was the source of bounty and nature itself.

By now we have grounded our stellar formulas, and we have tried parliaments, democracies, and capitalism. The industrial and socialist states of the modern world derive from this vision. And if we have not found what we were looking for, we have certainly learned the contents of that particular night sky.

The early hermetics and Rosicrucians, however, saw only the initial benign face of science. Hermes was an ancient Christ to them, a healer and a wise king. He was also the original star magus. If the great puzzle of motion in the astrum could be solved through mathematics, that same mathematics could show the way for troubled and unjust society. The old wars may have been Martian or Jovian, as man sought astrological explanation and legitimacy. The new revolutions, in the eighteenth century, were specific attempts to drive the lineage of kings from their thrones in the heavens down onto Earth, where scientific and rational man, common terrestrial humanity, could transpose the actual order of the stars. This is not the way history or the chronicles of the times describe it, but it is a possible way to understand the simultaneous evolution of astronomy, which describes the background against which man acts, and his moral order and society. A couple of centuries later, the task would be given to the proletariat, and Marxism would completely replace stellar law.

After the European revolutions against monarchy, with science providing a thousand promising paths to utopia, these ideas were secularized in the writings of the eighteenth-century philosophes and were embodied, in fact, in the Constitution of the United States. The idealism of America is, to a large degree, the idealism of the hermetic enlightenment, containing its belief in symmetry, the balance of power, and the harmony of the parts: a judicial, legislative, and executive system that mirrors the astral and elemental balance of forces. Thomas Jefferson was a possible Rosicrucian sage. We have long ago departed from the idealism, but it remains the one deep optimistic image in American society. The pyramid on our dollar bill recalls its quasi-Egyptian origin.

The historian Carl Becker captures what this process meant

to the eighteenth century, and what the United States inherited:

> The new heaven had to be located somewhere within the
> confines of the earthly life, since it was an article of phil-
> osophical faith that the end of life is life itself, the perfected
> temporal life of man; and in the future, since the temporal
> life was not yet perfected. But if the celestial heaven was
> to be dismantled in order to be rebuilt on earth, it seemed
> that the salvation of mankind must be attained, not by some
> outside, miraculous, catastrophic agency . . . but by man
> himself, by the progressive improvement made by the ef-
> forts of successive generations of men. . . . Posterity would
> complete what the past and the present had begun.[13]

The eighteenth century was no longer involved with astral
magic, but it was far more aware than we are of the consequences
of astronomical theory on society and vice versa. Enlightened
government was a transposition of "the regular and constant
order of facts by which God rules the universe."[14] Man had
inherited God's logic, so he could be like God. Furthermore, he
would *have* to be like God, for he was subject to the same universal law. And man had looked through a telescope into the
workings of the upper spheres, the operations by which creation
was held together. Gravity, light, and molecular structure had
shown how God works. If He could keep order in His kingdom,
containing such enormous objects and vast realms of space,
surely man could derive regional laws from the cosmic laws and
create a workable society.

The "starring of the Earth" is now complete (if we may call it
that by parallel with Charles Reich's 1960s fantasy of the "greening of America"). The explosion of nuclear weapons, imitating
the Sun's own fueling process, is finally the epitome of relocating
stellar law on Earth. The locomotives and early automobiles
share something with Kepler's vision of the orbit of Mars and
Newton's mathematicization of the gravitational force. Man
thought he saw a retrievable being in the sky, but when he captured it, it was an unknown intruder and the sky became incidental. In fact, the sky, in the sense of original forces of physics,
is everywhere, and it is no longer necessary to have reference
to the actual radiance. The preference for social programs in-

stead of the space program is a symptom of this dislodgement. Some want more bombs, others want more welfare checks, but they don't want the sky unless it serves them directly, either as a weapon or a controlled weather system. Our societies pretend to sit by themselves on their own terms, though the same universal laws, whatever they are and however we interpret them, hold everywhere.

Unquestionably, the space program is mechanical and external, but even machines are born after long incubation in the unconscious processes of our planet. The space program expresses the destiny of those machines in a way that psychotropic drugs and bailing out automobile corporations do not; it expresses *our* destiny within this dangerous technological adventure. The machines may be dumb and inanimate, but through us they struggle toward humanity and articulation. By their mute agency, men stood on the Moon and watched the rising of the radiant blue Earth against the infinite black. They stood outside the sphere of all human operations, looking back at the entirety of what they had been. Machines made this possible; machines from our minds placed our collective mind beyond the Earth. If they are mere technology, then such technology holds magical powers.

Abandoning Mars and Saturn voyages in favor of mental hospitals and MX missiles consigns our future to exactly those things, the ones we have chosen. We can use technology to turn our planet into an armed camp or a social drug center, and we can use it to explore the oneness of life against the infinity of the cosmos.

Life is so brief and fragile in the context of the durable and awesome scenery of night, and we have so little contact with the inner sky, that we do not dwell there long in our attentions. One turns away from the stars, fixes a meal, calls a friend. The lesson would be electrifying, refreshing, but we are not in the mood for such lessons. Instead we experience a kind of cosmic loneliness, and we put the stars aside to live our lives. But is this cosmic loneliness a result of the present infinite view of the ruthless stars and galaxies, or are they themselves a symptom of

the cosmic loneliness we already feel in a society which has lost
spiritual and ecological direction and which already has nothing
to offer man for this trip except, as in the beer ad: "You only go
around once and you'd better grab for all the gusto you can
get!"? No one could seriously believe this as stated; and yet all
of us do in some way, and pay a terrible price. The alternative
would be to express our own cosmic dimension; yet we have
forgotten how, and it is taught almost nowhere.

Astronomers were once our priests, and, whether they know
it or not, they still interpret the moral as well as physical structure of the heavens. And they have shown us a universe that
would seem to devour without rhyme or reason: stars crushed,
galaxies of stars destroyed, stars devouring other stars, black
holes devouring everything; they have shown dying suns swallowing their solar systems. Where ancient astronomers found a
divine whirlpool, modern ones received the news that the whole
of matter was created once in a giant explosion from a space
perhaps no bigger than a dime, and they said: there is no moral
structure; in fact, there is nothing at all.

After the fact, we can create science fiction stories about passing through black holes into beautiful other universes, but the
black holes given in scientific theory are no more habitable than
the Sun itself. Man could not pass through them, and certainly
consciousness could not. The vast explosions of space dwarf
anything imaginable, though on our scale they seem to represent
the downfall of vast civilizations, like the fall of the West, the
decline of the Roman Empire, or the overthrow of the Aztec
Kingdom. Perhaps that is what they are intended to mean, their
esoteric nature showing through their material guise. But for
now, mankind has been asked to be present at its own funeral,
a funeral which took place billions of years in the past and perhaps billions of years in the future. It is an atomic nightmare.

One is uncomfortable thinking about nuclear war; yet the
stars are nuclear war writ large—enormous fires whose death
throes will destroy planets and whose ultimate compacting (if
true as proposed) will mark the end of the material universe.
People who carry skulls and dress in death costumes throwing
ashes to indicate the consequences of humankind tangling with

this energy are enacting, on the one hand, a profound truth about something that has gone wrong in our time (the sloppy use of crude stellar energy in short-term schemes), and, on the other hand, a satire of what is shown in space: death of suns and stars too, death of the universe, which has been offered in place of religion, in place of internal process, and in place of life methodology. Our own age is threatened by a holocaust of man's own making (unless there be accomplice wizards and demons or extraterrestrial intelligences behind man himself), and it is no accident that scientific theology of this age proposes a cataclysm that will obliterate everything and what everything is—things which were ostensibly once brought into being by just such a cataclysm. We have hardly been less arbitrary and cruel to each other.

We have achieved the same proposition that the hermetics espoused for entirely opposite reasons: that Heaven and Earth are reflections of each other and the same laws prevail in each. We have made the sky our bedfellow and have put ourselves to sleep in the starry night. It is a coffin, and we no longer look because it is too horrible. The sky is our midwife and our interrer. It is our placenta but also our ashes. Unity is inescapable. The same elements and forces are everywhere. On the one hand, the meaning of the sky is reduced to a human scale, which makes it less mysterious. On the other hand, the scope of the sky and its possible moral structure are put utterly beyond men in a circumstance that is far more terrifying than even the old gods.

Unquestionably, the new sky set men free; the old sky had been a tyrant, ruling men's fortunes, taking away their rights, and setting corrupt priests and kings on their thrones, all in the name of cosmic myth. But it also kept the cosmos sacred and intact. Now we are treated as a speck in a puddle that must be influenced by whatever raindrops, detritus, or lines of force happen here. Coherence has become accidental and random, even if it still exists to hold solar systems and galaxies together, as well as the interior of the atom. We are free men and women, free of the tyrannies of the stars and of those who interpret their will into repressive kingdoms and castes. We are now subject to vast amounts of meaningless information about bigger and big-

ger things. The sky used to set an example for moral structure.
Now it seems merely to permit a moral freedom in line with the
principle of shapeless creative hydrogen fire and universal entropy.

Because the sky is so big, it becomes a blank, a zero. Beside
it we feel we are innocent and wonder why all this misfortune
has befallen us. We feel we are decent people. "Why were we
not born in a better place at a better time? Why this planet, this
world, this violent history? Why should we be subject to wars,
earthquakes, revolutions, famine?" Since we feel we did nothing
to cause these things, since they are an interpolation of stellar
material into a terrestrial frame, we become isolated and alienated. We connect to nothing.

Isaac Bashevis Singer, the twentieth-century Yiddish novelist,
has Asa Heshel wonder about the universe on the eve of Hitler's
invasion of Poland. "Meteors shot across the sky, leaving fiery
trails behind them. Silent summer lightning quivered in one
corner of the heavens, foretelling a hot day. Fireflies shone and
were extinguished; frogs croaked; all kinds of winged insects
came fluttering into the room and dashed themselves against the
walls, the windows, and the bedposts."[15] This is the modern
empty universe. John Donne never would have seen it this way.
"Asa Heshel thought about Hitler; according to Spinoza, Hitler
was a part of the Godhead, a mode of the Eternal Substance.
Every act of his had been predetermined by eternal laws. Even
if one rejected Spinoza, one still had to admit that Hitler's body
was part of the substance of the sun, from which the earth had
originally detached itself. Every murderous act of Hitler's was
a functional part of the cosmos."[16]

Passive acceptance of the morally unacceptable is the lot of
modern man. From the perspective of ancient man, though,
birth in this zone and clime is no accident, and we are not innocent. We are the secret perpetrators, in the mind of matter,
of the conditions in which we find ourselves. On some utterly
primary level that we no longer experience because it is beyond
even the shadows of memory or the old wisdom, we chose and
created this. We put ourselves under this sky and sealed its lot
upon us. Not only are we destined, but we can view the track
of that destiny in the sky, a dark magical mirror of our course.

In ancient stellar culture, a revolution was visible in the changing of the sky. Perhaps this is still true. Today's sky allows that
galaxies and stars blow up from their internal forces. No wonder,
then, that societies do too. Hitler's ovens are the moral equivalent of a neutron star in a system which once held life. Starvation in Cambodia is the equivalent of a supernova. Why not
invade Afghanistan? Comets invade planets; galaxies invade other galaxies, killing a possible billion billion billion people. Why
not put the people out to sea in dinghies? That's what gravity
does. That's all that planets are anyway. That's how life was created from the trillions of chemical compounds in the original
sea.

In another Singer novel, another character views the starry
sky, wondering if there are concentration camps and starvation
out there too, or possibly some spark of hope. When he realizes
that modern astronomy proclaims the same universal struggle,
he is overcome with despair: "A rage against creation, God,
nature—whatever this wretchedness was called. I felt that the
only way of protesting cosmic violence was to reject life. . . ."[17]

In the last fifty years in particular, we have done away with
the remaining vestiges of public morality. The sky stands as a
moral lesson only to thugs, looters, and terrorists. It expands ad
infinitum; it explodes without caring for the innocent victims;
and it enjoys itself without thought or fear of tomorrow. It has
no plan for the future. How strangely like ourselves!

Our own economies expand, and the value of money dissipates with the galaxies of the night sky. Inflation and the expanding universe may be light-years apart in terms of their apparent origins in the modern system, but they share a realm of
thought. They indicate equally the inability to set value, the
sense that all value is relative. As we find nothing but violence,
relativity, and destruction in the sky, we find ourselves surrounded by depravity, rioting, starvation, and advanced weaponry. The
"starring of the Earth" is right up to date. Family structure crum-
bles with the stable Solar System. What is there to live for if the
stars no longer care? Why even try to behave decently, with such
a ruthless bandit on display every night?

Our knowledge has snowballed, and our means for dealing
with nature have put us in an environment mostly of our own

making. Yet the basic mysteries are as impenetrable as ever. Our
civilization sits beneath the same sky as uncomprehendingly as
Stone Age man stood beneath it in his own loneliness. And by
the clock of the heavens, a brief second has passed from then
till now.

Our ability to transform scientific information has been far
outweighed by the amount of that information and its very
gloomy implications about our species. Even our local Solar
System is disclosed, planet by planet, as a sequence of hellish
environments in which our potential survival, if we should suddenly be transported there, would range from a matter of mil-
liseconds to a matter of minutes at the most. The rest is explosions and radiation. The beauty of space is overshadowed by the
sense that it is nothing but a noisy brute. It explodes galaxies
and worlds in the way that we build and put out campfires.
The planets in our vicinity are not neighbors; they are fires,
storms of poisonous gases, and dry meteor-pummeled stone.
The Martians and Venusians of the 1930s and 1940s, even of
five years ago, now seem fantastic wishful follies. Their "remains" are strewn on bouldery plains and around 500° carbon
dioxide volcanoes. The old mythologies, whether they be of Ice
Age man, the mediaeval astrologers, or science fiction writers
of the rapidly passing twentieth century, serve a crucial purpose
we may only dimly understand. And it is not enough to say that
they explain us instead of outer space; it is not enough to reduce
them to projections of our own habitation into the uninhabited
void.

In the introduction to *Hamlet's Mill,* Giorgio de Santillana
and Hertha von Dechend take up this issue from a different
perspective. They first acknowledge that the ancient star-wisdom tells us something of cosmogonic beginnings, of "the breaking asunder of a harmony" and the tilting of space. Then they
add:

> This is not to suggest that this archaic cosmology will show
> any great physical discoveries, although it required prodi-
> gious feats of concentration and computing. What it did
> was to mark out the unity of the universe, and of man's
> mind, reaching out to its farthest limits.[18]

Life attempts to express its own innermost truths, and these, if they are not expressed, will lodge more deeply in unconsciousness to make themselves known in other ways. If we ignore the stars, we ultimately feel the loneliness and mortality even more deeply, for the sky is a fact. The stars are there, like them or not, and though we can hang out in a covered city all night and greet the Sun as a kind of electric light in the morning, we must ultimately come to terms with who we are and the nature of the scenery here.

Just because we are no longer archaic does not mean we no longer require a cosmogony or that we have solved the problems of the ancient priests. Our position is more tenuous than we realize. De Santillana and von Dechend continue:

> Einstein said: "What is inconceivable about the universe is that it should be at all conceivable." Man is not giving up. When he discovers remote galaxies by the million and then those quasi-stellar radio sources billions of light-years away which confound his speculation, he is happy that he can reach out to those depths. But he pays a terrible price for his achievement. The science of astrophysics reaches out on a grander and grander scale without losing its footing. Man as man cannot do this. In the depths of space he loses himself and all notion of his significance. He is unable to fit himself into the concepts of today's astrophysics short of schizophrenia. Modern man is facing the nonconceivable. Archaic man, however, kept a firm grip on the conceivable by framing within his cosmos an order of time as an eschatology that made sense for him and reserved a fate for his soul.[19]

It is not a case of primitive wishfulness or lack of appreciation of the harshness of the cosmos. Archaic cosmology was just as fierce and merciless as our 250-miles-per-hour Jovian clouds and black holes swallowing light itself. The Hindu gods retain some of the original clarity of that mythic universe. Shiva is the sentinel of both love and death, the devourer of life and the source of life. As Shiva dances, the whole cosmos shimmers as his reflection. His throat is blue from a poison that he drank in order to save mankind. And then there is black Kali, goddess of disease, murder, evil, wisdom, revelation. "It was a prodigiously vast theory," according to de Santillana and von Dechend, "with no concessions to merely human sentiments. It, too, dilated the mind beyond the bearable, although without destroying man's role in the cosmos. It was a ruthless metaphysics."[20]

Anu fulfills his promise to scorned Ishtar by flinging a Bull of Heaven onto the Earth, a bull whose every snort eradicates hundreds of warriors. Enkidu rips the right thigh out of the animal and hurls it back in Ishtar's face. Disease itself is sent to punish this brazen despoiler. The body of Osiris is shredded through the cosmos. Triton blows back the flood with his radiant conch shell. Marduk shoots the Hyades into the squadron of cosmic monsters, dispersing them into the heavens. Isis flees Typhon, sprinkling the ground with ears of wheat. Odin sends a storm through the Milky Way. Samson pulls the house of the Philistines down on himself. Surt bursts from the divided heavens with a sword of fire. Phaëthon drops the reins of the Sun's chariot at the sight of the Scorpion, and the zodiac is shattered, the forests scorched; the body of the usurper lies in the Eridanus. King David sings to bring the waters up from the Abyss. Quetzalcoatl disappears into the great sea. The ancient Shah Kai Khushrau fades from the mountaintop into the sunless sky while the five paladins sleep. He is the last of his kind. "Farewell for ever!"[21]

It is no accident, in a mythical view of things, that an aroused Islam tries to drive the Western World out of the Near East, i.e., out of the sacred sky of ancestry and myth. Revolutionary Islam, in Iran, old Persia, virtual homeland of astrology and the Kings of the Sky, now attempts to break through the meaningless marketplace static and peg things again to a holy event. Public beheadings are acceptable, but eroticism and hallucinogens are not. If the Ayatollah Khomeini seems utterly rigid and unyielding, it is because he imitates that old sacred political way of doing things. His rules make no sense for human beings as we conceive them in the modern world, but they make total sense for planets and stars which must guard absolute orbits. In exile in Paris, he had no power to take over Iran, but Iran chose him as a figure for itself. The people, the Revolution, chose him, not apparently because he was eloquent on their concerns or educated on the type of society they wanted, but because he represented the old gods and the strength of ancient times. He brought back the unyieldingness of cosmology that preceded this modern tumult of races and values and marketplace politics. From the point of view of Islamic revolution, Big Bang Theory and pornography and crime are sworn accomplices in the Western World. The ostensible neutrality of astrophysics and international law merely obscures that.

It is not simply a matter of spiritual development and personal meaning. If we were more star conscious, we would be ecologically more astute and politically and economically more cross-cultural and wise. The false boundaries and passing meanings of decades and ways of life would be guided by something more central and enduring. It would help our energy crisis if we thought more clearly and profoundly about how energy itself originates in the stars and finds itself located on the planets.

People don't conceptualize energy resources in any realistic long-term sense. Michael Collins, the astronaut who stayed in the capsule during that 1969 lunar visit, understood as he watched the Earth from space. We are like ants, digging up everything under the surface, oil and coal, as if it were limitless and as if this behavior were enlightened, or even sane.[22] The only future that man can have at this rate must be set imaginarily in future worlds of outer space. In terms of the Earth, man has failed to grasp in any economically or politically viable way that it is a planet, a single planet. There are no others; to imagine them does not create them. And what have we made or left for our children, our children's children, and their children? They certainly will know and understand when time has thrown it into shocking focus.

Meanwhile, science has given us another sky with the seeds of a new ecological morality. The fossil fuels are solar energy, altered by photosynthesis and aeonic chemical activity. The winds are also solar, or gravitational, in their origin. The tides are lunar gravitational energy. Life is stellar chemistry. All the rivers flow into all the seas, and all the clouds arise from the whole and stand against it atmospherically. The lightning and the radiation of the ionosphere are aspects of a single field. It is one boundaryless chemical droplet, steaming from its seas and lapping up into ice, with clouds strung through the invisible winds. "Brown-red is the color," wrote the poet Charles Olson, "of the brilliance of earth."[23]

This was the first gift of Whole Earth consciousness. We were allowed to see a unity directly, and it was a unity expressed throughout mankind: in other ways in the writings of the alchemists and Taoists, in Zuni creation myths and the I Ching. Nature is a one, a harmony of diverse elements, and it acts as a one: the clouds, the Arctic ice, the open seas, the Sun penetrating the whole thing, making its radiance in the guts and giving it a blue aura that separates it from the surrounding space as a fine engraving is different from the unmarked jade around it. If it were not for our fearful greed and fatal existential doubt, we could almost come home in this century.

The same night sky poses unlimited energy to an energy-starved world. Or how is it energy-starved when photosynthesis, winds, and global tides are its daily gift from its immediate cosmic neighbors? The two must go together: death by too much energy, panic from too little energy—panic and starvation.

We may not wish to take the Shiite path ourselves, but we can see where contemporary science and morality have taken us. It is not even certain that any of us, or any living thing on this planet, can survive them, despite the billions of years that were put into getting us here. We live now with the knowledge that our civilization will be buried even more deeply than the temples of Rome, and that we will be showered by more than just the dust of winds and human forgetfulness and ignorance. Our heavenly city must be covered with the debris of an exploding Sun and the electric dust of a dissolving universe. We can no longer pretend to be making unlimited progress, so we war and murder in the cosmic void. No hope and no place to go; such is our disappointment and rage. Denis Diderot became deeply troubled by a forerunner of this notion in 1765; what got into his brain like a tiny insect that he could not dislodge until it threatened to topple his entire encyclopedia was the possibility that an unnamed comet, tearing out of the random blankness of the cosmos, might destroy the Earth in a cataclysmic collision. It did not relieve him to think that it was not likely to happen, certainly not in his lifetime. It bothered him that he could not put away the worry and that he could come up with no simple solution to such a pedestrian and almost light notion. In its sheer simplicity, it must mask something terribly profound.

It did. What was a whisper to Diderot would become a gong in the center of another city only two centuries later. It was no idle thought; it was the forerunner of a madness, an obsession in which man would become trapped.

Diderot feared that knowledge of this comet would take away all mankind's reason for noble activity and self-development. "No more ambition, no more monuments, poets, historians, perhaps no more warriors or wars. Everyone would cultivate his garden and plant his cabbages."[24]

He got the details wrong, but he certainly captured the mood. When the implication of universal Darwinism became clear to George Bernard Shaw, he wrote: "If it could be proved that the whole universe had been produced by such Selection, only fools and rascals could bear to live."[25] And such is the case, though we do not think of ourselves as fools and rascals; instead we are the mutants and accidents of directionless turmoil.

Without initially being aware of it, man severed one thread that held him to the sky, and then followed the other into the future; by now it has expanded to replace the original cosmos with new blueprints from the heart of matter. Since we are born and die within this technological nexus, and since we could not survive without it, many of us may laugh at the idea that the old magical sky held anything true or important in it. But we are biased, being the very interested partisans of the present order and not having lived any other way.

It is not simply that we have moved into spiritual darkness. By learning natural laws and creating a technological society based on them, we have become more humane and gentle in many ways. We have broken the tyranny of some of the cruelest of the old gods. Persian and Incan societies may have been in

touch with the heavens in ways we are not, but those paths led
to star-justified wars, slaughters, slavery, and sacrifice. In any
case, even the last of the old human magi emphasize that this
was the path that man was meant to travel, and he could no more
evade the current transition, the initiation into the conscious
knowledge of matter, than he could evade being incarnated in
the first place. The dream is still that we can keep the best of
the new order, and, through long painful discipline and meditation, reexperience the basis of the ancient wisdom—not recover it from texts and magical lineages, though these will always
be clues and guides along the way, but create it anew in terms
of the actual condition of the present Earth in the cosmos. This
means that the next hermeticism and astrology will have in them
aspects of astrophysics and microbiology. And they will not be
initiated in pop images of black holes and extraterrestrial intelligences. These may come into play in totally unexpected ways,
or they may wither into period pieces of our troubled times.

We have reached a turning point. It is a priority of the new
consciousness—the society emergent in the occultism, radical
politics, and Whole Earth philosophy of the sixties—that only
a breakdown of the current technocracy, with its laws of time
and space, will lead to a greening of America and a new heavenly
city on Earth. It will be a nonnuclear city, a city derived from
Zen, telepathy, perhaps the vital power in pyramids, and old-
fashioned solar energy (it will be Città del Sole). It may even
get energy from black holes and quantum physics. It will be a
science fiction city which may speak to other intelligences,
though not necessarily by radio telescopes. It will restore the
botanical and healing power of the Earth. It may be all of these
things, some of these things, or none of these things, but these
alone as images stand for the new heavenly city, the new order.
It cannot happen any longer as pure astral magic and with dis-
regard for the laws of the universe we now know from physics
and biology. But these sciences must give birth to occultism and
religion anew, borrowing something from a past golden age of
which most has been lost and most had already been lost by the
time of Plato, presiding over the birth of a new star-wisdom, a
new music both arcane and modern, so that the fields of flowers

and grains and the body of man and woman can once again be a primordial reflection of the starry firmament. In these fields, greening and starring can be the same thing.

Where we stand today is in need of a theory of the heavens, complex enough to contain all we know, yet beautiful enough to encompass all we are, cosmic enough to include modern science, yet true to all we are and have been, including Pawnee star maps on buffalo hide, space probe photographs, notches in bone of Moon phases, and replicas of the Scorpion and the Scales.

5

Ancient Astronomy

Perhaps time does not exist at all, but for those creatures who live and die and in whose company we are numbered, time is everything. The sky is our one universal clock. With one hand, the Sun measures the hours of the day, and the stars measure the hours of the night. With their other hands, they measure the seasons of the year. The Earth's wobble gives a third hand to these clocks, and they measure the epochs of history. The changing heavens are a great calculator wheel lodged between our transient world and the cosmos at large.

The Earth *is* the sky again, and vice versa. The sky houses the Earth and provides numbers for its movement through space and time. As violent and portentous as the sky can be, it is the only trustworthy guardian of the Earth. It is the one assurance that we can never fall entirely out of this incarnation. If we were transported, kidnapped, to another world, another dimension, another system, the first reference point would be the sky. If the sky were partially lost, partially twisted, we might find our way back to the Earth or have some understanding of what had happened to us. If the sky were totally unfamiliar, we would be lost forever. The closest we come to this without starship travel is in the migrations from one hemisphere of our world to another. As seafarers enter unknown waters, stars close to the horizon behind them disappear, while, in front of them, new stars appear. Only on the approximate celestial equator do some horizon stars and star-groups remain in this altered company. It must have been a great shock to ancient navigators to find the sky as well as the sea changing, but it was an event in keeping with the mythic scope of the journeys. Clocks and calendars were not the only ancient practical astronomies; there were also sea maps of stars and compasses of celestial navigation.

The aboriginal inhabitants of Micronesia, Polynesia, New Zealand, and Australia journeyed there by canoe from Southern Asia by stages through Indonesia, the Philippines, and Melanesia. No doubt a certain amount of blind adventuring and chance landfall occurred during this millennial process, but the systematic migration of clans of men, women, and children took place by celestial navigation according to a system of star compasses the fragments of which still survive. The knowledge was passed down from generation to generation over so many aeons that the peoples at one end of the migration no longer resemble the peoples in the homelands. They retain each other only as myths.

The sky is another vast "ocean" filled with myriad luminous beacons and hieroglyphics. The naked night is awesome enough to us on land, and despite our knowledge of the shape of the globe. Think how powerful and inspiring it was to peoples who knew only eternity and who found their way via the stars to their present homes and understood where they came from only by the mythology of guide stars passed down from their ancestors. It is as true a science fiction story as we can imagine. And it is also Earth history and ethnoastronomy.

In Hawaii, certain stars are called "guiding stars" because they rise over certain islands as seen from given locations—for instance, on a specific route, Arcturus rises over the Hawaiian Islands themselves, and Cygnus rises over Tahiti. For longer voyages, sequences of stars, i.e., star-paths, are necessary. One passes from zone to zone, with navigation realigned according to successive fixed points at sea.[1] In 1774, Andia y Varela described Polynesian navigation:

When the night is a clear one they steer by the stars; and this is the easiest navigation for them, because, these being many in number, not only do they note them by the bearings on which the several islands with which they are in touch lie, but also the harbors in them, so that they make straight for the entrance by following the rhumb of the particular star that rises or sets over it.[2]

In Tikopia, the 70 miles northeast across the sea to Anuta was traveled by successively pointing the bow of the canoe toward nine stars. A star is followed only when it is low in the sky, after which its successor is picked up. The necessary stars come up over the horizon all through the night, with the earlier guides having set. Only the last star or two remain when the Sun breaks through the map and floods the Pacific with daylight.[3]

The Samoans used a method based on two stars close to the horizon with a difference in azimuth of 180 degrees. The canoe could be aligned with its head on one star and its tail on the other. The Scorpion's tail was a common mark. A voyage begun with the Scorpion could be continued by steering directly on the culminating Belt of Orion. This would take one from Nokunono to Atafu.[4]

For the Carolines, a sidereal compass survives, with the rising and corresponding setting points of nineteen stars, including single stars from Scorpius, Crux, Cassiopeia, the Big and Little Dippers, Aquilla, Corvus, plus Vega, Aldebaran, the Pleiades, and so on. Polaris stands at the North; the upright Cross can be used to interpolate a southernmost point; and Altair and Orion's Belt mark the equator of the chart and the true equator, respectively. What makes this compass so useful is that it contains an unlimited number of possible relationships between stars that appear at different heights above the horizon and that rise and set at different times. The whole visible heavens are represented; hence, the compass contains, by correspondence, the "Whole Earth."[5]

In a rather obscure monograph entitled "The Astronomical Knowledge of the Maori," Eldon Best gives the Maori sequence for the voyage to New Zealand as passed down in oral tradition: "Atutahi (Canopus), Tautoru (Orion's Belt), Puanga (Rigel), Karewa, Takurua (Sirius), Tawera (Venus as the Morning Star), Meremere (Venus as the Evening Star), Matariki (the Pleiades), Tama-rereti (the Tail of the Scorpion), and Te Ikaroa (the Galaxy)."[6]

This was the sea-road once taken through the sky to the homeland from the ancestral land of Irihia. The blazing lights over the Pacific were the present manifestation of a phenomenon that lay behind the Maoris' whole history and made them, in a sense, space voyagers, ancient mytho-astronauts. The heavens were made up of circular domes, or cupolas, set one in another, the various skies raised by pillars and set in enveloping tiers. The roundness of the heavens was created by the intersection of these tiers with the Earth. To travel across the sea is to travel from heaven to heaven.[7] Maori myth has it that the ancestors forced their way through the hanging sky. The Samoans called the Europeans *papalangi* (heaven-bursters).[8]

The mariners of prehistoric times were astronauts insofar as their passage broke through cosmological systems and placed them in new ones as remote to their experience as we imagine other habitable planets to be. They did not know the sky as an extension of pure space. But they traveled through the sky as they understood it to exist.

The intertwining of number systems, stellar observation, and sacred architecture is a hallmark of ancient astronomy. The Meso-American temples are so complicated that dozens of stars and planets, as well as the Sun and the Moon, are built into their architecture. The vast plaza of Teotihuacan is as much the night sky as the Earth. This is a cosmological necessity. If men were not free to construct and visit representations of stellar relationships, then they could not study their own destiny. They would be cosmologically illiterate. Teotihuacan was apparently constructed so that the Pleiades passed visibly from its Eastern to its Western cross; this is the same star cluster that rises with the Sun on its first annual passage across the zenith in that locale. The Zapotec site of Monte Alban appears to have its baseline set according to the path of Capella for exactly the same reason.[9]

The Caracol is a prehistoric tower in Yucatán later used by the Mayans and named in historical times for its resemblance to a snail shell. Inexplicably asymmetric, it speaks architectural nonsense but stellar wisdom. Many of its windows and structural angles mark positions of Venus, including the extreme northern and southern points reached every eight years. Another window allows a direct line of site to the equinox sunset; while another series of windows and staircase openings lines up with the star Achernar. What is misshapen on the ground is caused by a building "in" of the sky. The Caracol contains other viewing lines for Castor, Pollux, Canopus rising, and Formalhaut setting, events which could seem almost compelled by the zigzags of the structure, as if the stars had no choice but to obey the ancestor-architects generations after their death. But it is not man compelling the stars; it is man in harmony with them, tying his own span, as a single ripple to the wave of eternity.[10]

To the North are American Indian mounds, many of them, if not all, set in the ground in the exact pattern that stars form in the sky. Some of the large conical mounds represent individual stars of great importance. Other effigy mounds trace out the constellations by the paths of their protrusions. These are both better and worse than telescopes; they do not reveal the actual bodies of the stars, but they bring the experienced and imagined essence of those stars down to Earth where man can experience them.

The Great Serpent Mound in Ohio could well be the Little Dipper; nearby bird and bear effigies suggest the Big Dipper and Canopus. Mounds and posthole circles in central Ohio, southern Illinois, and the East St. Louis area seem to mark extreme northern moonrises, and also sunrise at the solstices and equinoxes. Some of these mounds were still used in historic times by the Plains Indians of central Kansas. The Big Horn Medicine Wheel is set like a proper observatory 9,600 feet up in the clear mountain air of Wyoming. It is a series of rock cairns and postholes 90 feet in diameter. Lines drawn through the central cairn to the outer spokes mark summer solstice sunrise and sunset and also the rising of Aldebaran, Rigel, and Sirius just prior to the Sun in summer, i.e., their heliacal rising before the dawn drowns them. From the heliacal period of Aldebaran, at summer solstice, to the period of Rigel is twenty-eight days; it is another twenty-eight days to the period of the beacon Sirius. Twenty-eight is also the approximate number of days in the Moon phase and of ribs in the buffalo; the Big Horn Wheel has twenty-eight spokes.[11]

One of the East St. Louis sites is a star observatory at the center of a pentagram. Mounds are situated at the various angles and on lines bisecting each other passing from angle to angle. In these hillocks are buried the officials and players of an American Indian game like hockey and lacrosse, played in historical times by the Creek. It is a kind of prehistoric Indian Cooperstown, and also a museum in which the pattern of the burial ground is determined by the stars. The athletic stars are buried with the celestial stars, whose brightness they perhaps reflected with their scintillating plays. It was not as tame a sport as either lacrosse or football. Archers with slings were poised on the field to shoot down the ball-carriers. The main purpose was not to kill the runners but to stop their progress; nevertheless, there was still a high mortality rate. The corpses enshrined in East St. Louis very much suggest young players felled at the height of scrimmage.[12]

The mathematics of prehistoric peoples are evident in the astronomical systems of ancient Middle Eastern civilization. Timetables in clay tablets date from the fourth millennium B.C. in Mesopotamia. By the first millennium B.C., it is clear that precise observation of the stars and planets as well as the Sun and Moon is taking place. This is, as it no doubt had been for millennia, in two integrated systems: the movement of the stars and planets marked the carrying out of spiritual process and the passage of divine energy into the world; but it also measured and divided secular time, which inspired the simultaneous development of celestial mathematics and the calendar. A Chaldean ephemeris from 568 B.C. shows the precision of calendrical measurement:

> On the eighteenth of the month, Dilbat (Venus) was 2° 55′ above the King (Regulus in Leo).
> Night of the eighth, evening, Sin (Moon) stood 6° 15′ under the Scales of the North.
> The tenth, Mercury at evening behind the Great Twins enters.

The cycles of the planets are particularly important for the history of astronomy:

> Appearance of the Goddess Dilbat, 8 years behind you
> she will return, 4 days you subtract, you observe.
> Mercury 6 regular years behind you returns.[13]

Mercury does not have a cycle of six years, but Venus is accurate: there are eight years minus four days before it returns to its exact place in the night sky. The figures for Mars (47 years minus 12 days) and Saturn (59 years) are relatively accurate. These are given by the astronomer Labashi in a "book" called "Appearances of the Planets, Behind You It Will Return," dating from 577 B.C. Whatever they believed the wandering stars were, astronomers knew that they were cyclic and moved both forward and backward. It was not in the Chaldean, or later in the Babylonian, interest to explain these motions; they were proper because they happened, and the number systems they gave rise to were integrated into the calendar and the daily world.

The sky itself is animate and magical. Bright fiery beings in the sea of black literally dance out their will:

> Year VIII, Simanu 10, the goddess Dilbat in the evening
> into the head of the Lion entered, Simanu 27 at morning,
> in the place of the Crab she made her appearance.[14]

It is an entry from a tablet of 523 B.C., but it has a music to it, even in translation. One can read it over and over again. Venus is wearing a gown; she is moving through a wondrous realm. She appears one place after sunset, another place sixteen days later before sunrise. In and out of the houses of the sky (the constellations), the planets pass, all along that same band into which the Sun and the Moon rise too.

In the year 379 B.C., a clay tablet describes the following action in the night:

> November 25, the moon made his appearance; 58 minutes
> before sunset was the appearance of the new moon. Night
> of the 26th, Anu (Mars) turned to the west on his return
> below the first star of the constellation Ku. The moon god
> Sin was below the last star of the head of Ku 2 cubits 10
> fingers. Night of the 5th, beginning of the night, Sin was
> before the star Mat-sha-rikis (in the Fish). Night of the 7th,
> the midst of Sin was surrounded by a sheepfold; Anu stood
> in the midst.[15]

Without any instruments for measuring time or viewing space, the Babylonians calculated with remarkable exactness the positions of the Sun, Moon, and planets. The fourth-century B.C. astronomer Kidinnu corrected earlier turning points of the seasons to bring them in line with the precession of the equinoxes, a phenomenon itself undiagnosed at the time. He developed an arithmetical progression for the deviance of the position of the Sun from one full Moon to another. He calculated the period for the Moon's movement along its path closer to and further from the ecliptic, where eclipses were more likely, and he measured synodic periods for conjunctions of the Sun and Moon. All of this he did with an accuracy only fractionally off modern calculations—and better, in most cases, than the accuracy of astronomers through the nineteenth century, who, of course, because of the gaps in historical influence, had to repeat these experiments.[16]

The astronomy of Kidinnu came to the Greeks through the Persians, who knew him as Cidenas. It was brilliant mathematics, but it was mathematics to serve the gods, carried out by a priest. The Greeks were different insofar as they were the first people in the continuity of Western science to wonder what those things up there were made of. It was not enough to predict and derive their positions by number. Those positions themselves hid motive of some kind, impulse sacred or earthy. Somewhere within the flat tablet of deities sat a spacious world of bodies. If they were bodies, they had to be made of something. The Greeks never resolved this dichotomy, but they always worked towards its resolution, a process we inherit from them. They never gave up the notion that the planets and the stars were gods, but, in not giving it up, they never clung to it as passionately as the astronomer-priests of the Near East. Almost unconsciously, they committed a gradual act of sacrilege. They considered, at the same time, that the planets were gods who were cosmogonically bound in sacred paths, and also that they were bodies which must be substantial and must use the sacred circles of geometry to carry out their motion.

Hesiod's version of creation was predominantly mythological and shared as much with the Sumerian as with the later Greek versions. In the two centuries following Hesiod and leading to the Ionian astronomers of the sixth century B.C., an elemental philosophy gradually supplanted the theogony. The meaning of divine Eros was transformed, and the burden of Creation was taken on by the humors and elements. No one told the gods that they had been displaced, and no one told the Greeks. But with the old Eros went the Chinese box version of matter generated from matter, day from night, sky and stars from Mater Gaea. Elements now separated the dark and light, the cold and hot, the wet and dry, extending the properties of raw nature into matter. In the aeons since, we have only temporarily lost sight of these elements. They are surprisingly modern and inextricably woven into the later molecules and atoms. Our historical relationship to creationary principles and their etymology through different cultures and languages is a facet of the complication of Creation itself.

The pre-Socratic philosophers had the first visions of how the universe might work mechanically. At least they are the ones we place at the beginning of our own techno-historical sequence.

One of the earliest Ionians, Thales of Miletos, floated the Earth like wood on water. Aristotle later complained that Thales did not solve the logical problem of what the water rests upon. Thales also predicted eclipses from the Babylonian tables and deduced from the lunar phases that the Moon is lit by the Sun and travels concurrently with it. He reasoned that eclipses of the Moon are caused by the terrestrial shadow cutting off the Sun's light, and that eclipses of the Sun occur as the Moon, from the perspective of the observer, cuts across the Sun's light.[17] Like so many early ideas, Thales's propositions were discovered anew rather than inherited from ancient times, though, on some deeper level, each historical occasion (even those which are totally lost to us, of which there are far more) adds to the context of discovery and rediscovery. The texts we inherit, especially in fragmentary condition like those of the Ionians, stand for millions of others as the one extant clue to a profoundly unconscious and collective process.

For instance, of another sixth-century B.C. philosopher, Anaximander, only a one-sentence fragment remains, but we know of him from his later classical and Christian critics. St. Hippolytus writes in his *Refutation of Heresies:*

He [Anaximander] held that the earth is a body suspended in the sky, not resting on anything else but keeping its position because it is the same distance away from all; that it is in the shape of a cylinder like a stone column with a curved top surface; and that it has two faces, the one of them being the surface on which we walk, the other opposite to it.

He further held that each of the heavenly bodies is a wheel of fire surrounded by air, which separates it from the fire at the extremities. The air has little breathing holes somewhat like the holes in a flute, and through them the orbs are seen.[18]

According to St. Augustine in the fourth century A.D., Anaximander "believed that worlds are infinite in number, and that they contain everything that would grow upon them by nature. He held further than those worlds are subject to perpetual cycles of alternating dissolution and regeneration, each of them lasting for a longer or shorter time, according to the nature of the case."[19] Augustine regretted that Anaximander, like Thales, did not attribute this activity to a divine intelligence.

In the sixth century A.D., Aetius of Constantinople wrote: "Anaximander held that the stars are hoops of fire, compressed by air, and that they breathe out flames from little openings in the air."[20]

Another Ionian, Heraclitus, explained the stars as bright exhalations that ignite in the concavities of pure space. The Sun is hotter and brighter only because it is close to us. The Moon is a similar exhalation, but, since it is nearer the Earth, it is darkened by the Earth's impurities. Heraclitus proposed that bright exhalations in the hollow orb of the Sun are turned into flame, but that when the dark and moist exhalations take priority, the Sun is extinguished and night ensues. He is most remembered for his conception of a fiery principle within matter such that the world is a continuous flux and one never steps into the same river twice. The whole cosmos is such a river. Not only do we not challenge this, we still approach it.[21]

Another school of the sixth century B.C. followed the work of Pythagoras into a different aspect of the cosmos. Perceiving that it was the different lengths of strings in musical instruments that gave them their notes, the Pythagoreans discovered the harmonies as a regular progression of simple numerical ratios (the octave, the fourth, the fifth). The moving planets must equally form a musical harmony, they thought. Pythagoras himself assigned the intervals: from the Earth to the Moon was a tone; from the Moon to Mercury was a semitone; from Mercury to Venus was also a semitone; from Venus to the Sun was a minor third; from the Sun to Mars was a tone; from Mars to Jupiter was a semitone; from Jupiter to Saturn was a semitone; and then from Saturn to the sphere of the fixed stars was a minor third.[22]

The Greeks believed that something qualitative lay behind the cosmic manifestation, so they interpreted matter as form rather than quantity. The fifth-century B.C. natural philosopher Democritus proposed a theory of atoms that continued to interest Werner Heisenberg in his search for a unified field theory of physics. All of creation, said Democritus, is made up of an infinite number of tiny particles. These move around in the Void. Of different shapes, they become twisted, snarled, and entangled with each other as they bump and brush. Their contacts generate all substances in the world. For instance, the fire of the Sun and the stars comes apparently from those round particles which generate heat and light as they interlock. The atoms also create the human senses. It is the elemental atomic aspect of man's knowing that recognizes the elemental atomic aspect of things in nature.[23]

Democritus laid the basis for understanding the symmetry of the universe, said Heisenberg, though the Greek philosopher mistakenly assumed that the protean principle was a particle. But our elementary particles go back to Democritus and to Plato's *Timaeus*. "They are," according to Heisenberg, "the original models, the ideas of matter. . . . These primitive models determine all subsequent developments. They are representative of the central order. And though accident does play an important part in the subsequent emergence and development of a profusion of structures, it may well be that accident, too, is somehow related to the central order."[24]

In the last century before Christ, atomic theory in the context of an infinite universe attained a startling clarity in the work of the Roman poet-philosopher Lucretius. As the Platonic and Aristotelian branches of the great Greek river passed into the Christian Middle Ages, Lucretius wrote at the end of a small Latin tributary:

> In all dimensions alike, on this side or that, upward or downward through the universe, there is no end. . . . The nature of space makes it crystal clear. Empty space extends without limit in every direction and seeds innumerable in number are rushing on countless courses through an unfathomable universe under the impulse of perpetual motion. . . . Our world has been made by nature through the spontaneous and casual collision and the multifarious, accidental, random and purposeless congregation and coalescence of atoms. . . . There exist elsewhere other congeries of matter similar to this one which the ether clasps in ardent embrace.[25]

The atoms are in continuous movement and process; otherwise all matter would be lying in heaps. Instead:

> Each thing is born and emerges into the sunlit world only from a place where there exists the right material, the right kind of atoms. . . .
> Atoms of matter bouncing up from below are supplied out of the infinite. There is therefore a limitless abyss of space such that even the dazzling flashes of lightning cannot traverse it in their course.[26]

Objects and species may vanish or perish but the indestructible seeds remain. "Nature does not allow anything to perish till it has encountered a force that shatters it with a blow or creeps into its chinks and unknits it." These seeds, however, must have become inactive, for the Earth now seems unable to produce even animacules, let alone new beasts and tribes of men.[27]

From the fragments of the fifth-century B.C. philosopher Anaxagoras, we can see the early understanding of the relationship between the physical universe and the complexity of the mind:

> Neither in speculation nor in actuality can we ever know the number of things that are separated out.[28]

In everything there is a portion of everything else, except of mind, and in some things there is mind also.[29]

By the time we reach the fourth century B.C. and the work of
Plato, the mainstream of the West had turned from elementalism
and atomistic psychology to an archetypal and numerological
idealism. Plato hypothesized that the World-Soul transmits a
harmonious order from which the individual properties of the
visible world arise. The atomic templates are: cubes (earth), oc-
tahedra (air), pyramids (fire), and icosahedra (water); the Cosmos itself is a dodecahedron. These are not things in themselves
but qualities which mix together like Democritus's atoms in the
composition of substances. They are unchanging, ungenerated,
and indestructible; they are also imperceptible and in perpetual
motion.[30]

Plato was not a notable astronomer. His night sky was a giant
clock created by the Demiurge in order to bring Time into
being. The Sun and Moon and five planets were harmonic units
of this time. The Sun was created to "fill the whole heaven with
his shining and so that all living things might possess number,"[31]
learning it from the zodiac, the phases of the Moon, and day
and night. The overtaking of the Earth by Venus, and of Venus
and the Earth by Mercury, was a peculiar subtlety of the divine
clock. All of these events had esoteric and profound causes that
were hidden from common people because they would cause
panic if they were known.

> This was the plan [wrote Plato] of the eternal god when
> he gave to the gods about to come into existence a smooth
> and unbroken surface, equidistant in every direction from
> the center, and made it a physical body, whole and com-
> plete, whose components were also complete physical bod-
> ies. And he put the soul in the center and diffused it
> through the whole and enclosed the body in it. . . .
> And when he had compounded the whole, he divided
> it up into as many souls as there are stars, and allotted each
> soul to a star. And mounting them on their stars, as if on
> chariots, he showed them the nature of the universe and
> told them the laws of their destiny.[32]

Plato's circles and souls are ultimately psychological and epistemological, but if they are taken as natural and scientific, they trap mathematical astronomy in an impossible search for their coordinates. It is from this that the systems of Eudoxus and Ptolemy arose in the following generations and passed into the Middle Ages.

We find Plato interesting again in the contemporary context created by Jungian psychology and quantum physics. Prior to the twentieth-century reinterpretations, Platonism threw a cover upon the heavens.

It was Aristotle who surrounded an immobile Earth with nine concentric spheres, each transparent and showing through to the next: the Moon, Mercury, Venus, the Sun, Mars, Jupiter, Saturn, the fixed stars, and the Prime Mover. The Prime Mover of Aristotle is the Deity of Aquinas and Augustine. As one moves out through the planets to the stars, toward God on His throne, spirituality increases. The elemental chaos of the Earth extends only up to the sublunary sphere and the Moon itself and includes clouds, rain, snow, meteor storms, and comets. The stars are pure and perfect. The planets are less pure, but they are set eternally like gems in their mild powerful circles—circles that led mathematicians to go on imagining complicated contraptions of wheels on which these perfect forms could be manipulated into the paths in which they occurred in the actual sky with both retrograde and forward motion.[33]

The late fourth-century B.C. Aristotelian universe breaks with the Ionians and the Atomists in being finite, with the Earth at the center. No wonder Anaximander and Democritus were disowned. Heavy bodies now move toward the center of the Earth only because the Earth and the universe have the same center.

Though Platonic and Aristotelian astronomy trapped European thought in an artificial cosmos for almost two millennia, there was another Greek tradition whose fruits were ignored and all but forgotten. A scientific renaissance flourished in Alexandria, notably in the third century B.C. This Egyptian city was the crossroads and marketplace for the flourishing Hellenic culture that followed the conquests of Alexander the Great. At that time, Greek culture spread to and incorporated Egypt, Persia, and western Asia; the Hellenic world-view was actually a pan-Eurasian synthesis, gathering the wisdom of both classical civilization and the so-called barbarians of Europe and Asia. The science of Alexandria was a cumulative achievement of the many traditions that coalesced there. The Greeks inherited what was left of the Sumerians, the Egyptians, the Persians, and the other empires from past golden ages, but, even as they extended Hellenic civilization to the northeastern and southern Mediterranean, it was transformed by local cultures.

In pure technology, Alexandrian culture was a marvel for its own time: among other things, it had the chain pump, the water-lifting screw, the threshing drag in the fields, the sternpost rudder, a copying machine for sculptors, and a lighthouse at the port of Alexandria whose fire could be seen for thirty-five miles. Holy water was dispensed in the temples by a slot machine.[34] Some persons claim that if the Hellenic scientists had prevailed, we would now be traveling to the stars, perhaps even to other galaxies, for two thousand years of almost total ignorance intervene between the academies of Alexandria and the post-Copernican revolution in Europe. This is no doubt a misreading of history. Although certain surface features suggest the possibility of a shortcut, other more profound elements obviously required the long years we now call mediaeval. It is still an interesting fantasy that has us exploring the Solar System at the time of religious schisms and the Crusades.

The library of parchment scrolls at Alexandria was the major depository of the knowledge of the world to that point. Centuries later, in A.D. 415, religious fanatics burned and destroyed the library, and we retain only tantalizing fragments. The desecration of the Alexandrian library is notorious as an act of blind sacrilege against the planet; it robbed us of Heraclitus and most of Greek physics. But how many other crucial documents and species have we lost without even knowing of them? Civilization is as much a process of returning to unconsciousness as it is one of bringing to light. Our modern astronomies tell us this. And the poet Robert Kelly seems to be reminding us of both the dark gods who rule history and the frustratingly provocative quality of the extant fragments when he laments: "The only trouble with the person who set the torch to the library at Alexandria is that he didn't do a good enough job."[35]

We can review the achievements of the late Greek world as a prelude to the very different science of the Middle Ages. Even at the time of Aristotle, Heracleides put the Sun at the center of the paths of Mercury and Venus—the innermost planets, which circle the Sun faster than the Earth—though he still had the Sun and its satellites circling the Earth. Aristarchus of Samos, born the year of Heracleides' death, 310 B.C., and the last of the Pythagorean astronomers, declared unequivocally that the Sun was the center of a system of planets, including the Earth. His one surviving work is a treatise entitled *On the Sizes and Distances of the Sun and Moon,* a scientific work both in perspective and methodology.[36]

During the third century B.C., Euclid derived the basic formulas of geometry, and Archimedes discovered the mechanical laws by which machines would be constructed for more than a thousand years; he also taught the Aristarchan heliocentric cosmos. Using geometry, Eratosthenes, director of the library at Alexandria, computed the Earth's circumference to within less than one percent error by measuring the angles between the Sun's rays and the vertical at Alexandria and comparing these with figures taken at Syene after measuring the distance from Syene to Alexandria. The experiment came from the insight that the noon Sun on the longest day of summer shone on the bottom of a deep well at Syene but never in Alexandria.[37] This is not one of our modern mass-produced experiments with monkeys or computers. A moment of sunlight at the bottom of a well is a clarity and a mystery both. Such insight is repeated only as the overall aeonic conditions change. For instance, the astronaut Michael Collins recalls seeing the succession of night and day from space. Day is simply night with the closest star smashing light through the atmospheric window, but not all of it getting through, giving the illusion of sky.[38]

Every day, we can try to see our celestial habitat as Collins viewed it from outside. The Sun sets, and its bent rays scatter blue particles across the zenith while multicolored particles dance at the horizon. Then the air is quiet, and stars pop through the darkening veil, the brightest ones first, until night is complete and there are thousands of them. Meanwhile, the Earth itself is rotating, so that the ocean of sunlight continues to wash against a new tinted edge of dawn, crashing through the last shadows with brilliant morning light.

History changes everything, and we must struggle to regain primary experience, whether visionary or scientific.

The dimensions and distances of outer space which we now take for granted were not even remote possibilities to the ancient Greeks. It is those distances, and the sizes they portend, revealed by the optical telescope and the radio telescope, that separate our universe from theirs. The Greeks could not have known the scope of nature because they had nothing with which to discern creation at such vast distances and in such irregular pockets. The hierarchy of matter, from large raw suns to infinitesimal creatures in droplets of water, eluded them, but they perceived a basic elemental set of relationships.

It is for us now to try to imagine the Greek sky as real, not by being childlike and pretending that we know nothing about space (which implicitly demeans their views), but by considering again that space could still be anything. Those who lived and died under such a sky are no more benighted than we who shall live and die under an equally abstract version. The richness of apperception supersedes a sterile kind of knowing. Most people today project a flat unvarying eternity upon the sky, and even astronomers approach the sky as an arena of contest in the competitive brilliance of their theories rather than as a real thing. It is the absolute cosmic priority of the night sky and our existence simultaneous with it that stirs us to knowledge and truth. We are indeed privileged to have the instruments we do, and they are a gift of time itself and of the collective human race which has led to us. But there will be yet better instruments, and they in themselves will not automatically enrich the sky. In fact, they may deplete it by calling to our attention so many more bits of data and events that we are thrown out of the remaining oneness and singularity into astronomical jargon and clichés.

In the second century B.C., Hipparchus, a Greek scientist in Asia Minor, upon discovering a new star, took to counting the stars in the sky, measuring their positions, and comparing these to the measurements of the Babylonians. This immediately revealed that the zodiac had become displaced. His instruments were so good that he determined the length of a year within six minutes and the distance from the Earth to the Moon as 33 Earth diameters (30 is the more accurate figure). By noting that the Sun and Moon were both sometimes larger and sometimes smaller, he concluded that their distance from the Earth changed. In all, he measured the positions of more than a thousand stars, and he put them into six categories of brightness. This task was not continued until Tycho Brahe began again almost two millennia later.[39]

When Ptolemy built his master system of Greek astronomy in the second century A.D., it was based essentially on the observations of Hipparchus. In every other way, the Ptolemaic System was a restoration of the Platonic and Aristotelian cosmos that Hipparchus's findings should have fatally fragmented.

The third-century B.C. mathematician Apollonius of Perga had used Euclidean geometry on curves like parabolas, ellipses, and hyperbolas, and he had shown how the irregular motion of Mars could have a regular motion at its basis. In the *Almagest*, Ptolemy placed the Earth at the center of the universe and derived the motions of all the planets and the Sun and Moon as combinations of circles with their collective orbit centered on the Earth—or almost on the Earth. In the Ptolemaic model, they actually moved eccentrically, with the center of their orbits being a point in the Void slightly apart from the Earth. Ptolemy used Apollonius's idea, but he added an extra overlapping circle to equalize monthly irregularities in the distance covered by Mars. "Uniform motion in a circle corresponds to divine nature," he said. "To reduce all apparent irregularities to such motion may well be called a feat."[40]

Ptolemy retained the moral basis of the homocentric system by replacing the Earth-centered spheres with complex eccentric circles and epicycles. This also preserved Aristotle's physics, since Aristotle had claimed that circular motion was natural and primary. Circular motion was prior to any rectilinear variation on it, so it must be the basis of the heavens.

Planets now moved in series of circles, cycles, and epicycles, abandoning one circular path for another not according to any discernible law but as the equations of the terrestrial astronomers required to "save the appearances," the sacred and divine appearances. To many, fact itself had become a sacrilege.

Geometry as a mode of reality was a particular obsession of the Occident. The Chinese had their own sacred astro-geometry, but they did not believe in circular occult motion and crystalline spheres. Taoism implied nonrepresentational algebraic motion. No further impulse was imposed archetypally. Motions arose from intrinsic characteristics in the chaos of the elements and in the powers of opposite interacting forces, yin and yang.

Ultimately, the Western theory of reality was to bear fruit, in physics and technology, but not before cosmology was recreated out of simple quantifications so that any number, however short of an integer, and whatever shape, however irregular, had a reality within the conditions that generated it. This could not happen until the sacred circles were broken and their natural circularity was separated from their theological circularity.

It is one of the paradoxes of historical process that this happened in Europe rather than China, in a tradition that had to wrench the vectors out of fixed archetypes rather than in a philosophy already committed to creative chaos. A different science developed in the Orient, for the East internalized sacred number and developed from it the mantras and interior alchemies and methods of yoga and meditation that led to a representation of cosmology not as the night sky and the universe of gravity, quantity, and atoms, but as an attention fixed within the universe of human physiology and transmental process. In the East, they discovered gravity and atomicity as laws of consciousness rather than laws of space and substance. They went into the meditational inside of cellular structure with reality fixed at their own being; the West went into the outside of cellular structure and external shape until reality was reflected in the starry heavens of astronomy. The machine age was the counterpart of those heavens on Earth. Apparently, the externalization of sacred number, however rigid and unpromising a path it seems in retrospect, was a more likely forerunner of physics and technology than the externalized algebra of yin and yang. But all this is not resolved. Meditation now enters the West and transforms astrophysics, and astronomy is practiced in China. If the outward stars do not compel the inward stars to change in the Orient itself, then they do in the West, where meditation is practiced in the context of physics. If humanity is willing, these two paths join in the future and lead to the new science promised back in Neolithic times to both the East and the West. A so-called dark ages stands in the way now, even as it did then.

Mediaeval cosmology was more than the theocracy of the Babylonians restored. Democritus and Archimedes had spoken, and their voice would not be quelled. The scientifically progressive Arabs surrounded the West geographically and economically. Throughout the mediaeval period, an Enlightenment hung in the wings, which is why it was so magical and so joyously proclaimed when it seemed to come late after the millennium. But that is also the reason why there is no clear Middle Ages and no clear Renaissance. Some of Europe slept in Christian cosmology and feudalism. Some of Europe kept loyal to Greek and Arab science and the hermetic magic which became alchemy and astrology. Some of Europe had remained pagan from long before ancient times; its loyalty was to the Atlantic and Mesolithic industries. Even as the Christian theocracy dominated cosmology, engines and machines were built, new currencies were minted, and the local knowledge of plants, animals, caves, anatomy, and navigation increased, setting a more substantial basis for a scientific revolution than a few Ionian philosophers. The remains of Greek natural science were the spark, but by the sixteenth century there was something to ignite; and when the explosion was finished, we knew about the stars, the circulation of the blood, and the animals inside a droplet of pond water. But then, the explosion is not finished yet. And, in any case, there is no more a way to draw boundaries and lines in this process than there is in the creation of the universe itself. It all continues to emerge from within as we explore without.

The Ptolemaic cosmology of the *Almagest* was the basis of the mediaeval universe, but flat Earth models were popular within the confines of Church doctrine. Kosmas's *Christian Topography* of the sixth century is typical. The originator was a merchant turned scientist-philosopher who had traveled in the Atlantic as well as the Mediterranean, the Persian Gulf, and the Red Sea. He declared that the Earth, on account of its heavy nonspiritual nature, must lie at the bottom of the universe, not the center. The cosmos itself was designed, he thought, like the Tabernacle of Moses, with Heaven raised on four perpendicular pillars joined to the edges of the Great Ocean and shaped like a semi-cylinder. The firmament was a veil separating the divine world from the dwelling place of man. The Sun, Moon, and stars were carried below the firmament by angels who had this duty until the end of time.[41]

It was no doubt incredible to watch angel-borne sparks nightly beneath the sanctum of God in the nonindustrial air of the Middle Ages. It was a vision. It was also a superstition. The translation of that vision into theology and cosmography had a deadening effect. It denied the Greek heritage of elements and stargazing, and it bound the European world into a narrow cloister. How could navigators sail very far on a flat ocean that simply spilled over at the arches of heaven? Kosmas Indicopleustes (the Indian navigator) might have known better, for he reached Equatorial waters. But the image dominated much of the Middle Ages and had a popular appeal among the uneducated. Columbus's men actually feared the "black horizon" that they would fall into as they continued to sail beyond known and recorded lands to the edge of the world. The old European seafaring tradition and even the round Earth of Aristotle promised something quite different, but clerical and scholastic tradition was paranoid and confining. It was a time that saw angels in the sky but the shadow of Satan across the night. Plato and Aristotle marked no golden age. They stood before dark times scientifically, and a whole other civilization had to pass before the West returned to the point it had attained at the height of Greek enlightenment.

Dante, for instance, six centuries after Kosmas, is still in the Ptolemaic universe. His passage through the spheres of the planets is a journey into more and more radiant zones of light, which represent not just increased brightness but the unveiling of the spiritual component of light. The *Paradiso* is a fourteenth-century voyage into the Solar System. With Beatrice—Eros—imparting divine motion, Dante visits the various planets: Mercury, Venus, the Moon, the Sun, and so on. Each one is inhabited, not by beings on a terrain but by souls in stages of transmigration. As one ascends through the stars, or into the celestial fabric, the light of God which "impenetrates" the cosmos becomes direct and blinding. Even the stars wash out beside it. This spark contains the pure flame of God's love.[42]

There are also elements of Christian topography in the *Paradiso*. One sails across the ocean to the conical pit at the center of the Earth. Hell is a geometrically defined position, a bottom to the universe, sucking all that is antispiritual into its core. Mount Purgatory arises out of the sea directly beneath Jerusalem. Climbing this mountain, one ascends into the celestial spheres, the planets.

This cosmology leads one way into a totally tabernacular universe; but on another path, the hermetic magicians were transforming the Ptolemaic spheres into zones of the astral world, and the stars impregnated plants, animals, stones, and all of nature with pagan influences. The Renaissance astronomers came into this muddle and spent their lifetimes addressing it. They transformed the night sky, and they changed the West with it. Ancient astronomy ends in a single tradition leading across a few short centuries to men walking on the Moon. We should also note that, except for this single brilliant thread, it is still a dark sea surrounding us and we are in an aeon of war and ignorance. The Ice Age has barely ended.

6

The History of
Western Astronomy:
1: The Sun
in the Center

THE TRANSITION from ancient astronomy to modern astronomy is generally seen to occur through five main starwatchers: Nicolas Koppernigk (or Copernicus), Tycho Brahe, Johannes Kepler, Galileo Galilei, and Isaac Newton. Copernicus, the first, was born in 1473. Newton, the last, died in 1727. So the period we are talking about begins with the sixteenth century and ends at the beginning of the eighteenth century. It is specifically European, but it is pan-European. Copernicus was a Pole of Slavic ancestry. Kepler was a German Protestant. Brahe was a Dane born in a region which is now Sweden. Galileo was Italian. Newton was English. The thread from one to the other was clear and unbroken, although it was not a single tradition, and the work of each of these astronomers contradicted the work of one or more of the others. What they stand for as a whole is the transition from the Ptolemaic sky of the planets and Sun and Moon and stars moving around the Earth in perfect circles, driven by spiritual agency and composed of numinous crystal, to the pre-modern sky of planets, including the Earth, all moving around the Sun in ellipses established by gravity and centrifugal force and composed of the same basic matter.

Copernicus came too early to consider the ellipse, but there is little doubt he would have rejected it, as did Brahe and Galileo, because it violated the perfect circular movement attributed to the heavenly spheres. Kepler implicitly rejected gravity as being too mystical a force to assign to physical motion. Other contradictions underlie this astronomy, but the overall impact of a single new system is carried into the eighteenth and nineteenth centuries.

It is also important to see what these theoreticians did not do. They did not abandon the idea of God behind the heavens. They did not perceive the real distance of the stars or their arrangement in galaxies, though they understood that they were a great deal further away from Earth than the last planet, Saturn. They did not abandon the view of the heavens as an harmonious arrangement of perfect movements inspired by invisible occult sources and orchestrated by a Prime Mover (though Galileo came right to the threshold of the modern secular sky). These men sought to know how an esoteric agency had set physical matter into eternal motion and elemental exchange. The mathematician in their center, the German Baron von Leibnitz, was a bare shade from Pythagoras on this issue. The latter saw God wrapped in geometric forms; the former saw Him interacting with His Universe by calculus.

It is far too easy to credit each of these astronomers with the wrong discovery, by seeing their activities mainly in modern terms. The heliocentric revolution of Copernicus is apocryphal. Copernicus did not put the Sun in the center; it had been done before him by Aristarchus, among others, a fact that was general knowledge in educated circles. Copernicus was not the only "astronomer" to attribute motion to the Earth. Nicholas of Cusa, for reasons having little to do with physical astronomy, had concluded a century earlier that the Earth was in motion and that this was unknown to us only because we had nothing fixed to perceive it against. Cusa also said that since the universe has no boundaries, neither the Earth nor any other place can be the center. That Cusa arrived at these insights for theological reasons means only that his system was not in the modern lineage, but the heliocentric model of Copernicus was.

Copernicus was less theological, and this, above all, sets him at the head of the lineage of modern astronomy. He put heliocentricity and a moving Earth into a form that led them to be taken seriously by both the Church authorities, who banned his work after his death, and the astronomers, who followed him.

Copernicus was not a stargazer; he was a mathematician and church cleric. He sought to put the heavens in order, and to do so he created a better bookkeeping system for the stars. There is little doubt that he realized how flawed his own system was. He had set out to simplify Ptolemy, but he ended up with more, not fewer, epicycles and artificial devices to save the appearances of the heavens. Ptolemy's system required thirty-nine spheres and one for the fixed stars. Copernicus used at least forty-eight epicycles. The *simplification* of the Ptolemaic system is one achievement erroneously attributed to Copernicus.

Copernicus made only twenty-seven observations on his own: twenty-seven measurements of the stars, most of them inaccurate. All the rest of his system was based on Greek and Arab texts which he never checked even for the inevitable errors of translation and transcription. He was a frightened devout churchman, and perhaps the sloppy data on which he constructed his system allowed him not to take his heresy seriously.

In addition, he had neither the equipment nor the deep curiosity about the sky to make more observations and base his system on his own sightings. From the outset, he chose to work with secondary materials: the Ptolemaic system, the catalogues of Aristarchus and Heracleides, and the star observations of ancient times. Those twenty-seven observations of Copernicus stand out because they represent twenty-seven discrete moments at which this man looked into the actual sixteenth-century sky and tried to see it for what it was, tried to measure it. Otherwise, he assumed the heavens as a fixed imprint and worked in tables.

Ptolemy had created imaginary points in space—the equants—from which uniform motion would seem to exist. However, if uniform velocity were actually imposed, the planets must give up their circles. He must have known he was making a fiction, but, like so many other scientists, he no doubt assumed the fiction was better than the chaos that preceded it and would give some future astronomer a basis on which to make corrections. This was Copernicus. He set out to adjust the Ptolemaic schema of circles and equants by using a central Sun and a moving Earth. To his orderly mind, the violation of uniform motion was blasphemy greater than the heresy of a moving Earth. The equants and epicycles he took as nothing more than a calculating device for appearances. He intended his own device as a better underpinning for the holy firmament. He never abandoned the doctrine that the planets moved "with uniform velocity in perfect circles."[1]

Yet, Copernicus did something slightly more than adjust an illusory heavens. He made it possible for large numbers of people, especially educated people, to see the apparent motion of all the stars as stillness against a moving Earth. He did not initiate heliocentricity, but he wrote it in such a painstaking pedantic manner that it left a special imprint on the European mind not only in his own time but for centuries to come.

Since the Earth cannot be the center of the orbits of the other planets, and since they obviously move both toward and away from the Earth, the Earth must have "another motion in addition to the diurnal rotation." Beside rotation, the Earth "wanders with several motions and is indeed a Planet," a view which, Copernicus points out, was ascribed to Philolaus, the Pythagorean philosopher. The heavens, on the other hand, "if we assume them to be infinite, and bounded internally only by their concavity, so that everything, however great, is contained in them," could hardly move about the Earth. It would be like a vast eternity circling about a precise point. "Why then hesitate to grant Earth that power of motion natural to its shape, rather than suppose a gliding round of the whole Universe, whose limits are unknown and unknowable?"[2]

Because Copernicus is a mathematician and argues from such a stubbornly pragmatic point of view, his argument takes on a particular weight. Yet, the Copernican vision had no great widespread public appeal at the time, and the thousand copies of *De Revolutionibus orbium coelestium,* published in 1543, never sold out. Reprints came approximately every one hundred years. The system was communicated to the world quite secondarily through other books, such as Thomas Digges's proclamation of the infinite Copernican universe in his *Perfit Description of the Caelestiall Orbes,* which had seven quick printings. The differences between Copernicus's original ideas and Digges's recapitulations became blurred with popularization. Copernicus had retained the cohesive orb of fixed stars, but Digges scattered the stars helter-skelter through the realms of infinite space. He intuited the major cosmic import of local heliocentricity: it was not Sun-centeredness as such; it was what the dislodging of the Earth did to everything else. On a mere mathematical adjustment in an illusory system rested man's whole place in the cosmos—but wasn't it always so, then as now?

The pious canon would have been shocked by his own image in the poetry of John Donne. The Copernican system had become the work of Lucifer, raising the Earth into the heavens and building a modern Tower of Babel to challenge God. Decades after Copernicus's death, the Church elders heard of this famous heretic and wanted him burned at the stake. That they were too late astonished them. How had he eluded them?

But Copernicus had other problems. By historical accounts, he was a troubled man, given to petty squabbles. A bizarre chain of entanglements led to his adversaries' overseeing the publication of his work and butchering the text for their own purposes. A preface was written in his name claiming that the system described in the book must be a fiction because the path proposed for Venus was an impossibility. Copernicus did not deny this. He was certainly aware, if from nothing else than the discrepancies in the positions of Mars, that he had failed to correct the Ptolemaic heavens. Yet, he refused to allow that his system was a fiction in the same sense as Ptolemy's, even though he also failed to do the work that would allow him to take it seriously as a real proposal of physical dynamics. He was trapped between his system's possible heresy and a host of errors on the one side, conditions which tended to balance each other, and its dramatic correctness on the other. He had done away with the disturbing retrograde motions of the planets by showing that they were simply appearances due to the Earth's simultaneous

revolution about the Sun. Also, by implication, he had declared
the fixity of the stars. Since they were no longer "responsible"
for movement around the Earth, they began to drift out toward
their actual distance from us.

But it is ironical that Copernicus never got as fresh a look at
the sky as he gave to others. He did not have cosmic imagination.
De Revolutionibus orbium coelestium is exactly what its title states:
a book on the revolutions of the celestial orbs. It is not a statement of how the planets actually move; it is not an attempt to
understand their nature; it is not even an attempt to give the
Sun its real size and central position in this sytem. It is a cor-
rection of tables and a way to view the mathematical properties
of the figures traced by the planets' successive positions.

In attempting to preserve order, Copernicus contributed to
dislodging it. It is peculiarly fitting that a conservative church
cleric should have created such a giant wave that so little befitted
him, for it shows how specific and concrete are the pins that
hold the background to the foreground in our world. We hardly
know what they are. While others screamed for various sorts of
revolution and change (and there were wars and famous heresies
in his time), Copernicus accidentally dislodged one of the bolts
in the mediaeval world. He displaced the stars; he introduced
the tiniest element of eccentricity, the merest wobble, and it
eventually picked up other wobbles and became an earthquake,
a skyquake.

Almost at the moment that Copernicus turned to the Sun,
the hermetic and Gnostic tradition in the West turned with him.
In fact, it had always been there, and the association with the
Sun of Hermes himself, planetarily as Mercury and theosophi-
cally as the source of light and the metal gold, was an ancient
and significant one. Like Cusa, and without realizing it, Copernicus had laid the basis for a new hermetic interpretation of the
universe too:

> In the middle of all sits Sun enthroned. In this most beau-
> tiful temple could we place this luminary in any better po-
> sition from which he can illuminate the whole at once? He
> is rightly called the Lamp, the Mind, the Ruler of the

Universe; Hermes Trismegistus names him the Visible
God, Sophocles' Electra calls him the All-seeing. So the
Sun sits as upon a royal throne ruling his children the
planets which circle round him.[3]

If we were not told this was Copernicus, we might have guessed
one of the hermetic or neo-Platonic philosophers.

The historian Frances Yates has traced the relationships between scientific and magical movements at this time. She sees
that Copernicus, from one vantage, was involved in reforming
the clerical scientific—hence Aristotelian—universe, but that
the hermetics, from another vantage, were interested in mod-
ernizing their symbolism and deepening its connection to the
pagan Egyptian roots by ridding it of the supposedly false classical influences that intervened. Whether these origins were authentically Egyptian or not is a central concern of Yates and a
major issue of her book, but what is important here, in terms
of star images, is that the centralized Sun was perceived within
the hermetic tradition as a fulfillment of Egyptian prophecy. The
fact that this "prophecy" became parallel to the development of
astronomical science in the following centuries did not at all
deter magical identification. Science was taken as a millennial
reawakening of an Egyptian methodology that would ultimately
empower humanity to overthrow the rigid Christian orthodoxy.[4]

The great powers bestowed on common man by machines,
electricity, and metallurgy, centuries later, were the magical realization of this astral Egyptian tradition. They did overthrow
the Church. They did arise from hermetic scientists: Copernicus, Newton, even Einstein. Of course, the magicians were no
longer around to observe the victory; their paradise was wiped
out in Bohemia by the Thirty Years' War, and the Eden they
dreamed of never came, even with the machinery of the pagans.
The malaise of industrialism is taken as exactly Western man's
loss of his own sources and his concomitant failure to credit
astral intelligence with its role in civilization: hence, it is a loss
of touch with the great principle of energy itself. So the hermetics of the twentieth century tell us.

Giordano Bruno, the Italian astral philosopher, was the first
to integrate the heliocentric proposition into a new system of

traditional "Egyptian" magic. Born a few years after the death of Copernicus, Bruno was a contemporary of Kepler and Galileo. He was executed by the Church in 1600 for his heresy.

The view of the heavens that Bruno proposed in the sixteenth century is so idiosyncratic and so nonmodern that it has been misinterpreted as a brave forerunner of an astronomy that was to develop only centuries after Copernicus, Kepler, and Newton. Bruno grasped intuitively at things which look like twentieth-century discoveries when we read them in excerpts of his writing, especially when these are chosen to portray an early scientist who died in the name of truth. No doubt Bruno did, but it was a different truth from ours: the truth of the Sun City and the Egyptian renaissance.

Bruno saw that the stars and galaxies must be infinite and eternal, that such systems must contain sensible and intelligible beings. He did not use the word *galaxy,* but he spoke of systems of stars with their own customs and beliefs and their own right to centrality quite apart from the position of the Earth. He was a "modern" for decentralizing the universe and getting not only the Earth itself but this whole region of the creation out of its special position as the center of the divine energy materialized.[5]

> Sky, universe, all-embracing ether [said Bruno], and immeasurable space alive with movement—all these are of one nature. In space there are countless constellations, suns, and planets; we see only the suns because they give light; the planets remain invisible, for they are small and dark. There are also numberless earths circling around their suns, no worse and no less inhabited than this globe of ours.[6]

What Bruno found attractive in Copernicus was both the central Sun and the moving Earth. He also felt that the Copernican vision was a kind of Promethean seizing of the true power and source of the creation. The artificial spheres of planets and stars which the Ptolemaic-Aristotelian tradition had imposed on the sky barred man from the heavens and kept the magical principle gradated away from human access, up toward the angelic sphere where only the Church could mediate. But the Egyptian universe, or at least the universe of Hermes with its Egyptian affinities, allowed man to travel in astral spheres on his own, gave him formulas for drawing upon the stellar energies, and populated the celestial sphere with alien intelligences and powers unlimited. To de-Christianize the sky was not to blaspheme God; it was to allow God to create more than just a Christian universe. It was, in fact (and here is the blasphemy for which Bruno died), to imagine a universe in which God made things that could not be known by scholastic and Thomist law but could be derived by magicians and hermetics using equally divine principles. Said Bruno:

> Open wide the door for us, so that we may look out into the immeasurable starry universe; show us that other worlds like ours occupy the ethereal realms. . . .[7]

The inhabited galaxies of Bruno were not modern; they were simply pagan, but pagan in a different way than modern science is. God rustled through the universe transforming and moving and empowering everything everywhere. Ptolemy had attached the stars to envelopes, but Bruno said: "It is not to be believed that there is any firmament, or foundation to which are fixed these great animals which form the constitution of the universe, the infinite material of infinite divine potency."[8] The Earth moves in order to stir itself, to transform its materials, to increase its attributes, and because it is first and foremost alive and has a soul which it must express by movement.

Infinity is what makes Bruno most astronomical. He had an early vision of the great bestiary into which telescopes would later delve with wonder. He saw it as an *anima mundi,* angelic beings spawning stars out of their ensouled whirlpools like naiads, the force spilling through stars and worlds that it spawns and into which it pours its eternal virtues as elements, demonic influences, imprints hidden in species either by color, number, shape, sound, habitat, or minute signet. So the true art of the stars is not astronomy but astromancy and talisman-making. Intimacy is what makes Bruno least modern. He did not mean outer space in the modern nihilistic sense; he did not mean infinity dwarfing man. These vast reaches of creation are available to humankind by magic and astral power. Man is not relegated to a remote corner, for there are no remote corners.

Newton believed likewise when he set gravity between each particle and every other in the universe.

Bruno regarded the failure of man to stargaze creatively as his failure to ascend, with Copernicus, into the spheres of original creative energy and destiny:

> Some men [he wrote], resembling the dim-eyed mole, who, the moment he feels upon him the open air of heaven, rushes to dig himself back again into the ground, desire to remain in their native darkness; others are like those birds of night which, because of the weakness of their eyes, retreat into their shadowy haunts as soon as they see in the brightening east those bars of crimson which are the sun's ambassadors. All those creatures who may not gaze upon the lights of heaven but are destined to dwell in the infernal circles of Pluto's dark prison-house, when they hear the dread summons of Alecton's furious horn, spread wide their wings and veer away in rapid flight toward their abodes. But those who were born to see the sun, being full of thanksgiving when they come to the end of loathsome night, dispose themselves to receive in the very centre of their eyes' crystal globe the long-expected rays of the glorious sun, and, with unaccustomed gladness in their hearts, they lift up hands and voices to adore the east. . . .[9]

This theme echoes in the poetry of the twentieth-century hermetic Robert Kelly—once again the call to the Sun-star:

> & if we do not get up and destroy all the congressmen
> turn them into naked men and let the sun shine on them
> set them down in a desert & let them find their way out,
> north, by whatever sexual power is left in them, if we do
>   not
> seize the president and take him out in daytime and show
>   him
> the fire & energy of one at least immediate star, white
>   star,
> hammer that down in his skull till he can hear only that
> rhythm & goes and enters the dance or makes his own,
>
> we will walk forever down the hallways into mirrors and

stagger and look to our left hand for support & the sun
will have set inside us. . . .[10]

But Bruno died at the hand of mediaeval senators; and three
hundred and fifty years later, Wilhelm Reich was to die in fed-
eral prison in Connecticut for the medicines he derived from
observation of galaxies and research in the atmosphere into
cosmic energy. The terms of the heresy may have changed, but
we still have an astral paganism which challenges a clerical establishment. Bruno refused to recant before the Church, Reich
refused to appear before the Food and Drug Administration. It
is not the stars men die for; it is the radical effect of stellar
visions on society. Bruno's last words echo across the centuries:
"I await your sentence with less fear than you pass it. The
time will come when all will see what I see."[11]
And we might wonder if that time is still in the future.

Heliocentricity and the discovery of the New World by European mariners went together in the transformation of cosmography. Just as Copernicus did not discover the moving Earth,
so Columbus did not discover America. Cyrus Gordon makes
a case for Phoenician trade expeditions to Brazil as early as
800 B.C.[12] Carl Sauer suggests that there was Irish settlement in
North America by A.D. 900, following the Norse invasions of
the North Atlantic in 850.[13] Both of these "discoveries" could
have been earlier. In 1000, the millennial year, the Vikings sent
a polar bear from North America to the Sultan of Egypt.[14] The
connection could not have been more blatant. No doubt there
were other relics, even as rune carvings in stone have been found
clear to the Mississippi, traded inland by Indian groups. It was
a strangely cosmopolitan time.

By A.D. 1200, the Vikings are settled in the New World and
Basque fishermen are bringing back their catch from the North
Atlantic off Newfoundland to Spain. The Norse finally aban-
doned Greenland and the West in 1400.[15] So when we come to
1492, that famous date, we must truly ask: what is it a date for?
Surely not the discovery of the New World by human beings.
The Indians were there for at least twenty-five thousand years

before. Surely not the first Europeans in the New World. The "discovery" of America is as problematic as the Copernican "revolution," and it belongs to the same era in the West.

1492 is the date for fusing two contradictory European images of the world. One Europe was grounded in the old Mediterranean culture with lingering hopes of restoring the Roman Empire (or at least the Roman cosmology), perhaps through the Church, and thus starting a new golden age. It was aware of the riches of Asia but ignorant and afraid of the Atlantic—the direction (West) of primitivity and darkness. It was a Europe concerned with international finances, trade fairs and markets, and rearranging national boundaries for political purposes. It was the Europe of Verdun, and it became the Europe of King Philip of Spain, De Soto and his ravages of Southeastern Indian civilization, Cortez, and Napoleon (even that late, with his desperate sale of Louisiana, the one strategic land he held).

The other Europe was specifically grounded in the old Atlantic; it never entered into Christian orthodoxy or mediaeval philosophy. It was forever pragmatic, pagan, and tribal. It was represented most purely by the descendants of the Druids, the fishermen of Biscay and Bristol,[16] the Cretans and Basques, and those otherwise educated "Christians" who searched for Hermes, incorporated him alchemically into Church liturgy, and saw Egypt as the base of an ancient and powerful magic.[17] In this other Europe, the Irish priest-voyages were known, and there were secret maps and routes, old "scientific" documents. It was the Europe not of Plato and Aristotle but the Arabic and Persian encyclopedias—the Europe of John Dee, John Smith, Hesiod, Homer, and the Norse *Sagas*. It became a Renaissance Europe relatively unconcerned with either Christian orthodoxy or the Reformation, and it rejected the scholastic uses of ancient humanist philosophy.[18]

But neither Europe held America as such. The first one was afraid and ignorant of it; the second was involved in astral magic and navigation without a complete cosmography. Columbus took the Atlantic from its natives on both sides, Algonquian and Basque, and gave it to Spain and Rome, to Cortez and Pizarro. He brought together the round world and the flat world, the pagan world and the Christian world; he merged the secret trade maps and unknown kingdoms with public grants and acknowledged sources. By so doing, he lost the Homeric sea and its wondrous peoples, even as we have lost the angelic heavens since, and by the same process. He set sail into the old Atlantic and found lands in it in such a way that they stayed found, not as mere rediscovery of the Indies. He made it impossible for Europe to ignore what it already knew.

The year 1500 was a turning point. Columbus and Copernicus were both stubborn enough to change the world-view and make it stick, but rigid enough to believe in the old cosmology to their dying days.

7

The History of Western Astronomy: II: The Planets

IF THERE IS one astronomer whose work marks the watershed between the ancient occult system and the modern scientific one, it is Johannes Kepler. Kepler was that rare combination of cynic and mystic. He was an astrologer. In fact, he attributed his own perspicacity in solving the problem of Mars's orbit to the arrangement of the planets at his birth. More clearly than any historical figure since Pythagoras, he heard and transcribed the music of the spheres. He wrote some of the most beautiful and enduring testimony to the mediaeval cosmos. Yet, he alone of his contemporaries was pragmatic and resourceful enough to break with the perfect circular orbits and the inherent divine motion and discover the actual laws of the movement of the planets.

It is difficult to know whether to credit Kepler with discovering the harmony of the spheres as occult music or as the mathematical properties of their orbits, because to him they were the same phenomenon. He understood the physical basis for the movement of the planets better than anyone before him; yet his interpretation of that movement was spiritual:

> The sun in the middle of the moving stars, himself at rest and yet the source of motion, carries the image of God the Father and Creator. . . . He distributes his motive force

119

through a medium which contains the moving bodies even as the Father creates through the Holy Ghost.[1]

And elsewhere:

Why waste words? Geometry existed before the Creation, is co-eternal with the mind of God, *is God himself . . .* ; geometry provided God with a model for the Creation and was implanted into man, together with God's own likeness—and not merely conveyed to his mind through the eyes.[2]

In his epic work on the history of Western astronomy, *The Sleepwalkers,* Arthur Koestler places Kepler at the heart of the book, in the center of the series of chapters entitled "The Watershed." Koestler's portrayal of Kepler is profound and thorough, a far more accurate and insightful case of applying psychology to an historical figure than the more heralded work of Erik Erikson on Martin Luther. Koestler understands that Kepler was unlike anyone else of his time. His insights were far more radical and sustained than those of Copernicus. The laws he discovered had barely been prefigured, if at all.

What Koestler captures is the combination of the mystic and the scientist: a man who believed in astrology enough to write criticisms of the corrupt astrology of his time; a devotee of astral magic who had nothing but contempt for superstition and who gave up years of his life to defend his mother against a charge of witchcraft, preparing the defense with the same care he had used on the positions of Mars; a scientist who abandoned previous theories because of minute flaws, in an era when most people were competing to save the appearances only; a cranky husband and father and friend who blamed much of his troubles on astrological influences, yet wrote brilliant psychological self-analyses in the characterological language of the zodiac; a compulsively careful mathematician and theoretician before any other astronomer understood the usefulness of painstaking exactness.

Kepler's mind remained clear throughout innumerable exiles and banishments occasioned by prejudice, superstition, and war. He lacked access to the best data of his time, but, unlike Copernicus, he could not accept a partial system. He could not finally perpetrate a cosmos sustained by a circumstantial combination of actual mechanism and traditional belief. Vital forces lay at the source of the heavens, but their translation into physical motion was absolutely physical and thus describable without recourse to authority or orthodox cosmology. If the symmetry of the skies could not be maintained by circles and natural uniform motion, then the Creator must have set some deeper and more perfect riddle within.

The moral basis for Creation was a central issue through all of Kepler's work. When he discovered, later, that the distant stars were immobile in relation to the Earth and that this might be a result of their great distance, he argued that this disturbing infinity could not affect the moral consequences of man's life. Otherwise the crocodile and the elephant, for being larger than man, would be more in affinity with the Creator. This is reminiscent of Herman Melville's later insight that whale and insect are each obedient to a single volition, i.e., a single nerve impulse.[3]

Kepler accepted Copernicus's model with the Sun in the center, and from there he tried to work out the mathematical secret contained in the orbits of the other planets. Initially he meant to establish a ratio between the sizes of the principal epicycles of each planet. This led nowhere. He placed an unseen planet between Mars and Jupiter, then a second one between Mars and Venus, thus violating the numerological laws based on the seven bodies of the night sky (six planets and a moon). He tried trigonometric ratios between orbits; he applied different astrological principles, then various forms of geometry. But he was plying an impossible riddle. The orbits were not circles, and the placement of the planets was not the key to a Pythagorean harmony.

At this stage, Kepler did not distinguish between the attempt to arrive at a mathematical solution to the problem as a description of physical reality and the attempt to arrive at a numerological solution to the celestial music. The two skies were the same sky to Kepler. The wonder is that he was able to observe the "hermetic" sky closely enough to discover mathematical principles that had no basis in traditional occultism.

He constructed his first hermetic Solar System in *Mysterium Cosmographicum* (1597). The full title states the basis of the work: *A Forerunner to Cosmographical Treatises, containing the Cosmic Mystery of the admirable proportions between the Heavenly Orbits and the true and Proper Reasons for their Numbers, Magnitudes and Periodic Motions.* Kepler's solution was to place the orbits of the planets within the five perfect solids, which separated them from each other:

> The earth is the sphere, the measure of all; round it describe a dodecahedron; the sphere including this will be Mars. Round Mars describe a tetrahedron; the sphere including this will be Jupiter. Describe a cube round Jupiter; the sphere including this will be Saturn. Now inscribe in the earth an icosahedron, the sphere inscribed in it will be Venus; inscribe an octahedron in Venus; the circle inscribed in it will be Mercury.[4]

Kepler recalls the moment of discovery as rapturous. So convinced was he that the same God who created only five symmetrical solids could not help but place them between the six planetary orbits, he expected a perfect fit. When he got only an approximate fit, he assumed that the data was inaccurate and he corrected it (i.e., changed it) to fit his hypothesis. Having evaded other magical universes, he created one of his own. From this cosmic model, Kepler went on to derive astrology, numerology, the geometrical symbolism of the zodiac, and finally the Pythagorean correspondence between the perfect solids separating the planets' orbits and the harmonic intervals in music.

Years later he was to make a small but significant shift in his concept of the movement of the planets as conceived in *Mysterium Cosmographicum.* From assuming that the planets were driven by souls, he switched to the image of a force emanating from the Sun. The difference between a soul and a force was a small one, but he had made a subtle adjustment and was now honing in on the physical universe. Copernicus had set the corporeal center in the Sun itself. If the Sun was in the center, perhaps a force radiating from the Sun held the planets in their orbits and gave those orbits their shapes and frequencies.

For Kepler the quest was a lifelong meditation on the spiritual fount of the universe. He was directly engaging his own mind with the Mind of God. He understood almost at once that his geometrical universe was another myth. There was still a real solution, a purely physical solution to the problem. It would not violate sacred law because sacred law was inviolable. Whatever shape God was, He had put there in the heavens to be seen and known. So Kepler rejected his own theory, and in that he stood apart from his century.

Mysterium Cosmographicum was written when Kepler was twenty-four years old. His major scientific work, *Astronomia Nova (A New Astronomy Based on Causation or A Physics of the Sky derived from Investigations of the Motions of the Star Mars Founded on Observations of the Noble Tycho Brahe)* was written when he was in his forties. The title tells the story. Kepler had finally gained access to the astronomical observatory and star tables of Tycho Brahe.

Tycho was a wealthy court astronomer; he had been adopted by his childless uncle and given a rich estate. His interest was pure observational astronomy. He had the best equipment in the world assembled in his dwelling, which he renamed Uraniburg. According to Arthur Koestler, Tycho mapped the accurate positions of 777 stars, though he added 223 approximate places and guesses to make a table of an even 1,000. He also determined that the 1572 nova in the vicinity of Cassiopeia was a fixed star and not a tailless comet or a symbol of God's wrath.

Tycho shared precision and fastidiousness with Kepler but little else. Tycho was a proud noble; Kepler was a poor commoner. Tycho worked for his own ego and fame, to make astronomy a noble calling and to glamorize his otherwise idle existence. Kepler worked to solve celestial mysteries. Tycho was superstitious and lacked any insight into either physics or hermeticism; Kepler was deeply mystical.

Kepler was a man in a trance. He felt that he could solve the stellar mystery, and he was obsessed by it. It could not be done just by abstract mathematics, geometry, and intuition; the failure of *Mysterium Cosmographicum* proved that. Kepler required accurate figures and good instruments. Tycho wanted his work to go into a great heavenly synthesis, but he lacked the imagination. When he hired Kepler, it was to complete his own system. He was the nobleman, Kepler the commoner. Hence, it was to be Tycho's theory. Deep down he might have understood that Kepler had the better mind, but he lived in a courtly world, centuries from such an admission. Kepler would have to serve him.

Kepler sought only the freedom to work on his problem and to have unhindered access to the records. The collaboration was interrupted on numerous occasions by temper outbursts and Kepler's flight; but, in the end, Tycho gave in, and what he did not give to Kepler, Kepler either stole from him or whisked away after his death before the survivors could get their hands on it. For years afterward, the noble family of Tycho Brahe tried to hinder Kepler's publications or to attach their name rather than his to them because the observations themselves, the entries of the night sky, were considered family jewels. It was upon these jewels that Kepler based his new astronomy.

Very early in the relationship of these two astronomers, Kepler wrote:

> Tycho possesses the best observations, and thus so-to-speak the material for the building of the new edifice; he also has collaborators and everything he could wish for. He only lacks the architect who would put all this to use according to his own design. For although he has a happy disposition and real architectural skill, he is nevertheless obstructed in his progress by the multitude of the phenomena and by the fact that the truth is deeply hidden in them. Now old age is creeping upon him, enfeebling his spirit and his forces.[5]

This is the story of mankind—the multitude of the phenomena, the lack of a cohesive theory, and a brief period alive among these phenomena to solve them. It was as true of Einstein as of Tycho or Kepler.

Just as the Moon was to be the key planet for Newton because of its location in the Earth's gravitational field, and just as Mercury was to be the key planet for Einstein because of its passage close to the disk of the Sun, so Mars was Kepler's planet because of the eccentricity of its orbit, the most elliptical of the six inner planets (Venus and Neptune, by contrast, travel around the Sun in almost perfect circles).

Kepler waged a personal "war" against Mars—Mars who had made a career out of mocking astronomers, who brazenly kept his secret, who defied mathematical resolution even when the other planets obeyed. So long as Mars was a planet and not a chimera, Kepler had to deal with it. He suspected that it held the key. For all its inscrutability, Mars must follow the deepest signature of the law; and when its puzzle was solved, then the other planets could be understood on Mars's terms.

Mars's positions told Kepler that it moved in toward the Sun and then back away from it. But if the orbit was circular, its center could not be the Sun. The Sun's influence could only be uniform, so if Mars traveled about it in something other than a circle, then another force, originating in the planet, pulled it off course. A circle still lay at the bottom of things, but a circle distorted by some other shape.

Most accounts tell us that Kepler brilliantly deduced that the orbits of the planets were ellipses. Koestler actually follows the logic of the *New Astronomy* and shows how Kepler arrived at his ellipse painstakingly and only after many years. First, he tried different circular orbits. He came quite close to a "solution" in the old approximate terms. But now he had Tycho's appearances to save also, and no matter what orbit he came up with, it was contradicted by some corroborated position of the planet.

Of course, Mars's positions are determined by its own movement and the Earth's movement. Kepler needed both, so he took to computing the Earth's position as if he were an astronomer on Mars, and he found that the Earth did not revolve evenly around the Sun either. It seemed to move at velocities inversely proportional to its distance from the Sun, as if controlled by a solar force. In the course of working with this problem, Kepler articulated his second law, which gave him a basis for determining the position of a planet at a given time in its orbit: a line connecting the planet to the Sun will sweep out equal areas in equal times, no matter what the distance. When it is closer to the Sun, it will move faster at a rate that will increase the width of the area swept out to exactly the degree that its length is diminished.

Now Kepler could handle the deviation from uniform speed, but he still did not know the shape. For more than a year, he worked with ovals—or "eggs," as he called them. He made continuous errors of simple mathematics and transcription which magically canceled out, leaving him where he would have been anyway. Some deep unconscious guide watched over his quest. A chance perception of an odd number in two different contexts gave him a formula for the shape prescribed by the planet's variance in its orbit in accordance with its distance from the Sun. The semidiameter of the Martian orbit, where it varied most from a circle, was 1.00429 of the radius of the circle. At the same time, Kepler was exploring the angle formed by Mars simultaneously with the Sun and with the center of the Martian orbit as seen from Mars. If the distance from Mars to the center of its orbit was divided by the distance from Mars to the Sun, it gave a figure that was also the secant of this angle. In Kepler's own words: "I stumbled entirely by chance on the secant of the angle 5° 18', which is the measure of the greatest optical equation. When I realized that this secant equals 1.00429, I felt as if I had been awakened from a sleep."[6] (Hence the title of Koestler's great work on astronomy.)

Kepler had hit upon the formula for the ellipse without knowing it. He saw only that he had a curve with a bulge. After a geometric error led him through an excruciating battle with this shape, he tried an ellipse as a hypothetical stand-in, only to realize that the ellipse and his formula for the law of the planets' positions were one and the same. This is Kepler's First Law of planetary motion: the planets move in ellipses around the Sun. The Third Law, stated in *Harmonice Mundi* (a work in which he also tried to develop a notation for the heavenly music), is that "the squares of the periods of revolution are proportional to the cubes of the mean distances from the Sun."[7]

Kepler did not understand gravity, inertia, or centrifugal

force, but his laws contained everything needed to derive them. To him they were mystical and numerological relationships, so he went no further in uncloaking the sky. He had meant to show that the clockwork of the cosmos is inhabited by a soul which manifests itself in motions carried out synchronously between objects across distances without mechanical connections. This he demonstrated. It was Newton who made the connections, and even for him they were of a spiritual nature. Yet, we today, who consider them physical, have no clearer sense of their hidden nature.

Galileo lived during almost the same years as Kepler, but he was an astronomer in a different spirit, and he had almost no contact with him. Galileo was more like Tycho, vain and arrogant, concerned with reputation. Tycho may have wondered if astronomy was an important enough calling for a nobleman; Galileo had no such pretensions: he was an intellectual snob. The role of master astronomer and pioneer of the heavens was a lofty enough podium. He prided himself on knowing things in the cosmos before anyone else did, and he enjoyed pulling rabbits out of the night sky.

Galileo's contributions to a modern view of the sky are on two levels, the first of which was pure exploration through the best telescopes of his time. Through his eye, he walked on the Moon. He passed over deep craters, he saw mountain peaks covered in bright sunlight while their lower slopes were in shadow, and from the shadows he calculated their heights. He discovered the initial four moons of Jupiter and the appendages of Saturn; and turning his spyglass into the depths of outer space, he saw something that was truly awesome, which Tycho and Kepler had simply intuited: everywhere "other stars, in myriads, which have never been seen before, and which surpass the old, previously known stars in number more than ten times."[8] Each of the constellations is thus a far denser and more complicated object than had previously been considered. The Belt and Sword of Orion alone had eight additional stars. Galileo resolved the Praesepe cloud in Cancer, known as the Beehive

Cluster, into its component stars. This was the beginning of a barren infinity. But at first glance it was chilling and beautiful.

Galileo's book *Messenger from the Stars* introduced the notion of the infinite sky to the world at large in 1610. Since Galileo, the sky has been a dynamic opening into eternity rather than a flat projection of the code from the higher spheres. Now we more or less assume that the stars we see are the ones closest to us, the ones that happen to be in this part of the universe. Quasars, for us, appear to mark the end of the universe, but we do not have the divine sphere to place outside it that people still had in Galileo's time. If we should discover that quasars are part of our tiny corner of the universe and the creation goes on exponentially into other realms of matter, we might experience again a fraction of the shock that people received from Galileo's sky messenger. "The infinite is unthinkable," said Kepler.[9]

"The eternal silence of the infinite spaces terrifies me," wrote Blaise Pascal.[10]

We do not even bother to acknowledge it very much anymore. We have reached the point where it is worse than infinite spaces: it is the infinite without meaning. Milton would write of "a dark / Illimitable ocean, without bound, / Without dimension."[11]

It was as though we hung, in a moment of history awakening from one dream, between dreams. Galileo snapped the trance; he spoke what we already must have known. Look, he said, the heavens are not a vast clairvoyance or a diamond of our destiny; they are a fiery corruptible thing like the Earth. Even the brilliant Sun is pocked with decay when seen through the glass.

> What greater folly can be imagined [he wrote] than to call gems, silver and gold noble, and earth and dirt base? For do not these persons consider that, if there were as great a scarcity of earth as there is of jewels and precious metals, there would be no king who would not gladly give a heap of diamonds and rubies and many ingots of gold to purchase only so much earth as would suffice to plant a jessamine in a little pot or to set a tangerine in it, that he might see it sprout, grow up, and bring forth such goodly leaves, fragrant flowers, and delicate fruit?[12]

It is this very jewel that we were to search for later among the planets as soon as we fully understood they were worlds like ours—not angels, not astral signs, but the beginning of the carbon chain, our own elements, our cosmic brothers and sisters lost since the beginning.

Galileo's other contribution to a modern view of the sky was astronomical in a totally different way, having to do with the law of falling bodies: freely falling and rolling down inclined planes. Galileo showed that bodies fell to the earth at the same speed, not in proportion to their weight. But he persisted in the circular orbit of the planets, despite Kepler. His law of falling bodies was meant for terrestrial application only. What he actually had discovered was that the forces of the universe at large are not altered by transient matters of relative size and weight and that the Earth itself is no different from the heavens. It took Newton to generalize this finding into universal gravitation, and Einstein to generalize that to relativity and include time in the formula for space. These changed the Earth by changing the world line that ran through it from the universe at large.

Newton accomplished what Kepler and Galileo could not do, despite their contemporaneity: he brought them together by showing that there is no distinction between outer space and the Earth and that all bodies obey a universal Law of Gravitation. So Earth and Sky were brought together not in the hermetic axiom but by the realization that they are not separate domains.

Galileo's difficulty with the Church came not from the things he discovered or the new boundaries of the universe he proposed. These were accepted by religious people, enthusiastically by some, begrudgingly by others. It was Galileo's arrogance that trapped him. He came to see his own discoveries as more important than the whole Catholic Church with its millennial tradition, and he proclaimed that the Church could no longer have a say in matters of the sky. This gratuitously angered the elders in Rome.

Galileo's flaw was his inability to get a full measure of enjoyment from his discoveries without the attendant hoopla and homage. Perhaps the fact that it was *his* void made the void less fearful for him. The wonders he found did not destroy his universe, for he laid claim to them one by one with a flourish: The

Goddess of Love imitates the shapes of the Moon; the highest planet has a triple body; the face of the Sun is marred and corrupted. So the world learned that Venus went through phases, Saturn had a multiple body that would turn out to be rings, and the Sun had spots. These discoveries tore apart the remains of the mediaeval sky, for the planets and Sun and Moon moving through the constellations were the key to celestial harmony. Now there were things beyond our vision and knowledge which gave the universe its true shape. Kepler had merely applied mathematics to the visible. Galileo reported the secrets hidden by God Himself. When he insisted that these sights and wonders be made into dogma, the Church authorities balked. What right had this unspiritual mechanic to demand the absolute truth of things which were still hypothetical and whose meaning could not be absorbed so quickly! Like a practical joker, Galileo enjoyed shoving the telescope into the hands of disbelievers and Church officials, making them look at Jupiter's four captive planets and the crescent of Venus. "There," he would deride. "Challenge that if you want!"

It was not the heavens that disturbed people; it was Galileo's attitude. He was the prophet of doom for a whole world-view, but he did not handle his position with humility or sobriety. He did not even seem to know what it meant. He careened through town slapping people on the back, saying, "See, I told you!"— offending and frightening even Kepler. The skies were serious business. One could not announce that Pan was dead and then cheer or laugh. These were terrible visions. How terrible, time would tell. The authorities, in their aged wisdom, somehow knew.

The Church theologians cornered Galileo finally on the matter of the Earth's movement. They did not dispute that the Copernican model was an excellent calculating device and an hypothesis that might yet be proven true. They denied that it was proven beyond doubt. Galileo had to accept this and back down.

But it was the last time. The priests would not again have a chance to hold the secular scientist before his works and say, in essence, "Look at the consequences, look at what you have done to the world."

8

The History of Western Astronomy: III: The Gravitational Field

THE SEVENTEENTH CENTURY stood on the verge of a new universe much in the way we might again today. The pieces were in place, but no unified theory connected them. Copernicus's universe was not Kepler's universe, and neither of them were Galileo's Solar System or realm of falling bodies. Something was required to sew these into a single fabric, to reveal the shape that was emerging through collective humanity. In the early part of the century, Francis Bacon and René Descartes had set what seemed to be the poles of scientific inquiry. Bacon advocated exploration of actual physical systems and their components without recourse to metaphysics or abstractions and with an aim toward the ultimate technological improvement of society. Descartes had created an abstract and mathematical system: his universe was a thin fluid composed of minute dust particles which rotated in vortices and whirlpools around the Sun and distant stars.

Newton did not need to decide between Bacon and Descartes, even as he did not need to decide between Kepler and

Galileo. He subsumed them, and in so doing, he subsumed their contentions, which were real and are still real. The universe did not need to be *either* an abstract mathematical invention or a collection of limitless discrete causes and effects. These described the same reality. Newton combined the astronomical laws of planetary motion formulated by Kepler with the laws of falling bodies and projectiles developed by Galileo. He supplied the mechanism behind Kepler's elliptical orbits, which was also the basis of heliocentricity.

It is hard, at times, to distinguish the laws of Newton and the twentieth-century Newtonian universe from the work of Isaac Newton the man. The laws mean a different thing against a backdrop of mechanical theories of life than they did in the spiritual universe still bright on seventeenth-century nights. In his own time, Newton's laws were the solution of a divine puzzle. In the centuries following, they were the foundation for a materialist reality. The fact that any high school student knows them now hardly diminishes the achievement. It was not facts and formulas that made this moment in the history of science; it was Newton's sudden realization of the meaning behind the night sky—the physical agency of its rhythm and balance. To see this for the first time—at the edge of history, a new thing—was incredible. Now the laws are mass-produced; they are the mechanical bottom line from which all more complex events are derived.

The link between Kepler and Galileo was the Moon, which could be considered at once as a planet in orbit about the Earth and as a projectile which was fired from the Earth but which, for some unknown reason, did not return to it. This unknown reason was the Moon's tangential velocity, which created enough centrifugal force (as we have come to call it) to counteract the pull of the Earth. Conversely, what counteracts the Moon being pulled into the Earth (or the planets being pulled into the Sun) must be a force strong enough to hold satellites in place. The attraction necessary is staggering. A body the size of the Earth must be halted, as it tears at breakneck speed toward the outermost point of its ellipse, gradually slowed, turned inward, and drawn back until velocity and centrifugal force again carry it to apogee. Kepler had certainly proved that such a thing happens, and by a law which causes it to sweep up equal areas of space in equal times. But how? He thought that it could only be an invisible astral force emanating from the Sun.[1] He did not understand that this was the same force affecting all bodies in any space. It could be applied to balls thrown in the air, or rolled down a hill: these were "planets" too.

The law of universal gravitation proposed by Newton states that every particle—every particle of matter anywhere in the universe—attracts every other particle with a force varying inversely as the square of their distances and directly as the product of their masses. This held for stars and planets, and it held also for insects whirring their gossamer wings in the fields, and for pebbles washed up on the beach. Furthermore, it held all of these together in the same universal field. This was, in fact, the universe.

Newton laid the mathematical basis for gravity and the laws of motion and interaction, but he had no idea what gravity was. An invisible force transmitted millions of miles from its source with incredible power was so mystical a notion that it had only been idly considered or considered and rejected by scientists and mathematicians before him. The difference was that, for Newton, gravity was not an abstract concept in the tradition of Kepler or Descartes; he defined it only by its effect. "Whether natural or supernatural," he said (for it made no difference), it is that which has "placed the sun in the center of the six primary planets, placed Saturn in the center of his five secondary planets and Jupiter in the center of his four secondary planets, and the earth in the center of the moon's orb."[2]

The power of gravity was awesome. "It must proceed from a cause that penetrates to the very centers of the sun and planets, without suffering the least diminution of its force; that operates not according to the quantity of the surfaces of the particles upon which it acts (as mechanical causes used to do), but according to the quantity of the solid matter which they contain, and propagates its virtue on all sides to immense distances, decreasing always as the inverse square of the distances." The Sun's gravitation is made out of the particles of which "the body of the sun is composed," and although it weakens as distance from the Sun increases, it continues "as far as the orbit of Saturn, as appears from the quiescence of the aphelion of the planets; nay, and even to the remotest aphelion of the comets."[3]

The conviction that some great metaphysical truth lay behind gravitation did not cease for Newton's lifetime or in the decades that followed, and has ceased now only insofar as gravitation has been joined to relativity in a larger mystery. Newton believed that he had discovered how God was in contact with all parts of His Creation at once. Through this force, everything responded to the same will. In fact, God's will was a necessary component of gravity, to keep the entire universe from being pulled together and crushed.

Each point of matter, Newton realized, seeks unity at the center of a great sphere, which is the center of matter itself. This replaces Ptolemaic geocentricity as a statement of divine astronomy: "every particle of space is *always,* and every indivisible moment of duration is *everywhere,*" hence God is always and everywhere. "He is omnipresent not *virtually* only but also *substantially;* for virtue cannot subsist without substance."[4]

Newton at once turned the universe into both a mammoth field of influence which satisfied all idealist conceptions, spiritual or philosophical, and a simple machine which no performance of material effects exceeded or contradicted. He moved away from abstraction, either physical or spiritual. Words such as *time, space, place,* and *motion* were to be understood only in mathematical terms as actual measured relationships and quantities. These were constants, with their own nature, not requiring additional explanation. Absolute space occurred in a Euclidean geometry, and absolute time flowed equably from the past through the present to the future. Bodies occupied actual place, and absolute motion translated them from one place to another.

What follows are laws of motion: Every body, terrestrial or celestial, continues in a state of rest, or of uniform motion in a straight line, unless it is compelled to change that state by forces coming to bear upon it; if that happens, the change will be precisely proportional to the force and in the line of direction in which that force is itself operating; thus, two bodies always act mutually upon each other in such a way that every action has an equal and opposite reaction. Since Newton was talking about the masses of bodies, it was important to distinguish between weight and mass. Mass was a quantity of matter deriving from density and bulk taken together. Motion, as a numerical entity, required mass (an amount of matter) and velocity, multiplied by each other. Mass multiplied by accelerative force originated motion in a specific course and at a specific speed. Newton foresaw what was almost impossible to believe: that without the mass of the Earth, people would float away.

Another effect of Newton's laws was to dispel any lingering notion that geometry was somehow different from mathematics, with a special archetypal claim on nature. Kepler believed in the perfect solids; Newton did not. This is the fundamental difference between them, minor in its subtlety at the time and major in its implications for future times. Take away the special case of geometry, and mathematics replaces spiritual essence as the key to the universe. One need no longer look for spirit, only for number. In his preface to *Mathematical Principles of Natural Philosophy* (1687), Newton wrote:

> Therefore geometry is founded in mechanical practice, and is nothing but that part of universal mechanics which accurately proposes and demonstrates the art of measuring. . . . Rational mechanics will be the science of motions resulting from any forces whatsoever, and of the forces required to produce any motions, accurately proposed and demonstrated.[5]

If Newton could not have expressed gravity in mathematical terms and applied it to the actual mechanics of astronomical and terrestrial objects, it would have been dismissed as another mystical stopgap. Perhaps his interpretation of his own proposal was metaphysical, but those who followed him cast out the theological parts even as he had dismissed the geometric mysticism of Kepler and Kepler had discarded the circles of Copernicus. Newton's gravity became the foundation of a new system, and his sources were forgotten, his intention overlooked. The astronomers and physicists who followed him built a tidal and mechanical universe from the laws he gave them.

It took time, but Western science slowly began to see the web into which the secularization of Newton's theories had woven them, and the suspicion began to dawn that they would not get out of it for a long time; they might never get out of it. Before Newton, the night sky was a divine parchment, a demonic sigil, a display of cosmic philosophy. After Newton, it became a laboratory in elementary physics, a demonstration of simple large-scale interactions of gravitational fields, and a remnant of a primitive original system of matter. The night sky shows the universe as it is eternally under multiple influences, and, in a certain sense, as it *was* before the formation of galaxies and stars. The black heavens embracing the whirling compacted blobs of matter bare the fundamental symmetries of nature. In a hot universe, we have only the particles and their original structure. In a cold universe, as here on this planet, a jungle of camouflage grows up around this original atomic and pre-atomic scenery. Not only does it grow up around it; it incorporates it in itself and hides it in a diversity which is home to us but entirely foreign to the original atoms. This is where we enter, and it is the only way we could enter—latecomers to the mystery. At least this is how science chooses to explain us, its one inexplicable embarrassment. Beginning with Newton, we work our way out of the jungle into a clear sight of nature. It is inhospitable, but its saving grace is a gargantuan lucidity. We face the curious problem that, as we work toward protean nature, we work against our own nature.

The night sky not only demonstrates mathematical laws to the latter-day astronomers; it *is* those mathematical laws, written simply in things that are larger than we are and much bolder and less duplicit. Stephen Weinberg sums this up very succinctly in *The First Three Minutes* when he says: "That which we do now by mathematics was done in the very early universe by heat—physical phenomena directly exhibited the essential simplicity of nature. But no one was there to see it."[6]

We might also consider Bertrand Russell's warning: "Physics is mathematical not because we know so much about the physical world, but because we know so little: it is only its mathematical properties that we can discover."[7]

Newton left behind a thornier riddle than we have generally recognized, and one that expresses our own crisis of meaning and identity as accurately as the one which Newton addressed did for his own time. We have looked at Newton's night sky for three hundred years, following the rationality of a universal mechanics and measuring each new thing as we have uncovered it. And we have continued to find a machine which generates an abstraction which generates a machinery. Centuries after Newton reconciled Bacon and Descartes, the problem of mind and matter is a contention again. It was a Christian riddle; now it is a zen riddle.

It is incredible to realize that the only thing that stands between our mathematics and the night sky is ourselves. Otherwise, numbers and creation would embrace each other and the universe would be sealed. We are the only disturbance.

Newton did not foresee this. "Why there is one body in our system qualified to give light and heat to all the rest, I know no reason," he wrote to Richard Bentley, a theologian who sought to square gravitation with Christianity, "but because the author of the system thought it convenient."[8] This was not Church politics; Newton believed it. He made no attempt to construct a purely "Newtonian" universe. He wrote Bentley on another occasion:

> It is inconceivable that inanimate brute matter should, without the meditation of something else, which is not material, operate upon, and affect other matter without mutual contact. . . . That gravity should be innate, inherent and essential to matter, so that one body may act upon another at a distance through a *vacuum*, without the mediation of anything else, by and through which their action and force may be conveyed from one to another, is to me so great an absurdity, that I believe no man . . . can ever fall into it.[9]

For the next three hundred years, science has defined gravity exactly as innate, inherent, and essential, or, to the degree that it has not done that, it has redefined gravity as curvature of space and time according to Einstein's theory of relativity and has

passed the onus of agency ("material or immaterial," wrote Newton in the same letter[10]) on to an equally innate, inherent, and
essential characteristic of things. The face of night was shattered,
and when it settled again—the enigmatic smile of glittering
motes and dusky luminescent trails—it showed a new aspect of
its sphynx.

Newton did not do this to us, or did he? The current cosmos
is not his, even by extension, but his seeing was so clear, for all
of us, that it made it inevitable. This was clear in the century
following Newton's: William Blake's Newton is an enemy, an
enslaver of mankind and its vision. The telescope has replaced
the imagination as the instrument for seeing into nature and
spirit, and the simple coefficient it puts up against the night sky
becomes our only relationship to the wondrous forces there. In
fact, our very organs have been made dumb and sealed within
us. No longer do we see; instead we have an optic nerve regis-
tering disturbances. The grand connection eludes us.

In *Jerusalem,* Blake sets "Bacon & Newton, sheath'd in dismal
steel," terrors binding mankind. The "Loom of Locke" is
"Wash'd by the Water-wheels of Newton: black the cloth / In
heavy wreathes fold over every Nation: cruel Works / Of many
Wheels I view, wheel without wheel, with cogs tyrannic / Moving by compulsion each other, not as those in Eden, which, /
Wheel within Wheel, in freedom revolve in harmony & peace."[11]

But Blake, as those who follow him, can no longer attack
science from a pure theosophical position. Science has become
part of thought and part of seeing. All men and women are its
advocates, even those who deny it. The Rosicrucian enlightenment of the seventeenth century tried to invent a mathematical
nonscholastic magic. The critics of science today live under the
aegis of science and use it one way or another in their opposition.
There are no more saints. Blake's "strong wing'd Eagles" in "The
Four Zoas" are clearly post-Newtonian, and, in so being, they
also radiate Kepler and Descartes:

> . . . thro' darkness deep
> They bear the woven draperies; on golden hooks they
>   hang abroad

The universal curtains & spread out from Sun to Sun
The vehicles of light; they separate the furious particles
Into mild currents as the water mingles with the wine.[12]

In Percy Bysshe Shelley, too, are spirit and science merged:
the Earth is a planet, but it is also a zone of creation; light is
divine, but it is also tinted anew from Newton's experiments
with a prism; colors are qualities of the light itself, not objects.
Shelley writes of the "intense atom" of life, which "glows / A
moment, then is quenched. . . ." He tells us:

> The sun comes forth, and many reptiles spawn;
> He sets, and each ephemeral insect then
> Is gathered into death without a dawn,
> And the immortal stars awake again.
> ....
> Life, like a dome of many-coloured glass,
> Stains the white radiance of Eternity. . . .[13]

This is the real heritage of Newton, not the mechanical universe. It is a great irony that the Einsteinian universe is set as
the model of cosmic creativity and surprise against the universe
of Newton. It was Einstein who doubted God most deeply and
whom God failed, first in seeming to play dice with particles,
and again at Hiroshima. It was Newton who believed in the
spirit and who was the truer mystic.

Newton's laws were developed specifically in the context of
the Solar System and the Earth and were directly applied to the
motions of planets and moons about each other and the Sun and
to the interactive aspects of terrestrial substances. When Halley's comet arrived as predicted in the mid-eighteenth century,
showing a periodicity of 76 years, it was considered a confirmation of Newtonian physics and, in particular, of the significance of the Sun in determining the positions of all the orbs in
its immediate field. Halley's comet showed how big this field
might be.

Newton's method of formulation, a theory of fluxions
whereby changes of quantities were taken as infinitely small

variations, was rough and required constant refinement when applied to natural phenomena. Various astronomers worked with the path of the Moon, and others discovered, through the mutual influences of Jupiter and Saturn, that planetary orbits were incredibly complex and displaced from a pure solar-directed ellipse.

In his 1848 essay "Eureka," Edgar Allan Poe summarized Newton's relationship to celestial mechanics:

> He was forced to content himself with showing how thoroughly the motions of an imaginary Universe, composed of attracting and attracted atoms obedient to the law he announced, coincide with those of the actually existing Universe so far as it comes under our observation.[14]

Pierre Simon Laplace, the mid-eighteenth-century French astronomer, was the first post-Newtonian to complete a system of the heavens as a great machine. He pointed out that the incredible difficulties in squaring phenomena with Newtonian theory actually ended up proving it.

Laplace's machine operated eternally under immutable Newtonian laws. We continue to honor it. Though our intuition seems to tell us that the sky is something more than a housing of infinite fires held in place in a gravitational field, our knowledge knows of no other universe.

Laplace published his work in 1799 in five volumes entitled *Mécanique Céleste*. He imagined the Sun as having had a gaseous outer atmosphere of greater circumference than the whole Solar System. As this burning sheath rotated, it contracted, with an increase in the speed of rotation leading to the casting off of material. This was the birth of the planets: soot from the Sun. Further rotation contracted them into solid matter; and as the solid matter condensed, bits of it were thrown out and formed the moons of the planets. The Solar System was a clock—eternal, unvarying.[15]

But how had this clock been set in motion? Laplace (and later, Immanuel Kant) reasoned backward, as Newton had not. Since all the planetary orbits are in roughly the same plane, then this must once have been a flat, rotating disc of material, with the tidal force of gravitation creating the planets in their orbits out of coalescing matter. In "Eureka," Poe extended Laplace's theory outward to Neptune, the most recent planet discovered at that time, and suggested that the outer portions of the disc were originally broken into fragments, and that this explained the oddities of the new planet, its moon, and its phantom ring.

The self-regulating machine was so shocking that Napoleon Bonaparte said: "Monsieur Laplace, they tell me you have written this large book on the system of the Universe and have never even mentioned its Creator."

"Sire," Laplace replied, "I had no need for any such hypothesis."[16]

9

The History of Western Astronomy: IV: The Stars

WHILE NEWTON was developing a new "astrophysics," other astronomers were exploring the Solar System and the Milky Way. As lenses improved, Europe plunged through the dome of fixed stars into a sea of suns whose limits were not apparent. Persian and Greek deities crumbled and fell. The map of the West had been obliterated.

John Flamsteed, an English contemporary of Newton, marked the positions of three thousand stars. Another Englishman, Edmund Halley, catalogued hundreds of southern stars from an observatory in St. Helena. He checked discrepancies in position from the days of Ptolemy, and this revealed that the stellar sphere was not fixed and stable; the stars had moved.

Halley is best known for his discovery that comets have elliptical orbits like planets; and the return of the 1682 comet in 1758, thirteen years after his death as he had predicted, was perhaps the first new application of astromancy since the Babylonians, and was impressive enough to give that comet his name thereafter.

Meanwhile, on the European continent, the Sun King, Louis XIV, had assembled the great scientists of many nations at the French Academy of Science. A Dutch astronomer, Christian Huygens, became the new Galileo. He used Galileo's mathematics of the pendulum to control the rhythm of a gear and make an accurate clock and a small jewel-box planetarium of the Solar System. As an exploratory astronomer, he discovered that Jupiter had a bulge at its equator, Mars had polar caps that changed size, and Saturn's protuberance was actually a ring. He also discovered the first moon of Saturn.

Like Newton, he studied the nature of light, and he came to an opposite but complementary conclusion. Newton had decided that light was made of corpuscles passing through empty space. Huygens, accepting Descartes' ether as the substance of the void, decided that light "does not move; it merely strives toward movement" like a wave.[1] No material changed place, but motion was propagated through the ether as the waves through the sea. Newton's corpuscles better fit the mechanical universe of the time, but Huygens's vibrations and oscillations awaited the rays and radioactivity of a future science.

The Italian astronomer Giovanni Cassini, working outdoors with 150-foot air telescopes and lenses suspended from towers, participated with Huygens in deriving a rotation period for Mars close to that of the Earth. Huygens theorized that bulging Jupiter must be soft material rotating very fast. Cassini confirmed a Jovian day of ten hours. He also found a division between the rings of Saturn, discovered four more Saturnian moons, and mapped the hemispheres of Jupiter.

Cassini, like William Herschel in the following century, attempted to name new bodies after enlightened monarchs rather than mythological beings in order to distinguish the age in which these bodies were discovered from the superstitious aeon in which the planets and constellations were named. Mythological names, however, always replaced historical ones, especially within the Solar System. Simon Marius's method of naming the Galilean satellites of Jupiter after the lovers of the god was followed in the naming of Saturn's moons after beings of the Saturnian age. In this one way, the astral sky triumphed, for in astrological and magical work, names carry the archetypal meanings and influences of the worlds.

Meanwhile, the true distances in the universe were becoming evident to these astronomers. Most scientists then thought that light was timeless and instantaneous everywhere. Galileo himself was uncertain, so he devised an experiment with a lantern-bearing assistant. The results were inconclusive, and Galileo decided that, in any case, the speed of light was too great to measure with his apparatus. Olaus Roemer, a Danish astronomer working at the French Academy, arranged a celestial trap in which light would divulge its speed or instantaneousness. After measuring the period of revolution of the satellite Io around Jupiter at 42 hours, 27 minutes, and 33 seconds, Roemer persistently timed the reappearance of Io from Jovian eclipse between August and November 1676. If light had a finite speed, the reappearance of the moon might be retarded as the Earth moved away from Jupiter. A time difference of seconds would have proven the point, but light was even slower than that: there were a full ten minutes of lag at Jovian apogee, decreasing as the Earth reapproached Jupiter over the next six months. Now Roemer had a figure for the distance that light travels in a second: 186,000 miles. He derived it from the rate of retardation of Io's reappearance caused primarily by the Earth's movement in its orbit.[2] It was to become the unit by which all cosmic distances were measured. Huygens later figured that it would take a bullet from a cannon twenty-five years to reach the Sun. Looking at the Sun through a tiny hole in a plate, he concluded that it was 27,664 times as bright as Sirius by the laws of dioptrics. If Sirius were the same brightness as the Sun in its own vicinity, then it would take the same bullet almost 700,000 years to get there.

"What a wonderful and amazing scheme have we here of the magnificent vastness of the universe!" he wrote in *Cosmotheoros,* translated into English as *The Celestial Worlds Discovered or Conjectures Concerning the Inhabitants, Plants and Products of the Worlds in the Planets.* "So many suns, so many earths, and every one of them stocked with so many herbs, trees and animals, and adorned with so many seas and mountains!"[3] And this from a man who died before the end of the seventeenth century.

It was around the middle of the eighteenth century that astronomers began to explore the meaning of the Milky Way. The discovery of its nature is usually credited to Thomas Wright, who wondered why this belt was denser than the rest of the sky. Was it because we were looking along a single plane in which more stars were visible? Fantastic as it seemed, perhaps we were looking into the heart of a system of which we were also part. Furthermore, the system might be lens-shaped, so that we would see fewer stars out toward the rim, and almost through it like clear glass where there are no stars.

> Imagine [he wrote] how infinitely greater the number of stars would be in those remote parts, arising thus from their continual crowding behind one another, as all other objects do towards the horizon point of their perspective, which ends but with infinity: thus, all their rays at last so near uniting, must meeting in the eye appear, as almost in contact, and from a perfect zone of light; this I take to be the real case, and the true nature of our *Milky Way,* and all irregularity we observe in it at the Earth, I judge to be entirely owing to our Sun's position in this great firmament. . . .[4]

Wright was also a man after the heart of Kepler and Newton:

> We cannot long observe the beauteous parts of the visible creation, not only of this world on which we live, but also the myriads of bright bodies round us, with any attention, without being convinced, that a power supreme, and of a nature unknown to us, presides in, and governs it.[5]

Immanuel Kant, a contemporary of Wright, intuited that the stellar galaxy was the clue to cosmic evolution. Nature repeated fundamental shapes. If there was one nebula, then there must be more. Perhaps there had been a primal nebula at the beginning of the universe, a cloud containing molecules in random movement amassing by attraction. The stars fused within this cloud, compacting gravitationally so that space developed between them. Kant proposed this theory in his *Universal Natural History and Theory of the Heavens,* and, in a sense, he "waited" 175 years until 1925 to have it confirmed by Edwin Hubble.

Kant complimented Wright:

> He regarded the fixed stars not as a mere swarm scattered without order and without design, but found a systematic constitution in the whole universe and a universal relation of these stars to the ground-plan of the regions of space which they occupy.

. . . The eye which is situated in this plane when it looks
out to the field of stars, will perceive on the spherical concavity of the firmament the densest accumulation of stars
in the direction of . . . a plane under the form of a zone
illuminated by varied light.[6]

Once this system is established, we see that there must
be more Solar Systems, more Milky Ways, all from the
same primal nebula. . . . The worlds and systems acknowledge the same kind of origin . . . ; attraction is unlimited
and universal . . . ; in the presence of the infinite, the great
and small are small alike. . . .[7]

Millions of years may have passed before nature reached this
present perfection; millions more may pass before it extends
itself into new spheres and evolves new forms. "This infinity in
the future succession of time," wrote Kant, "by which eternity
is unexhausted, will entirely animate the whole range of space
to which God is present. . . ."[8]

Kant's faith in divine law was unshakable, but he did admit,
as more have admitted after him, that "there is here no end but
an abyss of real immensity, in the presence of which all the
capability of human conception sinks exhausted, although it is
supported by the aid of the science of number."[9]

And already Pierre Simon Laplace was on hand, creating stability without God.

The most famous astronomer of the late eighteenth and early
nineteenth centuries was Frederick William Herschel. He began
his adult life as a music teacher in Germany, and ultimately
settled in England. After constructing the best telescopes of his
time, he set to making a catalogue of celestial objects. Naturally,
he noted thousands of stars, but he also discovered the multiple
stars—that many sparkles contained two, three, or more discrete
sources. He estimated the periods of revolution of double stars
and put into the public imagination the idea of worlds with two
sunrises, twin shadows, and variations of night and day within
night and day. He realized that double stars were not merely
twins because they lay in the same line of sight. They orbited
about one another and were physically part of the same system.

So Newton's law of gravitation stretched deep into the sidereal realm. Not only could planets stand in mutual attraction to planets, and planets to suns, but suns could be impressed by other suns and must be in motion. Herschel discovered the movement of the Sun itself trailing the Solar System behind it toward an area of the sky marked by Lambda of the constellation Hercules. His inability to calculate solar movement accurately was the result of an incorrect hypothesis; he assumed that a star's apparent brightness was determined only by its distance.

Herschel resolved the Milky Way from whitish haze into small stars which he counted; and from just those that were visible, he dead-reckoned its shape as a grindstone with a diameter of six thousand light-years. That the Milky Way, the *via lactea* as he called it by the Latin, was a system of stars to which the Sun itself belonged became clear to Herschel as he went up and down its branches and swept across and through it, mapping its major and minor arms. He also became aware that this "stupendous sidereal system we inhabit"[10] with its millions of stars is itself detached from other nebulous clouds of stars. He saw that we inhabited a planet of a star in a group of stars in groups of groups of stars.

He discovered the first dark nebula, calling to his sister Caroline to come and see the hole in the Milk. He named it "The Coalsack." He also found other nebulous clouds that did not seem to be made of stars. "What a field of novelty is here opened to our conceptions!" he wrote. "A shining fluid . . . of a nature totally unknown to us . . . of a brightness sufficient to reach us from the remote regions of a star of the 8th, 9th, 10th, 11th, or 12th magnitude, and of an extent so considerable as to take up 3, 4, 5, or 6 minutes in diameter! Can we compare it to the coruscations of the electrical fluid in the aurora borealis? Or to the more magnificent cone of zodiacal light as we see it in spring or autumn?"[11]

Perhaps, thought Herschel, he was staring into the primitive yolk out of which stars themselves were born.

Herschel also studied nearby worlds. He explored the belts of Saturn, the polar caps of Mars, and he found satellites around Saturn. Most notably, though, in 1781 he discovered the Geor-

gium Sidus, which we now know as Uranus. "On Tuesday the
13th of March between 10 and 11 in the evening, when I was
examining the small stars in the neighborhood of H Geminorum, I perceived one that appeared visibly larger than the rest;
being struck with its uncommon magnitude, I compared it to
H Geminorum and the small star in the quartile between Auriga
and Gemini, and, finding it so much larger than either of them,
suspected it to be a comet."[12]

Later study showed no tail and a circular orbit. So this was a
planet. He named it Georgium Sidus because it was "a star which
(with respect to us) first began to shine under his [George III's]
auspicious reign. . . ."[13]

Sir Joseph Banks, in presenting Herschel with the Copley
Medal of the Royal Society later that year, extolled: "Who can
say but what your new star, which exceeds Saturn in its distance
from the sun, may exceed him as much in magnificence of attendance? Who can say what new rings, new satellites, or what
other nameless and numberless phenomena remain behind,
waiting to reward future industry?"[14]

In 1787, Herschel discovered two moons around Uranus,
which were subsequently named Oberon and Titania after fairy
and magical beings from Shakespeare. Of Oberon, Herschel
wrote: "I saw this satellite faithfully attend its primary planet,
and at the same time keep on, in its own course, by describing
a considerable arch of its proper orbit."[15] He made remarkably
close estimates of the moons' periods of revolution, and he
found that their orbital motion around Uranus was retrograde,
counter that of the Earth, the other planets, and the other moons
known at the time. This was a tremendous blow to the Laplacian
hypothesis which required a uni-rotational ring.

Herschel also participated in the discovery of the asteroids
during the eighteenth century, and, in fact, he gave them that
name. He was not notably involved in meteor work, but in 1798,
the year after the discovery of the retrograde moons, two German students compared their observation of the same meteor
from sites far apart and concluded that meteors were not "meteorological" at all, but must originate far out in space, beyond
even the Moon's orbit.

———

Herschel was an astronomer, not a theoretician. He adored the night sky, in which he said he saw "myriads of worlds springing up like grass in the night."[16]

Interestingly, he tried always to schedule his necessary visits to the royal court on Moon-lit nights. Royal support required that he attend, but he had only one lifetime of dark nights in which to see all the stars. Since he constructed telescopes for a living, he was often forced to work months upon months at a time in the daylight hours grinding reflectors for himself and others. The light-gathering mirrors in telescopes at that time were made not of aluminum-coated glass but of speculum metal. The glass eyepieces, in which the magnification occurred, were confined to a certain size by technology, but more light could be gathered by bigger reflectors. These required constant re-polishing to maintain their sheen. After painstakingly constructing a mirror of four feet, Herschel focused it on Saturn the first night and instantly discovered two unknown moons.

When he had to be away, he had his sister work with the telescope "every starry night on wet or hoarfrost-covered grass, without a human being within call."[17] She discovered eight comets.

His son, John Herschel, had a twenty-foot reflector built near Capetown, South Africa, and from there he catalogued over 2,100 double stars and almost 1,700 nebulae. By counting stars in different fields of view and then putting the fields together, he estimated that there were 70,000 stars in his telescopic sky. Behind the visible night, another sky was expanding exponentially. This would happen again when archaeologists uncovered semihuman bones in deep strata of that other ancient coffin, the Earth. There was another world of human creatures before this one, and there were other stars beyond the night. The universe was getting older and older, and man himself was becoming more ancient and more alien.

Stars were now everywhere unfixed, in various densities, double and triple, with no end in sight. Even the numerological basis for the Solar System was undone by a new planet. Herschel was born into a sky that would have been impossible for Kepler or Newton and, without realizing it, he made it impossible for anyone born after him to see that same sky. God was vanishing; there was no reason why, among millions of stars, He should not begin to seem further rather than closer, and less rather than more engaged in the Creation.

An 1803 astronomy book gives a contemporary picture of the new universe:

> The greatest number of stars that are visible to the naked eye, are to be seen on a winter's night, when the air is clear, and no moon appears. But even then a good eye can scarce distinguish more than one thousand at a time in the visible hemisphere: for, though on such a night they appear to be almost innumerable, this appearance is a deception, that arises from our viewing them in a transient and confused manner; whereas, if we view them distinctly, and only consider a small portion of the heavens at a time, and, after some attention to the situation of the remarkable stars contained in that portion, begin to count, we shall be surprised at the smallness of their number and the ease with which they may be enumerated.
>
> The number of the ancient constellations was 48; in these were included 1,022 stars. Many constellations have been added by modern astronomers; so that the catalogue of *Flamsteed* and *De La Caille,* when added together, are found to contain near five thousand stars. The names of the constellations, their situation in the heavens, with other particulars, are best learned by studying the artificial representation of the heavens, a modern celestial globe.
>
> The Galaxy or milky way must not be neglected; it is one of the most remarkable appearances in the heavens; it is a broad circle of a whitish hue, in some places it is double, but for the most part consists of a single path surrounding the whole celestial concave. The great *Galileo* discovered by the telescope, that the portion of the heavens which this circle passes through was every where filled with an infinite multitude of exceeding small stars, too small to be discovered by the naked eye, but by the combination of their light, diffusing a shining whiteness through the heavens. Mr. *Brydone* says, that when he was at the top of Mount Aetna, the milky way had the most beautiful effect, appearing like a pure flame that shot across the heavens. . . .

The number of the stars almost infinitely exceeds what we have yet been speaking of. An ordinary telescope will discover, in several parts of the heavens, ten times as many stars as are visible to the naked eye. *Hooke* in his Micrographia says, that with a telescope of twelve feet he discovered seventy-eight stars among the Pleiades, and with a more perfect telescope, many more. *Galileo* reckoned eighty in the space between the belt and the sword of Orion, and above five hundred more in another part of the same constellation. Antonia Maria de Rheita counted in the same constellation above ten thousand stars. Future improvements in the telescopes may enable us to discover numberless stars, that are now invisible; and many more may be which are too remote to be seen through telescopes, even when they have received their ultimate improvement. . . .

In speaking here of [Dr. Herschel's] discoveries, I shall use the words of M. De la Lande. "In passing rapidly over the heavens with his new telescope, the universe increased under his eye; 44,000 stars, seen in the space of a few degrees, seemed to indicate that there were seventy-five millions in the heavens." He has also shewn that many stars, which to the eye or through ordinary glasses appear single, do in fact consist of two or more stars. The Galaxy or milky way owes its light entirely to the multitude of small stars, placed so close as not to be discoverable even by an ordinary telescope. The nebulae, or small whitish specks, discerned by means of telescopes, owe their origin to the same cause. . . . Who can say, how far the universe extends, or where are the limits of it? where the Creator stayed "his rapid wheels"; or where he "fixed the golden compasses"?[18]

With the discovery of a seventh planet, rings, moons, and the nature of meteors, and then with Laplace's perturbation theory of the origin of the Solar System, the eighteenth century had come to a new understanding of the moving hands of the cosmic clock. One "local" problem was the gap between Mars and Jupiter. In 1722, Johann Titius had developed a mathematical progression for the distances of the planets from the Sun. That same year, Johann Bode, in his *Introduction to the Study of the*

Starry Sky, restated the progression with the specific recommendation that there was another planet at 2.8 times the Earth's distance from the Sun (or seven times Mercury's distance and four times Venus's distance). When Uranus fit the progression so closely, the search for the "missing" planet was intensified, but it was not until New Year's Day, 1801, that Giuseppi Piazzi, an Italian astronomer, found an 8th-magnitude star in Taurus that changed position over the next two nights. On January 14, it ceased its retrograde motion and began moving forward. Assuming it to be a planet, he named it Ceres. Then he lost it when Taurus passed into sunlight, and he became sick and was unable to continue the tracking. It was not found again until December, when Karl Friedrich Gauss, using an orbit computed from only three figures, relocated it. Thereafter, astronomers flocked to see this second new planet. Ceres fit Bode's progression almost perfectly, but it was so tiny that it showed no planetary disc. While astronomers were puzzling over this, H. Wilhelm Olbers, in April of 1802, found a second object in a proximate orbit, and this was named Pallas. Juno was found in 1804, and Vesta in 1807. By 1852, there were twenty known planetoids; and by 1870, there were 110. Once their existence was known, they were found all the way down to the twelfth magnitude, including some that passed out beyond Saturn and others that passed within the orbit of Venus. Hermes, Eros, and Icarus have all approached the Earth itself in recent times.

At the same time, comets were viewed more closely and their nature analyzed. Olbers noted: "Only in the vicinity of the Sun do they blaze up. They catch fire like a sulphur match, and . . . a bluish flame leaps forth."[19] Later in the century, astronomers discovered that the gentle pressure of light from the Sun is sufficient to create the comets' tails, dispersing their gases out behind them across millions of miles.

In 1842, during a solar eclipse, the Sun's corona, with its prominences leaping into space, was observed. "From the black rim of the Moon," wrote an observer, "there suddenly shot forth three gigantic, purple-red tongues of flame. They paused motionless, like jagged mountain peaks in an alpine sunset. Each was different from the others, but all were many times larger than the white circlet of rays. It was as if the Sun, behind the Moon, were flaring up in monstrous volcanic explosions."[20]

One can only guess at the incredible effect such events had in the ancient and tribal world. Oxen, asses, and cows stood still; even ants stopped moving. Flowers closed.

In this same period, curiosity about the inhabitants of these other worlds grew in parallel with the strange new peoples being found in the aboriginal worlds of the Americas, Australia, the South Pacific, and Africa. How did the rings look to the Saturnians? How did the many moons light the Jovian night? Herschel even believed that the Sun was inhabited and that it need not be as uniformly hot as some had proposed.

In 1846, John Adams, the British astronomer, and Urbain Leverrier of France simultaneously predicted the discovery of an eighth planet, using Newton's laws and computing its positions by the hypothesized perturbations that an unknown planet had caused in the positions of Uranus. Neptune was actually first observed, at least with awareness of what it was, by Johann Galle, a German astronomer using Leverrier's predicted position of September 23, 1846. After finding an 8th-magnitude star that was not in a new star chart he was using, Galle continued to observe it and found that it was moving in a retrograde direction in close proximity to Leverrier's estimates of size and speed as well as location. He then wrote to Leverrier that "the planet whose position you have pointed out *actually exists.*"[21] Leverrier's hypothetical planet was also a real planet. On September 10 of that year, Sir John Herschel looked through his telescope at this new world and said: "We see it as Columbus saw America from the shores of Spain. Its movements have been felt trembling along the far-reaching line of our analysis with a certainty hardly inferior to ocular demonstration."[22]

Later that same year, William Lassel, using a new mirror telescope, discovered Triton, the large moon of Neptune. Triton is so big (3,700 miles in diameter) that it is brighter from Earth than any of Uranus's moons. Lassel also found Ariel and Umbriel circling Uranus in 1851.

It is interesting to note that, even though a planet is discovered at a certain historical period, it is often known before that as a star. The ancients saw Uranus, but it was too faint and slow-moving to excite interest in its planetary nature. The American astronomer Sears Walker searched Lalande's eighteenth-century catalogue for unknown stars on the nights and in the positions where Neptune would have been visible, and he used these likely sightings in constructing his improved elliptical orbit in 1847. When Neptune was found to be way off its expected position from Bode's progression (30.05 times the distance of the Earth from the Sun instead of 38.4), the "law" lost any credence. It actually belonged more to Kepler's universe of geometric solids and Pythagorean harmonies, and its main historical role had been in encouraging the search for a missing planet.

The prediction of Neptune by two independently searching astronomers in the same year was not without controversy. Leverrier was the more famous and also the more egotistical of the two, and Adams's prior discovery went unreported for many months because the British Astronomer Royal, George Airy, did not believe in the existence of trans-Uranian planets and did not take his results seriously. When Adams's prediction was announced later, Leverrier and his French supporters vigorously fought against sharing the historical credit. In fact, Leverrier wanted the new planet given his own name and self-servingly suggested the name Herschel for Uranus.

This relatively insignificant competition masks another far more interesting controversy that has been forgotten but not resolved. The credit for discovering a planet generally goes to the person whose formulas predicted its position, often instead of the person who actually finds it. Galle found Leverrier's planet for him. But Galle's "star" also corresponded to Adams's prediction for the same night, even though, remarkably enough, Adams and Leverrier had different orbits for their planets, neither of which corresponded even remotely to Neptune's actual orbit, nor to each other, except at the periods when they all intersected. That the three ellipses should have come so close to perfect intersection (the hypothetical ones of Adams and Leverrier and the real one of Neptune the planet) on the night that Galle chose to look is a stroke of luck almost too fantastic to believe.

Both sets of calculations were based on Bode's inaccurate estimates of Neptune's size and distance from the Sun. They were also based on the extremely subtle calculations of not only Uranus's perturbations of the unknown body but also that body's perturbations of Uranus, and on an accurate Newtonian orbit for Uranus, with all of the other gravitational influences on it in the Solar System. This is a "solution" difficult to arrive at for many of the outer planets today, and it was impossible then. In fact, the hypothetical planet that lies between Mercury and the Sun, Vulcan, was "observed" many times throughout the nineteenth century because so many astronomers were looking for a body to resolve the anomalies in the motion of the perihelion of Mercury.

Given these difficulties, the officials of the time chose to credit Leverrier with the discovery of Neptune because it was found through using his formula, *even though* his hypothetical planet and Neptune crossed at only a few points. Having done this, the officials were compelled later to give Adams equal credit, since his planet crossed both Leverrier's and Neptune at the discovery point. The dilemma becomes far more provocative later, after it is clear that neither the existence of Neptune nor the later discovery of Pluto resolve the anomalies in Uranus's orbit. The Neptune situation is summarized well by the historian William Graves Hoyt, quoting from the American astronomer Henry Norris Russell: "Leverrier and Adams . . . had assumed too great a distance for their unknown planet from Bode's law, but their calculations also 'made the orbit considerably eccentric (although it is really very nearly circular),' " and this "spurious eccentricity brought the predicted orbit toward the sun in the region where the planet actually lay at the time, and went far to undo the error of the two original assumptions."[23] Apparently Neptune was ready to be found.

Toward the latter part of the nineteenth century, telescopic equipment improved, and, with the invention of the photographic silver bromide plate, modern astronomy of the heavens began as the painstaking recording of all regions of the heavens on replica film. The plates were so sensitive that they could pick up objects that the human eye would never see, even through a lens. Already the cameo of William Herschel with his sister Caroline standing in the night with hoarfrost on their telescope was quaint.

Furthermore, the world inside, or below, opened out as starrily as the night through the microscope. Both lifeless chemicals and fertile pond water showed stars and animacules as deeply as resolving power would go. No more than the telescope showed the face of God, or a Golden Compass in the Void, did the microscope show the vital force that guided all substance or the crystal sparks of primordial ether. It was the same instrument, only it enlarged things in a different plane. Atom and star were eventually to prove that. And man found himself in a strange new hierarchy with suns and nebulae above him to infinity and animals inside animals inside animals, and atoms inside everything, including himself. A lens made the night sky also the atom, and the atom filled the night sky with light.

As the poet Theodore Enslin taught: When we crack open the walnut, we find, not the kernel, but simply another husk. In order to find the kernel, we must change the nature of our perception and move into other dimensions.[24]

There was also another issue that troubled nineteenth-century astronomers. It was first known to be stated by Halley in 1720, but was later credited to Wilhelm Olbers, who put it forward as a paradox in 1823. As Halley realized it, the universe must not be infinite, for, if it were, the collective light of all the stars to infinity would fill the night sky to the brightness of the disc of the Sun. Galileo had concluded that light exhausted its "instaneity" over shorter distances, but this was no longer an acceptable solution. Olbers solved the problem for himself by attributing the blackness of the sky to the existence of dust and particles in space which would need only to dampen a small fraction of the eternal starlight to create the dark night. Even a substance much more transparent than water would absorb enough light over the great distances of space to eliminate sight of the furthest stars. To this degree, the nineteenth century still believed that there was sand to put its head into, and that the teeth of eternity must be blunted somewhere beyond the villages of Earth.

10

The History of
Western Astronomy:
v: The Elements

Aᴛ ᴛʜᴇ sᴀᴍᴇ ᴛɪᴍᴇ that the heavens were being explored by Herschel, Olbers, and Leverrier, other scientists were investigating the microcosm. A contemporary of Isaac Newton, the Dutch naturalist Anton van Leeuwenhoek, found that the minute world contained an unending chain of matter and structure: living beings and inorganic structures of fantastic intricacy to the very depths of sight. Joseph Addison wrote:

> Every part of Matter is peopled; every green Leaf swarms with Inhabitants. There is scarce a single Humour in the Body of a Man, or of any other Animal, in which our Glasses do not discover Myriads of living Creatures. The Surface of Animals is also covered with other Animals, which are in the same manner the Basis of other Animals that live upon it; nay, we find in the most solid Bodies, as in Marble itself, innumerable Cells and Cavities that are crouded with such imperceptible inhabitants, as are too little for the naked eye to discover.[1]

Leeuwenhoek was brought a ganglion from the leg of a woman, in which, it was reported, worms had generated spontaneously. Under the microscope, he recognized insect larvae, maggots from eggs deposited by flies, but the anatomist who had brought the leg was not satisfied. Leeuwenhoek removed the larvae to a piece of beef; they became pupae and hatched into flies; then a pair of these were mated and the female laid 115 eggs like the original ones. This was the natural cycle of generation, self-contained and without intruders.

The most important contributions to astronomy were not in the area of biology but in molecular chemistry, on which atomic physics and astrophysics were later based. In 1805, John Dalton, an English chemist, laid out the atomic theory of the elements. He said that basic substances are made up of atoms, which are indestructible and indivisible and from which all structure is assembled. Chemical combinations occur between the elements, based on the unions of atoms according to simple mathematical properties. The atoms maintain their essential identity through all physical and chemical changes. Atoms of the same elements not only have the same physical and chemical properties but also the same mass. They can join in more than one ratio to form entirely different compounds.

In 1869, the Russian chemist Dmitri Mendeleev discovered that the chemical properties of the elements are periodic functions of their atomic weights, i.e., of the number of protons in their nuclei. When he arranged the then-known elements in a series, he found that there were familial resemblances among elements at regular numerical intervals. For instance, carbon, silicon, and tin lie in a series for which the member between silicon and tin was then apparently missing. This was later found to be germanium. Fluorine, chlorine, bromine, and iodine constitute another family. Then there is a group of lithium, sodium, and potassium; another of nitrogen, phosphorus, arsenic, and antimony; and so on. Nature contains an intra-atomic periodic function which is basic to the order in the world. All elements are based on the simplest one, hydrogen with its single proton, which is also—we were to find out—the fuel of the stars. So, in a sense, there is only one element, one atomic building block, and the rest are formed as simple arithmetic interpolations that bring new and individual properties into being. Mendeleev's periodic table, and the reality that lay behind it, gave a new basis for understanding the history and evolution of matter. Mathematical relationships determined the seemingly limitless display of forms in nature, including plants, animals, and stars. It was hauntingly Pythagorean, as Heisenberg was later to remind us.

There was no reason initially to assume that man would ever be able to "touch" the stars and analyze them chemically, but with the science of spectroscopy, the elemental chart took on a special significance in astronomy. The expectation, left over from the days of an ethereal cosmos, was that entirely unknown elements abounded in the heavens, but this was not to be the case.

Spectroscopy began in the second decade of the nineteenth century when an optician in Munich, Joseph von Fraunhofer, noticed that the spectrum of the Sun, when passed through a slit and then through a glass prism, had hundreds of dark lines over it, each one a shadow of the original slit. With sunlight, these lines were always found at the same wavelength. They were also found there in the spectra of the Moon and the stars. Fantastic as it seemed, these minute scratches described deep and complex things happening to materials far away in time and space: namely, the absorption of light of specific wavelengths as it passed from the burning stars through their cooler atmospheres.

In 1859, another German, Gustav Robert Kirchhoff, discovered that each element, when vaporized, generates a specific spectrum. No two elemental spectra are the same. Not many stars had analyzable spectra at first, but the nebulae did, and they showed such familiar elements as oxygen and nitrogen, which meant that even at the great distances of interstellar space, the same chemistry was sustained on an elemental level. The sodium, magnesium, calcium, chromium, and iron found on the Earth are made of the same kind of atoms as those found in the stars. The first "exotic" element was found in the Sun and was therefore named helium, but it turned out that it existed on Earth too: soon after its discovery in the Sun, it was found in Texas.

Analysis of the stars showed that there was no great variety of material in them. If anything, they were less complex than the Earth, for they were so hot that only simple atoms and electrons survived in them. (A few red stars show compounds of carbon, oxygen, and iron, but nothing more intricate.) With a universal chemistry for a yardstick, astronomers could begin to see sequences of star types, and they even had a basis for uncovering the familial relationship between stars and planets. Charles Darwin, working primarily with animal fossils and living creatures, provided the theory that was to incorporate universal chemistry within a scientific history of the cosmos.

Until spectroscopic analysis, all the different kinds and shapes of nebulae and starry hazes were indistinguishable from each other. Lore from this moment in history persists when some people still call galaxies nebulae. William Huggins was the first to demonstrate, in 1864, that not all of the nebulae are star clusters; some are simply clouds of luminous gas. Today we know that the colored Great Nebula of Orion is a large gaseous cloud surrounding a number of stars. Other nebulae, the Pleiades for instance, are actual star groups.

We might also note that it was not until the 1930s that it was possible to analyze the composition of the planets from spectral light filtered through their atmospheres. To this day, with the exception of the Viking soil analyses on Mars, our spectral analysis is confined to the planetary atmospheres; these reveal great amounts of methane, ammonia, and hydrogen on the larger worlds of our Solar System, making them akin to small suns. Until such experiments, it was possible to imagine these planets as habitable by beings like those on Earth.

Charles Darwin was not an astronomer, but his concept of evolution was planetary, and he was one of the first physical or biological scientists to consider the Earth as a single world-system. By showing that creatures could evolve randomly through natural selection and that extinct forms might link various contemporary species of plants and animals, Darwin laid the basis for future scientists to demonstrate that life itself could develop mechanically from random chemical interactions. The followers of Darwin made this planet a spinning clump of star debris on which a particularly fortunate set of events had occurred—fortunate at least by the standards of those who were its beneficiaries. Gradually, Darwinian thought led to a new philosophy of the cosmos. Not only were stars and planets elementally linked, but life itself was a function of that filiation. There was no need to separate the animate Earth from the inanimate universe and look for a special cause for life. The Periodic Chart gives the elemental basis for making people out of stars (no new matter or energy was needed, the spectroscope proved). Life is a modification of the same hydrogen that burns in the star furnaces. The Law of Natural Selection peoples the planets of other stars with the kinds of beings that would be favored by their environments. Astronomers exist by grace of the same chemical mechanics as suns.

According to Darwin, species of living things come into being in complex interdependent relationships with their environments. Under the constantly changing conditions of nature, new organisms appear. Natural selection does not provide them; it is merely the circumstance whereby certain variations that arise accidentally are preserved. Order and harmony may seem to emerge later, in our own time, but anarchy and anomaly brought these present species and their accoutrements into being. Mutation and accident are the only "laws," and atomic and molecular morphology are the single foundation. Organisms always use ancient structures for new functions because there is no other place from which to obtain lungs or fingers, or gills and teeth, at earlier stages. Interactive properties of molecules lay the basis for food assimilation and genetic replication. Inanimate chemicals become cells, as it were, by imitating them first. The first cells incorporate "crystals," patterns of nonliving structure. Cells become organs and organisms, slight roughnesses become guts and spinal columns, fins become wings and limbs, primitive sensing cells become brain cells. Nothing is invented. Matter simply exhibits its properties in a cumulative chain or a series of cumulative chains; some of the links on some worlds grow and differentiate further, and others are shattered. This random evolutionary chain eventually replaced The Great Chain of Being, which hung down from the astral sphere and whose links were archetypes and could not be crossed by transitions of species.

Darwinian law claims that the ability to assimilate food and to have offspring, the distinguishing features of living organisms,

came about in nonliving chemical solutions from the chance
interaction of compounds. A generation after Darwin, Sigmund
Freud would show that the beliefs and customs of mankind were
a consequence of the same law. By the twentieth century, it was
clear not only that the world did not require a Creator but that
the concept of a Creator could be explained in purely mechanical terms as an aspect of primitive thought. In this way, science
finally dissociated itself from religion by devouring it.

Newton's gravitation lies behind Darwin's natural selection.
The mechanical universe has only one thermodynamic source,
and it cannot make special allowances for life or thought. Freud's
theory of the mind posits a mode of "natural selection" for
thoughts, images, and emotions. Even our ideas and motives
have a "gravitational" basis. Twentieth-century social science incorporates all human activity in this structural and statistical
universe. Stars, planets, plants, animals, human beings, tribes,
and civilizations are elaborations of a single force through a
secondary series of random processes. This insight, taken from
the sky by Newton, now returned to the sky with man's soul as
its prisoner.

The universe has become a sophisticated version of Laplace's
celestial mechanics. Hydrogen gas swirls into spirals, and knots
collect and condense under the force of gravity. Worlds harden
in the knots, and structures and compounds are elaborated by
the atomic nuclei through their molecules. The properties of
carbon, hydrogen, and oxygen lead to complex chains of molecules; proteins and amino acids form. Creatures crawl, blind
and dumb, out of the muck and sea salt. Those life forms that
are best suited to their environment, which is also changing,
survive to give birth to others of their kind, which are themselves altered by the changing universe in their exposure to
terrestrial climate, predators, the cosmic "climate" of mutations,
etc. After a few billion years, at least one very complex life form
uses its intelligence to invent society, language, and, ultimately,
science; or, more accurately, these things are unconsciously and
unintentionally developed, and individual creatures, like us,
awake to find ourselves in their midst. But not even this complex
creature has a spirit; it is simply a clever arrangement of chem-

icals. Mostly it is unconscious, but a minute portion of its being passes into consciousness against extremely strong forces of suppression. Such life forms develop societies, and some of these survive and amalgamate, mostly by harnessing greater amounts of environmental energy. Ultimately, they even develop theories of celestial mechanics and understand that the matter in their bodies came from the stars and that they themselves are nothing special, just debris in its chance assortment. It is a perfect circle.

Something in us may cry out against this common ancestry even for kings and queens and philosophers who were sired by the sires of earthworms and frogs. It may be an outrage, but there is little reason for hope and great expectations anymore. Our clearest statement of something else is our need to make a statement at all. The something in us that cries out may be just the illusion of a spirit in a puppet who thinks he is alive, or it may be the spirit of the infinite, whatever that is, and if it even has a spirit, and if we have a right to be that spirit through the glass darkly. Our outrage is either exactly who we are, or it is our most pompous and painful delusion. Soon none of this will be here anyway—none of it, none of it at all. What a surprise! What a comeuppance and surprise! A thousand writers have weighed it, but we will look again at D. H. Lawrence in *The Rainbow:*

> The purpose, what was the purpose? Electricity had no soul, light and heat had no soul. Was she herself an impersonal force, or conjunction of forces, like one of these? She looked still at the unicellular shadow that lay within the field of light, under her microscope. It was alive. She saw it move—she saw the bright mist of ciliary activity, she saw the gleam of its nucleus, as it slid across the plane of light. What then was its will? If it was a conjunction of forces, what held these forces unified, and for what purpose were they unified?
>
> For what purpose were the incalculable physical and chemical activities nodalized in this shadowy, moving speck under her microscope? What was the will which nodalized them and created the one thing she saw? What was its

intention? To be itself? Was its purpose just mechanical and limited to itself?

It intended to be itself. But what self? Suddenly in her mind the world gleamed strangely, with an intense light, like the nucleus of the creature under the microscope. Suddenly she had passed away into an intensely-gleaming light of knowledge. She could not understand what it all was. She only knew that it was not limited mechanical energy, nor mere purpose of self-preservation and self-assertion. It was a consummation, a being infinite. Self was a oneness with the infinite. To be oneself was a supreme, gleaming triumph of infinity.[2]

George Ellery Hale, one of the first New World astronomers, credits *The Origin of Species* with giving him a relevant model for the stars. "It taught me," he wrote, "to regard the sun as a typical star, a link in a long evolutional chain, and thus helped me to avoid becoming exclusively a specialist in solar research."[3]

Later, Hale summarizes the philosophical impact of the new cosmogony:

We are now in a position to regard the study of evolution as that of a single great problem, beginning with the origin of the stars in the nebulae and culminating in those difficult and complex sciences that endeavor to account, not merely for the phenomena of life, but for the laws which control a society composed of human beings. Any such consideration of all natural phenomena as elements of a single problem must begin with a study of the Sun, the only star lying near enough the Earth. . . .[4]

The Sun was like an animal to the nineteenth and early twentieth centuries. Science sought to understand its life and even seemed to foretell its eventual death. Baron Hermann von Helmholtz and Lord William Kelvin independently developed theories of the stellar atmosphere. The Sun was being compressed into its own center from the pull of its gravitational attraction. The energy for light and heat came from radiation released during contraction. As long as there was material to draw on, the star remained lit.

With this explanation came the shock that the Sun was

consuming itself; it could not burn forever. As material in the center was consumed and the star shrank, it would eventually extinguish itself. This would happen to all the suns in the universe.

The dying Sun is a prime image of our own cosmology. Born in the nineteenth century, it was another great blow to the mediaeval cosmos. Realizing the speed of light and the distances of the stars, astronomers began to understand that they were looking at bodies which might be millions of years dead.

They also realized that ancient explosions were visible in galactic spirals—for instance, a galaxy in Andromeda and another in the Hunting Dogs. It seemed both impossible and frightening that such bright and large explosions could appear from ostensibly so far away. It meant that devastating amounts of material, whole systems, could be destroyed. The nineteenth century could handle the orderly birth and death of stars and even the creation of new stars from nebulous material and interstellar dusts. It was not yet ready for supernovas, explosions beyond comprehension. In fact, the astronomer Agnes Clerke decided in 1890 that these were not so big and far away after all, that the universe was a single island with "the entire contents, stellar and nebular, [belonging] . . . to one mighty aggregation."[5] Unknown to her, other factors were working toward a far more violent and outcast universe.

In 1842, at the University of Prague, Christian Doppler constructed an experiment that was to give the single image on which the fantastic wonders of twentieth-century astronomy were to be based: the red shift. Using the changing pitch of a moving object as a clue to whether it is approaching or receding, Doppler created an analogous model for light. If the distance between the Earth and a star were increasing, the spectral lines would shift toward red wavelengths; and if the distance were decreasing, they would shift toward the blue. When we, nowadays, talk about an expanding universe, we should realize that it is the red shift of most of the objects in the universe that suggests this, and that it is the particularly great red shift of quasars that dates them close to the beginning of time.

A Dutch meteorologist, Christoph Hendrik Didericus Buys

Ballot, tested the Doppler effect in 1845 by using trumpet players on an open car of a railroad train pulled along through the fields by a locomotive. This strange cacophony was a forerunner to the music of remote stars.

It was not the color of star spectra that was altered by the Doppler effect, but, as was shown by William Huggins in 1868, the dark lines were shifted one way or the other from their normal position. The degree of shift, if interpreted as the same effect found in the moving orchestra on the train, was a consistent and unerasable clue to the stellar velocities. For instance, Capella, with a .01 percent shift, is moving away from us at that percentage of the speed of light.

In the 1840s, Michael Faraday, working experimentally with a magnet, discovered lines of force continuing into space from the poles. These seemed to support Leibnitz's image of space as the relationship of objects to one another, in direct contradiction to Newton's empty space. Moving a magnet near a coil of copper, Faraday excited an electrical current: the mechanical energy of the magnet had been transformed into electrical energy. The experimental work of Faraday and, later, of James Clerk Maxwell with electric and magnetic energies led to the concept of a force field. Outer space was newly conceived as a field with waves of electricity and magnetism as well as light. In 1861, Maxwell suggested that light itself might be a form of electromagnetic energy.

It was difficult for these experimenters to accept that fields were real phenomena. Previous models had proposed stress operating mechanically in a medium of space-filling ether. The ether had never been discovered, but it was ostensibly a real thing. Force was thus hypothetically real; scientists had something substantial to discover. What electromagnetism changed was the definition of "real." We know now that electrical fields are created by the mutual interactions of bodies with electrical charges. Magnetic fields are electrical in origin. All the light and radio noise from space are essentially electromagnetic radiation. Otherwise space is silent and empty. It took only Einstein, after Faraday and Maxwell, to add gravitation to the equation, cre-

ating the space-time continuum in which we are now located—
and in which our ancestors were, in their rock observatories and
stained glass cathedrals, without knowing it.

The immediate practical consequence of the work of Faraday
and Maxwell was electricity, a technology we can hardly imagine
the world without. On the one hand, it contributed to blotting
out the night sky with its cities and machines. On the other
hand, it created other "skies." Man generated a whole new planetary communications field with radio and television waves and
satellites, so that words, music, and images cross this planet in
the same way that the emissions of stars and galaxies cross the
universe. In fact, we imagine this to be more than a metaphor,
and we try to send the same electromagnetic signals to other
worlds, assuming that they send them too, in some pure language of numbers and geometry that we might intercept and
interpret—and we listen for their cosmic broadcasts. Sounds
come back to us from the stars, but they are nonconscious (if
the stars are nonconscious). It is in this area, of sentience and
language, that we retain the Keplerian prejudice of the inherent
meaningfulness of number and shape. But today our whole society is overwhelmed by the crisis of what constitutes pure noise
and what is information. We are showered with more data than
we can handle, and we are troubled when cause-and-effect is
"violated" by coincidences, equally so when great amounts of
information deteriorate into useless static. Computers are also
the legacy of electromagnetism, but, like Kelvin's star furnaces,
they solve nothing finally for us. Knowledge itself has become
the paradox and the dilemma.

It is misleading to think that space is different for being a
field rather than a concrete thing. There are no "things" anymore
in the old sense. Bodies are not solid concrete substances. They
arise only as singularities within fields, electromagnetic and gravitational, and the fields of their own nuclear forces. Matter is
nonporous only to our crude faculty of sight. If we could look
at it more closely, we would see something resembling the Solar
System or the galaxies. The twentieth-century occult astronomer Rodney Collin describes the Solar System itself as a fiery
train or body in about the proportion of a human figure standing

erect and racing toward Vega at 12.5 miles per second—that is, if seen by a being with a moment of perception eighty years long:

> The planetary paths, drawn out into manifold spirals of various tensions and diameters, have now become a series of iridescent sheaths veiling the long white-hot thread of the sun, each shimmer with its own characteristic colour and sheen, the whole meshed throughout by a gossamer-fine web woven from the eccentric paths of innumerable asteroids and comets, glowing with some sense of living warmth and ringing with an incredibly subtle and harmonious music.[6]

We have entered a world in which Newton's laws do not hold in the way that he originally proposed them. Potential has surpassed actual force, so finite equations must be replaced by differential equations describing fields in which this potential acts along a gradient, giving rise to the illusion of force.

Moby Dick could have been written as it was only during the profound global transition of the mid-nineteenth century.[7] Herman Melville's whale was a creature of early nineteenth-century biology—at least to the degree that its sheer size and power as a creature gave it the cosmological weight to carry the novel. It was also a forerunner of the alien intelligent whales of twentieth-century cosmology and a remnant of the sea monsters of eighteenth-century teratology. The nineteenth-century whale was one of the indisputable rulers of the animal kingdom at a time when both science and the humanities were committed to life—to the exotic creatures of the jungle and the ocean depths and to the tribes of precivilized humans in all their variety throughout the world. Human meaning lay in this realm.[8]

We have broken our agreement with the animal kingdom. We had already broken it by the time of Melville and Darwin, yet their works were filled with exotic beasts and tribes. This was the golden age of zoological and anthropological expansion, but it was also the death knell. Our search for original form has moved beyond the purely biological into realms of force fields and speeding star-systems. The genetic, where the whale reigned, is now inextricably buried in the morphological. Simultaneous investigations of primary elements and the physical makeup of heavenly bodies have married living and nonliving entities to the same chemistry, compromising not only the whale but the lion, the African shaman, and the Roman priest. As chemistry becomes universal, the whale merges with a new class of objects. In a cosmic framework, it is just another animal, neither chemically nor anatomically unique. Melville foreshadowed this in his drama, and he intuited it in other ways: for instance, in his discussions of the taxonomy, history, and mythology of the whale, which "interfere" with the narrative field of the nineteenth-century novel in the same way that Faraday and Maxwell interfered with the Newtonian field of simple "narrative" forces, or in the way that Janos Bolyai and Nikolai Lobachevski transformed the Euclidean universe into a universe of discontinuous fields and transformations. Melville could write of the "confluent measureless force of the whole whale . . . concentrated to a point" in its tail.[9] This is the new universe of fields and singularities. Or, elsewhere in *Moby Dick:* "Silence reigned over the before tumultuous but now deserted deck. An intense copper calm, like a universal yellow lotus, was more and more unfolding its noiseless measureless leaves upon the sea."[10]

The ladders and hierarchies of the nineteenth-century taxonomist, who presided over the whale's unofficial coronation, stand as trivial before the overall taxonomy of electrons, cells, polarities, and intelligence. But it is a mistake to think that the whale has lost its crown only because the stars are larger and presumably house larger oceanic beasts elsewhere, just as it is a mistake to assume that its size entitled it to the crown originally. The scope of the heavens had been known before. It is because the stars are essentially similar to whales that whales are no longer needed to mark the outer limits of morphology and mythology. Stars and animals bathe in a single elemental pool. Stars rival living systems in their complexities of transformation and discontinuous shapes, especially pulsars and quasars. At the same time that science has discovered the intricacy of stars, it has severely reduced its assessment of living and intelligent beings. Ethology and psychology have consigned the "free movements" of animals and people to deeply compelled patterns and activities. So the stars are no more "inanimate" and unwilled than we.

II

The History of Western Astronomy: VI: The Space-Time Continuum

THE TURN of the present century is marked symbolically by four events from the opposite ends of infinity. In 1897, the British physicist Joseph John Thomson demonstrated the existence of the negatively charged particle, the electron, and determined the ratio of its charge to its mass. Atoms were no longer just protons; they were systems. In 1899, the Andromeda Nebula was found to have a solar-type spectrum and a spiral shape like that of our own Milky Way system. The soft luminescence in its "arms" suggested that they bore stars in the process of formation. During that same year, Max Planck, a German physicist, discovered that the unsteadiness that appears in thermal phenomena and the atomic lattices of matter, the wobble or discontinuity, was not a problem having to do with imprecise equipment or interference; it was a basic and independent feature of nature. Planck's quantum of action allowed scientists to make a model for why two colliding atoms return to their "normal" states after collision when two colliding planetary systems obviously would not. The atom changes its energy by discrete quanta only, so it returns to its basic arrangement. In addition, the radiation from the atom produces wavelike interference patterns but particlelike photoelectric effects. And there was no way to describe either the position of the electron between any two observations or both its position and its momentum. One does not have to understand the subtleties of these matters to see the complexity of the issues raised. Also during that year, Sigmund Freud published his *Interpretation of Dreams*. As far as we look outward, Freud said (by implication), we do not see our actual condition, which is also infinite but in another dimension:

> One is inclined [he wrote] to regard the dream-thoughts that have been brought to light as the complete material, whereas if the work of interpretation is carried further it may reveal still more thoughts concealed behind the dream. . . . It is in fact never possible to be sure that a dream has been completely interpreted. Even if the solution seems satisfactory and without gaps, the possibility always remains that the dream may have yet another meaning.[1]

So it is, entering the twentieth century, not only for dreams but for stars, and in fact for everything. As man attempts to make the universe simultaneously conscious and complete, it will evade him in an absolutely new way that will make the original paradox seem minor. Like King Sisyphus, he has pushed his huge stone to the top of a hill in Hades only to have it roll down again. The universe cannot be made conscious and complete, Freud declared, but he did not deny that the attempt would still have to be made. From then on, we would have to be aware of the darkness of our actual location in the universe. No longer could the exploration be complete in its own terms:

> It is essential to abandon the overvaluation of the property of being conscious before it becomes possible to form any correct view of the origin of what is mental. . . . The unconscious is the larger sphere, which includes within it the small sphere of the conscious. Everything conscious has an unconscious preliminary stage; where what is unconscious may remain at that stage and nevertheless claim to be regarded as having the full value of a psychical

process. The unconscious is the true psychical reality; *in its innermost nature it is as much unknown to us as the reality of the external world, and it is as incompletely presented by the data of consciousness as is the external world by the communications of our sense organs.*[2]

Newton's riddle had finally come of age. As more and more data about the stars and the universe are discovered, the fabric begins to crumble in on itself. It becomes clear that what is underneath it all is a thing that is neither sensible nor knowable. Newton's laws had turned the creation into a laboratory, but there was no place in it for man except in his guise as objective scientist. Now he will look in three places, distinctly, for the thread which connects him to what he is. He will search to the ends of the night sky for his origins; he will look inside matter for the principle of formation; and he will explore his own mind through mathematics, philosophy, and psychology. Because these three share an equivalence in the riddle, they become faces of the same reality. The night of stars is also the night of cells and atoms and is the unconscious fabric of myth and dream and language.

Melville diagnosed the coming schizophrenia: "Better might one be pushed off into the material spaces beyond the uttermost orbit of our sun, than once feel himself fairly afloat in himself!"[3]

It was not the bigness of the sky that threatened man, but his own shadows and eccentricity.

With Freud, we begin to see that it is the stargazers, not the stars, that determine cosmogony. The stars are required, but as a face of the infinite, not the infinite itself. A zen law is operating here: the further we stare via instrumentation into what is meant to be complete and knowable, the more the basis of our being and the knowable will change. That is why stargazers and cell-gazers are important; their truths determine our relationship to the universe and its meaning. We cannot help learning at the same time that the bottom is bottomless and that the realm of concrete appearances will never resolve its own paradoxes. It will simply lead us on forever. There is no question that we have some ingenuous solutions to problems of matter, stars, and origins, but it is no longer enough to keep adding more knowledge; the factor of incompleteness is not going to change. We turn almost reflexively back to social issues, saying, "What have the stars to do with us?"

Everything and nothing.

We now find structural anthropology and its investigation of star and plant taxonomies and creation myths satisfying, for these take into account the properties of mind and culture. Truly the quest, even the urge to quest, engages us more deeply than the truth at the supposed bottom of it all. We are aware of thoughts, but the mind cannot be directly experienced anyway. We experience it as stars, as star myths, as language, as anthropology. We might almost prefer the moment in which we give up the illusion of scientific truth and seek the more human truth, like the astronomer who abandons physics for meditation. That such a thing is possible, and happens, is itself a statement of our profoundly ambiguous condition. We can replace the insolubility with contradictory solutions that have nothing in common except the distant and obscure link that we perceive and forge by our being: depth psychology, linguistic philosophy, zen physics, stellar art forms—whatever we choose. We are unconscious and *it* is unconscious, so that is where it will happen, for scientists as well as improvisational dancers. One makes models, the other moves: both are "stars."

Any astronomer wrestles not only with the stars but with his or her own nightmares, relationships with other men and women, and survival as a creature on the Earth, and all these things find their way into the theories, no matter how diligently he works to keep them out.

Early in the twentieth century, a system of classifying stars according to heat was developed. The hottest and brightest were the blue-white stars at 20,000 degrees C., typified by a star in Orion. This was followed by alabaster-white Sirius, only half as hot; then by pale-yellow Polaris; next by yellow Sol, our own Sun, at half the heat of Sirius; and then by pumpkin Arcturus, itself at twice the 2,000 degrees C. of poppy-red Antares. Generally, the temperature indicates the age of a star, with the young ones hot blue and white, and the aging ones red. A gradation was mapped, but not all stars fit the main sequence from small blue-white stars to large red ones. There was a cluster of red giants, including Betelgeuse, which would engulf the Earth's orbit were it our sun, and Antares in Scorpius, which would swallow Mars. A much smaller group of erratic stars consisted of the white dwarfs, including the companion of Sirius, which was discovered in 1844 from Sirius's wavy track on the celestial sphere. This was thought to be caused by its own orbit around and retardation by an unseen twin. Far too heavy to be a planetary system, it had to be a star. At the time of classification, it was found to be brighter than our Sun although a fraction of its size. Since this was "impossible," scientists assumed that they had made some mistake, but in the ensuing years more white dwarfs were found. They were then considered to be stars in the last stages of life, having collapsed and drawn all their material into a dense center.

The life cycle of stars could be seen strewn throughout the heavens even as the life cycle of animals could be found in the ocean: embryo, newborn, immature child, adult, mating beasts, older members, recently dead specimens, and fossils of extinct forms. Likewise, astronomers saw interstellar clouds of gas, young white giants, red dying stars consuming the last of their energy, eccentric white dwarfs, an abundance of common yellow suns, and almost all of them fossils by nature, fossils in light.

But scientists also faced more difficult questions: What is the shape of the universe as a whole? Is it fixed or changing, and to what degree either? Is it a single island of stars, or are there many galaxies? How can we explain the fact that the matter in the universe does not all come together from gravitational attraction? How far are the farthest things we can see? Does everything obey the same laws? How fast is matter moving? How did the universe begin? Did it in fact have a beginning? And how did it take on this particular shape?

Early in the twentieth century, astronomers discovered certain stars that changed in brilliance for inherent reasons. They were not double or triple stars. They were simply variables. The Americans Harlow Shapley and Henrietta Swan Leavitt were able to derive a period-luminosity curve for these stars, called

Cepheids after the test one, Delta Cephei. In other words, astronomers could calculate the absolute luminosity of stars by their periods, and if they knew the absolute luminosity, then they could calculate distance on the basis of apparent brightness. Suddenly the size of the Milky Way more than doubled, so that, in 1915, Arthur Eddington estimated it at 15,000 light-years, a mere fraction of its presently-estimated diameter but a staggering figure at the time. By 1923, Edwin Hubble had succeeded in finding Cepheids in the spiral arms of the Andromeda Galaxy. He measured its distance from Earth as 900,000 light-years. We now accept the figure 2.1 million light-years for the nearest galaxy.

The cosmology of the universe in the first decade of the twentieth century was leftover Newtonian mechanics, which were assumed to be able to handle all new phenomena. Newtonian physics had proved satisfactory enough in explaining dynamics within the Solar System, stellar mechanics, and galaxy formation. But there were shadows over the Newtonian model. One was cast by Faraday and Maxwell. The mechanical model is absolutely accurate only when the internal dynamics of the atom and the relationships of atoms are not taken into account. But there was another more immediate problem and one that Newton knew himself. If the universe were finite and matter were equally distributed in it, and if gravity were the only force determining the relationship of astronomical bodies, then everything would be drawn by collective gravity to coalesce at a single point. Only if the universe were infinite could this fate be avoided. The problem of gravity would be solved, but there would be the new problem of an infinite universe. Any brief consideration of it was not only mathematically staggering but emotionally chilling and dizzying. A universe that goes on forever is not only big; it stands against identity and reason. Not that a universe which ends has the redeeming virtue of explaining what happens then.

Meanwhile, there was still the Doppler Effect to deal with. The red shifts of stars boded something. Vesto Slipher, working at Lowell Observatory, had shown in 1914 that the spiral galaxies were moving isotropically outwards (away from us and away

from each other). This was not taken seriously until the late
1920s, when Edwin Hubble began to work on the velocity-
distance relations between our galaxy and others. An expanding universe did solve one problem: Olbers's paradox. Shapley
had concluded that space must be extremely transparent, too
transparent to resolve the paradox, or else other problems re-
garding the brightness of distant globular clusters would arise.
At the time, he said, "Either the extent of the star-populated
space is finite or the heavens would be a blazing glory of light."[4]
But not only was the universe infinite, it was expanding! Astronomy was desperately in need of a successor to Newton.

Albert Einstein confronted these difficulties brilliantly from
1917 through the middle of the century. The Newtonian universe, he claimed, should have a maximum density of stars in
the center; it should be "a finite island in the infinite ocean."[5]
He added that there was no place theoretically for both Newtonian matter and the Faraday-Maxwell field; the field is what
survived.

Einstein established that gravitation is a field, like electromagnetism. Mass itself is relative, depending on velocity: the
faster a thing moves, the more massive it becomes. Time depends on mass. If the force of gravity is great enough, time runs
slower. These were bitter pills: almost by the year, the universe
was becoming less secure a place to be born in, but at least there
was now a way out of the celestial machine.

Gravitation, Einstein added, is independent of things which
influence all other observed phenomena. Electromagnetic fields
are felt only by charged bodies. Gravity operates on all bodies
everywhere in the same way without regard for heat, chemical
makeup, or electromagnetic charge. It is the universality of
gravity that makes it impenetrable. We cannot see inside it. It
simply is.

Einstein did not construct an infinite universe. Using Bern-
hard Riemann's 1854 formula, adapted by Riemann from Karl
Friedrich Gauss when Riemann was presenting a paper as a
young job applicant in Gauss's mathematics department, Einstein made a universe in which time was added as a fourth dimension and matter was homogenously distributed (all view-

points were isotropic). Gauss's theorem had allowed the hypothetical two-dimensional inhabitants of a world of two dimensions to find the curvature of their world in three dimensions. Riemann used algebra to generalize this theorem so that it could be used in a space of any number of dimensions, i.e., to measure the curvature of an unknown space.[6]

Einstein developed a curved space for his universe, and he placed three terms—*space, time,* and *gravitation*—in an interdependent series. Gravitation was "explained" as an effect of the curvature of time and space; that curvature gave a limit to the universe with nothing outside. The speed of light marked the limit. Around the high gravitational field of a star, the curvature of space might be greater than in interstellar space. It was not an outside curvature, but an inherent one.

Because this universe was static, Einstein accounted for its failure to close in upon itself by a repulsion at large distances. This force between remote objects he called a cosmological constant. The expanding universe of galaxies required an expanding space ultimately, but Einstein's universe was adaptable because of its infinite curvature. The expansion could create space-time. Finally, Einstein gave his universe a negative curvature, with open and infinite space, like a western saddle with a radius of curvature of five billion light-years.

The nineteenth-century German physicist Hermann von Helmholtz foresaw this universe as a bright silvery Christmas tree globe whose distorted mirror transposes the whole of the space around it into a sphere. The further away a thing is, the tinier it looks and the closer it is to the center of the sphere. If we come up close to it, we can dominate it, but we lose our shape.

Relativity theory is *not* a metaphysical device or an image; it is a physical theory designed to explain observed facts and to bring different rules into one law. There are no more special laws such as the conservation of mass and energy or the principle of least action; these conservations are all included in the single equation of relativity. There are no more special fields; there is one universal field in which matter itself is a confluence. Einstein rested his theory on facts. He predicted the curvature of light close to the Sun when a simple experiment could have refuted him. His confidence was borne out during the solar eclipse of 1919. Relativity theory also explained why Mercury does not behave according to prediction at perihelion and why the dwarf companion of Sirius has such a large red shift.

Einstein's gravitational space was discovered mathematically, and the images we have of it are after the fact. We cannot imagine four-dimensional space simply by analogy with three-dimensional space to two-dimensional being. Another dimension would add a whole new quality to space itself. Things in three dimensions are radically different from things in two dimensions. The fourth dimension is revealed mathematically by tracks of material particles and rays of light. We can predict its coordinates, but we cannot experience its nature. Insofar as this four-dimensional world is "real," space and time as we know them are mere conventions. Events can happen either forward in time or backwards. In observing particles, we do not really know. Positive charge may simply be negative charge moving backwards in time. What we call force may be interaction. Two-dimensional beings might see the third dimension as something like time and attracting force, or it might add something totally different to their world. It has even been suggested that gravity is the fourth dimension and that this is why it pushes everywhere on everything equally from a source which is inherent but invisible. It shapes our entire universe and we feel it from within, but we cannot see it. How else would a fourth dimension act?

In the Einsteinian system, apparent time is also real time, and all time is relative to movement and space. Previously, it had been thought that the time showed by moving clocks was a local fiction. It is. But there is also no other "true" time.

Einstein demonstrated the primary relationship between inertia and energy: the electromagnetic energy stored by the electron increases its inertia and thus its mass. From this commutability of mass and energy, made famous in the formula that combines them with the squared constant of the speed of light ($E = mc^2$), substances and force become versions of the same thing.

In general, Einstein combined phenomena of gravity, mass, and energy in a four-dimensional space-time manifold. He understood the nature and relationship of light and heat and matter implicitly, and he was able to relate these to Planck's quantum. He intuited that radiation itself comes in quanta, and that they are also the source of pure light. The photon, which has the chemical energy of one electron volt per atom, is the intrinsic capacity of sunshine to engage in photosynthesis.

But Einstein balked at the uncertainty factor in quantum theory because he believed there was a real external nature quite apart from probabilistic functions. He demanded an objective night sky and a natural landscape of creation. Because of his involvement with the torso of space, he was able to paint the deepest night sky of the century. Time and space exist only as an inextricable pair, and the night sky is the visible form of them. The richness of this relativistic drawing stands out like the starry heavens themselves—utterly motionless, yet moving at the speed of light. We are post-Einsteinian by birth.

12

The History of Western Astronomy: VII: The Atom

THE TWENTIETH-CENTURY NIGHT SKY is an offspring of the field that arose first in the work of Faraday and Maxwell. Gravity preceded electromagnetism, but then both were integrated in the larger cosmic field of Einstein and the later intra-atomic field. The atom, in effect, both replaces and becomes coterminous with the star in determining the shape and meaning of the night sky.

In the first decade of the twentieth century, Ernest Rutherford bombarded atoms with alpha particles from radioactive substances, and he extrapolated the atom's structure from the way in which the particles were deflected in their passage through it. The atoms turned out not to be Democritus's hard building blocks of matter. They exhibited much empty space, which, in scale, suggested the vast regions of intergalactic space. Small planetlike charges moved about a sunlike center which held them by electric force—electrons and the nucleus, as they were named. Later it was discovered that the nucleus was only one hundred thousandth the size of the whole atom.

Exploration of this new primary unit during the 1920s and 1930s confirmed the existence of two subnuclear particles, first the proton (so-named) and then the neutron. The proton had a positive charge, the neutron no charge. Each had a mass two

182

thousand times that of the electron, and they were so close to the system's center that they sped continually through the nucleus at 40,000 miles a second. This kind of speed in so minute a space transcends our whole sense of reality. It also demonstrates clearly the limitations of our senses and our ability to grasp the actual relationship between matter and energy. Something moving this fast is not "matter," even if it is.

Newton had advanced the idea that there must be another powerful attraction in nature holding bodies together. The atom now stood at the threshold of that force. The elemental chart had intimated intra-atomic properties, and direct research showed that all chemical behavior arose from the electrical characteristics of the atoms. Elements were made by the addition of protons and neutrons to the simplest hydrogen atoms. The electrical charges of the electrons gave matter its distinct properties. Hence, the looseness of electrons throughout a metal allowed electrical current to move through it. Meanwhile, the atoms, in their struggle to recoup the lost electrons, crowded close together, making the metals hard and durable. With a different atomic structure, they would be crumbly or airy and porous.

Light was now understood as a very smooth mask for the chaos of electrons annihilating each other, which itself was only one possible way of looking at the complex interaction of opposite charges. The particles of light born in the Sun carry their electrical (electron) energy to the Earth, where they are converted into living materials by structures built out of previous atoms from the Sun and the local nebular cloud. The Earth continues to get an infinitesimal part of the unraveling Sun to incorporate into its structure.

A whole new science of matter arose from the work of Werner Heisenberg, Niels Bohr, Paul Dirac, Wolfgang Pauli, and their cohorts. The atoms were transformed from hard little balls into intricate sheathes of glowing auras. Heisenberg discovered that there was extra energy within the atom—not very much, but enough to make particles of light and gamma rays that lasted for fractions of a millisecond. The energy was fictional in that it never existed in a concerete locatable sense, but it was real in that the world stood on it. The light may have been borrowed, but the loan had been repaid in time since the dawn of the universe. Its absolute limits were set in a term discovered by Max Planck and called Planck's Constant. Along with Einstein's conversion of mass into energy, this inexplicable process laid the groundwork for the existence of nature.

It was around the quantum that formal uncertainty theory began; though as the twentieth century developed, uncertainty was to become a way of life stretching from the stars to the urban ghettoes. Light wrote the first case. These "virtual" particles were light itself. They were drawn between electrical charges and carried the message of the electrical force because they *were* the electrical force. Electricity was a substantial chain of transmission, not action at a distance. If an electron and its anti-electron actually exist, then they already have annihilated each other and left a particle of light. So, although no antimatter was discernible, somehow it was responsible, along with matter, for bringing particles into being. Scientists and science fiction writers imagined whole galaxies or universes of antimatter presently and necessarily separated from this one. By the 1930s and 1940s, force-carrying particles were hypothesized on the basis of the same borrowed energy. These were later found in cosmic rays. Named mesons, they came from the violent destruction of protons, prior to which they held the atomic nucleus together. Particles and forces were becoming in effect the same thing.

In the new universe of subatomic matter, particles collide continuously at high speeds. They are split into other particles, but these are not different or smaller or less; they are new particles of the same kind. There is no further partibility. Matter can be divided, subdivided, torn apart, but it never falls into more primary pieces, because the energy of its dismantling goes to create new particles. The perfect glue of light and the particle field holds together substance.

The structure of the atom creates other problems that we have touched on in this chapter and in the previous one. We cannot tell the position of an atom at any given moment, only its likelihood of being in one place or another. It is an underlying metaphysical problem which is resolved temporarily by the terms of any given experiment and, in general, by the existence of a world embodying this probability function. If one tries to give the particle a more focused locale, its velocity will take on the uncertainty.

It is the light quanta that give rise to the name quantum theory in the context of Planck's Constant, which gives a range to uncertainty relationships. Light quanta are neither a wave nor a particle, neither a singularity nor a radiance spread over space, and yet they are both. Matter has become like our experience of ourselves—it has a topology with qualities of dimensionality, orientability, and indivisibility. But it has no real locatability in time and space. Particles are not waves in three-dimensional space and time, but they are, in three dimensions, waves of probability. "Isolated material particles are abstractions," wrote Niels Bohr, "their properties being definable and observable only through their interaction with other systems."[1]

During the nineteenth century, observers of the Sun assumed that gravity alone bound it, and that as the Sun burned off its materials, it would shrink. This might be true if the Sun were a normal sort of chemical fire. But Einstein's theory of the convertibility of mass and energy and the discovery of a strong binding nuclear force grant the solar sea a totally different kind of fire. Hydrogen burns on an atomic level under the influence of the strong nuclear force. It consumes and radiates itself, making new material to consume, creating new particles out of energy. It is not immortal, but it is far longer-lived than the nineteenth-century sun-star.

But what is the strong nuclear force? We can no more answer the question than we can answer the same question of gravity. We know that the strong nuclear force works in the heart of the atom, in the nucleus, and that it holds the protons and neutrons together. It is a million times stronger than the electromagnetic force which holds the electrons to the same nucleus. All particles, not just those in the nucleus, have strong nuclear interactions, except the photon, neutrino, electron, and muon. The latter three are called leptons as a class, to distinguish them from the other particles called hadrons, which include the meson and baryon. The leptons interact by the weak nuclear force—a totally other characteristic of fields of matter, which neutralizes electric charges in about half the nuclear matter of the stars, thereby allowing atoms heavier than hydrogen to be created without annihilation first by the electric force. In a sense, the weak force creates the neutral basis of matter by changing protons into neutrons. It is a minor deed carried out in a very small place, but that small place is everywhere and everything, and without it we would not have much of a universe. It is the weak force inside the atom which causes changes in the atomic nucleus, protecting complex elements as they build up in the stars.

The tiny neutral particles called neutrinos are by-products of the weak force. Until 1980, they were thought to have no mass, but recently an infinitesimal mass was discovered, which becomes significant when we consider the number of neutrinos in the universe. Still, they travel right through the core of the Earth without interaction. They react only to gravity (and barely, because of their high velocity) and to the weak force. Since the weak force is truly weak, they do not act much at all. Predicted by Pauli in 1930, neutrinos were not found until 1956 in a nuclear reactor. They are far too flimsy to build much with, but without their tiny adjustments, the universe would have been too electric to complexify and differentiate.

In a subsequent model, the weak force was understood as a kind of meta-electrical entity. If the electrical force became stormy, the weak force would ripple through it. In the death of a star, neutrino pressure via the weak force would produce swarms of elements and ultimately start ripples toward breaking up the stellar body. In a very large universe, such brief disruptions make a lot of complex matter.

Compared to all this nuclear activity and even to the electromagnetic force, gravity is extremely weak, but its power is its universality and its action over a distance. It is not like a force at all but the cosmological constant of the whole creation, the spider whose web is light and time crisscrossing on eternity. Gravity is minimal with small objects; yet, as matter becomes denser, it overrides everything else and sculpts stars, galaxies, planets, moons, and their components out of the raw material, ignoring the subnuclear forces that alone give it material to amass. It is the enigma of enigmas, the central scientific koan. Newton was right.

In the 1960s, scientists came to prefer an alternate interpretation from the one in which protons and neutrons are the basic indivisible particles of matter. On one level, the weak force seemingly transformed a proton into a neutron. On another level, it changed something within the proton, a sub-subatomic entity that came to be called a quark. It was named by Murray Gell-Mann, an Israeli physicist working at the California Institute of Technology, for the James Joyce line: "Three quarks for Muster Mark."[2] Protons and neutrons were now said to be made of two kinds of quarks, up and down. The proton had two ups and one down, the neutron two downs and one up. This is what made them what they were. The weak force had a specific act assigned to it: it changed an up into a down quark.

Despite a subsequent worldwide search, including the bombarding of hadrons with extremely high energies, quarks have not yet been found; it is possible that they cannot be found, that proton and neutron are impenetrable. Moreover, there is a question of whether they really exist or are just a way of looking at the structure of subatomic interactions.

Where does this leave us? In molecules there are atoms, in the atom there is a nucleus, in the nucleus a proton, in the proton a quark. But is the quark the final denomination? Is the fact that quarks cannot be liberated from protons an indication that there is no more? Scientists have since hypothesized pre-quarks, called preons, that give the quarks their peculiar characteristics, but this can quickly become an endless path down another causeway. The eternal subdivision of matter, like the eternal universe, is a moral and cosmological issue. Mao Zedong, in fact, came out in favor of quarks and pre-quarks because he felt that the universe should go on forever down through the minutest zones.

The concept of quarks arose from a need to define an underlying symmetry in the world of particles. With three types of quark and anti-quark, baryon and meson patterns could be described as quark interactions. The quarks become actual points of singularity without structure but generating all structure.

They could not really have no structure or nothing would form, but they must go beyond the limits of our ability to detect structure.

The first patterning characteristic of protons was discovered in the 1960s before the idea of quarks; it was called strangeness by Gell-Mann. Strangeness was a real thing, not a metaphor and not "another thing" that was also strange. *Strange* shares a Greek root with the words *exterior* and *external*. Strange particles existed longer than others, but their strangeness eventually ended. Neutralized by the weak force, the particles became ordinary. There were nonstrange particles, strange particles, doubly strange particles, and even triply strange particles. These went on to have one, two, or three extra lives before emerging without strangeness. During the process, they shed particles. Eventually, scientists added a sideways quark (determining strangeness) to up and down ones to create a triadic structure for quarks. It may sound like puzzles and mazes, but it is meant to be real. Somewhere inside us, particles are shifting and shuffling quarks, keeping not only us but our atoms "alive."

In the mid-sixties, a new force was introduced to the quark realm: color. The quarks were not themselves colored (they could not be, as they are prior to light), but they behaved in relationship to each other in a way that resembled color in the building up of white light. The quark-dynamic binding force could be conceived of as chromodynamic, with six metaphorical colors: red with its anti-color turquoise, green with its anti-color mauve, and blue with its anti-color yellow. It is fitting that in the colorless sanctum of the proton, colorlike images should emerge.

Color force was no mild thing; in fact, if quark theory was used as the simplifying base for nuclear theory, then color force was actually the prime source of the strong nuclear force.

Particles themselves had no color: they were white; but they carried color, and color was what held them together. Any of the quarks could take on any color, and any of the anti-quarks could take on any anti-color. The color relations were conceived as stringlike, operating at close distances and indissoluble, held together by forces called gluons. The gluons would flow between the proton's quarks, and the colors would consequently change. As one got closer and closer to a quark, the color force, because of its stringlike quality, would not increase; instead it would grow weaker, because quarks too close would have no tautness. If the string were snapped, however, one would simply have new identical particles forming at each end. This is why we could not isolate and free the single quarks. They were there in the symmetry, but any disturbance continued to generate the symmetry anew.

To upness, downness, and strangeness, another flavor of quark was added in 1974, the charmed quark. It was a fourth kind of quark, whose property was to increase the formation rate of proton-category particles from combinations of other quarks. Charm was subtle, and it was named in keeping with its behavior. Even though we could not actually point to what its elimination would mean, we would have a totally different universe without it. It complicated the basic underlying symmetry of matter, adding many new possible kinds of particles to the substratum of the universe.

Charmed quarks combined with strange quarks in weak force interactions. They were heavier and had more energy than ordinary quarks. In fact, charm and strangeness were linked and interdependent. Thus, they are linked in us who have chosen to call them that in their invisibility. The archetypal fantasy runs so deep that some people have been willing to suggest that the left-handed predisposition of molecular life originates from a "left-handedness" in the weak force.

In the Big Bang, when the universe was tight and the nuclear and weak force dominated the actual deep sky of the heavens, when interstellar and intra-atomic were the same field, charm and strangeness were no doubt in abundance. Charm is a most ancient characteristic of the universe. It is pre-Cambrian in cosmic terms. Strangeness is more Palaeozoic. Both forces retreated to the microscopic range as the universe spread out. Then *we* formed to see the long-range dispersed sky and the foreshortened microscopic sky. Charm and strangeness were incorporated within, for they could not go outside into the thinness of space. We and they depend on each other, for they require beings such as us somehow to emerge from the Flux to define them as symmetries and number pairs, and we then require them to have been in existence virtually forever for beings such as we are to arise and describe them instead of some other sterile or vagabond universe.

There was no center to the explosion that created the universe. Everything detonated at once. Everywhere was the center. Everything was blown from everything else, spreading the conflagration into space. But the original substance was so dense that it took billions of years for it to thin out into our present array of black night with patches of creationary sludge. The sky, by this proposition, is a splatter—not a splatter *against* something, as white paint on a dark wall, but a splatter *into* waves of gravitation and time-space created by the electro-atomic composition of the stuff itself. It spread radiatively, vibratorily. And now it hangs there, ingots still burning, hot stars. Some of the original mulch is still stuck together in nebulae and galaxies, but even those are rushing apart.

The dynamics of the night sky are not that different from those of the Winnebago Indian creation myth in which the sky was "shat" by Coyote against the deep black, with the Milky Way the main stream of cosmic defecation. The old Greek image of milk squirted from Hera's breast, giving rise to the Via Lactea of ancient Rome and the Middle Ages, has some of the sense of splatter and streaming too. A deluge filling all space and time simultaneously is not a possibility in either Greek or Siouan mythology, but the explosion and the vibration are. The poet Gary Snyder takes an Asian image into a cosmic fertility vision:

> Our portion of fire
> at this end of the milky way
> (the Tun-huang fragments say, Eternal Light)
> Two million years from M 31
> the galaxy in Andromeda—
> My eyes sting with these relics.
> Fingers mark time.
> semen is everywhere
> Two million seeds in a spurt.[3]

The unintentional lewdness of the "Big Bang" is appropriate to our identification with star violence and star ecstasy. The pulsing, gushing qualities of living tissue connect it to a primordial pollen. Our flood of consciousness in awakening is also the cosmic dawn. Even the famous peeing in the grass under the full night of white-hot ash brings on a oneness astronomers do not always experience in their eavesdropping upon the immortal act. The sheer coursing and warmth of fluid with its *chi* ember upon the ground and its whisper of molecules returns the sense of all fire as water. Flying squirrel, penguin, gibbon, rattlesnake—each softly fashioned upon the spine of yin and yang—contain the symmetry of the original universe.

Isotropy is established by the structure of the explosion: everything is rushing away from everything else; thus, all galaxies are fleeing from each other, as seen from any place in the universe. There was a moment in physics when it was thought that we were back at the center of things: they were all rushing away from us. They are. But we have no special privilege.

The Big Bang theory was formulated in the late 1930s and early 1940s after Hubble's interpretation of the red shift. The theory might have remained obscure, as at the beginning, but it has grown on us, and in recent years it has taken over astronomy. We had no real alternative. The sky was not static; it showed recession in telescopes and radio waves. The initial implication was that some innate force was thrusting creation into new zones, but no such force has been found. The universe is expanding because everything was tossed outward by an ancient explosion of unknown origin. It is as soulless and unredemptive as that. We just happened to get mixed up in the middle of it—perhaps at the beginning, surely when we discovered it. Now it seems that all those ancient bison at Lascaux and Egyptian pyramids and Mayan astrological temples and Ming vases are part of the terrible affair too. So are the Australian Aboriginal dreamtime beasts and the Bushmen hunters pursuing giraffes and zebras. There was a shoot-out on Times Square. Principals unknown. Motives likewise. And here we all are.

The Big Bang minimizes the problem of whether the universe was infinite or not at the beginning or is infinite now. If it was infinite at the beginning, the explosion was infinite too. If it was not, but still gave the galaxies escape velocity, then they are moving infinitely into a space-time that is determined by their properties, or, more accurately, by the properties of their subatomic particles.

The universe has no net electric charge. It does not annihilate itself electrically. The numbers of electrons and protons in the whole thing must be exactly equal, not 99.999 percent equal but exactly equal. This is a condition for us to have a universe at all, or for matter to form without being destroyed in the embryo. It is necessary that powerful electricity be balanced and at bay for the relatively weak charges of gravity to take over the molding process and to shape a "big," or at least a chunky, universe, with atoms containing complex composite nuclei. Electrical charge is such that whenever it is changed locally, it creates its opposite charge in perfect and continuous balance. It is the powerful underlying yin-yang which allows an overlying amorphous geography.

If the explosion was not sufficient to propel the galaxies outward forever, the universe will eventually contract, condense, and bounce back out again. In such a view, there is no distinction between our past and our future. We can look forward, cosmically, to exactly the thing that gave birth to us. Suddenly, the nearby galaxies will begin to blueshift, while the more ancient light of remote galaxies will continue to redshift—or, actually, we will see its red shift longer because it will take time for news of the change out there to get to us by light. Millions of years will pass, and the contracting universe will not affect us any more than the expanding universe does now. All of the hydrogen and much of the helium that provides the fuel for the stars was created in the Big Bang. There is no other way to create hydrogen that we know of. Without the Big Bang, its origin is a complete mystery, and the posited explosion merely gives the mystery an agency. Millions of years from now, most of the interstellar gas will have been consumed in the stars, and few, if any, new stars will be being born. When the universe has reached a hundredth of the size it is now, we will have the night sky that Olbers saw in a conundrum or a nightmare once, as bright as the day sky. Eventually, molecules will break down into atoms, atoms into electrons and other nuclei. It will take thousands of years for big changes, but as the cosmos becomes a plasma millions of degrees hot, it will begin to change in a matter of days, rising by millions of degrees per hour. Not only will all matter disappear, but the more complex particles will vanish with it—the work of star and atoms—and stars and atoms will merge (the telescope will show the same thing the microscope does); the microwave background will collapse once again into a single howling roar. This will last for either an eternity or a brief fraction of a second, depending on how one views the obliteration of time. And then the Big Bang will occur again.

Wrote the poet Edward Dorn:

> every change of placement
> the shift of every leaf
> is a function
> of the universe which
> moves outward from its composed center
> 40 bilynyrs. Then returns. . . .
> our given pulse
> hits inside this
> everymoment we live
> to hear this
> COSMOS[4]

It is a pulse touching inside every mountain Ainu chanting, every juggler holding three or four stones in motion about him, every pair of lovers seeking their rhythm, every fern and starfish, every dervish dancing. It all happened one starry night, and we do not know if it is our faraway vision of spirit or simply, inside us, the complication of matter hung on the loom to the end of the universe. Gravity carries it to the wheels against iron in the clatter of the train along its tracks. It is our heartbeat. It is an avalanche. It is also delicate beyond measure, which is why we feel heartache as well and can neither relieve nor locate it. We must drift in a multiplicity. And then:

> the moment
> approaching when all of it
> will be stilled in a shimmy[5]

The ripple in the pond is also the explosion creating the universe. It begins and ends and hangs for an eternal second—the same one inside us when the insight comes and when we feel ourselves a unity.

The universe begins at an incredible temperature of millions of millions of degrees. Such a universe cannot be described, even hypothetically, for it is a universe only of quantum mechanical relationships. Gravitational fields would have been so powerful that particles themselves would be created by such fields, but that presupposes that the concept of particle has any meaning at such a temperature. No message about anything could get even as far as one wavelength, so size, shape, and location would be meaningless. There would be only one of each of them, and that one would be everything and everywhere. It is in perhaps this first ten-thousandth of a second that something primordial comes into being—the quarks. They buzzed around. This was their universe, their home. The strong and weak nuclear forces had as much range as gravity and electromagnetism. The Big Bang, with its quark-charmed strange universe, is the moment of determinative structure, and the millions of millions of years and other temporal units since then are nothing more than the particles fulfilling their potentialities as heat and pressure diminish.

To form the present universe from this bath of superheated matter, the first few minutes of cooling were crucial, if we can accept the eternity of minutes in the timeless flow before there was a Sun or an orbit in which to find units of time. The temperature first cooled enough for there to be protons and neutrons in the complexity of atomic nuclei. Hydrogen stands at the upper end of the pre-atomic series at a moment when it is doubtful whether atoms will be formed at all. Once the crisis is passed, cosmological and stellar nucleosyntheses begin to manufacture denser nuclei.

The early universe of the first few minutes was made primarily of photons, electrons, neutrinos, and anti-neutrinos. It was made of light and radiation, the same light and radiation that continues to flow from stellar centers. About a millionth of it became nuclear matter at first, and all of that was hydrogen and helium, about 75 percent hydrogen. After a matter of years, perhaps hundreds or thousands, a cool gas began forming, the gas of the galaxies and suns. Electrons joined with the nuclei to form atoms. Gaseous matter drifted in among the radiation, gravitation wheeled it off into galaxies, and galaxies spawned local space and systems of stars and planets.

A possible contradiction of the Big Bang theory is posed by the question: why were the thermal components not blown to bits far beyond the point where they could condense into galaxies? Theoretical physics requires that the universe have been in a state of statistical thermal equilibrium at a point before the formation of galaxies and stars. All subsequent prediction about earlier or later states comes from an assumption of an intermediate uniform state. In that sense, the Big Bang theory, like so many other modern suppositions since the application of natural selection to genetics and Emile Durkheim's discovery that suicide occurs in predictable percentages, is a statistical theory.[6] The Big Bang is not a concrete thing. We know it as the resolution of the distribution of things in time and space and their mathematics. It is a demographic conclusion about the universe. The 3° Kelvin microwave background of space, recognized first in 1965, is considered to be an echo of the explosion that occurred ten billion years before. It is a prediction of what would be found if a fabric, namely everything, had expanded a thousand times, with equivalently homogeneous cooling, from a time when it was 3000° K., at which time matter and radiation were in thermal equilibrium. The universal background of radiation is the universality of the explosion and the evenness of the dissipation from an opaque superheated space. In such a pure universe of heat and number, matter develops only as a contamination. That is a favorite word of contemporary cosmologists, and its irony must be intentional. It is lucky that this contamination is ultimately capable of feeling relative heat, looking into the fabric to see the portals of time, and developing "numbers" that must, in some way, be crude replicas of the aboriginal sky.

Once matter forms and coalesces into clumps and islands, the rate of expansion is handed over to gravitation. We return, almost nostalgically, to the Newtonian universe. If we go backward in time from here, we require Planck again and quantum mechanics—that is, we must go forward a few centuries in physics. If we proceed directly from here according to Newton, we go through Laplace to James Jeans, who determined mathematically the smallest mass that was capable of condensing gravitationally, thus leading to a theory of star formation. From Jeans's mass, we go forward to Heisenberg and Einstein, toward spacetime, uncertainty theory, and the microwave background. Once we get this universe cooled off enough, we can return to our daily Newtonian lives. All of these images and ideas flow in a circle, giving rise to each other.

Big Bang theory is unrelenting and unredemptive. We are trapped in it by the fact that our minds, like the primal nebula, are too dense to let go of it, in the same way that they cannot let go of materialism, progress, consumption of materials, and even an idea of themselves as something that requires explanation. We hold to these images as we hold to war. And as our reason tries to pull us away from war and destruction, something else compels us to return or risk having it thought of by someone else, and to our own disadvantage. We are drawn equally to pornographic events and torture. If it is possible, we must do it; our minds decree so, and we are never the first. Almost as we think it, someone else is there before us. So men are torn apart on wheels and thrown alive to hungry dogs.

But it was also a cosmologist of the night sky, G. I. Gurdjieff, who said that if soldiers in an army could see their true cosmic position *for just an instant,* they would all throw down their weapons and go home. That is, if they could see themselves against the stars, and the Earth in the universe, and their own being born, being incarnated in that universe.[7]

We have reaped the materialistic wheel that we naively sowed, and we have learned something from it. That learning is now alone what can change us. We could also get stuck here, and it is a barren place. If our destiny remains such, we cannot help destroying ourselves, for, as Diderot and Shaw divined, there is no longer any reason to live.

In Big Bang theory, our identity is given only by such a cataclysmic event that it could be at best a scar, the earmark of a primal trauma that is borne by the individuality of everything. Thus, the echo of primeval fears in the jungles of ancient man was also the echo of our own matter forming at the bottom of our unconscious bodies and their simultaneous nightmare.

Steady State theory is still quite violent, but it does not require the single big devastation, and it even allows for creative fountains in multiple dimensions of matter, and for a stability and a grace. It is interesting and perhaps terrifying that all the new evidence is in favor of the Big Bang. But is the terror a cosmic one or a cultural one? And do we fear space more than our own nihilism and its residue throughout our civilization?

Touching and powerful, and also sad, is the ending of a popular modern cosmology by Steven Weinberg: *The First Three Minutes*. As Weinberg reviews the implications of Big Bang theory, there is rebellion from the readers in my library copy, with insults in the margins and at the ends of paragraphs. People seem to feel that if the author had had some imagination, in terms of uncertainty theory and black holes, he could have created a "happy ending" in the same way that *Star Trek* episodes discover a psychic universe within the dregs of this physical one. Whenever the warmongers and the materialists are about to have their way in the *Star Trek* universe, another aspect of creation emerges, usually personified by highly evolved telepathic and even bodiless beings who have found immortality and a collective nirvana. We have been brainwashed by these endings. They are our inheritance as much as Big Bang, but for a scientist committed to seeing the present era through, there is no other outcome than the one Weinberg resigns himself to:

> However all these problems may be resolved, and whichever cosmological model proves correct, there is not much of comfort in any of this. It is almost irresistible for humans to believe that we have some special relation to the universe, that human life is not just a more-or-less farcical outcome of a chain of accidents reaching back to the first three minutes, but that we were somehow built in from the

beginning. As I write this I happen to be in an airplane at 30,000 feet, flying over Wyoming en route home from San Francisco to Boston. Below, the earth looks very soft and comfortable—fluffy clouds here and there, snow turning pink as the sun sets, roads stretching across the country from one town to another. It is very hard to realize that this all is just a tiny part of an overwhelmingly hostile universe. It is even harder to realize that this present universe has evolved from an unspeakably unfamiliar early condition, and faces a future extinction of endless cold or intolerable heat. The more the universe seems comprehensible, the more it also seems pointless.[8]

Since quarks and atoms bear so little relation to who we are now, except for the fact that we have dreamed them up from sparse evidence and use their mathematics, it appears almost as though we have originated from something alien, something that has no moral value. The cosmology of ancient and tribal peoples did not have this problem, because they began from moral value and moved outward. The myth hero of the Jicarilla Apache of New Mexico speaks:

This earth is my body. The sky is my body. The seasons are my body. The water is my body too. . . . The world is just as big as my body. The world is as large as my word. And the world is as large as my prayers. The seasons are only as great as my body, my words, and my prayer. It is the same with the waters; my body, my words, my prayers are greater than the waters. Whoever believes me, whoever listens to what I say, will have long life. . . . Don't think I am just in the east, south, west, or north. The earth is my body. I am there. I am all over. Don't think I stay only under the earth or up in the sky, or only in the seasons, or on the other side of the waters. These are all my body. It is the truth that the underworld, the sky, the waters, are all my body.[9]

In Qabalistic cosmology, the creation emanates from God in such a way that everything is contained in everything else. A single thought from the Divine Mind becomes many thoughts, and the many thoughts become boundless creation. It is another isotropy. Where anyone stands, he stands in the center of all worlds. The stars may be the detritus of an explosion, but that is the illusion of one layer; they are also the candles from which angels light worlds. They are the image through which we see such candles.

For some Oriental philosophers, our incarnation itself creates the world illusion. In Buddhist lore, this manifestation and our desire for it are the same thing and serve as a creative emanation of each other. From these perspectives, the Big Bang is a great paradox and a test for man.

Weinberg concludes his book:

> But if there is no solace in the fruits of our research, there is at least some consolation in the research itself. Men and women are not content to comfort themselves with tales of gods and giants, or to confine their thoughts to the daily affairs of life; they also build telescopes and satellites and accelerators, and sit at their desks for endless hours working out the meaning of the data they gather. The effort to understand the universe is one of the very few things that lifts human life a little above the level of farce, and gives it some of the grace of tragedy.[10]

Farce and tragedy are the two great muses who dance upon our century, and always together. Samuel Beckett provides us the same axiom. *Murphy* opens: "The sun shone, having no alternative, on the nothing new."[11] And at the end of *Waiting for Godot,* Vladimir says:

> All I know is that the hours are long, under these conditions, and constrain us to beguile them with proceedings which—how shall I say—which may at first sight seem reasonable, until they become a habit. You may say it is to prevent our reason from foundering. No doubt. But has it not long been straying in the night without end of the abyssal depths? That's what I sometimes wonder.[12]

This premonition falls like a shadow over all of human history from here on in—because we know so much about everything and because our despair cannot even contain in it the hope of a future golden age. The formal seriousness with which Weinberg states it almost belies the real seriousness of the problem. It is not a new problem at all; it is not a new paradox. Hindu sages thousands of years ago would have predicted exactly such an outcome for big State-funded stargazing programs in the West.

Estragon replies to Vladimir: "We are all born mad. Some remain so."[13]

13

The History of Western Astronomy: VIII: Pulsars, Quasars, and Black Holes

Astronomers of the early twentieth century, in having inherited such enormous breakthroughs into a new sky, did not realize the degree to which they still clung to the old model. They knew that the stars are distant suns, colored differently for their temperatures, that they are created from the incandescing of galactic material, and that the planets are thrown off them in the centrifugal force of their formation. But they still believed in simple experienced matter, space, and time.

The microscope and the cyclotron changed our understanding of the relationship between all matter and all energy, and they laid the basis of derivation for everything, for which the sky is an infinite exteriorization. They also had accomplices in the heavens.

The 200-inch Mount Palomar mirror was proposed in 1928, but it was not attempted for years. The glass was originally poured out of quartz by General Electric at half a million dollars' expense. It cracked, and Pyrex was used instead of quartz. Corning Glass did the pouring in New York State, and then the expensive disc was sent to Pasadena, where it was ground and polished and the mounting was built. Twenty years after it was proposed, this great eye stared into the galactic sky, and instantly man stood billions of light-years further out in space. Almost immediately, though, the radio sky, along with the X-ray, the infrared, and the ultraviolet skies, began to converge with the remote visual sky and overlap it.

The ancient universe was constructed of information from visible light sources and terrestrial interpretation. The modern astronomical universe was also made from light and the Earth laboratory. But the postmodern astrophysical universe is constructed primarily of information from radio signals and other invisible wavelengths plus data from experiments in subatomic matter and post-Einsteinian relativistic equations. When radio telescopes are aimed into the infinity of space, they record events that give off radio waves; these events may also give off light, but there are some that are either invisible from here or whose radio emission far exceeds their visible component. Used locally in the Solar system, radio telescopes have picked up disturbed regions in the outer layers of the Sun and the immense radio noise of Jupiter, especially as broadcast in bursts during the passage of its moon Io. Used to scan within our Galaxy, radio telescopes have picked up the voices of remnants of exploded stars, new embryonic stars, pulsing stars, and stars with flares, none of which have a visible display resembling the radio display, except for optical pulsars like the one in the Crab Nebula. If the radio "light" could be made visible, these stars would increase in brightness and transform the sky. Radio emissions have also been useful in "seeing" through the clutter of dust in mapping the structural features of the Galaxy itself, notably its spiral arms. Turning beyond the Galaxy, the radio astronomer discovers portions of other galaxies that ring in the radio parts of the spectrum ostensibly because they are exploding or are the collision points of two galaxies. Quasars also show up, although what they are and where they are located is anyone's guess. And then all about us in our egg is the microwave background containing the echo of the fireball that shaped our present cosmology.

The sounds from the electromagnetic spectrum of space were disruptive, confusing, and humanly troubling. We heard the crash and clamor of subatomic particles in their radio waves and

X-rays, for these dwell in and rule the centers of suns. From his analysis of their dreams and unconscious mind, Freud had taught his generation that this was a species in trouble. Barely three decades later, the radio telescope showed that this was a universe in trouble—renegade and violent in its conception, unable to keep order in its parts, and careening toward fresh disaster.

We were shown shapes of awesome capacity, perhaps safely in the distance for now—these ferocious and relentless beasts—but also hot upon us because the expanding universe cannot hold them at bay forever. It was not just a case of being consumed by these creatures but of having our whole universe consumed. Excited atoms scream like geese in slaughter when galaxies collide. No doubt the geese or quasi-white-feathered-birds of these other brilliant worlds are slaughtered too.

Where were the gods now? Where were the divine power and the perfect geometries that ruled in its stead? Where were the uncompassionate but just laws of nature? They seemed to have vanished from a universe in which everything had suddenly become possible.

Dreams and the psychology of the unconscious had shown man that his instincts and desires were limitless beyond his will and that every failure to express them would express them anyway. They would generate his societies, his laws, his art, and his international crises. But at least they had meaning; at least they shared with man his inner nature. Even the cruelty in them was the cruelty in his destiny, or the cruelty and resistance through which he had to pass to achieve his destiny. Whatever in them was alien would be made familiar by internalization and cathexis, even if it changed his nature by becoming familiar. He knew that he would experience his destiny and his meaning as part of himself, and that he would arrive at it by the continuum of association and consciousness in his own mind.

The sky, on the other hand, offers little that is familiar, and that which we borrow from it deceives us as our dreams cannot. The major technological adaptation of the model of the heavens is itself apocalyptic: atomic energy. But there is a twist in it. Solar energy is atomic energy too—not the direct explosion in imitation of the star core but its medicinal by-product passing

through space. We can call it medicinal without fear of metaphor
or sentimentality because the process of photosynthesis is the
protean medicinal process. It weaves the strands that become
the self-healing replicating cells. It creates the flesh and blood
of the nuclear scientists and engineers and the antinuclear dem-
onstrators counterposed in the atomic sunlight. The problem of
the sources of matter and energy is a far more complex one than
the pros and cons of any politicization reveal. We are the products of explosions, we contain explosions, and we keep ourselves
going with a tinder box.

To accept solar energy and reject atomic energy may seem a
contradiction, but it is a practical strategy. It also relives an ancient mythology. Solar energy is what the universe gives us of
itself at this distance: Take this and you will be enlightened, take
this and you will be healed. And we have not been wrong yet.
We have waited to be born, and the seas have filled with life.
We have waited while life crawled onto the land and established
itself, and we understood that we were born already, and then
we came more fully into being and built our farms and manors,
our astronomical observatories and our cities. In these we
understood the Sun again, the measure of our place in the cosmos—as simple as units on a sundial, the fields of barley and
bulgar in the Near East, the vast rainbow corn of the New World.
Our solar society existed for millennia. It was a society of flowers, grains, fish pools, tonics, mirrors, and delicate parchment.
All of this came from the stark abyss of fiery hydrogen gases a
mere stone's throw away. Gravity covered it, and light dispersed
through the sky into colors which formed eyes to see them. It
couldn't have been a better universe. It couldn't have happened
to a better universe. It said: wait and I will happen. And it did.

The new atomic universe of radio astronomy and particle
physics is a terrifying one, and we have become its dull-witted
targets. We are blind to the particles we are meant to avoid,
radioactivity and decayed nuclear matter, and we cannot see,
even with our finest telescopes, the chaos and violence that is
destroying the cosmos. Its warnings and prophecies are all about
us, yet we are somehow spared and allowed to go on living in
what is essentially a Greek city.

The priests have given us nothing. They have failed us. The very sound of radio noise in the sky is the crackle of our own anxiety, and it is also the crackle of our present cosmological insufficiency. The great violence we perceive in space may be more than our own destructiveness; it may be the suppression of our creative abilities to harvest inner space, a perception that the inner spaces are in turmoil and we are cut off. But what if we are not? How dread the responsibility then to make a decent world and recover our birthright.[1]

We stand before an incredible task. It would be something for even a planet of supermen who could fly into space. We must, if we too are to survive, avert the destruction of the universe. We must reverse the Big Bang. Which is to say, we must prevent the destruction of our own planet and its systems of meaning. We must pass through the Big Bang, even as we must pass through existentialism, Marxism, capitalism, materialism, and all the other tricks of the atomic age, and we must make a new universe, something like the Ionian and Hindu ones but without exactly those features that lead inevitably and rightly back to the present condition. The darkness is not something that we can go back on. Its riddle itself is our destiny.

Pulsars were discovered in November 1967 by a British graduate student, Jocelyn Bell. Because of their extremely regular bursts of radiation, they were first thought to be intelligent signals from civilizations in space. Every possible source for such a pulse was checked: local static, equipment malfunctions, pigeons' nests in the telescope. It was not suspected until the very last that they were themselves stars.

Since it was accepted that stars contract and die, astronomers considered that a very large star, with enough density to convert its material into neutrons, could, instead of becoming a white dwarf, collapse into a superdense object. Such a neutron star would throb in the sky, giving off radio noise and brilliant X-ray emissions.

The American astronomer Thomas Gold developed an hypothesis in which a rotating star collapses into a neutron star. An old star, ripe in material, would spin more than a hundred times a second, its pulses gradually slowing down as it throws off its remains. The pulse itself would come from the whirling envelope of plasmas held to the star by a magnetic field strengthened ten billion times by the compacting of materials and the conserving of their magnetic force lines.

The original pulsar showed up, in the words of its discoverer, as "this particular bit of scruff" in the constellation Vulpecula (The Little Fox), a modern figure which the seventeenth-century Polish astronomer Johannes Hevelius wedged in between the Arrow and the Swan at a point where the Milky Way splits into two branches. "I wished," said Hevelius, "to place a fox and a goose in the space of the sky well fitted to it; because such an animal is very cunning, voracious and fierce. Aquila and Vultur are of the same nature, rapacious and greedy."[2]

The swiftest and most powerfully-driving pulsar is the one in the Crab Nebula; in fact, it may have strung the cloud of filaments making up the nebula. Another young one lies in the constellation Vela, The Sails, of Argo.

Thomas Gold adopted pulsars early, and he used them to explain the cosmic rays which travel the universe at speeds approaching the speed of light. Composed almost entirely of atomic nuclei, these rays are recorded in mines deep within the Earth's subterranean regions. But how did they get their acceleration? Suspecting pulsars, Gold compared cosmic ray density with pulsar density in the Galaxy and found that these two figures perfectly interrelated. Nigel Calder, the science writer, compares using supernovae to create pulsars with using bombs to make glass goblets.

Neutron stars and pulsars are still models, based on the concept of a stellar body that is dense but does not have enough mass to form a black hole after its supernova explosion. Its insides are dying, but its skin keeps on burning, emitting particles. In the constant decay and regeneration of stellar material, there are many different types of cataclysmic events, each contributing its own grades of matter to the milk of the nebulae and galaxies from which new suns and stars are born. Scientists can predict ostensible sources, but we do not see the actual seeding.

I attended one of Thomas Gold's first lectures on pulsars in Ann Arbor, Michigan, in 1968. A local radio astronomer had invited me, and I in turn got his permission to invite the local astrologers. At the end of the talk, there was a formal line of people congratulating Gold on his discovery. The astrologers had seen what they wanted: stars giving off vast amounts of energy. They, too, congratulated Gold, to his shock and dismay; he did not even see the humor, let alone the irony, in it. Those same astrologers went on, over the next ten years, to use the computer at the University of Michigan to document the astrology of high-energy radio sources in the sky and, in a sense, to invent a radio astrology.[3]

The discovery of the first quasar preceded the discovery of the first pulsar by seven years. It was noted first as a very strong radio source, but there was no visible object associated with it. It could not be identified with any star or galaxy. The area of the emission was pinpointed during an experiment with lunar occultation of the radio source. A ninety-minute exposure of the suspicious area of the sky was taken with a five-meter reflector at the Mount Palomar observatory. What showed up was 3C 48, a bluish star accompanied by an elongated speck of material pointing back at roughly the 2:00 region of a clock. It was an ordinary dim star with a number assigned to it in the Cambridge catalogue. It had been photographed thousands of times since 1886, and, though its brightness had changed radically over that time, this variation had not been noticed. Faint stars are common enough in the unmagnified sky. In the telescopically enlarged sky, there are far too many for all of them to be monitored.

Right from the beginning, 3C 48 caused problems. None of the normal spectral lines for a star appeared; yet, it was thought of as a star. For one, galaxies, made up of hundreds of billions of different light sources, do not vary radically in brightness. Seyfert galaxies sometimes resemble stars because their centers are so much brighter than their arms and they have a slight variability, but they are not nearly so bright as quasars. When more of these strange objects were identified, they were found not to be stars in the conventional sense. They did not rotate with the Galaxy, so they lay outside it, and they had enormous red shifts, indicating that they were moving away from us at very high percentages of the speed of light. There are no objects known or imaginable among the stars and galaxies that enable us to solve all the problems of quasi-stellar sources.

Later explorations of 3C 273 from Australia showed that the radio noise from the quasar has two components, one from the star itself, stronger and fairly typical of other radio sources, and the other from the wisp beyond it, which was absolutely atypical. The wisp was actually moving directly away from the star; it was a jet shooting out of the star. This has become the characteristic image of the quasar: an irregular star accompanied by a jet.

The earliest spectra taken of quasars were fuzzy and inconclusive. Later ones showed the unusually high red shift. The first rough estimated distance from us was between one and two billion light-years and rapidly increasing. Later examination of quasar spectrum lines increased this to between three and ten billion light-years; 3C 286, for instance, was receding at 55 percent of the speed of light. This means that we are seeing these objects as they were close to the beginning of the universe. They are the Titans, or because of their asymmetry, the Cyclopses, vast personages left over from an earlier cosmology before the modern world, i.e., before the present universe as we know it.

We should be forewarned when the letter Q appears. In languages that come from Latin, Q is famous for trouble. As we enter a fundamental mystery, Q appears. Quarks and quasars may have other excuses, but the Q knows better. If it is not chosen consciously, then unconscious fantasies govern its appearance.

Whether apocryphally or not, the Q is said to come from the apple, from whose shape it was fashioned—the apple, called quert in many of the old languages, which Adam and Eve ate to get to the bottom of things at the beginning of mythical space-time. Look at our inheritance of Q's from Latin:

Quis: Who? Quid: What? Quantum: How Great? Quinam: Which? Quando: When? Quam: How? Quanam: By What Way?

Quia: Why? Quoties: How Often? Quot: How Many? Quotus: Which in Number? Quorsum: To What Place? Qualis: What Kind Of? Qua: Where? Quin: Why Not?

When we say quasar, i.e., quasi-stellar object, we are invoking the root: Where if? What supposing that?

Not only do our written letters reveal us, but our spoken sounds do too in a whole other way. If the letters are archetypes, the sounds are creatures, which are archetypes too. "Who?" is semantically simple. But try chanting it with normal rhythmic breath from deep in the throat and chest and the belly where it originates. Each breath will change it until a being you barely know is asking the real question you cannot answer. It may even be "Ha." Sound changes into a thrust out of the center of being, as if an embryonic self could speak through its whorls.

There are sounds and lights coming out of the belly of the cosmos. The models are only the products of high-paid researchers scanning the perceptible veil. What's out there is unknown and will remain unknown. Just because we do not have access to radio telescopes and not all of us are mathematicians does not mean we do not hear them.

The relationship between music and the night sky is an ancient one. The stars, in their silence in the vacuum of space, are also an eternal cone of sound—sound first postulated in the Pythagorean number systems and orchestrated by Kepler in the music of the spheres. This same sound recurs in the system of the Russian mystic scientist Gurdjieff: the deep octaves carry something prior to matter through the dimensions of creation into this present realm of star-suns that sit receiving them like haystacks in a field, changing them as "sunflowers" work an octave down through photosynthesis, deriving matter from the progression. The music of the spheres is a figure for the harmonic and orderly universe as late as the dawn of twentieth-century astronomy. The music of Bach and Mozart and Haydn is starry in the Kepler-Newton tradition, and even Chinese classical music suggests a highly ordered ethereal realm. But then radio astronomers began "hearing" this light and radiation, the discordant noises from the bellies of dying galaxies and stars. The modern cosmos of quasars and pulsars is also the primeval cosmos in its birth and death throes. It is the music of the primitive Earth: African drums, Balinese Ketchak, Australian Aborigine emu chanting, and the mantras of the Two-Horned Priests of the Hopi behind the kachina dancers. Jazz, now, as a modernization of folk forms, is the stars.

Human creation must somehow reflect the deep cosmic sky. The artist is a "radio telescope" on a cellular level. He cannot see or hear star birth and star death and the passage of materials across dimensions, but he is the creature in whose senses these patterns are recorded and ordered, and he is the inner mesh of the stellar material of which distant atoms and suns are also made. Cubist designs show one aspect of atomicity; impressionistic landscapes show another. Abstract expressionism has stellar coordinates; Joan Miró's creatures are not science fiction, they are aspects of our own incarnation as we peel back toward unconsciousness and molecularity and toward the origin of thought. Dancers drop their weight suddenly and fall, then scoot across the floor. An arm extends one way, a leg another. One dancer carries another asymmetrically. Why? Is it simply decorative aesthetics, or do both the dancers and the audience reach out to the limits of gravity and anatomy? Where these meet, what exists?

As a jazz band plays, atoms and electrons seem to fly from their primordial sequences of notes. Centers emerge; then they disappear. Saxophone and keyboard grind out sound; we hear the violent atonal birth of stars. We hear the archetypal tune trying to break into the present chaos of matter. The drums carry bursts of protons into energy, and the bass imposes the weight of gravitational fields across the night black. Wrote the poet James Bogan, in his rhapsody for musician McCoy Tyner:

> Neptune's moon
> red Aldebaran
> far Hercules
> drawn now
> into our range
> the sufferings of our Sister
> Galaxy Andromeda
> felt by spiraling correspondence.[4]

Quasar theorists have imagined collisions at the fringes of space between antimatter galaxies and galaxies of normal matter. They have talked of black holes squeezing material out of the universe which then shoots back in at the distance of quasars. They have mentioned leaks from a universe further in the future than ours, a future universe slipping back over the time barrier. They have proposed collisions of huge groups of giant stars or multiple supernovas. They have imagined that the quasars are the residue of black holes or vast amounts of matter condensing into a black hole. Perhaps they are even raw chunks of dense matter still reeling out of the explosion at the beginning of the universe (if there was such an explosion or beginning). Perhaps they are remnants of a past universe never included in the Big Bang because they escaped too far into space or created a new dimension of space and time.

Black holes are the most extreme example of theoretical objects. They are mathematical predictions of what might happen if matter were squeezed to the point where its intrinsic structure collapsed to infinite density. As the gravitational field becomes stronger and stronger, all the mass of an object, no matter how big it was originally (i.e., it can be as big as the whole universe) is reduced to a minute speck. Since the effects of relativity increase with density, the curvature of space would fold in upon itself, with infinite red shift. The object would be so dense that several billion tons or more could fit inside an object less than the size of a pinhead. The black hole would continue to have the mass of its ingredients, but the actual matter would be crushed. Hence, some stars upon burning out may go on collapsing indefinitely. The waves of light, bent and elongated by gravity, would become infinite, so that no visual information about the events inside the black hole could escape. In fact, a black hole leaves behind only its gravity. Rays would fall back even as water from a geyser returns to the ground. In relation to this star, we would be nowhere at all.

This hypothesis comes directly from Einsteinian mathematics and was originally proposed by Karl Schwarzschild, a German astronomer, in 1915. It was meant to be a theory only and had come about by considering possibilities using supernuclear densities and large gravitational fields.

Einstein and Nathan Rosen had proposed, in 1935, that points of infinitesimally small size such as atomic particles might be viewed as singularities within which density could become infinite. A total singularity would raise immense difficulties, so they proposed that the gravity-influenced curvature of space could become so warped that it would bend into a whole other plane of space-time before actually entering the impossible singularity. This is the famous brook that comes bubbling up in another universe, or in the supposed fourth dimension.

Einstein and Rosen had been talking about the quantum effects of particles in the subatomic realm. They were not dealing with massive crushed stars. By the psychedelic sixties, the idea of a bridge between different regions of time-space had become a chic ornament for astrophysicists, science fiction writers, and popular metaphysicians of science.

Black holes, with closed event horizons, light sucked back, wormholes to other universes, and bending of space and time, are curious mixtures of the observable physical effects in the realm of stars and the consequences of applying mathematics to topography. William H. Press of the California Institute of Technology proposed that if through some asymmetry or deformation the event horizon of a singularity broke open, then the laws governing nature and its phenomena would break down completely and utterly. Anything could come out of a black hole somewhere out in the universe—even, said Press, items ranging "from television sets to busts of Abraham Lincoln."[5] It is hard to know whether science fiction got ahold of this before science proposed it or whether it was borrowed from science or developed simultaneously. Clearly, that bust of Abraham Lincoln ended up on *Star Trek,* along with the possibility of riding black holes into other dimensions of reality. In fact, it became a companion notion to the one that mind is all-powerful and can dominate and change anything that matter presents to it. Yaqui shamanism and black holes became equivalent paths to another reality. But this is a simplification and a very optimistic reading of our lot. Black holes are also truly black, and they have darkened our philosophy more than brightened it. What has happened is that we have seen a destructive capacity that goes beyond anything imaginable, so we have begun to hope that it is possible to transcend destruction in ourselves. We seem to stand a far greater chance of acting out our destructive potential and blasting right through it than of retreating from it. Black hole journeys suggest such transcendence. Once we have trashed this universe—if we trash it absolutely to the bone—we will be blown into another universe. It would be foolhardy to trust this, though, and expect that, as at the end of *Dr. Strangelove,* the music accompanying the atomic bombs will be: "We'll meet again, don't know where, don't know when."[6]

Black holes need not be created by collapsing stars; according to the British astronomer Stephen Hawking, minute ones could have been formed in abundance in the Big Bang that led to the universe itself. The meteorite that hit Siberia in 1908, if not a comet exploding in the atmosphere, could have been a black hole that continued right through the Earth. The entire Solar System could be following the Sun around a black hole, or several very tiny black holes could be orbiting the Sun at great distances like planets. These would have to be the variety of "mini-black hole" formed in the Big Bang, for anything with more mass would have an appreciable gravitational effect on the bodies in the Solar System. Most of these "mini-black holes" have supposedly evaporated by now (if they existed in the first place). It has also been suggested that the universe itself is a black hole, exploded from a singularity. Or perhaps the material for the universe has rushed in from black holes in other universes. Quasars, correspondingly, are possible faucets or white holes at the end of passages linking different orders of space-time. Some astronomers have suggested that one kind of black hole with an ergosphere could be captured and used for energy. Waste materials could be discarded into it, and the energy released by the addition of mass could be harnessed in its acceleration out of the hole. One of the possible technologies of the future is based on a dynamic network using the recoil from captured "mini-black holes." Charles Misner, Kip Thorne, and John Wheeler described, perhaps fancifully, a black hole contained within a sphere upon which a great city was built, with gravity from the hole firmly supporting the city.

Hawking also did much of the work on the escape of particles from black holes and their destruction of information. During this time, he was confined to a wheelchair with a nerve and muscle disease, and it is almost as though the paralyzing complexity of the system arises from the depths of his own mandala, his sense of an originary force engulfing him and information trapped at the surface—beyond thought and feeling—from the beginning of time. This is not to diminish his work. In fact, it is to honor his courage to stay in touch with a universe passing through him in a dark phase and to report so accurately through the entanglement.

Scientists do not invent the probabilistic location of electrons or put tons of materials in a volume the size of a thimble because they find these things in the universe, and they also do not do it from sheer creative imagination. These things arise from a repeated inability to express physical phenomena in conventional mathematical or experiential terms. The inability arises not from a lack of instrumentation or a primitive technology; it is the consequence of the entire tradition of Western logic and science.

Contemporary physicists and astronomers are not unlike the Ptolemaics who struggled to find enough epicycles to save the appearances without abandoning the circle, except in this case it is the whole of Western logic they are trying to save, and at a time when the future of industrial society rests on the application of that logic. When Ptolemy "saved the appearances" of the sky in his day, he was trying to save the world of meaning that had developed under that sky. Subatomic particles, black holes, antimatter, pulsars, quasars, and the expanding universe are mythical representations of the present meaning of physical things. When we admit that we cannot know these things as they are but must make models of how they might be, we have moved back again into a universe of ideal representations of unknown things.

14

Language, Mind, and Astrophysics

W<small>E EXIST</small> in a confusing time in which ambitious things are proposed and scientists and philosophers make grand syncretisms of things in mind and nature. We pretend that we are up against the borders of reality itself, but these might be different borders, within thought and within language, that merely seem like the borders of the whole. When geometry had problems with curved space, we extended into non-Euclidean geometry. Now we are learning, as Kepler did, that no geometry resolves all the issues. Nor any mathematics.

Things exist for ontogenetic and epistemological reasons as surely as for cosmological ones. The new physics is, in many ways, primarily an inquiry into the origins of Western thought. On the surface, it uses the tools of measurement in the most rigorous manner to make an objective model of the universe, methodically correcting itself when new evidence is found. But still, that model gradually incorporates the contradictions within any attempt to objectify, and scientists are unwillingly included in their own equations. We end up with two overlapping systems: one of them is a cosmology based on the ostensible properties of matter and energy that essentially ignores the disruptive role of the observer and model-maker (this includes the study of stars, atoms, light, gravity, electricity, radiation, etc.); the other is the joint epistemology of the observer and observed.

There is no way to describe reality without acknowledging the participation of human intelligence and ethnocentric categories in the description. Gravity, time, space, and even stars are

215

not absolutes; they are the images that man has from within of a vast unknown creation. Different kinds of beings make a totally different universe, even if they share this one with us. If we were stones of the Moon, it would not be the Moon and we would not be stones. The history of language alone proves that. There is a concrete reality, no doubt, but it is always in flux, and continuously interacts with categories of thought, language, and belief, to generate the universe of any one people or system.

"We have agreed," said John Wheeler in a symposium at Cornell University on the nature of time, "that the world is built according to certain rules. We cannot answer the question why the rules are just as they are, but that they come from our experience we could not deny. We are faced with the problem of man in the small and the universe in the large. The two are not completely disconnected from each other, because for life to exist with its entropy-decreasing biological mechanism, there must exist temperature difference. We could not exist for long without the sun. So from that point of view, man is the tail that is wagged by the rest of the universe. But, from another point of view, the universe is the tail that is wagged by man; when the man observes, he creates a cut between himself and what he sees around him, and this cut is governed by himself."[1]

Man is what balances the rest of the universe and its gargantuan collection of matter. He is the specific counterpart to the stars.

R. Buckminster Fuller explains this insight:

I found myself in 1951 having to write in a book, which I was about to publish, that the mind of man seemed to be the most advanced phase of antientropy witnessable in universe. And if there is an expanding universe there logically is a contracting universe. Possibly man's mind and his generalizations, which weigh nothing, operate at the most exquisite state of universe contraction. Metaphysics balances physics. The physical portion of universe expands entropically. The metaphysical contracts antientropically.[2]

In his Copenhagen interpretation of quantum theory, Werner Heisenberg reminds us that the way in which classical physics views the universe is the inheritance of both our constructions of nature and reality going back through Greek times to the dawn of man and our ongoing phenomenological interaction with reality. Physics seeks to free itself of bias, but that is impossible. Without bias it would have no history and no perceptual basis in the world. Language itself is prejudiced by clandestine syntactic structures. It is not a neutral tool. It creates reality. The complex structures of nouns, verbs, conjunctions, tenses, and moods, and their equivalents in other languages, compel us into views of motion, time, and relationship that are unique to their own systems. Mathematics may be pure, but it is hardly divorced from the linguistic patterns of the mathematicians.

The linguist Benjamin Lee Whorf gives an interesting case of a non-Western syntactic division of the universe in his discussion during the 1940s and 1950s of Hopi grammatical categories. Hopi verbs, for instance, have many "aspects" revealing the universe implicitly in a state of motion and unfolding that we require semantic changes for. In other words, the transformation is carried unconsciously in the rules for verb change rather than in a conscious decision of meaning. One set of rules involves the punctual and segmentative aspects of verbs. The punctual aspect *ri'pi* (it gives a flash) generates the segmentative aspect *ripi'pita* (it is sparkling). This alone insures that no native speaker of Hopi has ever seen the same night sky as a speaker of English or French. The differences may have been exaggerated by the romanticists who used Whorf in the 1960s, but minute differences make enormous differences in the construction of a science, as Kepler, Newton, and Einstein knew. Whorf offers other examples of punctual and segmentative aspects: *pa'ci* (it is notched) versus *paci'cita* (it is serrated); and *ha'ri* (it is bent in a rounded angle) versus *hari'rita* (it lies in a meandering line, making successive rounded angles).[3] Some noteworthy pre-Whorfian examples can be found in an obscure dictionary at the back of Alexander Stephen's *Hopi Journal* of 1892: *ta'pa* (it gives a snap) versus *tapa'pata* (it is snapping); or *re'ke* (it makes a grating or scratching noise called by the Hopi "rek!") versus *reke'keta* (it goes rek-rek-rek!).[4]

Whorf summarizes the implications:

> Language first of all is a classification and arrangement of
> the stream of sensory experience which results in a certain
> world-order, a certain segment of the world that is easily
> expressible by the type of symbolic means that language
> employs. In other words, language does in a cruder but also
> in a broader and more versatile way the same thing that
> science does. . . . Hopi language maps out a certain terrain
> of what might be called primitive physics.[5]

It is important to remember that it is language which does
this *prior* to any conscious attitude about what constitutes nature
or the meaning of natural phenomena.

In the first book of his science fiction trilogy, *Out of the Silent
Planet*, C. S. Lewis describes the confusion of the character Ransom when he lands on Mars as a kidnap victim. Because he has
no language for the phenomena he sees and cannot separate the
foreground from the background, he does not know what anything is or even how far away or close to him it is. He sees a
purple mass and takes it at first for a heather-colored mountain.
It could also be a nearby animal or house. There is a rose-colored
cloud that he finds exquisite in tint and shape; it is like a red
cauliflower or a bowl of red soapsuds which might be above him
and beyond some unintelligible jagged upright shapes. After
looking at the "cloud," he turns back to the "mountain" and is
startled to see it swaying softly on tall thin stalks like an underwater jungle in the air.[6] This is science fiction Mars, but it helps
us to imagine the Hopis first entering Arizona and seeing in the
distance sand blowing over mesas on which they were to make
their millennial homes; migrating Apaches coming from high
ground onto their first herd of buffalo; Tlingits pushing down
the Pacific Coast during that "first misty spring" after the Ice
Age; or Bell Beaker peoples of ancient Europe reaching the vast
Atlantic, seeing it across the coastal plains of Portugal. We might
also recall the disorientation of our first sight of the infrared Sun
or the flow and movement inside a cell. Syntax reflects both
prior syntax and new reality. In imagining the extraterrestrial
now, we are expressing a simultaneous wish to encounter the
origins and meanings of our own structures of thought.

"The Hopi," writes Whorf, "actually have a language better equipped to deal with vibratile phenomena [like waves, vibrations, and chemical processes] than our latest scientific technology." The Hopi verb forms oblige "the Hopi to notice and observe vibratory phenomena, and furthermore . . . to find names for and classify such phenomena. . . ."[7]

> In [the] Hopi view [Whorf continues], time disappears and space is altered, so that it is no longer the homogeneous and instantaneous timeless space of our supposed intuition or of classical Newtonian mechanics. At the same time, new concepts and abstractions flow into the picture, taking up the task of describing the universe without reference to such time or space—abstractions for which our language lacks adequate terms. . . .
>
> The metaphysics underlying our own language, thinking, and modern culture . . . imposes upon the universe two grand COSMIC FORMS, space and time; static three-dimensional infinite space, and kinetic one-dimensional uniformly and perpetually flowing time. . . .
>
> The Hopi metaphysics . . . imposes upon the universe two grand cosmic forms, which as a first approximation in terminology we may call MANIFESTED and MANIFESTING (or, UNMANIFEST) or, again, OBJECTIVE and SUBJECTIVE. The objective or manifested comprises all that is or has been accessible to the senses, the historical physical universe, in fact, with no attempt to distinguish between present and past, but excluding everything that we call future. The subjective or manifesting comprises all that we call future, BUT NOT MERELY THIS; it includes equally and indistinguishably all that we call mental—everything that appears or exists in the mind, or, as the Hopi would prefer to say, in the HEART, not only the heart of man, but the heart of animals, plants, and things, and behind and within all the forms and appearances of nature in the heart of nature, and . . . in the very heart of the Cosmos, itself.[8]

What if the whole of classical physics had been developed by speakers of the Hopi language? Would they not have seen everything in manifestation differently from the beginning, and thus come to the dilemmas of subatomic particles, quantum relationships, and quasars on an entirely unique basis, or not at all? Given a billion years each, the Hopis, hypothetically, might reach Andromeda before the American Space Program (though the Americans would beat them to the planets and even perhaps to a few close stars), because space in the universe is the same as time, and the Hopi space-time verbs could eventually create a vehicular gestalt that would make all times equal and simultaneous in the universe, hence allowing an individual to choose his position in the universe. In other words, there are certain distances that man cannot travel unless he is unencumbered by phenomena and mass as we know them.

This is, of course, a fanciful and impossible comparison. Our attempt to imagine an alternative Hopi physics is also an attempt to disentangle ourselves from the dilemma of our own physics and American Indian linguistic theory, as well as from the moral dilemma of our time with which these are synchronous. The fact that Hopi verb metaphysics lie "hidden" behind tiny farming communities on Arizona mesas, in devotion to corn maidens, dancing kachina gods, multicolored prayersticks and rattles, and sand-painting rainclouds, connects our cosmic projection to our ecological idealization. We cannot help feeling that what is more complex metaphysically is also simpler and more balanced ecologically, which means that the powers we leave to unknown supernatural entities and extraterrestrials are those that we have lost ourselves. The visitations of Hopi priests and Martian wizards are simultaneous in Western culture: they lie in kind with the search for the lost universe. In that sense, we have already been to many other planets without ever leaving our own.

The French anthropologist Claude Lévi-Strauss carries this hypothesis beyond language to primitive systems of ethnoscience and totemic classification. These, he points out, are at least as complex as any mathematics or physics we ourselves derive. Their inferiority to them is based only on lack of simple data, usually about microstructure and infrastructure, knowledge we have gained only gradually through use of scientific instruments. Native cosmology understands the connection, coherence, and transformation by which the natural world is manifested, but it does not usually distinguish between complex information clusters and physically deterministic ones. The principles of interpretation are absolutely in accord with the nature of reality, and they are so potentially useful to us because they reveal aspects and features of things unknown to us forever. It is no wonder that we should intuit some latent relationship between the mystery of quantum physics and the mystery of totemism. Our images of things among the stars and within the atom—black holes, ghost particles, etc.—themselves generate ceremonies and symbols, anthropological and linguistic shapes; and these come to resemble the totemic categories of non-Western thought as they emerge from exotic languages and ethnic codes and attach themselves to the simplest and most innocent phenomena: insects, plants, animals, clouds, constellations, the Northern Lights. This is why ethnobotanies and myth cycles are implicitly astronomical and cosmic.

The meaning of any one of these systems is unique, and though they all relate to some core reality in nature, they cannot be translated into one another; they share few concrete features. For instance, in Osage Indian cosmology, animate and inanimate things are divided into three categories: the sky, water, and dry land. The sky includes the sun, the stars, cranes, other heavenly bodies, night, the Pleiades, and has a significant relation to turtles in some rites. The eagle, on the other hand, unlike the crane, is a dry-land being, along with the porcupine, the black bear, and the deer. Lévi-Strauss explains:

> The position of the eagle would be incomprehensible were it not known that in Osage thought eagles are associated with lightning, lightning with fire, fire with coal and coal with the earth. . . . The turtle with a serrated tail, an animal of no practical use, is often involved in rites. The reason for its importance could not be understood without the further knowledge that the number thirteen has a mystic value for the Osage. The rising sun emits thirteen rays, which are divided into a group of six and a group of seven corresponding respectively to right and left, land and sky, summer and winter. The tail of this species of turtle is said to have sometimes six and sometimes seven serratures. Its chest therefore represents the vault of the sky and the grey line across it the Milky Way.[9]

Stellar affinities are generated from the most ancient and thus the most layered aspects of the system. In *From Honey to Ashes,* Lévi-Strauss gives a sidereal transformation from South American Indian mythology:

> Star is an opossum, a forest animal in the first place in its food-supplying capacity and then a savannah animal in its capacity as a polluted and polluting creature, which brings death to men, after bringing them life through revealing cultivated plants to them. . . . From the astronomical point of view, the opossum shows an affinity with the Pleiades since, according to a Rio Negro myth, the opossum and chameleon chose the day of the first rising of the Pleiades to cauterize their eyes with pimentos and to expose themselves to the beneficent action of the sun. . . .
> . . . Just as the real opossum, a good wet-nurse, is congruous with bees' honey, so the figurative opossum, who is a bad nursing mother, is congruous with the wasp, whose honey is sour, if not poisonous.[10]

Through further mutual oppositions, involving the origin of honey, bees' wax (the dry, nonperishable part of the nest), and pineapples and plums (which mark transitions between dry and rainy seasons), we come to a transformation in which the opossum becomes a good wet nurse with an udder producing milk as sweet as honey, but with a desire for honey that is so great that it sticks its tongue into the tortoise's anus, which leads to a new set of relationships involved with the origin of the stars, fire in cooking, and disease.

Partially resolved pairs which are simultaneously natural and emblematic parallel the forever unmade cosmology of the universe and space and time. The same pairs map the different tribes and civilizations of men and women as they have spread and been transformed through the jungles and pampas of South America. They are like the stars of the expanding cosmos. The messages and meanings of their myths, which were first distorted by unconscious process and the natural discontinuities in the relationships they sought to express unconsciously, are further distorted by the physical disjunction between groups and the disjunction of any one version of a tale from the many historical versions lying behind it. All of this is inverted through different languages, environments, and interactions between historical groups bearing versions of prehistoric codes. And we have still not begun to touch the real layering and topological displacement. The Indians come to us out of something that looks like darkness, since we cannot see into it by seeing them in daylight; they become the night sky, or their artifacts and customs and tales do, as ours do to them in a different way. We must not shy from the relationship of these intricate patterns to the astrophysics of the modern cosmos, for they are part of the night sky in the same way that the Pleiades and honey are linked through Opossum. Constellations and language patterns are assembled within history, and it is through these structures, arbitrary as they are, that things as remote as other galaxies and quasars begin to reach us from the night sky. We have no choice in the matter: it is one of the natural initiations of the Western world, as William Blake knew even in his time. It laid the basis for the cosmic vision of the 1960s, with its galaxies and lotus plants, its gods and goddesses and naked torsos, and rock music and interior plant wisdom. Inside us we explore the divine, and always have. A tragedy of our culture is that this initiation comes with so little guidance and in isolation; our sages who prophesy it flee its raw presence, and it is often squandered in pop capitalism and cosmic fads which lose their archetypal connection, or else it is pumped for a final confirmation that it cannot give: hallucinogenic drugs lead neither to the stars nor the archetypes that sustain the sky, though trained shamans and priests do go on stellar and astral journeys with their aid. The combination of pop capitalism and drug culture leads also to heroin and war, and this is another cosmic function.

Yet, the sixties vision still contains the possibility of guidance from our disembodied and nonpersonal intelligence, as if some collective Western magus were trying to reach us and put us in touch with the joy and wonder that this planet has earned by the courage of incarnation. We can also dance with the stars ceremonially and chant their whale-songs. We can see the way in which we are all stars. It is a terrifying theophany of the cosmos, but it is far less alienating than the Big Bang. Its na-

kedness and mortality are our nakedness and mortality, and
those who experience it fully, like Hopi and Osage priests, never
return to the old universe.

Our age will not proclaim the great synthesis of all forms of
knowledge; it will barely survive its own paradoxes at best. Un-
avoidably, we must find parallels for the stars and matter in abstract mathematics, topology, Oriental religion, dreams, and parapsychology, for these are terrestrial things, and as we approach
the night sky, we also approach the boundaries of thought and
language, where celestial and terrestrial converge like non-Euclidean parallel lines. Let us not think, though, that by proclaiming a "tao of physics," we can unmask the underlying unity. We
cannot evade the riddle by pretending to solve it, or by pretending that it solves itself collectively and unconsciously across
the Indo-European and East-West gulfs.

We have come to see (like Sir James Jeans) that the universe
looks more like a great idea than a great machine, that our description of it resembles thoughts more than unintelligent matter. We no longer mean the thought of a specific deity or an
angelic energy within creation, as Kepler and Newton did; we
mean that something like intelligence is present in the universe
as a whole, or perhaps that we sense the progenitor of our own
intelligence in space and matter at large—that thoughts, like the
ones we have, shaped the universe. But how and why did it come
to this arrangement? Were we present at the beginning or created solely through the extenuating properties of matter? "The
atoms and molecules that make up the pages of this book are
also, within their own level, aware," Seth said through his medium Jane Roberts.[11] Consciousness precedes matter and creates it. No wonder yogis legendarily materialize food out of the
"air" to feed hungry people—but not often, it is said, because
of the cosmic consequences.

Mystics of all religions have told us that mind can shape matter, that we can make whatever we need. But to do this we must
take our incarnation seriously and not play at being alive. Science fiction lets us eat our cake and have it too. We get the great
power of mind over matter not through personal rigor and train-

ing but as the result of a collective exterior adventure or a technological invention. Parapsychology has shown us the possible rudiments of mind shaping matter in psychokinesis, telepathy, and other psi phenomena. Among those who believe in our ultimate transcendence, the battle is between the ones who would have us earn it individually only and those who propose that the human race can still be transformed *in toto.*

It is currently fashionable to show that modern physics and Eastern philosophy propose the same high-energy enigmatic yin-yang dance. The difficulty is to approach this as a fresh image with some potential meaning for us; at present it is little more than a symptom of global capitalism and New Age culture.

The universe is externalized only in relationship to the mind. And the mind is internalized only through its experience of the external forms of nature. Our breathing and perception change the universe, but phenomena burst in upon them continually and change them as well. It is no wonder that meditation and science come to describe similar events. Focus of breath and discovery of quasars are equivalent not because the systems are isomorphic but because the one universe generates the same crisis of perception.

Both modern physics and Eastern philosophy understand that we look at the night sky and inside ourselves at the non-origin. There is no justification or rationale for the present condition except what the present is. There is no answer to thought. We exist in the night sky as we exist in breath. Images pass through the sky, and we may temporarily use them to explain creation. Mental static passes through us as we try to create an ego and a personality. We may picture other galaxies and planets around other suns, or make a model for the beginning of the universe; these are like the realms of Oriental iconography. We picture gods as we picture electrons and neutron stars. We have a model for salvation and a model for creation. They are secondary images. Buddhism and astronomy are also pure imageless sciences.

Once upon a time, astronomy invented an ornate and bountiful universe, and it sought to locate us permanently in a cornucopia. Buddhism has, at times, found the same bounty in god realms and manifestations, if not in the stars. Each is now the cure for the other. Buddhism may not directly influence science, but the unconscious impact of the shape behind meditation empties the sky of hope and teaches us to expect nothing but the disruption and disturbance we perceive. This is how the East has cleaned the stars and blackened the night sky. The West has placed the economics and technology of its externalization as a yoke directly upon the Orient, so the rich god realms no longer exist. In fact, the current global epidemic of externalization has impoverished the actual lands in which internal "astronomers" traditionally dwelled. The symbolism of tantra and the mandala are compelled to integrate atoms and stars even as atoms and stars (in the West) are stripped to mere cognitive distortions and transient fashions of mind. With lamas in North America, physicists in New Delhi, and astronomers in Peking, it is possible, for the first time since the Eurasian split that formed the poles of Old World thought, to see through East and West to the star, or ikon, that shines behind both of them. Enlightenment and knowledge approach the same breath.

The balanced forces that make up the universe *are* the universe at any given moment, whether we know them or not. The Sun and planets and galaxies and so-called gravitation and electromagnetism exist and carry out their nature. We carry out our nature in imagining them. Breath separates mind from its attachment to images and forms; then both enter the eternal nullity and singularity. An externality grows larger and more complex as we stare into it; internality changes by our passage through it. There is nothing else.

Our pessimism is our projection onto the night sky and the gods when we see that they are not connected to our goals and do not take us into account. All such entities we fear and assume to be cruel. In our desire to create gods who share our values and destiny, we have created enemies who have turned back against us. There is a new sensibleness in letting the universe-that-is touch us like waves in our own silence, through our cells and through the radio telescopes. We can try to see deeper with more refined instruments, and in doing this we refine ourselves. We also see into the universe directly. We impose form on nothingness, but nothingness alone generates form. We fear the de-

struction of ourselves and everything finally, but even our awareness of being is an aberration in the placid void. We try to
perceive the concrete reality of matter, but all we experience is
the continuous alteration of energy. Clarity eludes us at both
the stars and the origin of being, but clarity also rushes upon us
as a sudden wind that cuts like ice to the root of existence.

The Western fantasy is to relieve this boredom with rocket
ships, to enter and explore an infinity of appearances. Even a
rocket ship, with or without men and women inside, and minds
inside them, has a consequence, direct and unadorned, in being
the thing it is. We are lucky in this; the object is always turned
back to within an altered field of perception. Otherwise we
would be stuck trying to force our way into a universe that might
not even exist. The certainty of the stars and matter, the appearance of a resemblance between Buddhism and astronomy,
the seeming thread of reason in this book are all bluffs and
converge in the aggregate illusions of coherence and identity.
The richness of the experience must finally stand alone for its
reality. That is the basic draw and desire of the stars.

The infinite energy that is exposed as being outside in the
universe is also inside and beneath our personalities. We recognize the cosmos by a projection of the psyche. Not only are
we atomic beings, but the sum total of all atomic fields everywhere is a larger collective unconsciousness from which we draw
limitlessly into our personalities. The illusion is that we must be
subject to the boundaries that we impose on ourselves at any
one time: material boundaries in a material time. But the stars
also give us a bigness to be big against. They give us the intimation that the consciousness within ourselves is not ordinary;
or if it is, the ordinary is cosmic and limitless.

As we try to see into our nervous systems, we have a sense
that our carnality, our incarnation in matter, shares properties
with the electrical network that we imagine in space. It is as
though a single originary idea lies near the center of the Milky
Way, where time itself is warped and the hottest and closest fires
burn so interconnectedly that everything is ramified in billions
of dimensions as soon as it exists.

The complexity of space and the complexity of mind are a single expression of the nervous system. Neutron stars and black holes describe the pressure we feel. On the surface our thoughts flit like dust motes and spit bugs, but we sense the powerful draw underneath, attaching us to anything at all. We know that we cannot concede our existence. We must work at the riddles of creation as they appear in us, and if we do not work at them, they work at us anyway, in the same way that they worked to bring us, and the idle thoughts we tag along, into being. This is why sages in the West practice astronomy. We cannot evade the gravity pulling us to the center. If we build the machines, we must proclaim their counterpart in the sky.

Vastness and complication are properties of the inner organs, not just their organic being but the entirety of space that evolves between them and within them, between them and the overall nervous system and the brain. Mind inhabits density and continuousness as breath and blood travel with it through the body. By the same rule, astral projection is the microcosmic counterpart of astronomical travel. The astral traveler perceives tremendous spaces internal to himself and enters these in exact correspondence, planet for planet and star for star, of the entire universe. It may not be the same universe as the external one, but it is the same universe as his internalized image of the external one.

We are made of our organs and our cells, and it is absurd to think that we can have images apart from them. We do not reflect them in simple literal symbols, the stars as eyes, the bloodstream as the Milky Way, etc., but we impose our collective inherited organ system upon the exterior world. The Milky Way may not be our intestines, but the profound inner experience of such a long winding passage is our basis for imagining the inside of such a spiral anywhere. Small cavities in our bodies create the infinity we imagine in space.

Charles Stein, in a discussion of alchemy, gives a methodology for intuiting the astronomical:

> Our whole going on includes realms that are beyond any possible scale of perception out of which, nonetheless, all of our possible experience is, in some sense, constituted.

Since we are also, even in the scientific view, physical beings, we have some primary intuition of that, we feel a connection. When you read about microphysics or astronomical spaces or periods of time calculated in billions of years, that produces a specific reaction in you, that is imaginary in one sense, but is on the other hand, *precisely imaginary.* The world of fantasy that is awakened in you when you think ten billion years is different in a precise way from the world of imagination that's produced in you when you think six thousand years. That has something to do with the actual physical data of the universe and our relationship to it, as any kind of real data. Subjective fantasy isn't something that has to be, in an ultimate sense, severed and separated off as a process from the process of natural investigation. The actual investigation of one's own subjective experiences in relationship to matter is of primary importance in itself because the content of the fantasies you have will be true of the physical universe as such. They are ways of revealing structures of the particular way in which our constitution exists in relationship to the rest of the world. . . . The scientific view of wanting to separate, radically, the fantasy from the data for the purpose of establishing general universal external structures, is itself a phase in a process, which has to be reunited.[12]

To Wilhelm Reich, the spiral shapes of the galaxies revealed a series of cosmic superimpositions in which the collectivity of the starfields surged with sexual energy (orgone) and attempted to unite and breed fresh stars. In looking through telescopes, Reich said, man departs from his inherent humanity and participates vicariously in a cosmic harmony he would express if he were free to carry out his natural human functions. The spasms of sexual intercourse are not only prefigured in the rhythm of galaxy formation; these two events occur at opposite ends of the scale of creation *simultaneously* as aspects of the same pulse. As the galaxies shoot out stars, creatures shoot out their kind. As the galaxies long to superimpose and connect their orgone streams, men and women long to love and connect their orgone streams and either heal by their natural medicine or give birth to new men and women. The streams of energy at large form the universe, the streams within generate cells and thoughts. Man experiences in his mind and in his organs the desire to procreate that is the original desire of the universe to spread and differentiate. The buildup of sexual excitation prior to release is itself the universe surging to continue, to spurt out new seeds and suffuse itself with its own elixir.

Reich came to see hurricanes, galaxies, the northern lights, cell growth, jellyfish, worms, and orgasm as the same function. The spiral is a spiral of excitation, imposition, and fulfillment on any scale. Even the rings of Saturn are an aspect of it. The blue sky is not light diffraction alone but the color of atmospheric orgone descending on the Earth. Sucked into the yellow resin of bion water from the Sun, it becomes green, as in plants. But plants lose their orgone to the atmosphere in the winter and turn yellow or brown.[13]

In *The Rainbow*, D. H. Lawrence has Ursula emerge from lovemaking under a magnificent night sky to find the magnificence gone: "Gradually she realized that the night was common and ordinary, that the great, blistering, transcendent night did not really exist."[14]

She had found it inside herself, so the stars no longer represented it. She had moved to the center of creation without them.

When the night sky appears in dreams, the infinite universe is projected through the imagination of infinite space in the collective unconscious density of the cells. Dreaming settles deeply into our own tissue as stargazing presses out into the tissue of the universe, and both enactments merge into a vision.

Sometimes the dream sky is blacker than night; a heavy darkness permeates even the air. We find that the lake shore is just as black as the forest we have emerged from. The stray stars in the sky seem innocent enough, but at any moment a brilliant and intelligent set of constellations will burn their way through the ignorance and beam down on us. We must be ready, or escape. Flying saucers are looking for us; they will become so big, as they approach, they will be unbearable. They will take us into the arcane system of planets and suns. But are we ready?

No, we are not. Not ready as Moses was for the burning bush. We must close our eyes to the darkness, stumble, and awake. And the question remains: Was this the astral universe in which our presence was so lucid and terrifying? Was it another universe whose name and place we do not know? Is that sky a blowup of our cellular tissue, fashioned by symbolism into night? Or is it some alien and primordial sky retained as a memory in the DNA of our species?

Star dreams are rare, and usually mythic. A notable one is the poet Robert Duncan's dream of 24 April 1963:

> All the stars of the cosmos had come forth from the remotest regions into the visible. At first I was struck by the brilliance of Orion, but as I looked the field was crowded with stars, dense cells of images and then almost animal constellations of the night sky. It was as if we saw the whole over-populated species of Man and in that congregation of the living and dead, the visible and invisible members of the whole, we began to make patterns of man, animal entities whose cells were living souls.
>
> "We see these skies here," the Poetess said, "because we are very close to the destruction of the world."[15]

The poet has left ordinary space and time. He is in a place where more than the naked-eye constellations are visible. This could be because he is seeing the Earth's skies from all of history, hence the same stars in their many appearances from the precession of the equinoxes, or because he is seeing through night and through the limits of the speed of light into centers of creation extinguished from our sensory field.

These "animal entities whose cells were living souls" must, on one level, be the constellations of the sky, whose cells are suns and planets. If we move from the Earth, and then from this Solar System, to other locations in the universe, the Sun becomes a member of our most familiar sky-beings: Cassiopeia, Ursa Major the Great Bear, Aquila the Eagle, Cetus the Whale. These forms, encoded as animals and mythological beings, are so large that they include us at the same time that we lie outside of them. If we go far enough to lose them, they break apart only gradually, and in the process they give birth to other figures in other skies. The poet's vision seems to encompass this transformation. In his intuition of astral and angelic and cellular intelligence, he acknowledges, even creates, the zodiacs and star temples of other planets, of other galaxies. He is not forcing it into being from knowledge, the way a science fiction plot-writer must. It comes to him, literally, from the center of the whirlpool, as he allows himself to fall into it, or as his unconscious becomes the petals of it, and he leaves his social identity and travels in parts that men do not commonly know. The feeling is that mythological entities, like the Titans themselves, must go on, long after these things are obliterated from the chronological Earth, and long after all our seeming obsessions have broken us or been broken in the catacombs of this world's interior.

Far from the night sky itself the stars return, as organs of the body, god aspects, totem masks, ikons, archetypes, cells, gaps in thought and language, and visitants to dream skies. This is the true texture of starriness—blood and bark as well as cold fire and remote constellations. Where we stand, the stars can be mute figures who approach us with powers of divination and signs, or they can be cosmological furnaces.

Then there is my own dream of November 1975.[16] I am filming the water pouring into Peacham Pond (Vermont). Suddenly the image through the movie camera lens becomes wild fat bugs which burst into orange, yellow, and red splotches; these become venous and luminous. They seem to be dancing to a music, but I cannot hear it. Now I see an aged forest. A river of stars flows through it. There are giant trees, bared on black humus; they hang over the edge of something, damp and rooty and quilled.

A loudspeaker mentions a war report from far away, perhaps the Holy Land. Unexpectedly there are jets in the sky, jets of varying shape and density. They approach not by engines but as our world is drawn to them. They are the work of artisans far beyond us: single jets with flares and double dumbbells. One group of seven or eight approach, growing bristly and grainy, and I understand that this is called the Pleiades fleet. As close as their bodies seem to be, they are stretched and fuzzy in the way that enormous enlargements of faint star clusters are.

Yet they are not stars. They are jets, silver gray jets with emblems on their sides in the overcast sky. Their emblems are constellations. This image replaces and then is replaced by the earlier one; something seems to hold the two together.

The figures are irregular and amorphous to raw sight. I sense that they are regular underneath in a way I cannot understand.

I am in a deeper universe. The jets fly in clear formation out of their extradimensional airport. Their flares leap out of density and bend back through space itself. I see now that some of them are perfect circles with single leaks and others are twisted rings.

They do not bomb our land, but this says nothing about their intention or ultimate plan. They do not have to attack, for their positions are perfect and they are being drawn into history.

I think that I have filmed them at last, the arrival of the armada. Then I see that I have opened the camera by mistake in my haste to work it. Perhaps I have exposed the film. The cartridge is a pyramid, perfectly sealed, and I cannot open it to reverse the film and shoot the other side. My immediate response is to try to change things by closing the camera and shooting, pretending there is film in it. During this interlude the sky has changed. There are enormous clouds, cirrus and altocirrus, but delicately crafted and wild and sinewy in a way I have never seen before. The color of the sky is a gem blue that is almost iridescent. Far away are other clouds that stand in long bands, whipped into spirals and sucked into cones that stand above the whole planet like mountains. In their foreground are intricately etched ivory figures that look like the work of a Mesolithic craft guild. They start as miniature statuettes and then expand; they retain their shapes and become white sea mammals, hunters with harpoons, and even fur-dressed ancient Europeans, members of the same Maglemosian communes that carved the figures.

The cones are smooth and eternal, without a single shred or fray. The air does not leave a ripple in them.

I realize that I have seen into the mythological world of quasars and that it is different from the tapestry of visible stars. Something about the quasars, I realize, was presaged through all of history, and their irregular shapes, like cancers of ancient worn objects, their suggested radioactivity and violence, are not modern but a prophecy of ourselves from creations before us. Their inscrutability merges with that of the Sphinxes and the pyramids and the gigantic Eastern Island heads that sit on islands of the Pacific as if looking at something beyond us, if not at us. And still they look at us.

15

Astrology

ASTROLOGY is a millennial science; that is, it has existed from unknown origins in prehistoric times up to the present, changing its form by culture and by aeon. It is an archetypal science: we cannot say what its ultimate form is, for we know it only by the aspect it reveals at any one time. It is a mistake to stereotype astrology in the form of the daily horoscope or in any of the antique variants of it that we have from ancient, mediaeval, and Renaissance cultures. Each of these, as well as each of the contemporary philosophical and psychological astrologies, attempts to reconcile temporal and local images with the cosmic ones that lie behind them. Thus, we have innumerable astrologies, all of which share a core of thought and each of which is adapted to its particular occurrence.

In calling astrology a "science," we do not mean that it is a science in the same sense that chemistry and physics are. It is a science in the old etymological sense of "a system of knowledge." It is also a science in the mathematical sense of measuring quantities. Modern physics might take issue with the cause-and-effect postulates behind the measurements, but it could not challenge the basic algebra of chart-making and planetary relationships. Millennial sciences help give rise to the modern sciences that are often their partial namesakes. So astronomy shares something of its origin and mechanics with astrology, but it is basically a separate development, not requiring astrological thought. It is misleading, then, to think of astrology as ancient or primitive astronomy. There *was* an ancient and primitive astronomy, but it is more accurate to call it archaeo-astronomy or ethnoastronomy. There are archaeo-astrologies and ethnoastrologies which parallel and interact with their astronomical counterparts but which are also essentially part of a different system of inquiry and application. Archaeo-astronomy leads to calendar systems, the measurement of time, and astrophysics. Archaeo-astrology leads to astral astrology, Qabalistic magic, and the contemporary astrology of personality.

The most obvious other millennial and archetypal science is alchemy.[1] As an occult science, it has far less a role in the modern world primarily because it has such a large role as a physical science. Components of laboratory and elemental alchemy were taken directly into chemistry, physics, astronomy, and the industrial processes. In fact, alchemy is far more relevantly a forerunner of astrophysics than astrology is. The adaptation of physical alchemy to modern technology has legitimized the position of ancient and mediaeval alchemy as early historical chemistry and physics. However, it is exactly those elements which alchemy shares with astrology that were *not* incorporated into modern scientific thought: the vital source of the elements, the life force, the transmutability of matter, and the astral body.

Medicine and botany are millennial sciences in the same position as alchemy: their mechanical features laid the basis for their industrial counterparts, and their traditional and vital features were abandoned as primitive magical thought. Herbalism was looted for its chemistry, but its role in holistic native medicine was ignored. Healing became a training in concrete anatomy and pharmacy, and medicine broke off from shamanistic art. Yet, millennially, herbalism and healing retain their "primitive" features, and these will no doubt return in other guises in future times. Even today, certain of their aspects are recognized but are called parapsychological to distinguish the seeming laboratory effects of mind over matter, which have not been proven scientifically, from the ancient arts and rituals that used such ostensible effects to heal people, bring on rain, and tell the future. This is how millennial sciences are renamed and rediscovered. If astrology is ever adopted by a mainstream scientific community, it might not be called astrology anymore. In fact, some current attempts to redefine it call it "astro-biology." (Our other modern response to the occult is to change raw clairvoyance and spiritual practice into philosophy and therapy.)

The complex of millennial sciences is a unity in itself, including aspects of esoteric plant, animal, mineral, element, and star knowledge, with magic and healing as its "technologies." If healing has been turned into orthodox industrial medicine, magic has been abandoned entirely under the aegis of physics, or physics is the contemporary form of it. Aleister Crowley and the savants of the Golden Dawn practiced a twentieth-century version of traditional magic in which they considered the axioms of sympathetic influence the primary laws of the physico-spiritual universe, i.e., the actual universe; the particular application of these laws in physics and chemistry was said to be one set of their corollaries. To Crowley and his associates, magic was the real science, physics the transient one, although physicists had obviously made dramatic new applications of magical law.

In a holistic civilization, the millennial sciences would blend with the current technologies and, to a certain degree, with each other. The medical applications of astrology would merge entirely with herbalism and psychiatry, even as astrophysics would unite with the theories of celestial influence. The present age is a dark one in this respect, for everything is fragmented and knowledge has become a chaos of useless data. But if anything survives a dark age, the millennial sciences do. They have no allegiance to the transient forms, so they reemerge on the basis of their universal and archetypal principles. Either they are guided by the old texts or they are intuited anew. Some vitalists might decry the present order, but the millennial sciences helped bring it on by their corruption and superstition throughout the Middle Ages and the Renaissance. They allied themselves with religion and occult orthodoxy in a way that trapped humanity in useless orders of authority and fantasy. If vitalism is able to return after the aeon of mechanics and technology, it will be a far tougher and more powerful vitalism, and one that will use the lessons of physics and chemistry to reestablish a harmony of man on the Earth. The prior vitalism could not have done this.

The present nihilism of which astrophysics is king has certainly cleaned house. It may have killed a lot of priests and made the Earth virtually uninhabitable before it is through, but physical determinism and the power derived therefrom will have scraped bottom. Revolutionary gangs will not be able to lead mankind so easily back—especially if the vitalists can grow a garden again and draw energies from the cosmos.

Goethe may have intuited this when he put the torch in the hands of botany and asked it to carry the flame through the coming winter of mechanism. Kant had failed him, and himself, and had not provided the necessity of a moral order in the universe. The violent arbitrary galaxies of an amoral universe were about to invade, and the machinery of the Earth served them alone. Blake saw this too and addressed the readers of a future time, not immediately thereafter but after that, when the thing would have happened and been done. Even with his theory of light, Goethe would not have trusted physics, but botany was bound to be the first science turned back to in the search for life and the life principle in a universe darkened by machines and soot. When he spoke of the root of life, it might have seemed that Goethe had an archetypal intention. Was the Primordial Plant an image, a template (like those Plato drew) of the form of all later actual plants? No, said Goethe, the root of life is not only a philosophical and archetypal root, it is a real living plant. And he crossed the Alps into Italy to look for his Ur Plant (*Urpflanze*) in Europe's oldest botanical garden at Padua. He recognized it in the "humble" or dwarf palm (*Chaemerops humilis*). The tree is now 400 years old and encased in glass with the name "Goethe's Palm," or "the vital root of existence."[2] Botany was later to blur this classification with its own taxonomy: the palm was deemed primitive but not primordial. By the time Rudolf Steiner appeared, the spiritual-vitalist tradition was already "occult" and suspect; traditionary science had been cut off from modern science. But Goethe had kindled and passed on the flame. And it was picked up in many places, especially since the brief spiritualist revival of the 1960s and early 1970s from which embers remain—for instance, The New Alchemy Institute in Woods Hole, Massachusetts, and Prince Edward Island; the biodynamic gardens of Alan Chadwick in Santa Cruz, California; and the various homeopathic and naturopathic orders springing up in California and along the Northwest Coast. These are not symbols of revival; they are literal seeds of the Ur Plant.

Astrology stands apart from all this. It has shared in the revival, but it exists in an authentic archaic form that does not require the same rush of New Age images. It is more likely to supply New Age images, especially those of a synchronized and holistic cosmos. Esoteric astrology takes the "Aquarian" revival as a remote reflection only of a distant age yet to come—perhaps its remotest reflection into the dark ages that precede it. It was hardly enough of a tremor to register, so every succeeding tremor will be deeper and more resonant—fair warning to those who claim pretentiously that the "hippie era" is over. The "hippie era" may be over, but the Aquarian Age has yet to come; and when it does, we will not be able to tell the scientific from the occult. We may have been jarred by what happened, but that was shadow before substance, and the big medicine awaits us or our descendants. According to the esoteric tradition, it will crest over the threshold around A.D. 2376.

Astrology is obviously patient and long-standing. Its images try to coordinate large dynamic units of time, space, and personality, which is its unique posture. It is an attempt to say the impossible. It is a system for measuring the immeasurable. If it fails, it fails in the biggest task of all: to define the simultaneous meaning and relationship of life, thought, creation, and space-time. It is better to attempt such a measurement than to pretend it has no relevance at all. The more mundane uses of astrology should not be taken in any way as diminishments of its cosmic perspective.

What we think of as astrology is a system of star divination inherited by Near Eastern civilization from the older ancient world and passed on through the Greeks in Alexandrian Ptolemaic cosmology to mediaeval Europe, where it was combined with local star mythologies and general hermetic/gnostic science. Zodiacs, constellations, and forms of star divination were common throughout the ancient world. Very old systems appear at the dawn of Chinese and Egyptian civilization, and there are equivalent Mayan and Aztec star charts and cults. It is possible that some even more ancient Stone Age system underlies all of these, at least in part, and that the Old World systems share a relatively recent root (from ten to twelve thousand years ago) from which the New World systems have more substantially diverged. In Chapter 3, we discussed the connection of these astrologies to the origin of the alphabet.

Neolithic man built Stonehenge, Woodhenge, the Caracol, Monks Mound, the "akus" of Eastern Island, and various menhirs, cairns, and astronomical temples throughout the planet. The starry night was the original sacrament and government of our species. The stars were a deific reflection of terrestrial activity, for they returned in sequence, either with the seasons or according to esoteric mathematical formulas. Peoples could gradually move across Eurasia, even into the New World, floods could wipe out landmarks, ancestors could die, but these skymarks remained, changing infinitesimally.

How the gods and the planets came to be one is an impossible question. They were one almost from the beginning. The lives of the gods on Earth might seem almost human, with tales of treachery, heroism, and suspense, but their lives in the sky, i.e., their actual movements as planets, are fixed, ruthless and predictable. They pass through the houses and holy spots, setting the boundaries and conditions for all the events in our sphere of Earth, which lies inward and subordinate to their zodiac. The rest is folklore. It is clear that there are too many people and too few gods for the latter to be busy interfering in all our lives at once. There must be some other way. Mercury and Jupiter are occupied in the heavens; if they manifest as Earth-beings, they are subject to one location at a time. However, if they are formed within us, within our very personalities, then a single god may simultaneously bring his aspect of things to bear not only on many peoples' lives but on all peoples' lives and the lives of all things. In that sense, the vision of aspects of personality and destiny reflecting planetary archetypes comes from the fact that the planets appear to arise in our experience at the same moment that they pass in the heavens.

The zodiac we know and have built upon in Western culture was inherited from the Chaldeans and the more ancient Sumerian and Accadian peoples of Assyria and Babylonia. The Egyptian and Chinese systems have substantially different constellations, unique symbolisms, and idiosyncratic methodologies of divination. Although these are relevant in the widest terms, the astrological images of the West are basically Babylonian. We inherit, in some sense, their intuitions of darkness and light, the character of the signs of the zodiac (though we have changed many of them), and the twelve-stage cosmic season in which nature was manifested. The Chaldeans believed that the planets were the visible bodies of the gods. We inherit the symbols forged in that belief.

Astrology represents a synchronicity between the ancient calendars of the farming communities of the Near East and a theory of cosmic or celestial influence. From our point of view, it may look like two systems, and it may well have been two systems at various times, even originally, but in practice astrology treats the two systems as one. As long as the heavens are divine and the planets are destiny-bearing gods, the time they measure is identical to the influences they sow. The measurement of time, however, does not require a theory of celestial influence. They are linked in the Stone Age and in ancient civilization, but eventually the measurement of time becomes a secular activity. Calendars become astronomical tools quite separate from any system of astral cycles and rhythms. But astrology maintains the measurement of time as sacred, or, in present-day terms, psychic and archetypal, and it assumes time as a basic harmony in the linking of microcosm and macrocosm and in the functioning of the universe as a unity. As civilization moved out of liturgical and ceremonial space and into days, months, and years that were purely political, military, economic, and scientific, the sacred sense of time was lost. The theory of celestial influence does require the calendars and ephemerides, for they are the mathematical representation of the wholeness and interrelatedness of the cosmos. Without them the idea of celestial influence can be maintained and honored, but there is no "scientific" methodology for recording and interpreting these patterns, no way of perceiving them as specific functional rhythms and cycles rather than abstract convictions. So astrology remains the statement of the synchronous relationship of all events in the creation and the methodology of predicting and understanding fragments by their relationship to the whole. The stars, as the projective background of the creation, stand for the whole, and the zodiac, as the path followed by the gods in their establishment of harmony through motion, is the course of immediate terrestrial destiny.

Once the movements of the planets and the Sun and Moon in the zodiac are transcribed, the astrologer need no longer have reference to the actual night sky. In millennial terms, this is a severe failing of modern astrology. The present shining night does not engage the astrologer as much as his ephemeris. Yet, the original inspirations, psychic or emotional, came from viewing the sky by night. The deep understanding that made astrology a philosophical system more than a puzzle of personality types came from its daily and direct connection to the cosmos. Without that, astrologers like Copernicus and Kepler would not have discovered the location of the Sun and the orbits of the planets. Without the devotion of Herschel, Adams, Leverrier, and Lowell to the night sky, astrologers would not have the Uranian, Neptunian, and Plutonian factors that are so important in their charts today. As astrology changes with the eras, it always makes use of the new stars. The specific discoveries are unpredictable, but each of them—quasars and pulsars included—is in the universe somewhere, or in man's model of the universe, and so must be included in the dynamic chart of the whole. Astronomy has always fed images directly into astrology, and astrology has interpreted them in its own traditional terms. At the same time, astrology assumes that the stars speak to us directly— themselves at night, as symbols, and in the lives of our friends, lovers, and kin—and that we pick up such star wisdom quite apart from any knowledge of the system. Because astrology is the "science" of the whole, it is free to assume the basic unity of all events and images and their reference to the biggest field of all.

The moment in time is critical in astrology, for it is the precise measure by which the connection of events is established. Events are connected because they lie simultaneous to each other across the temporal axis of the creation. At the moment of an individual's birth, the heavens are also "born" anew; they have a unique configuration, and in that can be read the potential of that individual, the aspects of the universe he or she reflects in miniature. Although some systems argue for the direct tele-pathic or gravitational influence of the planets, this is not nec-essary. It is only necessary to find an instant in absolute time from which to locate discrete events in the cosmos. The stars—and, in particular, the planets in the zodiac—provided that for ancient man. In theory, though, the same image could be taken from the cells inside a leaf or the imprints on brain tissue. As-trology is simply a system of birth charts set against the heavens, and the symbolic meanings have been worked out through those images from the beginning. It is the only historical record we have of the application of a symbolic system to successive mo-ments in time.

Birth charts are not the only astrological instant. Conception charts can be made if the moment is known. Death charts can be cast to know what a person's death potentially takes back into the collectivity of the heavens, what the universe has "learned" from that person's life and thus will pass on to the unity of unborn that come from its eternal field. A chart can be cast for the potential of every moment, and the exact science of this is called horary astrology. Marc Edmund Jones explains:

> The universe is orderly because it holds a place for anything at all, according to the particular time and space require-ments of whatever general and specific relations are brought together in experience; that is, given a focus in an identifiable situation. Horary astrology takes the moment of an event in the ordering of the universe, which is pro-vided quite literally for all human beings by the celestial motions of the earth, and measures the relations of these heavenly movements with that horizon on the earth's sur-face which, in its turn, is established by the place of the event.[3]

Synchronicity plays an important role in any explanation of astrological influence. We no longer imagine the stars touching people with invisible rays or holding them by magnetic reins. The connection of circumstance between Earth and Heaven is fundamental and sufficient, so it becomes a connection of the deepest meaning. Carl Jung, both on his own and in collabora-tion with the physicist Wolfgang Pauli, attempted to make a model of synchronicity as a law equal to causality. Events with no other connection would be linked by the very chance or concurrence of their happening. The relationships could not be seen by us directly, except as accident or arbitrary intersection, but they could be known on an unconscious level where man is in psychosomatic identity with the universe. This is the justification of zodiac and constellation symbolism by analytical psychology. These symbols represent the collective historical recognition of the underlying unconscious process of the universe. The order and intelligibility that are visible in the night sky and the world of nature arise psychogenically as forms pass from the unconscious into images and ideas.[4] In the second book of his trilogy *Perelandra,* C. S. Lewis quotes the ancient hermetic prophecy that "there is no such thing as chance or fortune beyond the Moon." The name of the space voyager, Ransom, though it originated aeons earlier when his forgotten ancestors received it in its etymological root form, becomes the clue to his trip to Venus, his ultimate role there as a "payment that delivers." His sudden recognition of that impossible truth saves him. "Before the world was made," Lewis writes, "all these things had so stood together in eternity that the very significance of the pattern at this point lay in their coming together in just this fashion."[5] It is as though the primordial cloud in which the physical atoms were united was also a psychic nebula which has since spread to encompass time and space.

Synchronicity is more than a law. It is meant to identify that which seems impossible and yet appears to happen. Cause-and-effect is only one way that two events can influence one another. They can also be connected by "simultaneity-and-meaning." This is true of all orders of divination, including the system of the *I Ching* by which the participants draw oracular readings from a book of hexagrams by a method of casting yarrow stalks, and scapulimancy, by which they read the cracks formed in bones burned over a fire, cracks which correspond somehow to the tracks of animals in the forest. Innards, muscles, and organs are likewise read for simultaneity. And, of course, the sky. If we ask, what does astrology mean, we are really asking: what is meaning itself? Dane Rudhyar writes:

It matters not whether such symbols are dreams or mystical visions or omens or occult "signatures," or any one of the forms of life-interpretation and even divination that have been used for millennia. The point is that all life-encounters become endowed with significance. Man becomes thus Interpreter and Seer. He lives in a world of souls, in a world of significant wholes, because wholeness, or holism, operates through his consciousness. . . . When the operation becomes perfect, there is in the intuitive interpretation of the symbols of the moment the same certainty that exists in the biological instincts; a certainty which the intellect can know only in logic and pure mathematics—the certainty of a tautology; a certainty that comes from *evident identity*. . . . The perfect intuition is the result of an identification between the perceiving individual whole and the perceived whole situation.[6]

Post-Einsteinian astrology is anxious to declare that there are world-lines and time-lines that cross the universe and join its parts. If we could travel fast enough, in ships powerful enough, at close to the speed of light, we would actually be able, within our lifetimes, to reach the most distant galaxies imaginable. We are twenty-one light-years from our own Galactic center, twenty-eight light-years from another galaxy. If we built a ship that ran on interstellar particles and radiation and traveled at close to the speed of light, we could end up in cosmically remote regions that our birth in this part of the Milky Way would seem to have denied us forever; we could experience water dripping in a cave on another planet around a Sun in another galaxy. Upon returning to Earth millions of years later, we would find the constellations twisted out of shape and nothing at all on our home planet, even archaeologically, remaining from our time of birth. Yet we ourselves would survive.

This may not be possible after all, but if it is not possible, then that is so for technical reasons, and we can always imagine another technology that could accomplish it, and we can project it years into the future or to people in other galaxies who ostensibly visit us in UFOs. The point is that it is cosmologically possible. And so our imprisonment in matter is open along one subtle curve. This universe is somehow made up of present time distended and stretched out to eternity. We can break with planetary time and enter different time scales. We can survive this as biological entities, and, in fact, we do in long plane flights above the Earth's surface, where we may gain a fraction of a second in relation to other people's time.

Contemporary astrology and astro-biology also attempt to uncover a physical basis for celestial influence. For instance, the Sun, Moon, and planets could make contact with the different organs and hormonal centers of the human body, releasing fluids and setting the underlying rhythm for the combination of centers of anatomy and embryonic tissue into elements of personality.

Some astro-biological relationships are basic. The Earth is formed of the Sun's material; it is precisely the interaction of particles of solar light with plants in photosynthesis that creates all biological substance on Earth. Furthermore, the Sun holds the Earth in appropriate orbit to receive the correct amount of light and heat for our survival.

The Moon actuates not only the tides but also the liquids of the body and the brain. Since these are mainly water, they are subject to profound lunar influence. Watch the waves on the shore. Though these swell and crash with resounding display, they come from the lightest touch, the same touch that is applied within us and causes "waves" on a cellular scale. With its monthly (= "moonly") cycle, the Moon creates a series of gravitational points around which biological rhythms are organized. Removing the Moon from the sky would cause cataclysmic flooding of the Earth's lands by its oceans. Even if life could survive such a catastrophe, its subtle chemical and hormonal rhythms would be shattered. There might have been another biological clock that life could have used to organize itself, but since the Moon was there, it was the obvious choice, and it is too late now to disentangle our biology from the lunar cycle.

For instance, experimenters have found that oysters from Long Island Sound open and close themselves in Evanston, Illinois, "at the time the tide would have flooded Evanston, had the town been on the seashore—that is, when the moon passed over the local meridian."[7] The Palolo worm, of the Pacific coral reefs, responds to the Moon during October and November. In the last quarter of the Moon, the back half of the worm with its genital material rises to the surface while the rest perishes on the reef. Eggs and spermatozoa float together and mix at low tide for several days. This process is seasonal for that species of worm, and the whole sea turns color; the event is celebrated in Samoa on the sacred calendar. In Florida, eels swarm with the final quartering of the Moon. Insects, newts, worms, crabs, and seaweed have all been shown to respond to extraordinarily minute changes in gravitation, electrostatic fields, and magnetism, changes infinitesimally smaller than the louder information with which they are continuously flooded. The only explanation is that living beings become sensitive, through millennia of evolution, to the exact microrhythms they require for survival. These rhythms are wound in them embryologically and exist not in the raw physiology of even the brain but in the sensitivities of colloidal suspension. The influences are as liquid and "dissolved" as life itself.[8]

Although responses to the planets of the Solar System cannot be demonstrated experimentally in the way that patterning by the Sun and Moon can, we cannot overlook how much electrical, magnetic, and gravitational material is supplied by them, especially those that are particularly close to us (like Mars and Venus) or particularly large (like Jupiter and Saturn). Each of these bodies helps to maintain the overall equilibrium of the Solar System, and each of them gives off varying forces as it passes nearer to and further from the Earth. Jupiter cannot be seen by a bird in flight, nor can Mars be heard by a mole in its tunnel, but these planetary bodies create resonance, and that resonance makes up part of the overall environmental background in which the Earth occurs. Unquestionably, the influence upon us of Jupiter is small, and the influences of Uranus and Neptune are respectively smaller still, but they are not nil. It is not their present resonance that matters so much as the repetition, for millions of years, of the same complex pattern. This may register minutely but permanently in colloidal suspension on Earth.

———————

The zodiac itself is the systemization of a twelve-aspect sequence of transformation—from the moment in Aries when the
universe bursts into being to the absolute destruction of everything at all in Pisces, after which the cycle begins again in Aries.[9]
This describes not only the universe as a whole but any individual calendar year which begins truly in Aries (March) and ends
in Pisces (February). These aspects are also woven into every
personality, every event and nation, every conceivable aspect of
existence at every level. "Out of Pisces," writes the astrologer
Walter Sampson, "which is the limbo of decayed worlds, the
scrap-heap of former creations, that chaos of disembodied entities, dissolved, disintegrated, lost, the creative fire and shock
of Aries, burning away the dross, fusing the remainder into its
original elements, makes fresh substance, which is Taurus."[10]
The Bull conserves and gives weight and gravity. Like the Pyramids, he stands defiant on firm ground, thinking: "I am everything, I will last forever, without dilution or deterioration." Scor-
pio waits in autumn bearing Antares on its back, exactly counter
the Bull in the Earth's orbit. The Scorpion is transmutation. He
answers the Bull by saying: "Nothing is forever." Then he proceeds to tear the Taurean work apart; he resurrects it as something else. No wonder he is associated with passion, sexuality,
and wizardry. Gemini follows the Ram and the Bull, before the
summer solstice; the Twins develop connection and distribute
ideas. Then Cancer the Crab permeates these primary aspects
with watery Eros, breaks them down, and transforms them into
a real and habitable world. Leo the Lion, representing the Sun
at the heart of existence, steps out of the Cancerian collectivity
and boldly incarnates. He rebels against the oneness of nature
and declares his individuality and freedom. Virgo receives the
impact of this at the edge of summer and keeps it alive and well.
The Lion is eager and idealistic; the Virgin guides him into suste-
nance and work. Libra, a set of Scales, stands opposite Aries and
follows Virgo, bringing harmony and equilibrium to the tumult.
Against the shock of creation, it provides distribution, serenity,
and space—the conviction that all this is somehow okay as it is.
Libra makes creation bearable and even pleasurable. Then
comes the surprise and the weird energy of the Scorpion, who
was an Eagle in Babylon.

Sagittarius begins the last phase of the zodiac and the year, the collective phase. The bow-and-arrow-bearing Centaur is the sum of all truths and all human wisdom regardless of culture or perspective. It marks the breakdown of self-interest and the multicenteredness of Gemini and the beginning of selfless love and collective responsibility. Capricorn then crystallizes; the Goat is collective knowledge as the source of authority, representing science and technology, government; it is "final form forbidding further growth."[11] In some esoteric astrological circles, a Capricorn is the next great world leader. He is perhaps already born, will be born tomorrow, or at the beginning of the next century. He promises to unite the world, to bring peace to the warring nations, to feed the hungry; he makes technology work, and the result is universal prosperity, limitless resources, utopian world society, forever. All he asks in payment is acknowledgement that he is all there is and there will never be anything more. He asks abandonment of all spiritual systems for this one rich fling with mortality and utopia. But no one sign can take over the zodiac. Aquarius follows Capricorn and stands opposite the Lion. He is a Water-carrier, and he brings planetary oneness, true global culture, the end of all authority in creative intelligence. Seemingly, it would be beautiful if the Water-carrier ruled forever, but it would apparently not be beautiful, for Pisces the Fish comes, and with him, the destruction of everything in universal unconsciousness, in forgetfulness, in the space that exists between two universes. Sampson writes:

> It is a place of shadows, strange shapes, monsters, dreams of unearthly beauty and haunting poignancy. It is a dim indefinite region, opalescently lighted, in which forms come and go, across which mists float, through the veils of which nothing appears sure. . . . It is the place of vanishing, where all things melt and merge into the universe, return to their Maker. . . . It symbolises the final decaying processes by which things are resolved back into their primal elements, disintegrated, scattered, their identity completely vanishing.[12]

The zodiac is a path along which the Sun, Moon, and planets *appear* to move because the Solar System lies in a single plane.

The images and meanings of the signs are aligned with twelve star-groups as if the latter were of equal size and duration, though they are in fact of vastly disproportionate span (Cancer is small, Pisces enormous). But the explanation lies in the synchronicity between a system of archetypal psychology and a seemingly arbitrary grouping of star patterns. Once the system is established, people are able to think in terms of it, and layers of meanings envelop the original ones. All of these continue to interact until the system's mytho-historical bigness resembles, on our scale as a species, the bigness of the sky.

When critics attack one or another aspect of astrology, they miss both the absurdity and the grandeur of the whole proposition.[13] Zodiac astrology treats every constellation as the same number of degrees, i.e., as occupying the same size area of the apparent sky, and it describes only the exact match-up of actual star-groups and calendar periods (signs) that occurred thousands of years ago, once. Debunkers have satirized astrology as something like an apartment house in which every occupant has moved to the apartment directly above him, with the penthouse occupants closing the cycle by occupying the groundfloor suite. The only trouble is that no one has changed the names on the door, and the mail goes to the wrong people, visitors enter the wrong apartments, and everyone seems or pretends not to notice the difference. It is business as usual under this alias. If astrology were to change in accordance with the sky, it would lose its association of birthdates and signs and, equally, its seasonal correspondences.

Astrology has had an interesting answer for this problem, and one very much in keeping with its own principles and scale. The traditional formula is assigned to a branch of learning called zodiac astrology, and the corrected system of signs and constellations is given its own territory, constellation astrology. Constellation astrology specifically corrects these two errors, but, in so doing, it does not damage or eliminate zodiac astrology. The zodiac is considered to be fixed within Earth history and thus to express realities and potentials as they occur exactly within that history, i.e., within the Earth as it resists its connections to the heavens and maintains a local order. The meanings of zodiac astrology are social, occupational, artistic, political, etc., most of the things that people consult astrology for. Modern society is, in fact, out of touch with the sky, and although it sees that the constellations are no longer in their old places, it is hardly interested in them. It is more concerned to maintain its meanings from day to day. But then there is revolution in Iran and a volcano in Washington. These events are literally zodiac-crashing.

The zodiac stays within Earth history and tries to hold onto its meanings, but the sky rushes ahead into new time. Eventually, though, the Earth "adjusts" to its actual place in the heavens, and the two astrologies pull together. The continuous pattern of pulling away and pulling together produces a moiré pattern of effects, so that the truth of any situation lies somewhere between the two, depending on how true a given culture or era of history is to its absolute meaning in an objective perspective in the stars.

Constellation astrology describes the cosmic potential of the Earth in relation to remote stars and galaxies. It has little to say about secular or historical fate; its information predicts the adjustment of the Earth to real conditions and the resulting global changes. Its art and psychology are radical, suggesting the birth of new forms rather than development within existing ones. These forms are in alignment with the present panoply of the heavens and not the Earth's ever-rushing to catch up. For instance, the boom of oil cultures and their resulting political and social systems are considered, by the zodiac which attends them, in terms of the events which actually occur within those cultures. But the constellations read them only in terms of the limited supply of oil on the Earth and their ultimate contribution to an Earth that is adjusted to its entire history and destiny in the cosmos.

Esoteric astrology, like relativity theory, does not stop once it has discovered the first distortion of two simultaneous times. If it is hard to imagine events within constellation astrology, the new heliocentric astrology is almost inconceivable. By moving its point of focus from the Earth to the Sun, where the center of the Solar System is, gravitationally, it speaks of events which have the Sun for their center and the Earth as simply an influence (there could be any number of differently centered astrologies in the Solar System alone, including one for every planet, moon, asteroid, comet, etc.). According to contemporary astrologers, heliocentric astrology speaks to the basic and concrete reality of matter down to a subatomic level. Its horoscopes are of relations between the planets over millennia, perhaps communications between sentiences spread through the galaxy. It is corrected according to the gravitational reality of the Solar System, so it cannot be pegged to the scale of an individual life in a country on one planet. But that life must still intersect the plane of the Sun somewhere, whether or not the person ever comes in touch with the moment.

If we were to discover a galactic center and use that as our astrological reference point, we would be able to talk only of galactic potentials, which would be deeper than subatomic quarks on the physical scale, or of such fine intelligence as to be unrecognizable, except as pre-material, pre-sentient measure for all which is now material and sentient. Such a center exists, of course, and we have known, since early in the twentieth century, that it lies out in the bright Sagittarian direction of our viewpoint of the sky. Virgo looks directly opposite it. The Sun circles the galactic center every 250 million years.

No doubt the Milky Way and its sister galaxies circle a supergalactic center, presently guessed to lie in exactly the opposite direction, fifteen million light-years out through Virgo. The astrological mesh here would be all the finer, all the more exact at every infinitesimal point of location. It is beyond experience, but it is not beyond imagination. Ancient astrology intuited this. Modern astrology uses the material of relativistic physics and radio astronomy to say this again. Our lives are tied to an unseen harmony and rhythm; the zodiac is the coarse terrestrial duodecimo of that rhythm derived from local Babylonian time and sky, and for the purposes of daily divination it suffices. In the words of the Taoist astronomer:

Heaven's net is wide;
Coarse are the meshes, yet nothing slips through.[14]

It is no wonder, hearing the things we have.

Stars mold the universe in three dimensions of space and one of time. The original nuclear fires have been subsumed in the atom, and a thin smoke blows off the loom of gravity, leaving behind bright, tinted worlds; fields of wild clover; snakes and barnacles and flies; and seas of liquid and air. The flight of the space shuttle *Columbia* demonstrates the complexity of the star rhythms. We cannot flood space with our cities and fly off to other worlds yet. A barrier prevents such extension. We must train ourselves in the exactitude of gravity, progressing through its labyrinth one step at a time. The resolution of *Columbia* lies hundreds, perhaps thousands, of years beyond; but, if we do not infinitesimally creep into the star net, those who follow us will be disinherited. There is no shortcut, and no one can do it for us. What the space program demonstrates, the master of *t'ai chi ch'uan* has known for generations: there is only one form, one axis, one center; after each move has been internalized, a deeper move follows, and then another, endlessly, all in precise and absolute attention to gravity—whether it be rolling a ball of energy from the *tan t'ien* up the spine or re-entering the windy world in a giant glider. We scrape the surface of perhaps a fourth dimension whose naked force could place us in another galaxy or shoot an opponent forty feet into the air. We can no more touch it than an amoeba can swim out of the tide, but we can allow its current to carry us zone by zone across the sea.

Astrology is our rune on the hollow surface of infinity, or we are the shadow play of astrology upon the dream of cosmic night.

16

The Planets:
I: The Solar System

WHEN WE THINK of the Solar System, the nine planets come to mind—they and their moons, the assorted comets, asteroids, meteor swarms, and the sea of churning fire they all encircle. In the night sky, the Solar System would seem to be a few needles in a haystack, some of them invisible most of the time, most of them invisible all of the time. It took heroic efforts to discover the outer planets, their moons, and the asteroids, and, for all intents and purposes, these are invisible to mankind without telescopes.

There is another way to imagine the Solar System: it is the gravitational field originating at the Sun. This alone keeps the planets "alive." Without it they would be dead stones, drifting or motionless depending on how one might interpret their inertia through the immensity of space.

The Solar System is mainly empty interstellar space. It is a veil, an almost perfectly transparent veil housing the gravitational field through which we look at the background of the cosmos. If it were not for sunlight and its chemical trail, we would look through a perfect transparency. Light scatters in the atmosphere to produce the blue opaque hood, and the solar wind blows against the gases and particles, creating the faint ionization of night. Even in the darkest of nights, the Sun's radiation creates texture. A sky hangs between us and the cosmos. It may be as fiery as the Northern Lights or as muffled as the twinkling of stars.

The planets are infinitesimal compared to the stars, and they have no light of their own. They fill the void between here and eternity by reflecting light from their metallic and gaseous bodies—a fraction of the continuous waves which arrive at their shores. These reflected waves tell us, as they told ancient man in other ways, that the Sun's veil has bits of matter caught in it like gemstones. What the night sky does is to throw the billions of billions of miles of interstellar space in all directions into a single blackness, while the planets, asteroids, and comets stand out as the single moving objects illuminated by the Sun among the stars.

When Galileo and Herschel first looked at the planets through telescopes, they saw surfaces. The stars stayed remote, but the planets swelled into objects. Their features indicated that they were not the source of their own light but rather worlds of varying composition lit by day. Unlike stars, each of which shines with its own discrete light, the planets borrow their visibility from the Sun.

We cannot see a gravitational field, but we infer its existence from the things that are held in it and move strictly by its quantity in the mass of the Sun. With the discovery of Neptune, the Solar System was extended to a field thirty times the distance from the Earth to the Sun (which itself is an average of 92.9 million miles). At the time, this incredible amount was taken as the limit. Pluto carries that to forty times the orbit of the Earth. And we have gradually come to understand that it extends far beyond that, and that the actual gravitational field of the Sun may reach over a third of the distance to Alpha Centauri, the nearest star.

Comets are a striking testimony to the enormity of the Solar System. They come, seemingly, from the depths of space and pass to the heart of the System in eccentric orbits slightly perturbed by the planets according to their sizes and the proximity of their approach. Although some comets do not even go so far from the Sun as Jupiter's orbit, their remote swings can carry them to aphelion somewhere in space 150,000 times the Earth's distance from the Sun. Visually, from there, the Sun is only one more star. Gravitationally, though, it has enough force to hold onto those comets that remain.

The Dutch astronomer Jan Oort proposed that the comets were spewed forth by the same exploding planet between Mars and Jupiter that created the asteroid belt. Most of the material was blown out of the System, while that which barely held on formed an icy cloud at the limits of solar influence from which the comets now originate and to which they return. Although the idea of an exploded planet has generally been rejected, the Oort cloud of remote comets clearly exists, for unknown comets appear regularly, comets that must have last visited this region of the Solar System during human prehistory. The cometary cloud surrounding the Solar System is probably the outermost ring of the original solar nebula out of which the planets and moons were born. The lighter material was blown to these far-away orbits by the radiation of the condensing proto-Sun. As comets approach the Sun again, the fine gas and dust they leave behind is ignited, and debris from the edges of the protean cloud burns anew.

Untold other planets may exist between Pluto and the comets, invisible to us for the same reason that the planets circling other suns are invisible to us: their faint reflected light does not reach us. Their sizes are necessarily limited to a range where gravitational effects would not be readily apparent in the rest of the Solar System. Earlier in the twentieth century, these phantom planets received far more attention than they do now. Astronomers regularly "invented" them from unexplained perturbations in the orbits of Neptune, Uranus, and even Saturn, and from anomalies in orbits of comets. William Pickering, the American astronomer at Harvard, was the most notorious planet-maker. His first planet, "O," was placed at almost 52 times the Earth's distance from the Sun. It orbited the Sun every 373.5 years and had a mass twice that of the Earth's. Pickering derived "O" in 1908 solely from residuals in the orbit of Uranus. A few years later, he announced three more planets: "P" was located at 123 times the Earth's distance from the Sun, with a year of 1,400 Earth-years; it was based on variations in cometary orbits. "Q" was located at 875 times the Earth's distance from the Sun. It had a mass 20,000 times that of the Earth, a year of 26,000 Earth-years, an eccentric orbit, and a sharp orbital inclination.

"Q" was big enough to counterbalance the whole System, to operate, gravitationally, as a second, invisible Sun. "R" was located at 6,250 times the Earth's distance from the Sun. Its mass was half that of "Q," and its orbital period was half a million years.[1]

The "planets" that Pickering proposed between the years 1928 and 1931 were bizarre in other ways. "S" was located at 48 times the Earth's distance from the Sun, with five times the Earth's mass and a year of 336 Earth-years. "T" was invented to cover the few remaining anomalies in Uranus's orbit and was placed just outside the orbit of Neptune. "U" was later placed outside the orbit of Jupiter in an eccentric path that sometimes carried it closer to the Sun than the giant planet was; it was only 4.5 percent of the Earth's mass.[2]

Pickering's Solar System is interesting not least of all because it shows that we can imagine an equal configuration to the visible one based solely on the analysis of the gravitational field. The movements of known planets, moons, and comets reveal this field, but they also suggest unseen other influences.

Far from being a scatter of individual sun-stars, the Milky Way is a series of enormous overlapping seas with suns in the centers of them. Except for the suns, the seas are invisible to us, but the universality of gravitation ensures that they are there. They are most likely inhabited by planets, asteroids, meteors, and so on, if our Solar System is any measure. Some of these seas have clouds, both bright and dark, galactic mist of metallic vapors, and universal raw hydrogen. There is also cosmic dust and debris. Occasionally, according to the Newtonian formula, objects achieve the velocity necessary to escape from these waters, and they drift in the void until they enter another sea. Their hyperboloid orbits carry them into the space between the solar systems. They may continue to pass through countless solar systems on a journey through space, they may be perturbed into orbits in systems they enter, or they may be caught and consumed in stars. Most bodies carry only the archaeology of their own solar system and universal chemistry, but wanderers from other solar systems would bring with them messages of the formation of substances from other stellar clouds, and they would no doubt link us in some way to a more ancient common ancestor in the Galaxy. Von Braun and Ordway suggest such an origin for the Moon.

Compared to a terrestrial ocean of water, the solar system appears dry and sterile, but this is misleading and even contradictory. The oceans and seas of the Earth are part of the stellar ocean. So are the Earth's forests and the cells of its living creatures. This ocean of radiation and gravity generates the nurturing climate and chemistry of Terra and maintains them with delicate chords. If it does not seem to do so for the other planets, we must remember that Eden is particular to us, and what may nurture our botanical and zoological garden may be poisonous to other life forms. If the Earth is the only solar planet capable of biology, that capacity is still an effect of the solar sea. It keeps the algae and forests green and feeds them their light, which feeds us and nurtures the visions of philosophers and alchemists. Take this planet out of the stellar sea and the living layer would instantly contract and freeze into a black fossil.

In the early days of the Sun and of the nebula cloud at the heart of which it contracted and burned, there was also an abundance of tiny bodies that did not condense into full planets or planetoids. These are known as planetesimals, infinitesimal planets. Dense as mosquitoes at the beginning, they bombarded the whole of the Solar System. Most of them crashed into planets and moons, and the sky contains only relict meteor showers and comets from its prehistory. The Mariner 10 spaceflight which photographed Mercury in 1974 showed the ancient craters on the innermost planet, evidence that these planetesimals had penetrated to the core of the System. Every planet, asteroid, and moon with a surface was scarred, but on some worlds secondary processes covered the wounds with lava or rubbed them off with winds and water. We measure the age of features in the Solar System by the presence or lack of planetesimal craters.

The meteoroids are the moraine of this ancient armada. Some carbonaceous meteorites bear amino acids and other organic compounds, which suggests that such chemistry may have been present, or potentially present, in the original nebula dust of the System. It is hard to know what this portends in either mechanical or vitalist terms, but it is unexpected. The carbonaceous meteorites might also be carriers of templates from other systems. The Earth could then be showered with life chains that did not originate natively, and we might be strangers and invaders on our own world. Of course, this does not solve the riddle of the origin of life; it transfers it elsewhere.

The original gases of the Solar System were a form of plasma. As the spirals cooled, substance was precipitated out, like ice. We find this substance in various states, ranging from the micrometeors of dust to the gases of the large Jovian planets. Most of the mass is still in the Sun. Only if we looked very closely would we notice the rocks and pebbles scattered about the solar disc. We might well overlook all of them except the four largest planets: Jupiter, Saturn, Neptune, and Uranus. Our own blue-green gem is a very tiny if remarkable pebble.

The larger planets have more of the aboriginal solar material. The smaller planets are almost completely rocky. On Earth, though, the rock has been layered over and incorporated into history. The historical process engulfs us and spawns us, but it is only local. Outside it lies everything else, living and not living. It takes life, biological forms, to weave such a history, and once it is done, it is final, until it is destroyed. The rock on Earth contains the encyclopedic regional histories of our planet, from massive continuous features like plains and mountain ranges to the strata of a single site by a pond over generations and aeons, even when it is uninhabited or inhabited by mute creatures. Rock which is not imbedded with fossils of life contains the prior history of lands where species of animals and tribes of men and women arose later, or did not, and where ecological chains unfolded in accordance with climate and native resources, all of which were incorporated into subsequent systems and technologies. We do not think of the soils of Kansas, the tin of Bolivia, the uranium of New Mexico, the harpoons of Greenland, or even the Arctic ice from which Eskimos build their homes as nebuloid matter, but it is all rock and galactic dust condensed at different points on the loom and then subjected to the rigors and meaning of terrestrial history. The aboriginal corn of Mexico and the barley and rye of Mesopotamia share this heritage. Solar material works itself into our flesh and into the atoms and molecules of this planet on a continuous basis. This is our basic cosmic identity.

The kernels of corn are food, not Sun, but they are originally Sun. The solar aspect of ourselves is what finds them edible. Those sugars and "vitamins" that we assimilate are their solar aspects. And everything else in us and them is a solar aspect of another sort. If the kernel is Sun, so is the husk. If the golden metal is stellar excrement lodged in nebuloid lattices, so is the black lava hot from the cloud. And spiny spidery goldsmith creatures hammer away at ingots in the forge trying to represent something lodged shimmering within the solar archetype.

All the properties of this world rest upon the original material, its composition, density, and distance from the Sun. Planets that are mostly original condensed rock with planetesimal and meteoritic scars do not seem to us like worlds. When they are atmosphereless like the Moon or Mercury, we are in an ambiguous position. Will we stand simply on a stony platform in the void, or will we dwell within an albumen hemisphere? High-gravity gas giants do not seem like worlds either, for there is no bottom to their atmospheres and no thinning of their substance.

If the Moon is locally formed, then rocks brought back from it should give us a history of the formation of this entire region, for they are preserved from the first moment. Intense volcanic activity, water, and life have not significantly eroded or altered them, only meteoritic impact. They have sat, as it were, in suspended animation in the deep freeze of space, fossils of primordial cosmogony. The stars are even simpler representatives of a more ancient eon.

All our personal sense of complication, except for the topological and atomic complication of quasars and quarks and their kin, emerges from life and history within a world, more from riverbeds and family genealogies than from galaxies. Take that away and we have only simpler and older events. The history of the universe and the formation of the Solar System are easier to unravel than the migration of the Australian Aborigines in waves across the Pacific or the passage of Indian groups from North to South America. The blood types, languages, and myths of those groups are even more complicated. When Alex Haley worked his way back through the generations of slaves to the Gambian River whose name he had received intact along with the clan name of his African ancestor, and when the bard of his clan's tribal history sang his way back to the moment of Kunta Kinte's capture while out making a drum, a moment at which one face of creation was sundered from another, they had somehow gone deeper and farther than the Big Bang that is behind the universe itself.[3] No wonder Haley wept. He had an intimation of our lost beginning and our broken entanglement in the chain. It was like knowing that we have a beginning somewhere, that we are more than orphans of pond scum and galactic dust. Even the very different discovery of Australopithecus in a South African hill, testifying to the kinship of man with the wild creatures of this world, is more stunning than the origin of the Solar System. What Haley found may not even have been the truth, and if it was, it still stands as less than a candle against the night that lies behind us. But the real history of the universe and its complication is unconscious to us, and the part of us that knows it is unconscious too. So we experience it in replica as the fragments and roots that can be made conscious and visible. These have our trembling and our tears for the whole condition.

The sense of the five original planets as worlds came fairly late in European history, sometime between, roughly, Copernicus and Galileo. Copernicus demonstrated that it was mathematically simpler to treat the Earth as one of the planets than as a body in their center; in a sense, this marked the discovery of a fifth planet, on which we lived. Kepler then showed that all these planets belonged to a system. Bruno and Cusa had not distinguished between spirit realms and worlds. Galileo made it clear: the planets were places that one might go to physically. Until the meteorological criteria for life were fully recognized, it was possible to imagine the exotic inhabitants of any one of these ancient globes. The New World of the Americas, with its

"Indians," was still in the European psyche, and Asia itself was potentially as foreign as Jupiter or Saturn.

But the idea of the Moon as a world is very old and predates any clear sense of the hemispheres of the Earth. For centuries people imagined that the Moon was a continuance of Terran lands, reachable, if not by land or sea, then by some unknown topographic principle. With the occasional exception of the Sun, the Moon was the one place in the sky where it was possible to go without being transformed into a spirit.

For Plutarch, the Moon was a continent, close enough to be considered part of the Earth's lands. He wrote of great selenean valleys and shaded areas cast by lunar mountains. The Moon aborigines bathed in dark oceans whose Latin name we retain in the dust-bowl *maria* of the present Moon.

There is not so great a difference between the transits that science fiction writers now pose between galaxies and those which mages and sorcerors set between Earth and Luna: whirlpools and magical caves that link discontinuous regions, telepathic nodes that bring bodies across physical space, and so on.

Kepler's *Somnium* described a journey to the Moon through the northern Polar region of the Earth. It had magical elements but was essentially a secular journey to a physical place. Bruno's worlds could be reached only by sympathetic magic on a cosmic scale: no ignorant layman or lowly astronaut could travel in such a universe. Though condemned as a heresy, it was neo-Platonic Christian at its roots.

Kepler called his trip a "dream," probably to protect his pagan Copernican vision from the Church hierarchy. It is also a fairy tale that uses the nether elements of seventeenth-century Europe: a female magician speaking Icelandic summons a daemon, and the travelers leave the Earth at the Arctic, near the famed abysses of Mount Hekla. But Kepler looked upon the surface of the Moon and saw countryside, hills and valleys, living creatures. In a few more years, Galileo would peer through a glass and walk in the shadows of lunar mountain ranges. If the Moon was land, then the planets and their moons, after Galileo, were land too.[4]

Kepler's "Moonship" was constructed from the turgor of opiates and the upward rush of unencumbered mass; it was necessarily magical, for no one then could imagine a space vehicle or machine:

> The body no doubt escapes the magnetic force of the earth and enters that of the moon, so that the latter gets the upper hand. At this point we set the travellers free and leave them to their own devices: like spiders they will stretch out and contract and propel themselves forward by their own force—for, as the magnetic forces of the earth and moon both attract the body and hold it suspended, the effect is as if neither of them were attracting it—so that in the end its mass will by itself turn toward the moon.[5]

Kepler spoke of gravity here but did not recognize it.

While the alchemists watched the stages of scorching, whitening, and rainy deliquescence, Kepler dreamed a Moon of storms and seas, swift and sudden alternations of hot and cold. His Moon is spongy, serpentine, filled with "hollows and continuous caves." Life is shelled, long-legged, and serpentlike; the labyrinthine sublunar surface teems with aquatic creatures, rheostatic, subject totally to the flow of waters and their own somatic wetness—the pull of the Earth bringing them up into the cold evening, the release of terrestrial weight lowering them into the deep interior during the hot lunar day. "Growth is very quick; everything is short-lived, although it grows to enormous bodily bulk." This is Kepler's compromise between an occult Moon and its possible physical properties.[6]

The Emperor Rudolph asked Kepler one night as they stared at the orb in the sky if the Moon were not a mirror in which the lands of the Earth were reflected; he pointed out Italy. No, said Kepler, the Moon is a rugged wild land of its own. It is a place lying to the north of all known civilization, north of North. It appears in the sky only because air and other exquisite forces have lifted it.

The seventeenth century did not come to the planets as blank tablets. They had been astral unities for centuries; and before

that, they were gods, influences, spirits, and myth heroes. Every
world had already been layered with images and associations,
and, in a certain sense, had its peoples and its landscapes. These
were a translation of the astral and astrological influences of
these worlds on the Earth into local planetary sceneries. Mars
was martial from the beginning, red and bloody. There was no
way, after the fact, to distinguish Venus as a world from *primavera*
and the Rites of Spring. Every planet already had a metal, varieties of plants and animals, and an organ of the body. From
these the original planetary natures were drawn.

It is almost impossible to be true to both the astrological
tradition of planetary images and the later planetary landscapes.
The former stretch deep into the past and become richer, with
more associations, the further back we go. The latter start as
gigantic blankness, dark barges tugged in their orbits. The
blankness is there only in our projecting back to the imaginary
infancy of objective astronomy. The landscapes were always
more sparkly and flamelike than the speculative realms to which
we submit their remoteness and wilderness (by the same properties of the same lenses that resolve maria of viral molecules
upon their helical lattices).[7] They burn from the beginning. They
cannot help but emerge from an astral symbolism.

17

The Planets:
II: Mercury and Venus

MERCURY is the innermost planet of the Solar System. An eccentric orbit brings it as close as 28.5 million miles from the Sun and then carries it to aphelion at 43.5 million miles. During the "new planet" furor of the nineteenth century, a planet even closer to the Sun was apparently discovered—Vulcan, with an orbit of 13 million miles and a diameter of 1,000 miles. It was named by Leverrier himself, but it is doubtful that it was ever seen. What appeared to some as Vulcan might have been sunspots, and the fate of that world is unknown. It shares a place in history with that other mysterious planet that circles the Sun in the Earth's orbit in such a way that the Sun always prevents us from viewing it—the so-called anti-Terra, long ago dismissed.

Mercury is difficult to see. Not only is it small, but it reflects a mere twentieth of the light that reaches its surface. When it is closest to the Earth, only its unlit side faces us; and when it is furthest from the Earth, it is eclipsed by the glare of the Sun which stands in between. As the two planets inside the Earth's orbit, Mercury and Venus are both morning and evening stars, always closely accompanying the Sun. But Venus is closer to us, larger, and more reflective, and, in fact, very bright. Mercury is seasonally obliterated by the Sun's light, and it is otherwise so dim and elusive that Copernicus lamented on his deathbed that he had never seen it, a bizarre virginity for such a passionate

265

astronomer. Even Giovanni Schiaparelli, the nineteenth-century astronomer who mapped both Mercury and Mars, claimed that he struggled with an almost invisible object. Of the five planet-like stars of ancient cosmology, Mercury is the least visible, and it is a testimony to the perspicacity of the ancients not only that they saw it but that they realized it was on a par with the four more visible wanderers.

Ironically, Schiaparelli's maps of Mercury have held up better than his maps of Mars. They are no finer, but they are less ambitious, and we have not been able to improve much on his basic image. By contrast, his Mars, laced with *canali,* led to a whole mythology of Martians which was later abandoned, and the "canals" were never found. He participated in creating a different Mercurian mythology. After viewing the planet carefully over a long period, he decided that, like the Moon, Mercury had only a captured rotation. Thus, the same side was always turned toward the Sun. This was based on his impression that the surface markings did not change, and it gave Mercury a day and a year each of 88 Earth-days. We might then expect a planet with a parched molten side and a frozen side, with a possible twilight zone in between. If this zone truly existed, it might have temperate conditions. Science fiction writers peopled Mercury with creatures of fire warring against creatures of ice and with tribes of blind cave-dwellers in the central region, underground species who worshipped the Sun and had the same relationship to the surface of the planet that we have to outer space. In some versions, a race of sages dwells in the middle region, bearing, from their proximity to the Solar source, a wisdom that transcends anything else in the System. This is also astral Mercury, messenger of the gods and repository of the knowledge of the Sun.

In 1965, with a new technology of more powerful transmitters, this image vanished from astronomy. The planet was mapped from a radar-radio telescope at Arecibo, Puerto Rico, and was found to have a rotation period of 58.65 days. This creates a totally different Mercurian climate.

Before Mercury's axial rotation was computed, the planet was observed to wobble, a feature predicted by nineteenth-century observers on the basis of the eccentric orbit. Under the old axial period, the wobble would give Mercury as much as a quarter of its 3,000 miles diameter surface in twilight areas that move between heat and cold as the planet revolves around the Sun. On one side of Mercury, a temperature of almost 800° F. would melt lead and zinc, while on the other side, at − 280° F., the potential gases of the atmosphere would be partially liquefied and solidified into pools and slush.

In reality, though, Mercury has such a meager atmosphere as to be essentially airless. Until the Mariner 10 photographs confirmed this in 1974, one school of planetologists created a model for a stormy, poisonous Mercury based on the thin aura that appeared on the planet's disc against the Sun. We now know that the solar wind, combined with the low escape velocity of Mercury, swept this kind of material away long ago, but the model is interesting in itself. It gives an image for picturing Mercury's axial rotation, and it serves as an hypothesis for some planet like Mercury but a little larger.

On this hypothetical planet, the huge temperature differential would cause the winds to blow continuously at hurricane force, solidifying gaseous and molten metals and releasing exotic combinations of metallic gases. The relative thinness of the atmosphere would make the hurricane seem mild by comparison with the same wind velocity on the Earth, but it would still be appreciable, especially given the metallic sleet.

A rotation of 59 days is fast enough to prevent a purely hot side and a purely cold side, but it is not fast enough to balance the climates completely. Although temperatures on the sunward side of Mercury are now figured at a more "moderate" 600° F., it is hotter when the planet is close to the Sun; in regions that have been in the Sun longest, the temperatures may go up as high as 2000° F. The night side never sees the Sun for many Earth-months, and though it is far closer to the solar disc than anything on our own Equator, it may never get above − 50 F. Rock and metal are an effective heat shield.

A 59-day rotation is quite slow, so the Sun in its virtually black sky will crawl across the heavens in 176 days in a slightly zigzag path. Then it will set below the horizon, beginning 176 days of night. Because of Mercury's orbit, the planet actually moves around the Sun at perihelion faster than it spins, so some Mercurian zones will have two sunrises and sunsets in a day, and the Sun will appear to go backwards.

The originally-proposed thin but violent Mercurian atmosphere contained sulphur vapors, sulphur dioxide, krypton, xenon, iodine vapors, and the like, about as poisonous a mix as could be imagined for Earth blood and lungs. These materials would disperse into the atmosphere more and more rapidly as the day reached high noon at 90 Earth-days. As night fell, they would crystallize out of the atmosphere in a dirty rain that would soon become a metallic snow. If the planet's volcanic activity released any of the metal mercury, this would of course vaporize in the daytime, and would be one of the first metals to turn back into silver rain. Thus, dust, sulphur, and metal winds rush toward the dark side, and *from* the dark side come boiling gases as the Sun cuts away the solid edge with advancing daylight.

On Mercury as we now know it, there is probably not enough atmosphere to distinguish the night sky from the day sky; both are black, but the day sky has an enormous Sun in it, with a full corona visible. From this distance, the Sun is an ocean with turbulent waves, and its "wind" will blast most of the lingering or new gas molecules into space. If Earth colonists or scientists were to try what presently seems impossible and set up a habitation zone on Mercury, they would probably have to live underground to escape the Sun's radiation. The trick would be to use the heat of the long day to provide energy for the long night. It would be a solar energy paradise, the epitome of unlimited energy, but with all the dangers of a mammoth atomic energy plant. On Mercury the solar/atomic paradox is fully realized.

Man could do little there anyway except contend directly with the big energy source and make use of it. This points up the absurdity of wanting unlimited energy. Our mental image of Mercury captures much of our present resource greed, as befits the mythology of the planet of Hermes the thief, who steals everything from everywhere. Mercury is also a forge of metals, ready-melted and available in a low gravity situation. If there were a planet Vulcan, it would be an even hotter oven. The sky itself would be tumbling fires.

The Mariner 10 spacecraft came close enough to Mercury to begin photographing it in late March 1974. At first glance, the planet fulfilled expectations and showed a "lunar" surface with very old craters and some new rayed craters—streaks of light new material radiating over the ancient dark. Closer examination and more photographs showed Mercury not to be completely moonlike. The cliffs and scarps proved that the planet had contracted after formation and its solid surface had wrinkled. Mercury also has a magnetic field. How this is generated without faster rotation is still uncertain. The magnetosphere of Mercury was also without radio signals, and it was generated by the planet itself rather than by the solar wind.

On a second flyby a year later, the spacecraft passed to within 200 miles of the surface. Mercury was seen to be brighter than the Moon, with cratered terrain similar to the lunar highlands, but there were also very ancient plains underlying the craters, including some smooth lavalike plains crossed with ridges and cliffs. In the hot area of Mercury was a feature called Caloris Basin, which is a crater with an unusual lava floor. The biggest feature on the planet, the crater is 800 miles in diameter and was possibly formed by an asteroid collision. Its floor has ridges and complex radial and concentric features, inwardly cracking like a dried-up pond.

Most notably, the conception of a stormy Mercury was put to rest by the spacecraft. There was no appreciable atmosphere, so the metal hurricanes were consigned to myth, or to some other planet in an unknown solar system. Mercury is now known to be like the Moon, but denser, hotter, and more disturbed and complex geologically. Mercury is a dramatic case of Freud's law applied to whole worlds: "Anatomy is destiny." But we will see this again, planet after planet.

Pre-planetary Mercury is not only the messenger of the gods but the late European incarnation of Hermes-Thoth, who carried the magical lore from the ancient Near East and was directly associated with the origin of language. Hermes-Thoth is a wise but dangerous sorcerer, bringing things into being too fast for them ever to be used, like blinding sunlight and rivers of thorium, lead, bismuth, and antimony. In occult tradition, Mercury represents the intellect and is assigned the color yellow, with the white of magic bursting through a red robe of sensation in the tarot card. The card stands for transparent consciousness as a vessel for pure communication, hence Mercury as conveyor of the gods' messages and those of the deeper unconscious.

Mercury "invented" astrology, astronomy, mathematics, geometry, medicine, grammar, and music. An amoral destroyer, Mercury is also a profoundly capable healer. On the psychological plane, it is quick and brilliant, spirited and fragmented, full of merry thoughts, puns, half-words, sounds, phonemes on the verge of meaning but dissociating before it can occur. The metal itself is mobile, forming tiny soft globules. It represents the lungs, which are symbolically a mercury forest of droplets connecting all oxygen-breathing life on the planet.[1]

Venus is the nearest planet to the Earth and also the brightest "star" in the night sky. It reflects twelve times as much light as Mercury and twice as much light as the Earth. Venus is covered with white clouds that shine like a planetwide snowpack. The only way we knew, initially, that we were not looking at snow was that it was far too smooth to be a surface.

Like Mercury, Venus accompanies the Sun from the Earth's perspective and is visible in the dawn and dusk skies. Until the time of Pythagoras, it was commonly thought to be two stars, the Egyptian Tioumoutiri and Quaiti and the Greek Phospheros and Hesperos, the morning and evening stars.

From the beginning of astronomical observation, the Cytherean cloud cover was the most dominant aspect of the planet. Mars and Mercury had surface features, and Jupiter and Saturn showed cloud patterns. Venus revealed nothing. It was simply a gleaming white star enshrouded in mists. Otherwise it resembled the Earth more than any other planet. Its diameter of 7,700 miles is only 200 miles less than that of the Earth. Its year is 224.7 Earth-days. Its distance from the Sun is 67.2 million miles, and it comes as close to the Earth as 27.5 million miles. At the most optimistic, it should be a warmer wetter Earth, and this, in fact, was its image all through early astronomy. The faint bluish light (the aureola) that Venus gives off as it crosses the face of the Sun suggests an abundant atmosphere, a fact that was noted as early as the middle of the eighteenth century. In *The Destiny of the Stars,* published in 1918, Svante Arrhenius, the Swedish chemist who proposed that life was carried to Earth in spores from other systems (the panspermia theory), wrote that Venus was a warm misty land.[2] Swamps there would resemble those of the Earth's reptilian age. The vegetation would be unimaginably fertile from six times the Earth's humidity. Later in the century, some scientists proposed that Venus was a single planetary ocean covered with vegetation and filled with unimaginable varieties of sea creatures. It was difficult to avoid moving from Venus, the goddess of love and beauty, to a garden planet filled with primal dinosaurlike creatures and civilized fish-beings. These creatures might never have seen the sky, for as far as we know the clouds over Venus have not parted even for a second in all the years we have been viewing it. The creatures would never have seen the Sun, and they would have no explanation for the cycle of light and darkness. There is no starry night on Venus; it is in a different cosmos. One might wonder how incredible such a night would have looked if the clouds had parted for an instant at some point in ancient Cytherean history. What would the inhabitants have thought the stars were? And what would have been passed down from ancestral times of this wondrous vision?

Closer to the Sun than we are, Venus has been taken for our own mythical past, when the Earth was younger and covered with wild vegetation, only its seas inhabited. Cytherean science fiction repeats this image. C. S. Lewis's *Perelandra* is Venus:

> Enormous purple clouds came driving between him and the golden sky, and with no preliminary drops a rain such as he never experienced began to fall. There were no lines in it; the water above him seemed only less continuous than the sea, and he found it difficult to breathe. The flashes were incessant. In between them, when he looked in any

direction except that of the clouds, he saw a completely
changed world. It was like being at the centre of a rainbow,
or in a cloud of multi-colored steam. . . . All sorts of things
seemed to be coming down in the rain—living things apparently. They looked like preternaturally airy and graceful
frogs . . . and had the colour of dragon-flies.

All day there had been no variation at any point in the
golden roof to mark the sun's position, but now the whole
of one half-heaven revealed it. The orb itself remained invisible, but on the rim of the sea rested an arc of green so
luminous that he could not look at it, and beyond that,
spreading almost to the zenith, a great fan of color like a
peacock's tail. Looking over his shoulder he saw the whole
island ablaze with hue, and across it and beyond it, even to
the ends of the world, his own enormous shadow.[3]

Venus was thought of as a world of rain forests, jungles, tow-
ering clouds, gigantic plants like tree-ferns, telepathic tribes,
and mermaids. Yet, from the first spectroscopic analyses in 1920,
no water vapor showed up in the atmosphere; instead there was
an abundance of carbon dioxide. Reluctantly astronomers let
their hold slip on this attractive wet world we wanted so much
to exist. There were many reasons why water vapor might not
be detected, but the accompanying failure to find oxygen was
an ominous sign. A new model of Venus began to emerge: a
violent desert with storms whipping dust and salt up into the
atmosphere.

Scientists differed as widely as possible on the length of Venus's day. Some thought of it as short, like the Earth's; others
thought that Venus rotated with one side always to the Sun, and
thus that it had a day equal to its year of 225 days. The cloud
cover made it impossible to know who was correct until 1965,
when Venus's rotation was measured from Arecibo with a startling result that no one had predicted. Its day was found to be
247 Earth-days, longer than even its year. Furthermore, it was
found to rotate on its axis in a direction opposite to its motion
around the Sun. Several moons in the Solar System are retrograde, but Venus is the only planet. No explanation has been
found. The Sun rises on Venus in the West and sets in the East,
but, in any case, is not seen at all.

Seven spacecraft, both Russian and American, were flown by Venus during the 1960s, and four of the Russian ships either crashed or soft-landed on the planet. These explorations buried forever the notion of beautiful oceanic Venus. Whereas spectroscopic analysis had indicated carbon dioxide in the atmosphere, researchers felt that 3 percent would have been an enormous amount—100 times the carbon dioxide content of the Earth's atmosphere. Mariner 5 showed that Venus had 90 percent carbon dioxide, producing a greenhouse effect of unimaginable proportions. Venus was very hot; temperatures of 900° F. were measured. The cloud cover was solid and dense, twenty miles thick, extending to forty-five miles above a rocky or sandy surface. The intense heat apparently melted the Russian craft Venera 4. Living on Venus would be like dwelling more than thirty-five feet beneath the surface of a terrestrial ocean, for the surface pressure of Venus's atmosphere is ninety times that which we have. The density of the atmosphere so strongly bent the radio signals sent from Mariner 5 when it passed behind the planet that they circled Venus and returned to the sender, never reaching the Earth at all. Needless to say, clouds, winds, dust, and pressure make Venus an utterly arid planet of deserts with knife-sharp stormy air. Even spacecraft are melted and crushed, some before reaching the ground.

In June 1975, the Russian spacecraft Venera 9 finally parachute-landed a capsule, which then photographed a surface of young irregular rocks. The ship seemed to have landed on a hill on which rocks were rolling down (33° N. latitude and 293° longitude in a region noted as dark from radar mapping). Venera 10 landed in October 1975 on an older plain and found dark soil and pitted rocks, indicating erosion and weathering. The planet was also not as dark as the Russians had expected. At ground level there was at least as much sunlight as on a cloudy day in Moscow in June, and objects and details 330 yards away could be seen.

The surface air was found to be relatively gentle, but the enormous upper atmosphere whipped around the planet in four days, adding pressure to the surface. From spacecraft reports, the clouds seemed to be ice or quartz dust in their middle regions. At thirty miles up, the winds attain 160 miles per hour;

while on the surface just below, they blow at a mild 1⅓ miles per hour. Meanwhile, the uppermost clouds move at 260 miles per hour. Mariner 10 showed a specific polar hood and complex circulation patterns forming a planetwide complex; there was a particular stormy region at the point of direct sunlight. By 1973, new photographic techniques in the infrared range revealed the upper clouds as 75 percent sulphuric acid and the rest water. With fluorine also present in the atmosphere, this leads to corrosive clouds of fluosulfonic acid. The entire process is extraordinarily complicated, with sunlight heating the upper clouds, and surface and chemical reactions heating the lower ones.

Venus also showed no magnetosphere but a tremendous solar wind wake.

Although heat and chemistry alone had done away with the Garden, it was still surprising when radar mapping showed enormous craters, seemingly planetesimal markings billions of years old that had not undergone erosion or volcanic flow. However, some mountains, chasms, and very long lava flows appeared on the maps, and one huge cratered volcano. James Maxwell has the distinction of having his name on both the tallest mountain (Maxwell Montes rises 35,400 feet above Ishtar Terra, a northern hemisphere highlands) and the Maxwell Lava Flow, hundreds of miles long.

An American Pioneer satellite equipped with radar entered Cytherean orbit on December 4, 1978, and it proceeded to map the planet's surface. No distinct plates have shown up in the crust of Venus—hence no grinding collisions to produce earthquakes and volcanoes. It is one continuous continent. The surface rocks are much thicker than Earth's, and the hot plastic material beneath them is unable to break through. The satellite has also mapped a rift 1,400 miles long and 9,300 feet deep cutting across Aphrodite Terra.

Venus seems as though it should be like the Earth, but it isn't. If both started with the same amount of carbon dioxide, the Earth reassimilated its supply in the carbon of the rocks in the planet's crust and in the oxygen of the atmosphere. Also, aboriginal sea creatures and water itself took carbon out of the air and put it into the ground. Since the carbon cycle apparently never took place on Venus, perhaps because of the greater heat keeping the carbon in the atmosphere, the same chemical endowment could have led to carbon dioxide remaining a gas, which would have increased the planet's heat even more. Life-giving on Earth, where it formed the central node of protoplasm chains, carbon was life-smothering on Venus. Perhaps the oxygen lost from boiling water vapor on Venus combined with carbon that was not bound into the crust of the planet to form more carbon dioxide.

On Earth everything went right, at least for us: hydrogen and oxygen went into water; carbon went into limestone and other rocks. On Venus carbon dioxide remained gaseous; heat increased; and water vapor reached the upper atmosphere, where the molecules lost their hydrogen, giving rise to a hydrogen corona. The Earth loses water this way only fractionally, but Venus, which is almost baked dry, still loses another million tons a day. The greenhouse effect is a vicious cycle; yet it could have begun from only a slightly warmer temperature in the beginning. Such is the subtlety of planetary chemistry.

In current times, Venus has been anything but a Garden of Eden. It is a warning of the possible fate of Earth if industrial waste products continue to pour into the atmosphere, adding to the carbon dioxide while the carbon-removing forests of Africa and South America are bulldozed away. On one side we may be threatened by another ice age, but on the other we are forewarned by Venus that whole oceans can boil off and that this begins with a subtle temperature difference.

Some planetologists have suggested seeding the atmosphere of Venus with carbon dioxide-consuming algae that thrive in high temperatures. If these found Venus tasty, and if there were no native life (at least in the upper atmosphere) competing with them, they would multiply and cover the Cytherean sky, turning it green and working their way down in the atmosphere. Since they thrive in hot springs, these algae could perhaps survive the temperatures on Venus. Photosynthesis would release oxygen, and great millennial rains would begin. For thousands of years it might rain on Venus, and we would get our garden after all.[4] Maybe. The idea is perhaps more symptomatic of our condition than a realistic response to another world, but who is to say of people who have come this far down the path?

Immanuel Velikovsky, an often discredited scientist, interpreted the conditions on Venus very differently.[5] Long before the present spectroscopic and radar discoveries, Velikovsky theorized that Venus was not a sister of Earth at all but a comet that had been torn out of the planet Jupiter and arrived in the vicinity of the Earth three thousand years ago, reversing our magnetic field and causing global cataclysms. Velikovsky specifically traces this comet to Athena, born from the forehead of Jupiter and Astarte with her two tails. He also cites other mythological evidence from cultures throughout the Earth.

Such an origin might explain the climate and composition of Venus, its dissimilarity from the Earth, its retrograde motion, and its nonexistent magnetic field, none of which are satisfactorily handled by present theory. Velikovsky died embittered that, as new scientific evidence appeared to cry out for a revised model of Venus, his was summarily dismissed. The scenario of planets as moving actors jumping out of one another was too outlandish and radical, and this far outweighed any circumstantial evidence.

His comet Venus had a violent history after it emerged from Jupiter. It disturbed Mars in its orbit and showered both Mars and the Earth with radioactivity. Part of its tail was captured by Mars, another part was torn loose by the Earth and became petroleum clouds which settled into the ground. Velikovsky assumed that the petroleum came from the decay of a species of vermin that inhabits Jupiter and Venus. This would mean that our wealthiest oil sources are not terrestrial but Jovian in origin, carried here by a comet that became Venus. Stealing some of the Earth's oxygen, Venus set its own petroleum on fire, and this continues to burn, giving off the white carbon clouds. Velikovsky's followers have created a whole theology out of this planetary event. Note the following from a pamphlet handed out in New York City in 1964:

> None have sinned, not one. No one is to blame for *any* of the atrocities of the past 6000 years, nor for any that are to come. There was no sin in Sodom and Gommorah. The

flames came down from a comet. It was nobody's fault that the flood came down. The water came from a comet, not a god.

It was a comet, not a person, not a hand, not an eagle, not a snake, not a demon, not a holy father, not a holy mother, not a witch, not a cat, not a wolf, not a ghost, not a vampire, not a dragon, not a sword, not a bull, not a cross, not an angel, not a phantom, not any of these things.

It was a blind unthinking and unhearing comet. It was sent by no one. It intended no evil and no good. It had no intentions at all relevant to the human species. It listened to no prayers and accepted no sacrifices. It made no promises and chose no special people. Those who were destroyed were destroyed by chance alone. Those who were spared were spared by chance alone.

. . . It was a comet, not a god.[6]

This is the modern prejudice anyway, though not on the basis of Venus's origin as a Jovian comet.

In the traditional occult, Venus is the goddess of love and ripeness, tranquility and charity. It represents the desire within nature to grow and spread and become wild fields of plants and herds of beasts. It is subconsciousness, generating ideas, creating form out of Mercurial fragments. Even minerals are spawned by the archetypal intelligence of Venus.

The metal of Venus is copper, which is associated with both water and plants—water by its ability to absorb fluid, and plants by its green color. Venus the goddess emerged from the ocean like copper in foam.

Venus was once cohesion and beauty, creation through eros. But now we have a twentieth-century love as a parched inferno, beauty as a hellish desert. Traditional symbols do not lie. Is this the disappointment of industrialism mirrored back in the enigma of radar Venus, which still lies beneath an inexplicable white mist? Is this the terror we have turned love into in our race to get beyond ourselves into an immortal machine?

18

The Planets:
III: The Moon,
the Earth,
and Mars

No body in the sky has been more devalued in the modern transition from the spiritual heavens than the Moon. Luna was once an equal partner to the Sun. Sol ruled by day, Luna by night. Alchemically, the Sun was gold, the Moon silver; the Sun was the King, the Moon the Queen. Together they bred the metals. The Sun brought fiery intelligence and conscious seed; the Moon brought memory and unconscious growth. Between them, they made man. From this throne the Moon has tumbled into a replica of crude rock hammered by meteoroids since its birth.

To ancient astronomers, the Moon seemed to be the same size as the Sun. It is actually only a quarter the size of the Earth, with a diameter of 2,160 miles. Its proximity to us, not its size or brightness, gives it a central place in our mythological and physical systems. As a satellite, the Moon is an anomaly. No other planet has a moon even close to a quarter of its own size; in fact, the Earth and Moon comprise a double planet system, with each having substantial influence on the other.

The Moon's overbearing mass leaves the Earth vulnerable to a powerful lunar internalization. The engagement of these two is carried out in the one way possible for bodies in space: gravitationally. Our surface seas, biological waters, and molten metals are tugged back and forth by the Moon. Inanimate materials record this force through their own mammoth structures on the Earth, transposing lunar rhythms into grand topographies, selenean grottoes and palaces. Caves are hollowed out by the Moon's tides, and sediments are built up in lunar cycles. Glaciers accumulate the icy tides. Animate materials "remember" the Moon and store it in cellular and psychic phases that go on for the lives of organisms and the histories of species even when these are broken from the rhythm of the actual Moon. Inanimate tides can only respond to the Moon as it is. Living things can record the lunar music, dance to it in other phases, and pass it on through chromosomes to their remote descendants, so that *they* will embody both the ancient Moon and the Moon of their own moment in time. Between the old and the new phases, complex lunar patterns emerge. And the visible Moon is taken into folklore and myth, where it finds itself again, symbol against biological rhythm, and reemerges with new myths, deeper and more remote lunar music, and the traditional chalices, coins, goddesses, and temples.

Lunar effects are so scattered and so imposed and reimposed on each other, melodically and amelodically, that we can no longer find them, but there is a Moon present in every one of us, and in every natural event, in every stone and piece of dust—a Moon of some significance. The Moon leads subtle psychosomatic currents through our waking and sleeping, our consciousness and unconsciousness. Passing overhead, the Moon lightens the ocean by one ten-thousandth of its mass. The entire waters are lifted together in a single coherence, and the tides slide out. Organic liquids are molecular, and the lunar response is intensified in their high-pressure capillaries. Lunar sensitivity is excruciating. The tides may seem like raw neutral events when we regard waters on a bare rock ledge, seas receding to show long tidal flats and shellfish beds, but every internal shift within us releases profound sensations, images, and shapes, transforming the most basic aspects of what we are. The Moon stirs creatures with unintentional movement, endless aimless activity or wandering. The Solar System is woven with tidal effects, but the Moon's are the most powerful because they share the same solar orbit with the Earth. The bodies grind against one another to sustain a harmony. If the Earth is animate and the Moon is dead, surely this is only part of the picture—the Earth must share in the Moon's deadness, and the Moon must share in the Earth's life. The first photographs of the Earth from the Moon remind us of an original indivisibility.

The occult Moon stands for the stream of consciousness that flows between the manifested world and the hidden world. As spiritual silver, it is the source of regeneration and reproduction: in crystals, as cellular somatic material, and as thoughts, numbers, images, ideas. It embodies the colloidal basis of life and mind. The use of silver in photography reminds us that the Moon itself is like a photograph of the cosmos. Sunlight, starlight, and meteorite obliteration fall on it, and it is a perfect mirror, a photograph of everything that has happened. The autonomic Moon functions in the personality as instinct, desire to touch, and also as fear and flight. These are quick silvery gestures. Astrologically, the Moon draws out of the other planets their strongest tendencies. It is a mirror, and the mirroring is an eternal deepening of their own individualities.[1]

There is an old hermetic/astrological belief that the Earth is bound by the Moon, imprisoned by it. Occult practice demands the making conscious of blind responsive and reactive movements. The counterlunar disciplines are the most difficult, yet crucial, for men and women to master. They include meditation, awakening within dream, precise choreography, prescribed ceremony, poetics, the martial arts, and all those other disciplines that seek to break with the Moon by imitating it and imposing it back on itself. An infinitesimal amount of being is made conscious, and through that man adds directionality to his life.

Luna stands for the enslavement of man's will in blind, meaningless, destructive activity, mechanicalness, and habit. The Moon sustains life, but unchecked lunar flow becomes simply an agony and a spasm. William Faulkner writes of being born, trying to act, and finding all these other people and their arms and legs in the way, and one's own arms and legs in the way, and

all of them animated as if by puppet strings.[2] Although he did
not intend it as such, this is a description of the negative astrological Moon in the collective personality of the Earth.

In Gurdjieffian philosophy, the Moon sucks people's souls
into its body at the moment of death, and this endless transit is
the living link between the Earth and its dead animator. It is the
ultimate basis for the association of the Moon with death. The
souls are living electric things, built up by the transformation of
stellar matter through digestion and breathing into thought and
spirit; they can be attracted magnetically and physically by a
proximate body.[3] That body need not be sentient; it can be as
oblivious of dreams and fantasies as a comet is, but it will eat
souls as we eat the animals we kill. The Moon is one of those
beings of whom Juan Matus warned Carlos Castaneda: they stalk
us and we are a gift for them, even as the rabbit in our trap is
a gift for us.[4]

The Moon is the first obstacle to be overcome by the soul
after it has been separated from organic nature, for it must recognize that it will be sucked into its own habit, into automatic
response, and thus into oblivion of any individuality it has developed. The Gurdjieffian dances hammer away at lunar sub-
jugation and teach the dancers single free movements from
among the Moon motions they defiantly mimic back. Freedom
is formed of lunar activity made conscious. Otherwise all bursts
of freedom are illusory, mere sublimated lunar gestures.

Gurdjieff was a ruthless and severe guru because he felt that
the chances for preserving any of this after death depended on
absolutely unswerving training, to break down the Moon's ha-
bitual pull on Earth life. Action had to be made conscious. Men
had to see their true situation in the universe. "The earth," he
said, "is a very bad place from the cosmic point of view—it is
like the most remote part of northern Siberia, very far from
everywhere, it is cold, life is very hard. Everything that in another place either comes by itself or is easily obtained, is here
acquired only by hard labor; everything must be fought for both
in life and in the work."[5]

He had no pity for those who suffered. Pain was a means of
waking people up, momentarily startling them out of lunar tyr-

anny. Those who suffered needed not sympathy but training to make the suffering conscious. Pain located them in the real universe.

Everything consumes and transforms. Man must convert elemental material back into spiritual substance if he is not to die unredeemed.

But perhaps there is also a Boddhisattva function in the universe; perhaps there is one who does not himself enter paradise until all the other souls have gone before him. So he has a long wait. The cows are sentient as they stand in the field, carrying in the heat none other than their own heavy bodies, their tails swishing the flies. He will wait for them. Pine needles, maple leaves, catkins of momentary flowers; he will wait. Three men in a car in L.A. shoot a child on the sidewalk for kicks. He will wait.[6] "In every particle of dust," we are told, "there are present Buddhas without number."

The astronomical Moon clearly stands for the beginnings of this present system. Some say that it came out of the same nebula cloud that formed the Earth. Others say that it was captured from deep space. It is slightly less dense than the Earth, so either it got the lighter material out of the swirl or it originated elsewhere.

"The Moon is more than our lamp of night," wrote Rudolf Thiel, "more than the generator of our tides, more than a frozen, lifeless satellite. It is a surviving document out of the first day of Creation, from a day that perhaps even antedates the birth of light. It bears upon its face a runic script that tells us of how in the darkness of earliest genesis the heavenly bodies of the solar system, moons and Earth, and all the rest, emerged out of the primal nebula and grew great under a hail of meteorites."[7]

In the captured Moon scenario, the original Earth was roiling with radioactive fires; water from underground steam was beginning to collect in pools, and the primeval ocean was formed. It rained and rained and rained, eroding rocks, producing clay and mud and swamps. Shorelines emerged. Mountains built up in the sea. Enormous cumulus and nimbus clouds sparked lightning in the deluge, ultraviolet light rained down from the Sun, and the first amino acid chains came tumbling through the broth. The fertile water washed up on the clays, where new elements were incorporated into the DNA strands. Then this runaway planet swept into the Earth's field, swallowing the original moons in tremendous explosions. Gravity grabbed it and tore it, and continues to hold it with one face on the Earth. Tides stirred and volcanoes burst under the stress. But the runaway was caught. And so were we. Fiery stones showered the Earth. Hot lava spewed from the belly of this dead thing and spread across its primal craters. Now two planets were locked into orbit around one another 93 million miles from a sun-star, circling each other at a distance of 240,000 miles and orbiting the sun in 365¼ days.

A local origin for the Moon is far more likely. In either case, our satellite is an example of what happens to stellar material when it is cooled and exposed without an atmosphere. Nothing keeps the meteoroids out and nothing erases their marks. Trillions of tons of rock have been added to the Moon since its birth, leaving a world of craters and craters-within-craters. The biggest one is 800 miles in diameter, now filled in with lava and called a "sea." The impact must have nearly fissioned the Moon. The next biggest craters are 185 miles in diameter, and the smallest can be found in beads of Moon rock viewed through an electron microscope. The seas (*maria*) are actually old impact craters covered with lava. One-third of the Moon's hemisphere that faces us is made up of these and of the lakes (*lacus*) and marshes (*paludes*). They are all lava, with a layer of dust.

The fact that man went to the Moon in his ships, collected stones from its actual body, and returned to tell of it is a great tale, one that a Pawnee priest with his ancient medicine rocks would appreciate. We are committed to artifacts by our history. We value the oldest things: coins from the tombs of Egypt, the jade of the Confucian emperors, and the gold and silver pots of Asia Minor. Archaeologists have sifted the dusts of the Earth looking for relics of past civilizations and the early peoples of the New World. It is no longer a matter of rubies and gold, and it never really was. More valuable are the chipped pebble tools and molar teeth of creatures who lived and died millions of years ago, whose thoughts we cannot imagine, yet who began thought and so must be contained rudimentarily and fundamentally in our own thinking. We have scoured the Great Plains, Borax Lake, Frightful Cave, and Five Mile Rapids, looking for clues to migrations that took place following sacred constellations across whole continents. We have collected Clovis points, manos, hammerstones, scapula bones, Thule harpoons, medicine bundles, prayersticks, and Mandan poles. So we have voyaged to the "Moon" before, or to aboriginal sites that give our succession meaning. Because of the history of science in the West, the Moon rocks have a meaning they could never have in Pawnee or Hopi culture. They are the actual Moon. They are the completion of a question asked over thousands of years.

In analyzing the lunar artifacts, we are the same people who recreate the sequence of Indian cultures in the Great Basin from their broken tools. We accept that matter is never created, never destroyed, at least in our time. The Moon is an alternate version of ourselves, with a different destiny. In the Moon rocks we see the mark of the beginning of time—the formation of our own world and the other worlds in this System. And we have fulfilled the consequence of that kind of logic by going there to get them.

Several different types of rocks were brought back. Igneous rocks, mainly of calcium and aluminum silicates, were evidence of a once-molten Moon and the planetesimal and meteoroid deposits that began at birth more than four billion years ago. As the Moon's crust was forming, meteorites fell into its glowing red ingot. Although the Moon is not volcanic in the sense of having eruptive cones, it is volcanic insofar as igneous material breaks through cracks in the lunar surface. Basalts and rocks of potassium, phosphorus, and rare earths were formed in the following billion years from deep lava flows working their way to the surface. The oldest basalts have high percentages of titanium, a fact still unexplained. The glasslike and beady rocks also indicate some unknown agency. Despite this, and despite the Moon's lack of an iron core, the chemistries of the Earth and the Moon are remarkably similar, suggesting that these two worlds originated in the same whorl of the cosmic nebula.

As a lifeless, airless world, the Moon has been consigned to the planetary junkheap, but then fair Venus has proven to be a wasteland of another order, and the Moon has other redeeming qualities. Those who advocate space stations point to the Moon's low gravity, unimpeded diurnal solar energy, and abundant metals. Material mined on the surface of the Moon could be tossed directly into space by machines; there it could be smelted by raw sunlight and constructed into enormous dwelling and research units in the virtually gravityless void of outer space. With far less energy than on Earth, millions of people could be housed and fed. Using the Moon, we approach the life-giving Sun. And we begin to imitate the supercivilizations of our science fiction, who engineer great wheels and tubes about their planets in all directions, intricate cosmic mandalas dwarfing the original world.

But when we reduce worlds to mines, we reveal our ultimate prejudice toward ceaseless resources and expansion. We are callous capitalists, even the communists among us. We will use anything we can claim. This is our brilliance. If there are no Selenites or Martians to dispossess, our job is all the easier. But that does not mean we will look long and hard for them, and in places where men would not go. We will shoot first and ask questions later.

Is space construction the next step of cultural evolution? Or is the industrial age a false trail that contains the terms only for its own reduction to entropy? Can the Earth's biosphere, down to the subtlest life-chains, insects, and critical traces in soil and bacteria, be duplicated on artificial planet-moons? Has it already been duplicated by agribusiness in its monocrop farms? Or are these another mistake that risks ultimate famine for temporary plenty? Gurdjieff argued that we cannot mine even the Earth without disrupting our psychospiritual life, for all the deposits of minerals and metals have vital counterparts in the balanced personality of the planet. Global derangement comes exactly from dismantling the Earth's mineral psyche. It is clear, in any case, that industrialism, and the collective salvation that it proposes, can expand only into outer space. And if it can't go there it can no longer lead us, and another prophecy awaits our coming.

We cannot defile the lunar imagery that we have accumulated in our being. We can no more change what the Moon is by spaceflights than we can hide the real nature of the Earth by factories and cities. The old nature myths and gods remain, hidden within us and in sacred regions. The Moon goddesses remain, and the Moon itself in the sky continues to mold and initiate us.

Some 7,927 miles in diameter, slightly oblate and inclined on its axis, 8⅓ light-minutes from the Sun, the Earth is a living planet, geologically and biologically. Like the other planets, it was formed in a molten ball, and its solid parts developed as plates floating atop the original incandescence. New magma continuously erupts within, moving the plates and spreading the continents to new locations. They crash together, raising mountains and sinking coastlines. California and Egypt are temporary lands on a world that has seen Atlantis and Lemuria come and go thousands of times.

Biology and its consequent chemistry make the Earth what it is. Plants capture sunlight by photosynthesis and create a living layer above the stone. The oxygen they release may have been poisonous to the earliest life forms, but later creatures used oxidation as a means of releasing energy from substance, which led to complex animals of many cells. These then created another level interpenetrating the plants.

Water is the key to the chemical cycles which occur above the lithosphere. Water covers three-quarters of the Earth's surface, and most of that is ocean water filled with salts, metals, and dissolved gases—sixty of the ninety-two natural elements. Less than 1 percent of the planet's water is fresh; 2 percent is frozen in glaciers and ice caps. Some of it is contained in the atmosphere in complex cloud patterns that are integrated into cohesive weather systems by temperature zones and the ocean streams and currents. Water has a continuously moderating effect on climate, cooling hot areas and warming colder zones.

The oxygen in the atmosphere is critical to most living beings, but it is mixed with three times as much inert gaseous nitrogen. In the upper layers of the atmosphere, the oxygen becomes ionized, forming an ozone layer which protects the surface from radiation.

Blue oceans, white clouds, and brown-red land masses dominate the Earth that is seen from space. For all that we do in our divided nations and philosophies, we create this one lovely coherence and survive within its nurturing. One gets the illusion, said the astronaut Michael Collins, that there are somehow many worlds, many possibilities of this one world, if from nothing else than from the number of photographs there are of the world and the number of different ways in which it is referred to and discussed. But it is neither arbitrary nor multiple. Collins saw a single globe sitting there in space, as its clouds and oceans changed.

Two millennia earlier, Lucretius saw this realm from the surface:

Showers perish when father ether has flung them down into the lap of mother earth. But the crops spring up fresh and gay; the branches on the trees burst into leaf; the trees themselves grow and are weighed down with fruit. Hence in turn man and brute draw nourishment. Hence we see flourishing cities blest with children and every leafy thicket loud with new broods of songsters. Hence in lush pastures cattle wearied by their bulk fling down their bodies, and the white milky juice oozes from their swollen udders. Hence a new generation frolic friskily on wobbly legs through the fresh grass, their young minds tipsy with undiluted milk. Visible objects therefore do not perish utterly, since nature repairs one thing from another and allows nothing to be born without the aid of another's death.[8]

To enter the Earth by metal craft is a vibrating, shattering experience, and this is how it should be. Gravity protects this special place, a zone removed from its surroundings by more than simple space and the invisible fields and belts that issue from it. It is a wet hole in a desert trillions of miles long in all dimensions. And within that larger moistness are billions of moist bodies, jellies held together by hydrostatic tension and their own tough cellular networks, impermeable by simple water. Within them are still tinier bodies: eggs, spores, genes.

Being born into the Earth through this chain of matter is also a vibrating, shattering experience. The newborn infant crawls as a pagan newt from its mother, choking on its own blood. It is also an astronaut reaching this world in a ship made of the finest materials: earth, air, fire, and water. For us, the Earth is where incarnation and creation meet. We lie here watching shapes form and dissolve as the cumulus clouds blow in from the ocean and out over the hills.

As surely as Venus, being closer to the Sun and younger, became the Earth's mythical past, so Mars became our legendary future—a dying civilization on a planet grown old, a planet whose magma had cooled sooner, whose life had formed earlier, which had civilization when the Earth had only one-celled animals, which expended its air and water sooner, and now is in the last throes of existence after millions of years of history. Our hypothetical Martians were alternatively wise and peaceful, expansive and invading. Some of them were like Earthlings, others were based on the chemistry of silicon because of its bonding affinity with carbon and its ostensible abundance in the Martian sands. But silicon creatures would be alien to us from the cell on up.

From the time that Schiaparelli saw the lines in 1877 and Percival Lowell drew the waterworks and imagined an ancient civilization trying to preserve itself by drawing water from the polar caps, Mars has, to our minds, been inhabited. The Martians were our cosmic neighbors whom we strove one day to have the pleasure of meeting.

It has often been pointed out that the idea of Martian canals arose first in a mistranslation of Schiaparelli's term *canali* as "canals" rather than "channels." Lowell, conceiving these as artificial structures, published two provocative books: *Mars and Its Canals* and *Mars as the Abode of Life*. The Martians, he speculated, not only built these canals to irrigate their increasingly dry planet; they also launched two large satellites, the moons Deimos and Phobos. In Lowell's own words:

> . . . The lines start from points on the coast of the blue-green regions, commonly well-marked bays, and proceed directly to what seem centers in the middle of the conti-

nent, since most surprisingly they meet there other lines that have come to the same spot with apparently a like intent. . . . The lines appear either absolutely straight from one end to the other, or curved in an equally uniform manner. There is nothing haphazard in the look of any of them. . . .

A mind of no mean order would seem to have presided over the system we see—a mind certainly of considerably more comprehensiveness than that which presides over the various departments of our own public works. Party politics, at all events, have no part in them; for the system is planetwide.[9]

Lowell's Mars spawned the "mediæval" desert civilizations of Edgar Rice Burroughs to which John Carter, his fictional hero, astrally projected. This kingdom gave way to the more peaceful telepathic sages of Robert Heinlein and Ray Bradbury, but Lowell lay behind all of them. His image was that compelling.

Until the first space probes, Lowellian Mars was still a possibility, though analysis of the density and composition of the Martian atmosphere during the 1950s seemed to all but do away with it. The later version was perhaps not exactly as Lowell had conceived it, but was rather a combination of his conception and Bradbury's and those of hundreds of other science fiction writers. If the red planet did not hold intelligent beings, at least it must have life—a fact which would be almost as stunning in its actuality as the imaginary monuments of long-dead civilizations. From the beginning, Mars betrayed us, almost exactly in the way the whole second half of the twentieth century has, which is the way in which we have betrayed ourselves.

Mariner 4 reached Mars on July 14, 1965. It took twenty-two pictures, covering about 1 percent of the surface. The part photographed was heavily cratered and not unlike the Moon. Mariner 4 also showed no magnetic field to deflect the solar wind and an even more minute atmosphere than was feared, 0.4 percent that of the Earth.

In July and August of 1969, Mariners 6 and 7 reached Mars. Although they showed some evidence of more complex terrain, including mountains and deserts, they in essence confirmed the earlier message: Mars was covered with craters. There was nothing to explain the dark features on Earth-based photographs except dark crater bottoms. The atmosphere turned out to be 90 percent carbon dioxide and a little heavier than previously thought. There was some water vapor fog. Temperatures near the South Pole went as low as $-189°$ F., while a hot equatorial day reached 68° F., sweltering by Martian standards.

Mariner 9 arrived in November 1971 to find Mars covered in its entirety with a dust storm that had arisen in the southern hemisphere a couple of months earlier, when the ship had been partway to Mars. A yellowish cloud emerged in the desert and crater region of Noachis, just west of a mountainous zone called Hellas on early maps. With Mars at perihelion and with trapped heat increasing the winds, the storm reached 100 miles per hour and required a month to settle as the planet slowly traveled further from the Sun. When the dust cleared, there was a totally new world. Now that we had lost Lowell's Mars for good, a strange nonlunar landscape began to emerge. Four dark areas, with deep circular rings of craters, stood above the sand. But they were not impact craters, they were volcanic craters—the biggest volcanoes seen anywhere on any world. The largest, Nix Olympica, was three hundred miles wide at the base from its lava flows and stretched eighteen miles in the air. Its name was accordingly changed from "Snows of Olympus" to Olympic Mountain (Olympus Mons). Another volcano, seen in the clearing dust, was 910 miles wide across its base cliffs.

And these volcanic caldera were not all. Mars was covered with channels and complex lined geography. Something had lifted the crust in some regions; in others there was erosion. And there were things that looked suspiciously like dried-out riverbeds, meandering and feathery. Later spacecraft saw more. Mars had a canyon so vast that its tiny tributaries were larger than the Grand Canyon. It stretched across the equator as long as the Mississippi River. The icecaps were found to contain a significant amount of water on top of a layer of carbon dioxide permafrost. (The water ice evaporates seasonally.) And there was clear evidence of water erosion in the canyonlands beneath Olympus Mons, dendritic patterns stretching for 3,000 miles and in 450-mile-long channels that seemed to deepen and widen downstream. These were ancient Martian rivers, now waterless, reminiscent of Lowell. Mars was an arid land shaped by water, filled with gulleys and canyons like the American southwest. Where this water went no one knows.

As the whole surface was photographed, the old craters were in abundance too, but there is a large amount of surface area on Mars, the same amount as there is *not* covered by water on the Earth; thus there is land for many distinct topographies, climates, and regions. The North Pole was surrounded by a gigantic dune field, probably wind-shaped. One area was filled with inexplicable "pyramids." Extensive clouds of water ice capped the volcanoes. There was even a mackerel sky one day over Labyrinthus Noctis. In some areas, the clouds were very complex, running from cirro-cumulus to cumulus with fog and mist beneath, or in cyclonic spirals from which volcanic shields dramatically emerged in the dawn as the spacecraft raced across sun and darkness. The southern polar region showed ledges and wind erosion of the ice. Mars was not an eternal photograph like the Moon; it had days that were different from other days and for local reasons, not because some new meteorite had fallen.

The cloudiness in such a thin atmosphere actually indicated an incredibly high humidity, with the atmosphere almost saturated and ground fog everywhere. Water was found in all the rock samples tested by the landers. But most of the potential Martian atmosphere was trapped in the polar caps.

Mars is roughly within the Earth zone of temperatures: at perigee it is 35 million miles farther from the Sun, at apogee it is 60 million miles farther away. It is somewhat smaller than the Earth and Venus, 4,216 miles in diameter. Schiaparelli and all later observers saw Martian seasons, with dwindling and expanding polar caps. But seasons need not mean great poppy fields or irrigated grains. On Mars, seasons are apparently duststorms, reflecting climatological change with movement through the yearly cycle, intensified by the inclination of the planet on its axis. Because of the thin atmosphere, the temperature plummets swiftly after sunset. On a warm summer day, the Martian night is well below zero. This means that any life form would have to sustain this temperature range. Since the polar caps should be able to refreeze at night, their rapid seasonal shrinkage indicates that they are quite thin.

The first Viking lander rested on a desert in Chryse Planitia strewn with boulders of all sizes and small ridges. Sunset over the summer plains was a brilliant magenta, the color of our first alien sky. The topographic contour lines on the picture gave the illusion of a jewel-filled geode, radiating in concentric circles of delicate pinkish, violet, and magenta shades until the last ring disappeared into the ebony Martian night. The redness of the ground was from a relatively thin coating of hydrated limonite. The iron oxide influenced Mars's image from the beginning. In 1644, when it was newly imagined as a planet, Father Athanasius Kircher described it in his book *Mundus Subterraneus:* "The surface is extremely hard, rough, sooty, and sulphurous, but incombustible, sweating tar and naphtha, surrounded by poisonous vapors. From mountain gorges brownish flames burst with a frightful stench; the seas are viscous sulphurous mud."[10] Mars does show a hundred times as much sulphur as the Earth.

The second Viking lander rested on the more northern tundra of Utopia Planitia among rock-free channels. The test for life had ambiguous results. The spacecraft drew some of the Martian dirt into its laboratory and reported that Mars was virtually teeming with microorganic life or minute insectoids. After the previous disappointments, this was almost too good to be true. We had come to terms with a barren Mars; then a new mystery arose. Of course, "life" was only an interpretation of broadcast codes, and later interpretation was that some substance in the Martian soil "mimicked life," to use the words of planetologists. How can something mimic life? Were they saying that the experiment was flawed? Were they saying that they had found something neither dead nor alive?

Ultimately the experts concluded that Mars did not have even the organic compounds found on some meteorites. It was as dead as dead can be. As for the activity, they decided that some aspect of the Martian soil seemed to digest Earth's offering of organic molecules for unknown reasons.

If the "Martians" were radically different from us and were to send a lander here to ask "Is there life on Earth?", would it report that, from a Martian standpoint, we only mimic life? Our present assumption is that they would recognize the Earth as teeming with organisms, and that even if their lander rested on the Arctic plains, it would record the existence of microorganisms. This is why *our* experiment concludes that Mars is lifeless.

The moons of Mars were discovered during August 1877 by the American astronomer Asaph Hall, who had previously complained about the planet's moonless condition. Deimos was found on August 10, and Phobos a few days later. Both are extraordinarily faint, and Phobos (alone of all the moons in the Solar System) whips around its planet in less time than it takes the planet to rotate on its axis. Hall named them after the god Mars's attendants (Panic and Fear), and Lowell later considered them satellites launched by his intelligent civilization. Mariner showed the moons to be objects composed of one of the darkest materials known, heavily cratered, irregular in shape, and very old. They are utterly different from the Earth's moon, and they are probably captured asteroids made of dark carbonaceous material.

Still, we got to another planet, stood by proxy on its plains, watched its pink or blue sky, and saw its sun set. John Carter and the "Martian Chronicles" were not dead, but evidently they belonged elsewhere, or they belonged to this Martian world in another, supernatural way. The fragments of different Martian novels rush by: the computers of Deimos; ice-skating home along the canals in the subzero Martian night; furry balls of creatures bounding across the desert; colonies by the dead sea; the windships, the wonderful windships, like great Phoenician vessels, one after another across red sands; the metal books with raised hieroglyphs; the electric spiders; the palaces; the battles in dry sea bottoms; the poisonous showers that the Martian dictators made Flash Gordon take; the freezing dawns with twin moons; the theft of Phobos; the ruins of stone on vast deserts; the hypnotists who created Illinois towns there; the remaining jewels of the Martian dynasties; the invisible telepaths in the atmosphere; and finally, the abandoned Earth colonies falling into ruins like those of Lowell's Mars, and then all of them covered by sand and craters and boulders, and never having existed, so that we come to Mars ourselves in the sixties of America and the West all differently.

In the words of John Carter:

> I am of another world, the great planet Earth, which revolves about our common sun and the next within the orbit of your Barsoom, which we know as Mars. How I came here I cannot tell you, for I do not know; but here I am, and since my presence has permitted me to serve Dejah Thoris I am glad that I am here.[11]

But this was another America, before World War II, just as it was another Mars. John Carter's intrigues sound as impossible as the heroism of the CIA in the sixties. And the more ancient Mars has died at the hands of post–World War II space science.

In occult terms, Mars is transforming and regenerative. It is certainly the bloody planet of war—not war for war's own sake, but war as the inevitable conflict of forces involved in change. Mars has a vigilant and a processional quality. It is a lawgiving force that structure must obey; Mars is unrelenting. If it relented to save a single sparrow outside the law, the structure of matter itself would cave in and all would be lost.

Mars is rhetoric as well as law—social order, personal property. It is a planet of embodiment whose metal is iron, which gives shape and structure to substance and generates spherical and radial forms. Iron is simultaneously associated with blood and magnetism, with the dodecahedron-pentagon shape of pyrite crystals and the iron will. It forms very strong chemical bonds. In the martial sphere, these are implemented as weapons of iron. This may be incidental to Mars the planet, but it affected the imagery that Burroughs gave his world—chivalry and battle—and it served the implacable designs of the Martian invaders who appeared on the radio suddenly on October 30, 1938, as *War of the Worlds* was broadcast:

When I came in my son said, "Mother, something has come
down from Mars and the world is coming to an end." . . .
I heard 40 people were killed and there was gas and every-
body was choking.[12]

The enormous gulf between Mars and Jupiter is filled with
thousands of small airless rocks, the biggest of which, Ceres, is
450 miles in diameter. In one sense, the asteroid belt is like the
lost continent of Atlantis. Some great world may have been here
and exploded. Or the asteroids may be the remaining planetes-
simals, embryos kept from forming their own world by Jupiter's
bulk. As such, they would be an exposed cross section of the
origin of the Solar System, as Olduvai Gorge is for the history
of Africa and the origin of man. They cluster in groups, some
highly perturbed by Jupiter, like the Trojan asteroids which developed colinear libration points with their giant neighbor. The
asteroids might contain relics of the prebiological chemistry of
the nebula, or they might hold the barely recognizable remains
of a civilization which destroyed itself or was destroyed. It would
be a sad and shocking moment to realize that the first solar
empire was here and that something cataclysmic befell it before
we were born. We would wonder: are we its survivors? More
likely, we will find only rocks and badlands, as in the science
fiction image of the asteroid belt as a kind of scrub outpost of
mining villages where outlaws hide.

As we pass beyond Mars and the asteroid belt, we leave the
golden age of science fiction and the Terran planets, and we
enter the true center of our System. Mars and Venus represent
the myths of a previous generation. The outer Solar System
stands for the 1980s and beyond.

19

The Planets:
IV: Jupiter
and Its Moons

O F ALL THE PLANETS , Jupiter is the one whose image has deepened most in the last decade. For a long time, its sheer hugeness dominated every other sensibility, and, in a Solar System where we were looking for delicacies like the Earth, Jupiter was a monster, an insensitive bully, indiscriminately capturing moons and crushing everything that got in its way. Our Martian imagery was so developed that Mars actually seemed vaster, though Jupiter is thousands of times the size of Mars. There was little to say about the giant planet except that it was an ocean of cold poisonous gas.

Through telescopes, Jupiter shows up as richly colored bands: brown, light orange, amber, and reddish. The red spot itself is a single persistent feature, unexplained scientifically. It alone could hold more than three Earths; three times the diameter of our whole planet, our whole world, could fit in this one feature with room to spare, and more than thirteen hundred whole Earths could fit into Jupiter itself.

The fact that it is gaseous, with helium and hydrogen dominating, has come, in itself, to be interesting. Mars, like Mercury and the Moon, seems sterile and lifeless. After becoming worlds in our imagination, these bodies have lost much of their worldhood and hang in space as huge metallic shields bombarded by random stones—virtually skyless, and without the interesting softness of liquid or the subtle blendings of distance against a rich sky. Venus has an atmosphere and a sky, but they are its curse.

Jupiter is at least wet. If we could sit inside an imaginary house with windows, at the point on Jupiter where there might be a surface, the windows would be whipped by brilliantly colored liquids moving at terrific speeds. The storms would splatter and interact, and the light from this weather would be a constant variance of auroral sparkling and faint rainbows of bent sunlight. Photons rushing onto the Earth smash into the blue sky, fall into the oceans, and some are drunk by green plants. Photons falling onto Jupiter are swept into a continuous 300-mile-per-hour storm that has stirred everything up from moorings nothing ever held and by these many millions of years has found an equilibrium in which everything, torn in chaos, is actually sifted into precise belts of affinity and order. The light enters and is torn into colors and food for this pattern.

We also know now that Jupiter is not quite so cold as we had thought appropriate for its distance from the Sun. It gives off more heat than it receives, and in some images it is a miniature Sun, not large enough to burst into incandescence, but large enough so that something like solar heat is coming from the planetary body. The Sun itself is fire, and Jupiter is liquid and air, which is a big difference. On the Sun everything is obliterated and simple. Jupiter plays with the complexity of matter right down to its core. In a wild chemical dance, Jupiter keeps substance on our own side of Sunhood, exploring it in methane and hydrogen alchemy, spinning it around in mirrorings of solar storms. We cannot imagine a furnace as a world, but we can begin to accept a storm, for we have seen how Earth itself can terrifyingly turn colors and stir up hurricane winds and blow chemicals upon ships and houses and begin to twirl everything into funnels of liquid, wind, and light. After it quiets we look at its debris, the littered planks and torn rags. What repose could we promise the Jovian debris in unceasing gale?

With Jupiter we are entering a different realm of meaning, for this is not a planet with a surface; it is a sphere of contained swirling gases that may get thick enough to form a ground only at the bottom of an enormous dense sea. Nothing could have prepared us for the tumultuous tapestry of cyclonic movements visible at all levels of Jupiter as it was photographed by Voyager. We saw a land of ceaseless churning activity, each minute pattern of it larger than the Earth, with an eerie coherence of internal movement. From the "Whole Jupiter" perspective of Voyager, we could see these maelstroms as connected streams of an intricate meteorological system; yet each of them contained patterns as complex and coherent as the whole system, and each of those patterns contained patterns. The visible swirls were knitted by invisible swirls, right down to the size of an Earth ocean, a mere pond by Jovian standards, and, from there, down to minute pools. All of these were fused in the magnificent ikon glowing at night's distance.

White blobs passed in and out of the red spot, dissolving and reforming. How? Currents circulated in circles and countercircles, like paint in whirlpools. Some of the waves seemed almost ornate and cushiony in their splotches of foam and scrolls 50,000 miles long, bearing gentle Jovian wombs in their centers. Brilliantly blue and green, their counterwaves rushed out behind them. Red and white and greenish storm spirals with dark interzone channels thundered against and through the scrolls. Viscosity tore out the top of the red spot, its last layer of yolk, turning yellow, blue, and white in doing so. Then, over a space the size of whole planets, it splashed down into a brilliant white flood beneath a white oval cast off by a similar painted wave.

Billows and swirls crashed against each other, and each interference produced a dominance of one or another design, or dissipation into some totally different pattern.

And this is just one area of the planet around the red spot. The complexity of chemistry defies description. If we could survive an entry of Jupiter, Arthur Clarke seemed to be saying at the end of his *Space Odyssey*, we would pass through an endless undulant rainbow in which lands would come into being, surfaces shimmer, all to be swept away into deeper and deeper mirages and distortions until time and space were turned into something else.

The new images of Jupiter emerge from a sixties counterculture, though, in fact, they are far older and more archetypal. They include "inhabited Jupiter," "Jovian resources," and "Jupiter, gateway to the outer worlds."

Inhabited Jupiter came into being as we let go of the prejudice that this simian shape of ours is the one intelligent symmetry that nature can make. In prior decades, we had imagined humanoids maintaining the canal systems of Mars, nursing their dying civilization. UFO encounters were usually with beings of human or semihuman shape. And, whether we believe in the ancient astronauts or not, our prejudice has been to see them as beings like ourselves, their hominid images cut on stones of the Sahara and in the temples of South America: Erich von Daniken's great white gods.

But as we observed other species on our own world and noted man's less than glorious behavior in the local ecosphere, we became more objective about "destiny's angel." The whales and dolphins of the Earth's seas are intelligent beings of another kind. Why might not intelligent water-beings arise on another planet?

Evolution of the mind has been placed back at the feet of the raw cosmic materials: hydrogen, oxygen, nitrogen, carbon, and silicon. The toxic whirlwind of Jupiter has become a bloody and fertile egg. Methane and hydrogen and ammonia gases are now understood in terms of their resemblance to life, to the crystalline matrix of living cells, rather than in terms of their deadly consequence if inhaled by terran lungs.

"We cannot imagine that Jupiter is inhabited," I wrote in an essay on the planet in a book of ecological thoughts in 1968. "Yet we imagine the ancient desert cities of Mars, as though Oaxacan or Egyptian, the canals bringing water from the polar icecaps to a dying empire. We can embroider Venus with dense jungles, an age of seeding ferns and lizards, rain forests and quaking bogs. But what creature breathes ammonia and swims under tons of icy atmosphere?"[1]

This is the old prejudice, the boastful certainty of our privileged real estate in the temperature range of the solar sea, our rightness as a species. But it was necessary then to begin to

speak for Jupiter, not for the Jovians, but for the dangerous
simplicity of our images of ourselves.

On Jupiter the universe is hardly getting down to something interesting; it is getting down to itself, what it is at
this distance and pressure, as on the Earth. But we believe
our own melodrama, hence the Garden between fire and
ice, between water and stone, between jungle and desert.
Jupiter is a Garden also. Life breaks like a crystal, grows
outward, a bud shedding protective hairs, knows itself in
sexual feedback; life is methane and ammonia, for methane
and ammonia are children of the sun as oxygen and carbon,
and are conscious but to other ends. Jupiter is now in the
middle of its ammonia and methane history. . . . The map
of Jupiter, belted in colored latitudinal zones like the forests and tundras and deserts of phytogeography, is an historical puzzle, a map left by unknown sea-kings of another
world of which we are dimly and always conscious, a map
we cannot deny by reducing it to literal chaotic vectors.
. . . Jupiter's history is as tragic as our own, as uncertain, as
needy of saviors and wisemen, these ammonia-hydrogen
life-forms assuming crystalline bodies as flesh but their own
flesh. [2]

This image softens us and puts us back in a living universe.
We are no longer astronomers first; we are creatures, and our
astronomy is as much a living protuberance as the cartilege of
the shark or the feathers of the owl. If it has something to say
about Jupiter too, all the better, but it is Earth looking back at
Earth through the Jovian possibility.

Looking out at the inhabited planet, we must realize that
from any particular ring of consciousness, any other, based
on different chemical chains, will look like a chemical hell,
as Earth does from the Jovian laboratory on Io. They claim
that no one could live in hydrogen, oxygen, and carbon; no
one could live on such a light world; everyone would float
to the sky. . . .
Jupiter leaves on Kodachrome a signature of history, of
use, of conscious dreaming to undo the enigma. And, as
we, the Jovians softly breed, and listen within for the voice
of their planet, listen from the North Polar Regions, yes,

and in the North North Temperate Belt, listen from the nations of the Equator and the schools of the South Tropical Zone. They are not Esquimaux and Polynesians; they are creatures of ammonia, and breathe ammonia and love ammonia bodies, the curse of flesh albeit, and their dreams are the eternal dreams contained in ammonia crystal and ammonia nerves.[3]

If we were gracious, we would extend to the unknown inhabitants of eternal Jupiter the same desires for peace and honor that we wish "them" to extend to us, the same humane curiosity that we, as Westerners, failed to use in Africa or the islands of the Pacific, turning the peoples into less-than-humans and pretending that we had a Biblical injunction to enslave them and steal their bounty. The Jovians should be so warned. And we should be warned too. This is the Air Force fear of UFOs, that they might actually be great galleons carrying conquistadors, the first vessels of an army larger than ours, to which we are vulnerable and naive. Is this a projection of an ancient cosmic terror? Are we so embarrassed for what we have done that we must continue doing it? Should we not find our own cosmic sympathy first and regain our dignity on Earth before we even imagine who goes thither among the planetary spheres?

The idea of "stealing" Jupiter is not as remote as it may seem. It is outside our present capacity but not outside the conceptualization of our technology or the scope of what seems to be our greed. For instance, in the 1960s, Freeman Dyson suggested that we could completely vaporize Jupiter and use its materials to create a shell around the Sun. We—i.e., the human species, the people of the Earth—would dwell on the inside of this shell, with a surface area one billion times greater than that of the Earth, utilizing every single photon emitted by the Sun.[4] This is certainly the present supertechnology writ large and applied to the two major potential sources of energy within our reach: Jupiter and the Sun. If not build an immense shell, then perhaps we could maintain a gas pipeline directly from the ammonia-hydrogen atmosphere. These images are fever symptoms. Whether we are astronomers, space physicists, or simply citizens, our feeling for twentieth-century Earth leads us not only

THE NIGHT SKY

to look back to simpler, more pastoral times (whether there ever were such), but also to fantasize endless windfall profits from new strikes. Our peoples seem too many, our bombs too big, our oil too depleted, our planet in general too small. For what, we do not know.

But Jupiter's size and composition speak to our Terran identity in another way. Jupiter is not just a collection of different storms, cloud layers of different colors, internal energy sources, and interphases, any of them many times bigger than the Earth. It is a single planet, and it gives us a sense of our own size, not in its largeness of resources or its dwarfing of our volume but in the way that any planet coalesces as a single system within the limits of its space and materials. The creatures of Jupiter, Arthur Clarke's science fiction medusas and mantas, no doubt face the same population pressure we do:

> It did not resemble a tree at all but a jellyfish—a medusa such as might be met trailing its tentacles as it drifted along the warm eddies of the Gulf Stream.
> *This* medusa was two kilometers across and its scores of dangling tentacles were hundreds of meters long. They swayed slowly back and forth in perfect unison, taking more than a minute for each complete undulation—almost as if the creature were clumsily rowing itself through the sky. . . .
> High intelligence could only develop among predators—not among the drifting browsers of either sea or air. The mantas were far closer to him than was this monstrous bag of gas; and anyway, who could *really* sympathize with a creature a hundred thousand times larger than a whale?[5]

We pretend that if the Earth were the same volume as Jupiter, we would still have millions of years left before expending our resources. This is not true. Material and volume expand at the same rate inwardly. We would be at exactly the point we are now, for all worlds are finally the same size. In seeing Jupiter as big, we see the Earth as a big world too. Volume is a law of space, girth of matter. It is how we inhabit and appreciate our volume, not sheer number or amount, that determines the depth of our existence.

Looking at Jupiter through the photo-satellite, we know that this is a space into which 1,318 Earths would fit, though the conception is meaningless. Our experience cannot be multiplied that many times. Nor are any resources limitless. Something else determines our crisis. We have already envisioned the mortality of the Sun, which is the mortality of all free energy.

The true Jovian image is not poisonous gas, ceaseless gales and whirlpools, or monstrous size. All of these lie beyond our comprehension, beyond both infinity and zero. Jupiter stands inside us as a ceaseless unconscious process and as a radiant unity. Jupiter is the self that prevails, clear of any threat of death and destruction or diminution—and in the center of this Sun System. We stare into it, single mind by single mind, each one of us a unity, an image of creation. Jupiter is not thirteen hundred and eighteen things; it reflects back our own mind, as if it were a mind itself.

When the planets were formed, King Jupiter claimed a full 70 percent of the material made available in the nebula cloud around the Sun. So it continues to hold much of the mass and angular momentum of the Solar System. Its diameter is 86,000 miles, but, big as it is, it rotates rapidly on its axis, once every ten Earth-hours.

Jupiter maintains a mean distance of 483 million miles from the Sun, which it circles every 11.86 Earth-years. It is quite cold in the outer atmosphere, − 184° F. on the average, which is one reason its storms last so long: their energy dissipates slowly. Another is the lack of surface features to modify tempests. Jovian storms have deep roots.

Jupiter has retained a large amount of the basic gaseous materials that the planets, moons, and Sun inherited from the Solar nebula in their formation. It is very young in the sense that it hasn't aged and very old in the sense that it is a living dinosaur, a planet in the primeval state. Its immense mass has held the lighter gases that escaped from planets with weaker gravitational fields, so Jupiter has an abundance of the "life" compounds: methane, hydrogen, water, and ammonia, as well as helium. By comparison, the Earth is made up of metals and minerals, with extensive deposits of iron and silicates. Dead or alive, Jupiter is an impressive nursery for natural selection and mutation to play in for a few billion years.

The center of the planet is very hot, 54,000° F., or five times the temperature of the surface of the Sun. The pressure on the planet is the equivalent of a hundred million Earth atmospheres, quite possibly enough to turn the hydrogen metallic. This may, in fact, be the Jovian surface.

However, as cloud layers are heated from beneath and transmit heat, a moderate zone fluctuates through the planet at different depths and in irregular currents. There is enough internal heat and external cold to produce intermediate climates, both tropical and temperate, poisonous by our standards but not by the standards of the organic compounds which would form on such a world. There are potentially hundreds of millions of microenvironments in the Jovian swirls-within-swirls in which life could develop. The atmosphere is strafed with lightning from end to end, and this could well jolt organic molecules into existence throughout the Jovian sea. It is indeed a strange birth for cells among the clouds, but all births into the world of light are strange. All are a sort of fire of waters. The "photosynthetic" brightening and darkening of the red spot in thirty-year intervals suggests a biological pattern, a thicket of vegetation in a cornucopia of edible molecules.

Jupiter has an extremely large and complex magnetosphere and intense radiation belts, some of them caused by the metallization of liquid hydrogen under great pressure. Visible Jupiter is enormous enough, but the magnetosphere extends 450 million miles around the planet. Some particles in the vicinity of Jupiter are so charged that they are hotter than the interior of the Sun. All of this is invisible in the Earth's sky, but if we could see it, it would be just about the most dominant feature of our cosmology; it would outshine the Moon and rival the Sun.

The immense radio noise of Jupiter was first heard in the mid-1950s and was thought to be associated with the rotation of the planet itself because of its ten-hour phases. It was later discovered to be the rate of rotation of the magnetic dipole field, which is inclined 10° from the physical axis. Each burst is at least the equivalent, in energy terms, of an earthquake or a hurricane. The broadcast cycle is linked in a doubly periodic system with the rotation of the magnetic field of the planet and the 1.77-day revolution of the satellite Io around Jupiter. As Io is bombarded continually with Jovian radiation, it emits an invisible torus of charged particles, so that it passes around Jupiter in a doughnut-shaped tunnel. At the same time, Io connects to Jupiter directly by a horseshoe-shaped flux tube of five million amperes. This makes Io and Jupiter a complex system of magnetism, radio noise, and radiation unlike anything else in the Solar System. The gigantic planet and its miniscule moon generate more energy between them than all of the Earth's electrical generators. If Jupiter is the chief god of the Solar System, Io is the radio and the forge; it is the immediate receptor of the Jovian power, which it transmits to the universe.[6]

Jupiter has a fantastic system of worlds encircling it as planets encircle a Sun. It is, in that sense, a second center to the Solar System, named appropriately after Zeus (Jupiter), who overthrew Cronus (Saturn) and the old gods, and who now presides as king over the present millennium. The Sun may have nine planets, but Jupiter has at least fifteen moons, the last two of them discovered by Voyager on the edge of a thin Jovian ring system. The four large moons are the Galilean satellites, formally discovered by Galileo but seen by sharp-eyed shepherds and sailors for millennia, and hence known esoterically from the dawn of time. With Venus and Mars having thwarted the fantasies of both scientists and science fiction writers, the four large Jovian moons became the mystery worlds of the 1980s, holding the promise of strange realms despite their low temperatures and high radiation. There was always the possibility of unknown heat sources in the Jovian system.

These satellites were visited by Voyager in 1979 and photographed one by one. Suddenly the Earth was showered with images of four "planets" that most people had never heard of. Their landscapes were stunning, though our survival on them would range from a matter of seconds on Io to barely longer on the other Galilean moons.[7]

Io is the closest large moon to Jupiter, at a distance of a little over 227,000 miles. It has a diameter of almost 2,000 miles, or 90 percent that of Mercury. Only tiny irregular Amalthea and the two unnamed 1979 Voyager moons (one within Amalthea's orbit and one outside it) are closer to the planet itself. Europa is a third again as far away as Io and slightly smaller. Ganymede is 36 percent larger than Mercury and over 500,000 miles from Jupiter. Callisto is slightly larger than Ganymede and a little less than twice as far away from Jupiter.

The other moons of Jupiter are very tiny. A second group, made up of Himalia, Elara, Lysithia, and Leda, revolve around the planet at between 7.15 and 7.27 million miles out. Their diameters range from 12 to 37 miles. A third group circles the planet in retrograde clockwise orbits at distances from 12.86 to 14.73 million miles away. None has a diameter larger than 18 miles, and the smallest has a diameter of 9 miles. Pasiphae, Sinope, Carme, and Ananke are so highly inclined that they are virtually leaning on their sides. They are perturbed in their revolutions about the planet by the other satellites, by Saturn, and by the Sun itself, with orbits so eccentric that they defy Keplerian ellipses. In fact, these moons change their orbits regularly like a mime of electrons. They may well be captured asteroids. The other satellites are tiny and unnamed.

Io was the first Jovian "planet" visited by Voyager. Its surface was the biggest surprise of the space program. It could have come from another galaxy. Mars and Venus had been pondered for decades in advance. But there was nothing to prepare us for Io. Instead of the expected craters, there were curious erratic zones and splotches of dark and light material, some obviously liquid flows, bright patches of color in sharp, irregular patterns, and regions where it was impossible to tell figure from ground or which way a current was flowing. Active volcanoes were shooting plumes 200 miles in the air. Here was the first geologically alive body and the first visible uncratered surface in the Solar System other than Earth's. Who would have expected the honor would fall to Io?

It is now assumed that Io's climate and topography are created by the intense relationship between it and Jupiter and the simultaneous gravitational pull between Jupiter and the other nearby satellites. This twisting back and forth causes tidal bulges and a crust that rises and sinks more than thirty feet per Ionian day (or Jovian revolution). There may also be a sulphur ocean within Io feeding subterranean sulphur lakes, or pure sulphur springs from aquifers. Io also has very black crescent shapes on its red hot surface, and blue clouds. The former may be lava flows.

This world is so continuously bombarded with Jovian radiation that it is a ceaseless crucible of lava, lightning, ions, and flares. Gas and ice clouds form everywhere, as over an imaginary industrial city. Io may be geologically alive, but it clearly has forfeited creature life as we know it.

Mythological names are automatically given to features on celestial bodies, with the difference that they now come from international culture and with a particular sensitivity for non-Western terminology and Third World divinities. So the first map of Io represents the global culture that photographed its surface; the volcanic paterae are Persian, Mongolian, Egyptian, Celtic, Iroquoian, Incan, Nicaraguan, Zambezian, Quechuan, Pawnee, Babylonia, and Hopi. One is named after the Japanese sun-goddess Amatersau, who reemerged from a cave to restore light to a darkened world. The volcanic peaks, shield volcanoes, and vaporous fissures are named specifically after fire gods and goddesses: Marduk (Sumero-Akkadian), Masubi (Japanese), Maui and Pele (Hawaiian), Prometheus (Greek), Surt (Icelandic), Loki (Norse), Amirani (Soviet Georgian), and Volund (the Germanic blacksmith god).[8]

Europa was only distantly glimpsed by the first Voyager, but the second photographed it closely. The pictures showed an enormous frozen ocean streaked with dark wiggly lines. The surface was as smooth as that of any world ever seen. The dark areas had so little relief that they might have been colored stains on the ice, but were probably fissures filled by material oozing from the Europan interior. Io was found to be a world of black lakes and riotous sulphur geysers. A walk across it would take us through intermittent yellow, orange, and blue snows. Europa would bombard its visitors with huge ice pellets shot up from geysers. If we crossed the entire planet, we would never leave the ice age; only the color of the crust would occasionally change from brown to white and back again. Some scientists proposed an active worm life beneath the ice.

Ganymede turned out to be an enormous meteor-ground glacier with primordial brown ponds, muddy and frozen for eternity and themselves pocked with craters. It may have been entirely covered by ocean earlier in its history. Part of the surface consists of long crosscutting and interfering chains of ridges. Twenty miles of such valleys are followed by thirty-foot-high shelves. An explorer might abruptly leave one such system and enter another going off at an angle or find the pattern interrupted by a crater but continued on the other side. Scientists have referred to these as possible tectonic plates, so that Ganymede is a frozen picture of continental drift.

There is probably no more pocked body in the Solar System than Callisto. It has recorded so many millions of years of meteorites in ice that it looks more like a chunk of conglomerate than a world. One impact basin is more than 100 miles across and many miles deep, with a smoothed-out bottom. Concentric circles run out from it for miles. It is one of the biggest collisions registered in the rock of the Solar System. In this case the rock is ice. Callisto froze early and deep. At the moment of impact, this world had an instant ocean, but almost immediately ice poured in and the ocean began to refreeze, creating the hundred-mile long ice castle of frozen splashes, eerie towers, and twisted ice shapes, with crumbling ancient ice renested in new ice formed of ancient ice melted and refrozen. This is probably a dead museum, but who knows? Who knows if man will ever walk here and shine his light through the colored ice and stand within this gargantuan monument to the unknown violent gods of this System?

Of these satellites, the three innermost, Io, Europa, and Ganymede, seem almost synchronized with each other. The sidereal rotation period of Io stands in a ratio to that of Europa of 2.0073, almost exactly the harmonic; and Ganymede's sidereal rotation has a ratio to Io's period of 4.0441, almost exactly double the first ratio. When Io and Europa fall on the same line passing through the center of Jupiter, then Ganymede also falls on the line or stands at a right angle to it, and this is true of any combination of the three: either all three are in a line if two are, or the third is at a right angle to the other two. The line of this conjunction rotates gradually around the planet, completing a cycle every one and a third years.[9] This would obviously be a focal point for any Jovian astrologers, and, in fact, Arthur Clarke seemed to use the lining up of the Galilean satellites to mark a moment in Earth-Jupiter time in *2001* just before the astronaut's descent into the giant world. The Galilean rebus discloses the entry into the Jovian temple.

Clarke's story begins when a remnant of intelligence is found on the Moon.[10] It points outward to Jupiter. The Moon is the base, the watchpost and signaling area for outer space peoples involved with our species, perhaps even ancestral to us. An enormous computerized spaceship is sent on an odyssey to the Jovian center, but, even from the beginning, there is the implicit problem of what to do when it gets there. Will the mission be self-evident? Surely it cannot land there. The whole voyage is undertaken within this unstated mystery, as if man is compelled to answer the summons, compelled genetically and astrologically.

After various disasters en route reduce its crew to one, the remains of the ship are sucked into the gravitational field of Jupiter. The moons line up. The ship, it seems, could not have arrived at any other time. Even though millions of years lie between the initial message to man (in the bestowing of intelligence on early hominid forms) and the arrival of the ship, this is a matter of seconds in the timing of planets. Imagine just one sailor alone on the stormy Pacific. This astronaut is flung into the unknown whole of Jupiter, thirteen hundred and eighteen times as big as Earth. He must fall through the layers of storms and colors buffeted like a feather in a hurricane until he is crushed and the small fragments of his ship and his own body enter, on about the level of a bug, the Jovian vastness. It is more than death; it is the whole cosmic history that lies behind each of us (in our coming to be at all) and before each of us in eternity.

This is not what happens in the film. Space and time change. The astronaut enters a room or is lying in a room. He has become a spore. He is an old man. The Earth and Jupiter are breeding together; a heavy cosmic sexuality hangs over the bed. As flesh and intelligence, these worlds spawn an infant who is returned immediately, in a bubble, to the whole of the Earth. He is the child of the astronaut-Earth and the Jupiter system; and he is the avatar of Jupiter-Earth connection. The astronaut is killed but not killed; he lives through his whole life in the density of Jupiter's seconds. The meaning of his experience is wrung out of his flesh, but it stands clonally for all of Earth, as raw material for this new being, equally formed from the unknown system of Jupiter, which was linked to the Earth aboriginally and unconsciously. This is Jupiter as guardian of the secrets, key to the Solar System, but also willing magus to the Earth, as willing as those on Olympus once were to make this world, from a mountain which dwarfs even the mountains of Venus and the volcanoes of Io.

The strong external images of the planets and moons become internalized over time. Science fiction landscapes and creatures are one aspect of this process. Dreams are another. While working on a final revision of this book in January 1981, I had a dream which sheds light on the imagery of not only Jupiter and its moons but the whole Solar System. The intense ikons of the planet and the moons penetrated a hidden archetypal layer and generated a startling dream sequence:

Returning to the village in Vermont where I once lived, I am wandering toward the river at night. I learn from an undisclosed source that I am now in the Solar System. Immediately I begin to look about for planets. I do not know what region I am in. Suddenly I see a huge bright object spinning in the front yard of a house by the river. I recognize it instantly from its markings as the moon Ganymede of Jupiter. It is radiant, enormous, and intricately engraved, and, as it spins, I see all the features of the Voyager photographs. Yet, it is somehow contained in this front yard. Now that I know where I am, I begin to look for Jupiter itself. I suspect it must be over the large hill that rises out of town to the mountains. In fact, I am drawn in that direction by an immense gravity. I try to look through the trees, but the forest is as dense as lead, and I can only feel the presence of Jupiter beyond.

I start at once to climb in darkness, and I am very careful. I feel that at any misstep I can stumble and fall into Jupiter. The climb is perilous, as if I am walking along a mountain ledge overlooking the sea. I wonder if there are any other moons about, and I turn to see a tiny ball spinning rapidly in a bush in front of a house. I think, "How cute. That's the tiny fifteenth moon." It is minute compared to Ganymede, but just as fiery and radiant. I realize that dozens of these moons might be scattered in the bushes all around here, and I feel as though I am a child in an Easter Egg Hunt.

The heaviness pulls me up the hill, and, suddenly, through the trees, I see an enormous limb of brilliance. It is so overwhelming that it seems literally to blow me back. But I push on, as if I am floating in space. I see the broad bands of the planet, and I struggle to get out of its way.

A voice is suddenly telling me that I don't understand gravitation at all. "These are not the real planets," it says. "They are painted balls." I understand that it is speaking about the actual planets in space; it is saying that they themselves are only painted balls and that these replicas of them are mere symbols of the internal planets. There is another gravity, inside gravity, which is the real core of substance. I feel a wholeness and a bigness, as if all that cannot be connected or realized in a lifetime is joined in a unity of self for this one moment.

Astral Jupiter is clearly the king of the present Solar System. He enters roaring, filling people with terror and laughter, solemnity and pomp. The metal of Jupiter is tin, which is involved in coagulation, condensation, and the formation of cartilege. It is bony, or grey like the matter of the brain. Tin stands opposite the fluid breath of Cytherean copper.[11] The Jovian contribution to personality is justice and interpretation, with an emphasis on prosperity and growth, completion.

If Jupiter is the new order, Saturn is the old dying forces. Outside temporal wisdom, says bearded enigmatic Saturn, lies ageless wisdom. Inside my temporal system, says mighty Jupiter, is magic and splendor and ceaseless procreation. For the present, anyway, Jupiter symbolizes the end of possibility. Saturn begins something that is beyond us. It will be a long time, in any case, before we see past the bigness of Jupiter in ourselves.

20

The Planets:
V: Saturn, Uranus, Neptune, Pluto, and Their Moons

As WE MOVE FURTHER OUT in the Solar System, toward other stars, our information about worlds dwindles. We have sharp images of the Moon and Mars, but Uranus and Neptune are faint and fuzzy. We see only shadows of their grossest surface features. For the outer moons and Pluto, we have no images at all. They are bare tincture stains on the black illusory curtain of night. Beyond these, there may be other worlds in this System, and there are surely countless other worlds among the stars, but those we do not see at all.

The night sky sits as an almost weightless cap upon the heavy Earth. Its meanings have been stretched thin over billions of years of time-space, the photons barely reaching us despite their capacity for long-distance travel. All of the sun-stars and all of their worlds shower the Earth with not even the energy of the creatures in a droplet of pond water. At this distance they are mere ghost-selves. But the thin skin of their collective image is an impregnable wall of cosmology—cosmology which locates all real weight and mass at enormous distances from our center. We are dependent upon light. Without it, we are blind and ignorant.

But most light does not reach us. Most objects are unimaginably far away. In our own Solar System, neighboring planets only a few orbits away are virtually invisible. There is distortion in our atmosphere, and we and they are continuously moving in relation to each other, blurring long exposures. Even our most powerful telescopes strain to see out beyond Jupiter, much as fish in the mesopelagic zone do to see the Sun itself.

Detailed information about the outer Solar System must come from space probes because we cannot "see" far enough into it to gather any but the most meager information. Pioneer 11 and the first Voyager have now completed photographing the Jovian and Saturnian systems. Voyager 2 will reach Saturn in 1981, and, as Voyager 1 heads out of the Solar System, its twin will attempt to visit the planets and moons beyond Saturn, worlds unknown until relatively recent times. We have had only a few centuries in which to consider their existence. Soon we will encounter them directly.

Voyager 2's rendezvous with Uranus is planned for 1986, and in 1989 it may well look down into the frozen seas of Neptune and fly by Triton, Neptune's large moon. Small and fragile as these insect robots are, they are transmitting to the collective consciousness of the Earth whole images of the unvisited worlds they skirt.

The night sky has always been a source of our deepest visions. It has provided, from aeon to aeon, in conscious and unconscious forms, the images that have changed us. These new worlds—planets and moons—are being seeded among us at the end of our cosmic summer. No scientist or seer can begin to predict the crop they will yield early next cosmic spring. None of us will be around to see it, but the seeds have been planted, and whatever they are to become has already begun to form inside us.

These space probes seem absolutely necessary for some unknown reason. Their rich and even generous images stand against a paucity that we have not yet recognized. And it is not only a paucity of resources in the ground or of funds for the space program. It may have something to do with the record of ourselves that we have placed on the vehicles for creatures who may cull them from the cosmic debris. Our world is an over-

populated armed camp, and yet we are lonely, we seek someone
to talk to, even after our death. We kill off sentient species even
as we seek sentient species to learn from and to teach. As Voyager flies toward Uranus, we struggle against minimal, almost
arbitrary violence and cruelty. Soon enough, it will stand naked
in the presence of Neptune, seeking revelation. And then, long
after it sends us images, it will carry one curiously precious and
ethnocentric record of who we are. We will be somewhere else
entirely. What all this suggests is that somehow we should know
better. And I cannot even say what it is we should know better,
or why. Perhaps it is this that our experiment will teach us, long
after we have forgotten it and long after the discrete images and
data have merged with ancient history itself.

For better or for worse, we are different now. And we will
change even more. But perhaps we have become so utilitarian
that our leaders and so-called representatives would be quite
willing to trade these visions in for a new line of missiles or a
percentage point or two against the national debt. Future space
probes to the outer moons may never be launched with the
present prejudice, but fate decreed that we should fire these
babes into the night before our minimality prevented it. Now
we are at their mercy and the mercy of the images they send. A
moment in our own technological development coincided with
a window in the heavens: a satellite lofted through it would go
on a grand tour of the Solar System. Historical factors almost
blocked the mission. Thousands of meteors, asteroids, and fal-
lible parts on two delicate machines still stood in the way. Yet,
both Voyagers have survived, perhaps miraculously, to send
back close-ups of Jupiter and its system of moons. Clear images
of hazy, ringed Saturn arrived immediately following the election of Ronald Reagan—an event the ancients would have ascribed to Saturn anyway. Who knows what events will coincide
with our images of those other remote worlds, worlds about
which we know so much less? Obviously the meteors and asteroids that let our machine through mean to leave us no choice.

Traditionally, we have known that Saturn, Uranus, and Neptune are Jovian planets, massive, gaseous, and primitive. They

retain the primordial planetary environment: hydrogen, helium, and other light gases blended in thick atmospheres with no surfaces in the usual sense. By contrast, these gases have escaped from the smaller worlds, leaving thin auras upon the secondarily formed rocky cores. On any gaseous planet, there is uncertainty about how deep the visible features go. Are we seeing just the outermost layer of the atmosphere, or are the features sustained with some profundity? Are we seeing clots of gas at the tops of convection currents and the anti-cyclones they form with the upper air, or are we seeing eddies in the tops of swiftly rotating clouds? This question can be asked separately of the bands and the ovals on each planet. Though they are written literally in the wind and in gas, they may persist for hundreds of years.

The history of these worlds, since the birth of the System itself in the galactic cloud, has been an increasingly entangled engagement of storm layers and their effects. The bright pungent bands and ovals of weather lines stand out, but there is no archaeology cut in fossils or stones. The differences among these worlds come from their sizes, their distances from the Sun, the local endowments of original gases, the random patterns of development that each zone on each world has followed, and the delicate and complex interaction of all these things for millions of years. One ecological gradient surely dominates: as we move outward, the temperature drops rapidly and the Sun comes to look like an extremely bright star. Day sky and night sky, from Neptune, are virtually the same.

Before Voyager reached Saturn, it was difficult to imagine how it would be different from Jupiter. But right from the earliest images, it was revealed in light as a unique never-before-seen landscape. Saturn's face appeared iridescent yellow, almost golden in the sunlight, with storms twisting and swirling across it in ribbons and bands of yellow, tan, orange, and darker brown. It is the familiar Jovian turbulence, but with its own zones and patterns and peculiar hues. Jupiter looks like the bloody innards of a beast or a richly colored oynx. Saturn looks like the unformed yolk and albumen of a young egg or like an ancient gold coin rusted from seawater. Beneath these cameos, no doubt, lie profound differences of nature and character.

The winds across the lemon cloudtops were measured by Voyager at speeds as high as 900 miles per hour. Tan and dusky ovals were seen, as on Jupiter, marking the deep churning eddies of gaseous material from below. The Saturnian cold no doubt slows down chemical reactions and storm interaction, which accounts for some substantial differences from Jupiter. Saturn also seems to be less dense, with a greater abundance of lighter gases. Its radiation belt is twenty times weaker than that of Jupiter. Saturn's seasons are also likely to be longer and more intense than those of Jupiter—longer because of Saturn's year (equal to 29.5 Earth-years), and more intense because of Saturn's greater inclination on its axis. Regional effects would probably develop more distinctly than on Jupiter. Perhaps these factors lead to Saturn's larger quantity of ammonia haze, the golden clouds, and the displaced bands.

On Jupiter, the bands and currents seem to move across the planet alternating from west to east and east to west in a manner consistent with each other and with the upwelling zones. On Saturn, they are displaced ninety degrees from the upwelling zones, and in general they are less orderly and more chaotic. In the southern hemisphere of Saturn, there is an oval akin to the large red spot on Jupiter. It is neither as big nor as differentiated, but it probably originates from the same kind of climatic and chemical conditions.

Other features of Saturn were known before the Voyager passage. The planet circles the pale Sun at a mean distance of 886 million miles. The Saturnian day has recently been recalculated to a length of ten hours and thirty-nine and a quarter minutes. Saturn's diameter is roughly 74,500 miles, and its volume would hold 815 Earths. Mostly composed of light gases, with some ethane, acetylene, and water, Saturn—like Jupiter— may have a tiny core of metallic hydrogen. Its low density, only 70 percent that of water, gives it a surface gravity barely more than that of the Earth. If one could find an ocean large enough, Saturn would float in it.

Although they are incidental to internal planetary dynamics the rings have been Saturn's distinguishing feature since Galileo discovered them. He never saw them clearly enough to discern their nature, and so he imagined that Saturn was a double or triple planet. Then, as the angle of the rings to the plane of the Earth changed, they apparently disappeared, and an astonished Galileo wrote in December 1612: "Has Saturn, perhaps, devoured his own children?"[1]

It was Huygens, in 1659, who disclosed their separation in a treatise upon Saturn: "A thin, flat ring, nowhere touching, and inclined to the ecliptic."[2]

Some early astronomers interpreted the rings as an aeromantic sigil, speculating, for instance, that ethereal Saturn was composed of gem material with a golden aura about it. In general, however, the rings were discovered too late for traditional magic to incorporate them in the astral planet before the Newtonians were well on the way to a gravitational solution. Continuous reexamination during the next two centuries showed that there was a system of rings, some of them faint and some of them dark. The rings were not a fixed crown; they were the cumulative effect of matter in motion. They were an orbital phenomenon like moons. This suggested, to the nineteenth-century astronomers, that the possible source of the rings was the fragments of a broken moon that had approached too close to the planet and shattered. From the slight differences in their orbital speeds, these fragments would follow a path; and as they collided with each other, the path would distribute into a ring. Maxwell showed mathematically that the rings could not be solid but must be made up of "an indefinite number of unconnected particles, revolving around the planet with different velocities according to their respective distances."[3]

From our new knowledge of the history of the Solar System, we have considered other possible sources for the rings: a wandering planetesimal or asteroid torn apart, a stillborn satellite, or the nebula cloud of the System itself. We have also found that rings are not unique to Saturn. Rings of a different and dark material were found around Uranus quite recently; amost invisible from Earth, they circle the poles of the planet rather than the equator. In 1979, very thin Jovian rings were discovered by Voyager. Clearly, then, rings betray a rather commonplace natural phenomenon and are not a special endowment of Saturn, though the Saturnian rings are a particularly glorious and complete demonstration of the phenomenon. From radar mapping, we now consider that their componential chunks are less like dust and more like boulders and stones covered with ice, or snowballs and hailstones, tumbling in their eternal circle, one behind the other. Inside the rings, we would not experience the smooth collective phenomenon. Instead, we would be pelted by irregular pellets of snow and ice as though we were standing in a cold meteor shower. The rings we see from the Earth are the same underlying Newtonian circles we find everywhere, whether on a supergalactic level or in the phases of the Moon.

From telescopic observation, we have been able to establish certain aspects of ring topography. For some time we have known that the rings of Saturn have an outermost diameter of about 171,000 miles while being only a few miles thick. Individual ring sections are visible, ranging in width from the faint Crêpe ring's 10,000 miles to the bright B ring's 16,800 miles. As early as the seventeenth century, one clear division was discovered between the B ring and the outer A ring. Later measured as 1,860 miles wide and named after its discoverer, Cassini's Division was assumed to be an empty space, a zone swept absolutely clear of fragments between rings. Other smaller rings and divisions were assumed as well. In fact, Pioneer 11 was originally charted to pass through Cassini's Division. Closer observation corroborated by satellite photography forewarned scientists: Cassini's Division was not a division at all, but an additional zone of rings. Voyager later found at least twenty distinct bands in the "Division." There are small gaps in the rings, however, and these are ostensibly regions swept clear by resonance from the satellites.

Although Pioneer did not approach the planet and take the dramatic close-ups that Voyager did, it managed to discover two new moons, and it began to disclose the complication of the rings. By measuring where the trapped particles of Saturn's Van Allen belt were blocked, Pioneer found a thin outer ring later named "F." Meanwhile, ground-based observations through the late 1960s and the 1970s had shown that Saturn had more than the traditionally assigned ten satellites and that there were a number of small irregular inner moons, intricately connected to the dynamics of the rings. In fact, if we add the Voyager discoveries, Saturn now has at least fifteen moons. Although it is presently impossible to attribute all of ring dynamics to planetary satellites, certain specific relationships other than gaps have been tentatively proposed by scientists. For instance, Jupiter's ring may be held in place gravitationally by the irregularly shaped satellite Amalthea. The F ring, only sixty miles across and 50,000 miles above the golden cloudtops of Saturn, appears to be held in place by the thirteenth and fourteenth satellites operating as Newtonian sheepdogs. One of the jagged moon fragments orbits the planet just inside the ring, and the other orbits just outside it. Since the inner moon is faster, a gravitational tug between the two of them develops, making it impossible for any of the "sheep" fragments to escape. Furthermore, the mutual gravity of these moons forces particles together in clumps. Six of these internal F-ring features were photographed by Voyager. Since they are not discrete bodies with separate orbits, these clumps cannot be called moons; yet they and the thirteenth and fourteenth moons show that the distinction between moon and ring particle, between sheepdog and sheep, in the formation of the ring and moon systems is a subtle and changing one.

Close-up photographs of these moons, taken as Voyager passed through the ring plane, showed them to be not only oblong but jagged in such a way that they could have once been a single body. The destruction of the single moon, perhaps by a meteor as big as the one that almost split Mimas, created not only the twin co-orbital satellites but the entire F-ring system.

The two satellites perhaps explain the F ring and the gravitational accretion of particles within it, but they do not explain one of the most extraordinary features of the Saturnian system discovered from the initial raw pictures. The F ring has three ribbons that are braided and seem to cross over each other in different planes like a helix. These twisted rings also become thinner and then thicker and are knotted in spots, indicating some totally unknown force. From the early days of the Newtonian renaissance, it was clear that multibodied gravitational systems are very difficult to describe and understand. The Saturnian rings are the most elegant local statement of that problem. So many bodies are caught in so many gravitational fields—Saturn itself, the moons both near and far and large and small, and the ring fragments of varying size and distance—that gravitational interaction cannot be predicted in terms of the collective outcome of systems.

One scientist remarked on television that these braided helices were certainly the only example of life viewed in the Saturnian system, implying ironically that gravitational complexity was mimicking biological complexity. "In this strange world of Saturn's rings, the bizarre becomes commonplace," said Bradford Smith, the photography section leader. "Those twisted rings seem to be defying the law of orbital mechanics as I understand it. They must be doing the right thing, be we just don't know what laws of physics they're following. . . . It all boggles the mind that it even exists. It's just weird."[4]

As Laurence Soderblom of the imaging team said, "It's the unthinkable that we're looking for—the unimaginable."[5]

This is the difference between the single unique expedition of Voyager and all the science fiction crafts of the imagination that preceded it.

Voyager gave us our first pictures of the ring system as a whole and characterized it as an actual topographical entity. What scientists once described as half a dozen ring systems with divisions became five hundred, and then a thousand, individual rings and ringlets as Voyager approached. The rings spread out from Saturn on a vast flat plane like an enormous phonograph record with extremely fine grooves. The flat ornament had become a three-dimensional landscape in stone, its actual bigness revealed in perspective as Voyager soared above its plane.

Inexplicable spokes appeared across ring sections, moving as the rings moved. They were dark as they spun between Voyager and the Sun, bright as the probe flew past their eclipse. These spokes were perhaps ice phenomena among the particles of the rings, forming on the night side of the planet, apparent as the rings emerged from shadow into their respective mornings, and fading as the ring "day" moved through "noon" into late afternoon. Additional freezing may occur in spoke patterns at night; the Sun then melts them back into slush.

Voyager also reported other ring phenomena. The C ring seemed to be made of looser assortments of particles, and to be semitransparent. In photographing the small thirteenth and fourteenth satellites, Voyager discovered the shadow of another unknown tiny ring, perhaps also held together by still tinier satellites. It found eccentric rings, dark gaps, and other irregular formations.

Recording 256 different degrees of relative light and dark, as well as nonvisible bands of the spectrum, the probe is simultaneously blind and far more sensitive than we are. As the grooves in the rings show up and the spokes turn from dark to light, we realize that we are looking at the infinitesimally fine detail of light itself. Intricate texture leaps forth as the angles of the camera, the Sun, the planet, the rings, and the moons change. We might think of ourselves driving through the terrestrial fields at sunset. Tinted shadows fall across the hills. The cows seem made out of rich brown mud, the lakes out of sky. The spiders' webs are soft mucous from the creatures' bodies, each morsel strung in taut geometry. The houses are arcs of energy, their walls ginger and transparent. Each smudge and leaf vein stands out, and the myriad insects above the field to the horizon are distinguished as ring particles. The blue ions of air seem molecular in their collectivity. Then we pass over the cusp into night.

In the delicacy of Saturn's rings, we see once again the grain and hue of this inhabited Earth. Through the alien unimaginable landscape of a remote and probably hostile system, we see the delicate watery home planet as we never have before.

Saturn has ten named satellites. From inner to outer, these are: Janus, Mimas, Enceladus, Tethys, Dione, Rhea, Titan, Hyperion, Iapetus, and Phoebe. They are named after Father Saturn's cohorts in the old world of the gods. Titan is the largest moon in our Solar System, but the rest are quite tiny. In fact, before Voyager, they were assumed to be mere dirty snowballs, more ice than rock. Voyager gave us our first chance to view planetary objects in the range of 750 miles in diameter in the cold reaches of the light gaseous planets. These bodies are far lighter and of different material than the ostensibly captured moons of Mars. The large Galilean satellites show obvious evolution and historical complexity, but some of the Saturnian satellites show surprisingly similar features.

Tiny Janus, 100 miles in diameter, was discovered by French scientists in 1966. Very little is known about it, and it is even unclear whether the present Janus, confirmed by Pioneer, and the original French one are the same moon. It is similar to the later unnamed satellites.

Mimas is a little more than 200 miles in diameter, and it orbits Saturn 115,000 miles from the cloudtops. It is only slightly heavier than pure water ice, and probably contains some silicate material. What is notable about Mimas is that it survives at all. A quarter of its diameter is filled by an impact crater eighty miles wide and many miles deep. A steep rim surrounds it, and a giant mountain rises to a sharp peak in its center. Other large craters, including some that are twenty-five miles wide, cover the Miman surface. Mimas looks like a big snowball that gathered cold out of nebula material and then was bombarded by planetesimals into a field of craters. It is a relic of the early days of our System.

Mimas was discovered by Herschel, as was Enceladus, the next moon in sequence orbiting Saturn. What is surprising is that a body about the same size as Mimas (Enceladus is 150 miles larger in diameter) and about the same distance from the primary planet is so different. Enceladus shows no large craters, only some faint stripes reminiscent of the internal evolution of larger moons in the Jovian system. Both moons may have water volcanoes.

Tethys, Dione, and Rhea, the next three moons in sequence, extend from orbits of 183,000 miles to 327,000 miles. All three were discovered by Cassini, who also found the next to outermost moon, Iapetus. These are the most complex of the small moons viewed by the first Voyager.

Tethys, 635 miles in diameter, is a block of ice like Mimas, and also heavily cratered. But there is other highly unusual topography on Tethys, including a lambda-shaped twisting canyon or fault valley running for 250 miles along a north-south axis and approximately fifty miles wide. There is also a huge white spot on the surface that may be a hill or just very bright ice. These are not crater mounds. They represent distinct geological processes local to the moon. Although topography in ice is rare, the ice was fluid once, and was melted and remelted by materials churning up from the interior.

As Voyager approached Saturn from the distances of the inner Solar System, Dione showed a bright spiderlike marking in its center, giving it the appearance of a star sapphire. This and other ropy patterns imply internal evolution from molten material, as on our Moon. There are "lunar" craters too on Dione, but this world recalls most the cracked surface of Ganymede. Rhea even more strongly resembles Ganymede, except that its surface material is brighter, indicating that something from very deep within the core of the moon is emerging. Rhea has complex streaky glowing areas and swirling patterns, which intimate not only impact craters but also rearrangements of fields of ice and ice cliffs. The surface has been sheared and torn apart. Dione is somewhat bigger than Tethys, and Rhea is almost 1,000 miles in diameter, but this is still remarkable geologic upheaval for such small icy moons.

The Saturnian and Jovian systems emerged from their segments of the nebula cloud somewhat differently. Saturn got lighter material; it developed a much fuller ring system; and its moons seem haphazard in arrangement. Jupiter has a small amount of moon and ring "debris" close to its surface, but for the most part the large dense moons are inner moons, and both size and density decrease as one moves away from the planet. This may or may not indicate the way in which the primordial material of the system was distributed, but it does strongly suggest a clustering of matter toward the center of the cloud. However, we cannot simply carry this model over to Saturn. There are many small inner moons around Saturn, as well as the rings, and there is only one moon of planetary size, Titan. This is four times larger than the next largest moon, and it is followed by three more of the Mimas to Rhea variety. It is also further from Rhea to Titan than it is from inner Janus to Rhea. That enormous gap of more than 400,000 miles is filled with a gaseous disk of squashed torus shape containing a very thin distribution of hydrogen atoms, probably blown off the surface of Titan, which continues to lose its original endowment at the rate of about a kilogram per second.

Voyager missed Mimas-size Hyperion entirely, as that moon was on the other side of the planet from Titan when Titan was photographed. There is a relatively small gap between the orbits of Titan and Hyperion. The next moon, Iapetus, was photographed at a distance, and it will be scanned more closely by the next Voyager. It has always been known for its erratic appearance, indicating either extreme irregularity of shape or discoloration. From Earth, one side of this moon is six times brighter than the other. There is probably some extremely dark material in its makeup; perhaps an internal process has forced dark material up on the faint side. From Earth, it appeared possible that Iapetus was shaped more like a cylinder than a ball, but Voyager showed a round world with a sharp demarcation line between the zones.

From all the moons except Iapetus (and perhaps Phoebe), the rings of Saturn would be only barely visible at the "razor" edge, for they would be seen along the same plane in which the moons themselves pass. Iapetus strays sharply from the plane. Anyone on this body would see the whole surface of the rings, like the wings of a butterfly, as the moon soars over the plane. Iapetus is 800 miles in diameter and more than 2,200,000 miles from the surface of Saturn.

Phoebe, discovered like Hyperion in the late nineteenth century, is six million miles further away than Iapetus. Only 800 miles in diameter, it is also retrograde and eccentric in its path. It may be a late addition to the system, perhaps a captured asteroid or comet.

The water of Saturn's moons is primordial—not later rain but original H_2O from the solar nebula. Since that ancient freezing in the darkness of space, the ice has been twisted, melted, refrozen, and pocked with meteorites, but it is cleaner than any mountain brook on Earth will ever be again. The moons of Saturn are cosmological water, planetary glaciers. They are frozen replicas of cosmogony, attending the god of time. That same nebula water on Earth remained liquid; and after aeons of chemical interaction with other substances, it became contaminated with life—life that returns, through Voyager, to view some frozen blocks of the original spring.

Titan is the largest moon in the Solar System (but see Neptune's Triton, below) and the only one with an atmosphere. More than 3,600 miles in diameter, it is bigger than Mercury. Even a decade ago, we could not have discerned the full significance of this moon. In some science and science fiction books, it was mentioned parenthetically that Titan might have life on it. But what brings Titan newly to the forefront is our recent appreciation of the uniformity of the Solar System—in particular, we have become aware that all the planets and moons evolved from relatively similar beginnings. Although Titan is a distant moon of a faraway planet, it is as much a sister of the Earth as of Saturn. With Saturn it shares distance from the Sun and the same ancient patch of elementally enriched star debris. With Earth it shares the conditions of surface and terrestrial-type gravity. In any case, the star debris was probably little different in the vicinities of Saturn and the Earth.

Titan's importance to us is also a direct reflection of the decreased organic potential of Mars and Venus. Mars has an insubstantial atmosphere, and Venus is apparently trapped in a developing carbon dioxide cycle quite remote from the chemistry of life. We have moved, in a sense, away from the old Solar System of proximity and ancient familiarity, and into a new Solar System of hydrocarbon action and primeval atmospheres. Suddenly, we find that we must search among the unfamiliar Jovian worlds for our likeness and origins instead of among the traditional inner Terran planets. The ancient plains of Mars are deeply cratered and show only traces of river valleys that dried up long before the forerunners of men lived in the Old World jungles. But Titan is covered with photo-organic smog, and organic compounds likely fall to its surface and drift across it like snow. If Mars is our long, bright visual planes and hard rock surfaces, Titan is the dirty and salty intimacy of our cells.

After Mercury and Mars, scientists were prepared for disappointingly thin atmospheres, and Titan's bounty surprised them. Voyager found that the Saturnian moon, despite a relatively weak gravitational pull compared to that of the Earth, held an atmosphere extending to three hundred miles above the surface (three times higher than the Earth's) with a surface pressure one and a half times that of the Earth. Telescopic observation had shown an atmosphere, but had not prepared scientists for its extent or its high nitrogen content. This photochemical smog, with thick clouds of methane and other hydrocarbons, apparently extends right down to the surface, with nitrogen rain and snow falling through it. The atmosphere totally obscures the face of the moon, and it will take a Titan landing to learn what it is like on the surface. One scientist said: "We might find nitrogen icebergs in a methane sea."[6] There also might be oceans of liquid nitrogen. Probably, though, Titan is too warm for these exotic topographies.

Although this is a ghastly environment for human survival, it is a rather promising environment from the point of view of universal organic chemistry. Titan might abound in the kind of swamps in which complicated hydrocarbons form. Carbon, oxygen, and sulphur have all been identified in the atmosphere, and a large amount of water is likely—as on the other Saturnian moons—to be locked in ice. If all this material is bombarded by the general cosmic radiation and by the pale Sun through a red hazy sky, then many of the more complicated hydrocarbon building blocks may be forming in seas and swamps, materials familiar to the water oceans of the ancient tropical Earth. Hydrogen cyanide and acetylene both appear to be present, and there is an unknown abundance beneath that smog.

Chemically, Titan appears to be a very cold and somewhat small primeval Earth. It retains a great deal of hydrogen in its atmosphere—witness the torus between Titan and Rhea. As on the gas giants, there are large amounts of helium, methane, and ammonia. But there is a surface. It may well be a surface of pure water ice.

Titan's distance from us is negligible in cosmic terms, although it is crucial in terms of a fragile life form such as we are. But it may well have its own fragile life forms. Severe cold is the most extreme problem. At the time of the first Voyager visit, Titan was just emerging from a deep winter, with temperatures recorded by Voyager as low as − 300° F. Creatures born during Titan's spring and summer, a period of five or six terrestrial years, would have to be able to survive the winter, or at least pass on genetic material that could survive it. Otherwise, all of the evolution of the chemistry of life would be crammed into a ridiculously short period, and new creatures would have to evolve each summer.

There is, however, some reason to be optimistic, from a human standpoint, about the summer climate on Titan. The moon shares Saturn's orbit around the Sun, and thus its long seasons. The − 160° F. now estimated for the height of summer is considerably more than was once thought. It is also possible that Titan's temperature rises even higher regionally from internal heat sources. In addition, there is a greenhouse effect from the smoggy atmosphere. Distinct seasonal changes seem likely, even from brief viewing of the upper atmosphere. There is a dark northern pole obscured in haze, and the entire northern hemisphere is darker than the southern hemisphere. Even at its brightest, the Sun does not shed any more light on the Titanian surface than the Moon does on the Earth's surface.

There is a remote chance that in areas of extended summer and internal heat, perhaps underground, ammonia and water lakes have formed. If these survive the winter, there may be a hydrocarbon paradise on Titan. In a certain sense, the search for life in our System has left the Mars era and entered the Titan era. We see ourselves differently, and we understand that the Earth's watery conditions are unique for a small inner planet in this cosmic region. We have come from further away in nebula history and cosmology and are more isolated than we thought.

Saturn stood at the end of the old Solar System, an aged king with a long white beard. Beyond him was nothing. He was organization, completion, age—the final and frozen arrangement of things. Even as revolution and radical and unconscious actions change things, Saturn still stands as a great rock fortress, within custom, within society, within matter, and within mind, holding to the original and eternal truths. The strength of the Saturnian gesture is overwhelming, but its invocatory images may be fleeting and misleading, like the election of Ronald Reagan. There is a coldness and sadness to Saturn because it is eternal, hopeless, and unremitting. In electing a Saturnian, we, in a sense, turn to and acknowledge our own inner darkness. Even the later Galilean rings fit the sepulcher image: Saturn is a ringed planet, the only one as seen from Earth. It is a closed mysterious tomb. Something has died there, and the spot in the sky is marked in such a way that the symbol could not have been missed by the earth's first telescopes.

The finality of Saturn is both its virtue and its curse. Mythologically, Saturn is the creator of time, which makes him a healer, a guardian, a shield. He protects the inner Solar System from the infinite chaos. In the body, he both creates density and disintegrates used materials, including the skeletal frame itself ultimately. His wisdom is like the oldest Buddhist teaching— the wisdom of suffering. Because Saturn guards time, he alone contains the wisdom outside of time. The encircling ring has come to represent, in modern times, the protective function of lead, the boundary around a boundary, so that something more remote and complex, cosmic in its sigil, stands on the ancient edge. Lead is heavy, sluggish, impenetrable, but also of a rich depth. When it is combined with the tin and copper of bronze, we can hear its profundity in the tone of the bells. That sound is not the wisdom of the copper or tin.[7]

From Janus and Mimas, the incredible golden planet fills the whole sky, drifting up as a buoy in the void. If the Gurdjieffian Moon steals souls, what must Saturn do to the poor creatures in its system! A night of full Saturn is brighter than the solar day. To the astrologers dwelling on the Saturnian moons, the planet itself is so dominant as to be meta-astrological. The other moons and the thin ring line would make up the local "zodiac" for the astrologers of Titan and Dione.

Ringed Saturn is the passageway both into and out of the modern world. And it is the gate in time to the ancient kingdoms of the Earth. Outside its orbit are only the radical occult planets, discovered in modern times, which represent different cosmic forces entirely.

————————

Uranus is the next planet, though a 300-mile-wide object was discovered in a planetary orbit between Saturn and Uranus in 1977 and named Chiron. It is probably doomed to become a moon of one of the two planets or to be caught by one and bounced to some other part of the Solar System.

Uranus circles the Sun in about 84 Earth-years, making its astrological circuit the measure of a long human lifetime. Its diameter is about 32,000 miles, and it is 1.78 billion miles from the Sun. From Uranus, the Sun has hardly any disc left, but is still a star brighter than any other.

The Uranian atmosphere of methane clouds reflects back 90 percent of the light that falls on it. Ammonia mists probably lie beneath the methane. The overall appearance is blue-green, or greenish with whitish belts in the equatorial region. At − 360° F., it is still fairly warm for its location and may have internal sources of heat. It is heavier than Saturn: 1.2 times the density of water.

Uranus rotates rapidly (10 hours, 48 minutes), but it does so on its side. The Uranian axis of rotation is almost parallel to the planet's orbital plane, so its North Pole faces the Sun for half a year and outer space for the other half. There is no terrestrial diurnal-nocturnal cycle. Day and night are forty-two Earth-years each, but daytime is distinguished only by the fact that the Sun prescribes a ten-hour circle in the sky. Other variations in this cycle come from the alignment of the planet's axis and orbit.

The five moons of Uranus have bizarre orbital patterns. Over 21-year cycles (part of the complex Uranian numerology of 84), they move from equatorial to polar orbits, circling the planet around its center and then above and below it. The outermost ones, Titania and Oberon, were Herschel's discoveries. Lassel found Ariel and Umbriel in 1851 while looking for the first two. Innermost Miranda was found on a photographic plate by Gerard Kuiper in 1948. Because of Uranus's unorthodox tilt, the five moons are retrograde even though they seem disposed to normal prograde orbits. The largest, Titania, is only 1,000 miles across. The rings of Uranus were discovered in 1977. These plus the Jovian ones give rise to the idea that large planets normally create enough debris to form ring systems when the temperature is cold enough for the ice. Jupiter's body heat might melt some of its rings, which would explain its paltry set.

Occult Uranus has strong magical affinities. Its discovery is associated with its message—i.e., its actual body became visible when man was able to respond to it. Insight into the hidden secrets of nature, fantastic inventions, elaborate machines, and unemotional thought are all Uranian functions. Uranus rules astrology because it generates cohesive laws of whole systems. It is an astrum of lightning and fast-striking change. Although its rearrangements are necessary, it can tumble lifetimes of work as it rotates topsy-turvy on its axis with its erratic interacting moons. It looks like an atomic nucleus, and it is the archetypal creator of atomic power. That swiftly do astrologers claim the astronomical images, as if synchronicity furnished them from the sky for their use. Since Uranus destroys the old order and creates a new one, even as it did on its discovery, it is the enemy of Saturn, guardian of the ancient Solar System. Saturn tries to hold the throne for the oldest lineage; Uranus is revolutionary. It either seems to be amoral or to act from motives that lie beyond the understanding or even the conception of ordinary people. Strange, eerie, magical, electric, it is one of the rulers of Aquarius.

Except for its more normal inclination, Neptune is similar enough to Uranus to be a twin. It seems to have more methane and less ammonia. 2.8 billion miles from the Sun, its year is 165 Earth-years, and it rotates in 15 hours, 48 minutes. Its diameter is 30,760 miles, and it is 1.67 times as dense as water. If Lassel's satellite Triton is as big as it seems (3,700 miles in diameter), then it, not Titan, is the largest moon in the Solar System. Triton also circles the planet in a very tight retrograde orbit of 5 days, 21 hours. Nereid, discovered by Kuiper in 1949, is tiny (300 miles in diameter). It behaves more like a comet than a moon: its 360-day Neptunian year carries it from less than a million miles away from the planet to more than six million miles away.

Piers Anthony uses Neptune as the central planet in his science fiction novel *Macroscope*. As the spaceship approaches the green gas globe, this is what the travelers see:

Its roiling atmospheric layers were horrendously evident. The great bands of color hardly showed now; instead there was a three-dimensional melange of cloud and gas and turbulence suggesting a photography of a complex of hurricanes.

   . . . [He] felt as though he were peering into a cauldron of layered oils recently disturbed by heating. . . . Gray blue bubbles a thousand miles across seemed to rise through the pooled heavy gases, while slipstreams of turbulence trailed at the edges. In one place the recent passage of a bubble had left a beautifully defined cutaway section of gaseous strata, yellow layered on green on pink and black. In another, masses of whitish substance—hydrogen snow— were depressing the seeming ocean beneath, ballooning downward in a ponderous inversion.[8]

Piscean Neptune is magical like Uranus, but more mystical than electric. In the personality it sometimes seems motiveless but with dreamlike visions of a hidden unity. If Uranus is a scientist and magician, Neptune is a dreamer, mystic, and prophet, more concerned with the hidden shape than the high-energy forces. It will create a vast work of art or philosophy rather than a machine or a technology. If Uranus invented the radio and the telescope, Neptune gave both a planetary and cosmic meaning. The global European migration and the spread of Western civilization is Neptunian; so are the airlines and multinational companies. Neptune is a medium and a musician associated with Venus. Uranus is a mechanic and an inventor associated with Mars.

Neptune is also dangerously unbalanced, tending toward schizophrenia, involved in drugs, hallucinating. Alcohol, opium, and cocaine are its astral flowers. "Normal perception is a jail," writes the poet Gerrit Lansing, "from which [Neptune] wishes to break out." He adds that the Neptunian dissolves to create. He is attracted to "the watery powers of the underworld," the "criminal, the forbidden, the untasted, always seeking to unveil, though not through the rational mind."[9] Neptune is a planet of mirage, rapture, enchantment, holy places, arcane speech, the relationship between sex and blood, communion, and communalism. Neptune was discovered in 1846, and the *Communist Man-*

ifesto was published in 1848. This is the astrological basis of the latter's planetwide effect on the modern world. The two events are locked in the heavens. When we fear Russia or China as hegemonous powers, we are intuiting the Neptunian influence now at large. Though no modern state may represent this influence in its pure form, the agency itself must be expressed, astrologers tell us, through Neptune's movement in the heavens.

The search for a ninth planet in our Solar System began in the manner of the search that led to the discovery of Neptune. But it was an exhausting, fruitless obsession over three decades, with an ambiguous resolution in 1930. Percival Lowell began the quest at the turn of the century from his observatory at Flagstaff, Arizona. Working with unexplained residuals in the orbits of Uranus and Neptune, Lowell calculated the probable orbit of Planet X, and he and his staff proceeded to search for it throughout the likely regions of the sky. But Lowell recognized "that when an unknown is so far removed relatively from the planet it perturbs, precise prediction of its place does not seem to be possible. A general direction alone is predictable."[10] He died in 1916, well before the discovery.

The man who would eventually find Planet X was Clyde Tombaugh, a self-taught astronomer who worked on his family farm in Kansas during the day and studied the heavens at night with a 9-inch reflecting telescope that he made himself. He wrote repeatedly to the Lowell Observatory for a job; Vesto Slipher was impressed with his drawings of Jupiter: "fairly good for such a chap working all alone."[11] So Tombaugh was hired. He was twenty-two years old, with a high school education. Slipher gambled that his raw intelligence would be more useful in the search for X than the usual submissive university type. Tombaugh was twenty-three years old when he became the last person to discover a planet.

Tombaugh worked by exposing plates on good nights and then "blinking" successive exposures of the same area on different nights in a special machine to see if any "star" moved. Searching down to the 17th magnitude, he found innumerable difficulties in exposing the plates and producing blinkable pairs.

Gradually, he worked toward resolving the fundamental problems. The most serious obstacle was the thousands of asteroids moving through the zodiac. Searching at this level of magnitude, he was plagued by their blinking. "The key strategy," he concluded, "was to take the plates within 15 degrees of the opposition point, so that the daily parallactic motion of the earth would cause all bodies external to the Earth's orbit to retrograde through the star field—the more distant the object the smaller the angular displacement during the interval between the dates the plates were taken. This solved the asteroid problem beautifully."[12]

After months of working with Lowell's orbit, Tombaugh began an exhaustive search of the entire zodiac in September 1929. He moved from Aquarius into Pisces, from Pisces into Aries, and then into Taurus and Gemini. In eastern Taurus and western Gemini, the average number of stars per plate increased from 50,000 to 500,000. By early November, Tombaugh was in Scorpius and Sagittarius and was encountering a million stars per plate. Disappointed thus far, he returned to western Gemini in January 1930. Blinking two good exposures of the delta Geminorum region from January 23 and 29, he saw the shifting star, Planet X.

Since it was found at Lowell's observatory, under the auspices of his search, by an astronomer using his tables, Lowell was given credit for having discovered the planet along with Tombaugh. But Pickering claimed that the new body was his Planet "O." Then, when he heard of its small size, he felt it should be discarded immediately as the perturbing influence on its neighbors. The perturbation on Neptune's orbit requires a planet of 50,000 miles in diameter, and Pluto is, at most, 4,200, and more recently has been mapped at 1,500. In fact, as recently as 1979, it was suggested that Pluto is no bigger than Ceres. The astronomers doing the photometric research on Pluto at the University of Hawaii, Dale Cruikshank, Carl Pilcher, and David Morrison, concluded that Pluto's mass was a few thousandths that of the Earth. This is "much less than would be required to perturb the motions of Uranus and Neptune measurably. . . . If this train of logic is basically correct, it appears that Tombaugh's discovery of Pluto in 1930 was the result of the comprehensiveness of the search rather than the prediction from planetary dynamics."[13]

But then, where is Lowell's predicted trans-Neptunian planet? For all intents and purposes, Pluto has been used to save the appearance of Lowell's discovery. Even the choice of the name, Pluto, instead of the more popular Minerva or Cronus, was partly based on the lucky accident that the first two letters of the name of a major available god also happened to be Percival Lowell's initials. The *PL* symbol for the planet could thus honor Lowell. But clearly it is no more his planet than Pickering's. And even Pickering was satisfied with the name, which he read as standing for Pickering-Lowell.

The minute Plutonian satellite, named Charon, was discovered by James Christy and Anthony Hewitt in 1978. This allowed measurement of Pluto's mass by Kepler's third law and confirmed the extraordinarily small size of the ninth planet.

Prior to the discovery of Charon, astronomers favoring Pluto as the perturbing influence on Uranus and Neptune had a number of explanations for the ostensible small size. Some hypothesized that it is such a black frozen planet that we see only a 3,000-mile-wide glint of its 50,000-mile-wide sphere, like a sparkle on a black Christmas ornament. Another suggestion was that Pluto is a white dwarf or a black hole, a burned-out cinder from the other half of a twin Sun system of which our present Sol is the remaining half. Pickering suggested that it might be a stray white dwarf picked up from another star system and thus the only body in the Solar System with an origin outside it. This would give it the necessary mass for the perturbations. For a planet so far away, we can imagine almost anything. But the perturbations remain.

From this supposed one-time sun, the Sun we know is just another star in a black sky. Pluto is 2.7 billion miles away from the solar disc, and takes 248 Earth-years to make its annual orbit. We know how fast light travels. The 186,000 miles per second is beyond conception. Yet, it still takes the Sun's light 3.22 minutes to reach Mercury. That same light takes five hours and twenty-eight minutes to reach Pluto. If we imagine light whipping off the Sun's surface at 186,000 miles per second, zooming down the corridors of interminable darkness and space so fast that it opens shafts of light that disappear into the distance even as they come from a remote darkness in another direction—past and beyond any observer so fast that he cannot see it but it makes the whole world that he sees visible—then we can understand how long is that five-hour-and-twenty-eight-minute passage to Pluto. The temperature at Pluto, $-369°$ F. or lower, would freeze any atmosphere. If it is truly a child of the primal nebula, it should be water, ammonia, and methane ice, with occasional haze, for these are the last substances to condense from the outer rings in the cold of deep space. Pluto perhaps has a water ice core, a methane and ammonia mantle, dead methane seas, and a frozen methane crust and atmosphere.

A Plutonian day is, of course, hard to fix without knowing its surface features, but variations in brightness suggest a possible 153 hours. Pluto is perhaps 88 percent the density of the Earth, in this respect being more like the inner than the outer planets. It might even be an escaped moon of Neptune. It is the only planet that lies outside of the ecliptic that makes up the zodiac, so that Pluto is at an angle to the whole plane of the Solar System. Its orbit is eccentric compared to Neptune's almost perfect circle, and, on December 11, 1978, Pluto moved within the Neptunian orbit. The small world will reach its closest point to the Sun on September 12, 1989. Neptune will be the remotest planet until the year 1999, when Pluto will swing out beyond it again, en route to aphelion in 2113.

Occult Pluto is a realization of hidden inner forces that have been operating secretly and suddenly burst into being. It rules transformation, but also regeneration, metamorphosis, and even reincarnation. Uranus marks the beginning of atomic power in the natural element uranium. Man-made neptunium follows on the elemental chart, and then the most dangerous of the artificial elements to be released into the oceans and the life cycle, plutonium. Hitler was said by astrologers to have brought negative Plutonian influences to bear following Pluto's discovery, i.e., the most horrendous aspects of buried human consciousness.[14]

Pluto also represents a bringing back of the least expected:

the ghoul, life after death. This is the appropriateness of the
name: Pluto, lord of the Underworld, with his boatman Charon.
"With his queen Persephone he held sway over the other powers
of the infernal regions, and over the ghosts of the dead. The
symbol of his invisible empire was the helmet that made men
invisible."[15] The black hole is a perfect image for Pluto, but so
is the frozen debris of Solar System beginnings. Pluto's whole
discovery was an enigma in a Plutonian way. Pluto is also, mythologically, the source of wealth and grain, both of which come
from the earth. His cruelty and inexorability are part of the
cosmic order, which must transmute radically. An eccentric planet, slightly out of the zodiac, passing slowly through the signs,
is the appropriate agent of change and upheaval.

Pluto also dispenses earthquakes, epidemics, world wars, and
magnetism; its magicians are fakirs and yogis. From its Underworld association, it bears the horror and gloom of images so
deep in the unconscious that we cannot reach them, or else we
receive them only as nightmares. They are shapeless and shade-
like, akin to death.[16]

Pluto's astral allies are the amphibious animals, the poison-
bearers, ants, spiders, and hairy plants. Black diamonds and
deep purple-blue stones—or anything undergoing metamorphosis (cocoons, stalactites, stones changing color)—are Plutonian.[17]

But there is another interpretation of occult Pluto, one that
more clearly represents the conjunction of the visible planet
with world history. Pluto's real message is neither World War II
nor the planetwide deployment of atomic power, though these
are Plutonian conditions. It won't be a mind-matter ray or psychic electricity either: these are other passing manifestations.

The psychologist James Hillman writes:

> Hades [Pluto] was of course the God of depths, the God
> of invisibles. He is himself invisible, which could imply that
> the invisible connection is Hades, and that the essential
> "what" that holds things in their form is the secret of their
> death. And if, as Heraclitus said, Nature loves to hide, then
> nature loves Hades.
>
> Hades is said to have had no temples or altars in the
> upperworld and his confrontation with it is experienced as

a violence, a violation. . . . He is so invisible in fact that the entire collection of Greek antique art shows no ideal portrait of Hades. . . . He leaves no trace on earth, for no clan descends from him, no generations. . . .

All this "negative" evidence does coalesce to form a definite image of a void, an interiority or depth that is unknown but nameable, there and felt even if not seen. Hades is not an absence, but a hidden presence—even an invisible fullness.[18]

Pluto's real mystery is unknown, and it will remain unknown, even if it is still marked by the tiny ninth planet when the conventional relationship between mind and matter changes too.

21

Flying Saucers
and Extra-
terrestrial Life

THE NIGHT SKY is like Homer's sea—vast beyond measure, mysterious, dangerous, but still navigable, and also inhabited by unknown, perhaps nonhuman beings. The prospect of interstellar civilization changes the very nature of the sky for us. The stars become ports in space; our own world is also a potential port in other people's skies, and a fair target for anything else which nature has formed in its diversity and extent.

The sea can be entered by simple beings in handmade vessels, like the Polynesian "astronauts." But a raft cannot be slipped into the interstellar medium. It requires a boost to beyond the home planet's gravitational hold, and also, at the very least, strong materials and an artificial atmosphere on the ship. These were impossible feats for the tribal cultures that have dominated most of human history, and for their primitive equivalents on other worlds. Civilization, however, progresses by exponential degrees. It was not so long ago that Leonardo da Vinci's "aeroplanes" were science fiction art, and not so long before that that the distances of the sea were too great for those who sailed them and perished when their ships were shattered or their supplies ran out. Rocket launchings follow the first flying machines by less than a human lifetime. Gravity and distance are fundamental, but they are also relative. We face a night sky that may hold magnificent worlds beyond number, but it is also an emptiness

338

of inconceivable vastness with high levels of radiation and widely separated suns.

We have yet to encounter beings from other worlds. Despite all the UFO reports and supposed close encounters of the second and third kind, the extraterrestrials remain unknown. Their existence has been proposed on hundreds of thousands of occasions, but it has neither been demonstrated nor proven. Like the various spirits and disincarnate entities sighted throughout history, they are an overwhelming presence on our world, but they have not moved from the shadow regions to an upperworld of political and scientific visibility.

From the depths of the Stone Age, we have had intimations of intelligences not our own, of visitations, but these have always been, in one way or another, internal concurrences: the allies of shamans, the deities of myth, the visitors from astral realms, the various demons and angels, and the ghosts of the dead. Even if these should turn out to have objective external existence, they are not beings who emerge in the universe in the same way that we do. They are not embodied as we are, and they are not our counterparts. Spirits are not informed in the way that we are, and they are not uninformed in the way that we are. Encounters with them change our sense of reality and of our own nature, but they do not broaden the physical and biological context of our species.

We have come into being in a cold and secular place without any guideposts or references to what lies outside it. Only those who have come into being in the same way can give us a reference for our human existence. Spirits do not share the flesh with us, and they apparently do not share the billions of years of evolution that are incorporated in our process. They clarify incarnation only as it relates to their different form of existence. The extraterrestrials may also have spirits and allies. There may be only spirits on some worlds, or in some galaxies. But these are not the extraterrestrials with whom we seek a meeting in outer space, though we may find them there all the same.

The potential impact on us of extraterrestrial life is unimaginable. We are misled by scientific supposition and science fiction into thinking that we have already gauged the possible aliens. We have not. The most conventional extraterrestrial would affect us more profoundly than even the exotic insects and crystal intelligences of science fiction. These latter are projections of ourselves, while the real aliens come from outside the entire biochemical and psychosomatic chain in which we have developed.

Whether we fully appreciate it or not, biology (life science) means to us the living forms on this planet only, the sequence of life originating in protoplasm and carried from the first cells into multicellular organisms whose interdependent fusion is embodied at the primordial levels of our own existence. It is only a single continuity of life forms. It does not include, for instance, life forms on Mars; even the simplest of these creatures, if they exist, are not protozoas in a terrestrial biology. They are something else. Biology does not subsume the life forms on any other planet orbiting any other star, even if that planet is blue, watery, and oxygen-rich, and its star is a replica of our own Sun. We would be most shocked to be visited by spacemen who resemble us, for if this did not indicate that matter has in it a template leading to the human shape, it would mean that the combination of environmental, pregenetic, and genetic conditions leading to man is duplicatable (and perhaps the only chain capable of intelligence); that we did not originate on this world; or that we are the lineal ancestors or descendants of people on other worlds. Unless there is some unknown quality in matter, life forms evolving elsewhere must have unique biological histories; they must originate differently from inorganic matter and non-living compounds, and they must continue to evolve differently every step of the way. Even the most minute differences in the original amino acids and DNA material would have profound consequences. Such differences would affect one-celled animals or their equivalents, and they would be incorporated at every level of plant and animal life, including intelligent beings and their societies. All the underlying biological strata would contain the structural components they inherit from their evolutionary predecessors; these structures would be ramified at each level of increasing complexity with new differences and unique variations. At the level of sentient beings in a society, the differences between us and any extraterrestrials would be inconceivable. We would share only the raw star debris.

But scientists assume that extraterrestrials would have to know the same laws of nature that we have discovered either to communicate with us or to travel here, since the intrinsic physical properties of the cosmos are universal. For this reason, astronomers broadcast mathematically meaningful messages to the stars, and listen for such broadcasts passing among the stars. One message we send and seek is a series of beeps marking the prime numbers: 1, 3, 5, 7, 11, 13, etc. Such a sequence is not produced by any known natural process, yet it apparently expresses a design which is fundamental anywhere in the cosmos: integers divisible only by themselves and by one. If we located such a prime number "broadcast," it would corroborate not only the existence of extraterrestrial civilization but the commonality of our scientific path.

In one optimistic scenario, beings from another world send or bring us useful information that speeds our progress and improves our planet. But even the bare statement of the existence of others, without any ensuing data, would transform us. It would demonstrate that technology is survivable; it would show scientists that they were on the right track. A mere series of prime numbers originating elsewhere would indicate that technocrats can lead us into a future that has already happened somewhere—unless, of course, the message comes from others in the same turmoil as ourselves when they broadcast. Then they might no longer exist.

It is also possible that life might take on such a different form that we would not recognize it, that thought itself might develop along such unfamiliar lines that we would not be able to communicate with it. The prime numbers and the spectral lines of the elements seem universal to us, and we presently take it for granted that they are known by any civilization able to send messages to the stars. But this could be a provincial assumption.

Unquestionably, the universe from our vantage reveals a uniform physics and chemistry, but even if this universality should hold up with travel to the remotest regions of the creation, it does not guarantee that anything resembling that uniformity is sustained in the biological, psychological, and social levels that have built upon the physics and chemistry. We already expect sex types, languages, and basic social institutions on other planets to be foreign to us, perhaps undefinable in our terms. But we might not even be able to tell that the living are alive, that intelligent creatures have minds, or that a certain feature is a civilization. The boundary between organism and environment, as we know it, might not apply elsewhere. The objects of conscious thought might not be communicable to our biological line.

There are perhaps only two ways of avoiding such a final cosmic isolation, and the dice are already cast: it is up to us to see how they have fallen. One way is for matter itself to contain a predisposition toward certain forms and archetypes. Despite random variation throughout the cosmos, ultimately the same basic structures would be expressed. The second, and possibly related, way would be for higher systemic levels to bridge the differences of content and of structure from world to world by similarities of function and of adaptation to the macroenvironment. Intelligence, as the apparent final layer, would bridge the greatest differences. Ideally, when intelligence is applied to the deciphering of nature, it generates commensurate images everywhere. If this is true, science would fulfill its own prophecies and become the galactic language. Through science, we might transcend terrestrial culture and enter a cosmic civilization. Then all of the years from the first walking apes to global technology would be understood as an early and primitive stage of our species. The next phase would be something like the coming of the Europeans to the Plains Indians, but it would occur all at once, as though Chicago, Detroit, and Indianapolis simply landed, fullgrown and operational, at their present sites, and the local inhabitants were immediately enrolled in schools and given movie tickets and taught to drive cars. Something exponentially larger than what happened here over centuries would happen almost instantaneously.

We should be prepared for the impossible. Even if the impossible never happens, the practice of it will sharpen our sense of the cosmos. The meeting with extraterrestrials would be different from a meeting with spirits, for we cannot bypass or belittle the physical cosmos. If there are extraterrestrial beings, they have their own spiritual life. But the physical fact of different creatures throughout the cosmos transcends spiritual issues on this one level: in the bigness of physical creation, there might be others formed like ourselves. They would have emerged from the enriched star debris along a totally different line; they would understand universal law differently. All our customs and beliefs would have to be reexamined in the context of their behavior. The meanings of our actions would never be the same. Key concepts would need to be rethought in terms of other types of intentional sequences and philosophies: justice, compassion, harmony, peace, love, power, and morality would have new applications. No government or religion would stand unchanged. These other creatures would have come into existence just as we did, by natural law. The differences between nations will be trivial beside the differences between life forms. How do you develop a commensurability of value systems when you are not even made out of the same material? Men cannot agree, and they virtually share a collective mind.

Christianity and Islam would face beings arising from cells or cell-like clusters, not our cells but cells of the same fundamental elements. Could the priests and imams tell these beings what they tell humans about creation and incarnation? Communists would have a similar dilemma with extraterrestrial social orders. These would not reflect the sequence from patriarchy through feudalism to capitalism and socialism. What would theorists who searched even the atom and its particles for the dialectic have to say? They could reject the extraterrestrial orders as alien and irrelevant, but to do so would be dangerous, for it would deny the same natural law on which they claim communism rests. By their very presence, the extraterrestrials would be subversive.

Having come this far through science, which we derived from universal laws in the heavens, we are in no position to reject the natural origin of thinking and acting creatures from those heavens, or the things they make and do.

If we even find someone to talk to, our isolation is over. We then experience a thing in matter and psyche that is larger than ourselves: even two orphans of star debris can hold an elegant conversation in these vast and hollow halls. We suddenly exist among the stars and their incomprehensible vastness and emptiness in a new and brighter way. We come as a species, collectively, to such a moment, but each one of us also becomes a different person.

Until then, we are alone. We are devastatingly lonely, and have been even since our gods were driven from the heavens and the night became an alien infinity. It is all well and good to talk about interplanetary meetings and to imagine them. Yet, our fantasies of extraterrestrial beings are still like our fantasies of a scientific future. We will have to experience them in person to believe them, or even to know what they are.

Meanwhile, science stands at least a century short of examining the depths of its own psyche. The true Earth scientist who will ultimately speak for us to those in the stars may be wiser and more compassionate than those who presently stand in his place. Hopefully, he will represent a multicultural planet, social and sexual justice, economic and ecological harmony, and a unity of spirit and matter. Perhaps he will also embody such virtues. Until then, we are asking our radio mechanics and some clever computer technicians to speak for us, with all their ethnocentrism, untested humanitarianism, and political naiveté.

And this is only on a matter of prime numbers and a civilized scientific dialogue. It ignores some of the more Gothic science fiction scenarios. What if the beings out there are represented by something more like the Mafia, the Rosicrucians, or some combination of those? What if we are wise and peaceful and they are bellicose? We could end up in much worse trouble and more lonely than before we began to look.

The shapes of our cells and brains and those of extraterrestrials will keep us forever and inalterably strangers. We may make each other less lonely, as different varieties of freaks formed by a random undirected process of selection among the stars. In transcending these differences, in overcoming the injustice done to both of us, in facing the cosmic joke together, we may meet sympathetically and discover our true biology and

humanity. The aliens will not teach us who they are as profoundly as they will teach us who *we* are.

Thus far, the entire literature on flying saucer contacts has
underwritten the enigma of our own identity and shadow selves
more than it has told us who the extraterrestrials are and what
they are doing here. The messages ostensibly received from
alien spacecraft have been diverse and contradictory. There have
been thousands of such reported transmissions since unidentified flying objects became legion in the terrestrial skies at the
end of World War II. In 1954, while flying a military aircraft in
pursuit of unknown spacecraft, Mel Noel was contacted over a
high-frequency VHF channel: "Our crews are made up of individuals from planets known to you as Venus, Jupiter, Mercury,
Mars, and Saturn. . . . Life does not and cannot exist on these
planets; it's all inside the planets, it's all in the interior, just as
the house of the Lord. This is the house of the Lord we live in,
the interior of the planet."[1]

He was told that our planet was entering a new cycle in 1958,
that there would be earthquakes and erupting volcanoes in the
1980s, "that there would be mass geographical, spiritual, political, economical change as a result of this cycle, and that the
planet would be moving from the third to the fourth dimension."[2]

Among the more recent transmissions is a sequence of messages received from spacecraft passing over Sweden in 1975; the
occupants of these UFOs claimed to be from planets in the
Pleiadian star system. These communications are particularly
interesting because they are sensitive to the diplomacy involved
in one biological line contacting another within this large physical cosmos. "It is very important," they tell the Earth-beings,
"not to think of yourselves as the only case of matter reaching
sentience in this creation." A "cosmonaut" identified as Semjasse
goes on to say: "We, too, are still far removed from perfection
and have to evolve constantly, just like yourselves. We are neither superior nor superhuman. . . . In no case do we come on
behalf of anybody, since creation, by itself, confers no obligation

on us. It is a law unto itself, and every form of life must conform with it and become a part of it."[3]

Flying saucers, or unidentified flying objects, express the quintessential puzzle of the sky. Their problematic existence combines the various celestial paradoxes in one epiphenomenal event. Occult heavens and astronomical night are brought together, not at one level but at all the different levels on which they are confused. Strange orderly lights and patterns of light streak across the sky. Enormous vehicles land in remote places, and humanoid or alien beings emerge. The vehicles look like two dishes with their tops stuck together, cylinders with chandelier protuberances, gyroscopes, vortex wheels, silver derbies with torus rims, radiant light bodies, or some combination of these. They appear suddenly and disappear just as suddenly. They often register on radar. They have been sighted by experienced pilots, Air Force personnel, and nonbelievers. Occasionally they have seemed responsible for the loss of aircraft. Some individuals claim to have taken trips in UFOs, either willingly or through molestation. Some visitations involve trance states, loss of memory, and sharply divergent reports from two people having the same experience. The whole mystery defies explanation. On one level, it would seem that the saucers cry out for a simple technological resolution, probably an interstellar civilization. On another level, there is no simple explanation. As long as we do not know what reality is or where exactly we are in the dimensions of the universe, things will break in; and this includes not only UFOs but all sorts of psi phenomena, ghosts, and outrageous coincidences. A resolution of the flying saucers may have to wait for the big resolution, of everything.

A quick survey of possible interpretations shows the range of the flying saucer phenomenon:

> They are spaceships of beings from another planet, perhaps around another sun or in another galaxy.

> They are vehicles or creatures from another dimension interaccessible to ours. This same explanation has been given for the Yeti and Bigfoot.

They are clandestine military craft or experimental weapons of terrestrial nations.

They are local spirit forms or life forms made of energy and light.

They are psychic phantasms caused by human telepathy or telekinesis.

They are the visible aspect of an unknown energy.

They do not exist at all; they are imaginary projections.

Other hypotheses are possible, but these are a diverse assortment to start with. Let us see what their most immediate implications are.

The spaceship hypothesis presumes that the UFOs are mechanical objects powered by some form of energy. They are real vehicles, like our own rockets and planes, only much more advanced. We have pretty much eliminated every planet in this System as a source of humanlike life, with the possible very remote exception of Saturn's moon Titan. Thus, spacecraft most likely must come from beyond the Solar System, or they must also be conceived and operated by an utterly alien life form.

If they come from beyond the Solar System, their technology exceeds ours by more than ours exceeds that of Neolithic man. We can begin to conceptualize interstellar ships, but we are far from being able to construct and launch them. We have no energy source that would carry us to other solar systems; nor can we attain the speeds necessary to get people there in a time even reasonably within the scale of the human lifetime. If the UFOs come from another galaxy, the marvelousness of the technology necessary increases exponentially again.

But what if the saucers do not come from outer space at all, but originate in another dimension outside our perception? It is hard enough to imagine how a universe of three dimensions plus gravity and time came into being. It is impossible to conceive how dimensions themselves came into being. UFOs from other dimensions would make the sky incredibly dense and complicated, with knots and invisible holes. Our existence in what seems to be real physical space would become an hallucination of temporary contingent space, interruptible by laws we do not begin to know.

Creatures from other worlds are serious enough. Creatures from a different biology would challenge the molecular continuity in which we exist, as well as the systems that have arisen from it. Creatures from another dimension would challenge even the fact of our being real. This is either a critical issue deserving of immediate discussion at the United Nations, or it is a great cosmic joke. But this has always been the wheel across which flying saucers stretched. We can hardly begin to take them seriously until we have to.

Already we have an identity crisis over who we are, as individuals, as countries and races, and as a planet. Our problems are complex and usually fatal: nihilism, Nazism, world war, resource depletion, global madness. Any one of these is as all-engulfing as the universe itself. But what if the physical and biological yardsticks are altered? The shock could be either fatal or evolutionary. Mankind could find itself far crazier yet, or it could find itself, period: it could find its cosmic destiny. Perhaps this is what the radical journalist Hunter Thompson meant when he said: "It hasn't gotten weird enough yet."[4] The cosmic is comic. If we survive long enough to laugh, our laughter will be a deep expression of the universe within us, of accepting the creation as it is—despite the very obvious deficiencies we have and the seeming paltriness of life against the whole of matter and the whole of time.

We do not know what UFOs are, so we only dip our feet in this dark cold water. We think about it or we create stories about it. *Close Encounters of the Third Kind*[5] was so powerful a cinematic experience because it tried to put to rest all previous imaginary civilizational contacts and to posit a single real one. But we were cosmic virgins trying just a little bit harder to make our fantasy real. It is not real. Or if it is, it has happened in such a way that we do not know if it has happened or not.

(At a UFO meeting that I attended in the basement of a bank in Hamtramck, Michigan, in 1966, the gathering was told that it was honored by visitors from Venus and Saturn. I looked around the room, and suddenly everyone looked strange and extraterrestrial. Everyone was a candidate. Someone said to me that his friend came from Venus. "How do you know?" I asked. "He drives with his eyes closed," he told me.)

Close Encounters was only the latest vicarious experience of the simultaneous realness and unrealness of the aliens. Remember how they looked at the sky without blinking in *It Came From Outer Space*. A 1950s cinema audience gasped. That was them! They weren't us. Those were the others.

These films pushed us infinitesimally closer to the contact even if it should never happen. We begin to understand what it is that never happened and what it should be like if it does. We begin to understand what in us expects or wants it, and what in us denies it forever.

We seem to know that we are in a crisis of meaning and a concurrent moral crisis, and we are ready to risk quite a lot on the hope of new perspective from outside where we are. We are willing to go outside of history in order to get outside of this present historical dead end. We are, at the same time, willing to postpone the debate of whether these epiphenomena are more mortal threats than godsends. We do not even ask ourselves if we are ready. The very shallowness with which we imagine the contact, in various films and other works of planetology and science fiction, suggests that we are not ready. Perhaps this is why it does not happen while it continues to seem to happen. Perhaps this is why the aliens always land in West Virginia or rural Argentina and never on Red Square, the White House lawn, or the United Nations Plaza.

Semjasse, the visitor from the Pleiades, ostensibly told us: "General public contacts are not in our own best interests at this time, and besides, they would not convey a correct significance for the state of mind in which we now exist."[6]

If this sounds mysterious and almost inexplicable, it is probably meant to. The explanations always sound strained, but then we are led to assume that we would not understand the real reason. Yet, the visitors speak in our local languages.

All indications lead to the conclusion that the aliens are friendly and peaceful beings, but the possible military threat is appreciable too. What if these ships bear beings no more or less

enlightened than the Spanish conquistadors who came to the
New World in the fifteenth and sixteenth centuries and destroyed whole civilizations as if they were hives of insects? What
hope is there for us that beings of another biology and a more
advanced technology would behave better toward us than we
have behaved toward ourselves and our own?

There have been many science fiction "invasions" of the Earth
by antipathetic expansionist peoples, H. G. Wells's *War of the
Worlds* being the prototype. *The Invasion of the Body Snatchers*
presents a more sinister strategy.[7] What if the aliens should invade from within, like viruses or mental aberrations? If they
could invade by spores, they could invade by anything. Some
people have even suggested that *we* are the invaders, and that
DNA came to Earth as a spore, accidentally seeded or consciously planted, but evolved somewhere else. That is a fearful
and bastard legacy, though it affects us not at all this far into our
"invasion" and history. The situation is like that of a child who
worries that his own parents are the kidnappers. What recourse
to any salvation is there at that point? Perhaps we think these
things and fear them as a projection of our current dehumani-
zation and materialism. We are alienated from what we are and
from what we used to be. The remains of our old humanity cry
out against this invasion of ourselves by bureaucracy and alien
machines. Or we blame ourselves for the invasion by assuming
that it lies in our own ancestry and happened because of what
we were in the seed. *The Invasion of the Body Snatchers* expresses
mainly our anxiety that we are so susceptible to such an invasion
and that there is no defense. If we are not safe from each other,
then we are not safe from ourselves. And if we are not safe from
ourselves, then who are we?

Enemy UFOs change the sky into a military zone, the aero-
space of the Pentagon—pointed outward toward infinity in
terms of the possible source of attack and the nature of the
weapons. Or the sky becomes a camouflage for cosmic intrigue.
Seeds fall, seeds disguised on meteors landing indistinguishably
in the night, or not even requiring such cover. Beyond the seeds:
aliens, armed battalions and interstellar warships. These images
are part of our heritage too; and World War II, when bombs fell

in great number from the sky, was like a proxy attack by aliens. Who could have seemed more alien to the British than the Nazi Germans? Who could have seemed more alien to the residents of Hiroshima and Nagasaki than the Yankee fliers? And ever since, we have lived day by day, even minute by minute, with the terror of atomic apocalypse from the sky. And even though it has not happened, it has spawned atomic energy in a time of resource depletion, so once again the feared invader has become ourselves.

For the first time, after World War II, outer-space weapons were created, weapons like those of the supercivilizations that could destroy a whole nation or a planet. In *Star Wars*,[8] we were given this image in a sinister realism that seemed almost pop because it had been done in comic books so often before. Furthermore, it was right after World War II that flying saucer episodes became legion. As we became cosmic, the threat to us became cosmic—though not necessarily from outer space. In fact, the aliens were considered better than ourselves. People pleaded with them to deliver us from the conditions we had created, by malice, blunder, or both. After Hiroshima, we began to solicit help from the outside. Where else? The majority of UFO reports indicate friendly, even helpful, deific extraterrestrials, usually anxious to keep the Earth from self-annihilation. Psychics have claimed that UFO intelligences have prevented a third World War on numerous occasions simply by altering a minor detail in circumstances—a detail so minor that it would be overlooked by everyone else and yet so crucial that its discrete alteration would circumvent atomic warfare. It might even be a thought projection into the mind of a national leader (Uri Geller claimed such an implantation by interstellars into Anwar Sadat during the 1973 Arab-Israeli War). The leader need not be a warmonger, and the suggestion need not be peaceful; it need only be the right impulse at the right moment, based on a clearer extraterrestrial perception of the overall situation.

Everything the aliens do is anonymous and secret, and (if they do not exist) protects the myth of their beneficent presence. They do not end hunger or brutality; they do not brazenly interfere by using their "superior" machinery. They do the bare minimum, or we feign the bare minimum in their name to allow some other part of ourselves to come into being by projection and externalization. Even when they come with prophecies of earthquakes and erupting volcanoes, or upheavals of government, they reassure us that we have entered a natural cosmic cycle—in, say, 1958 or 1969—and that we will be through it by 2025 or 2107. They tell us that they are Venusians or Saturnians and that their own planets have come through a similar cosmic evolution. "We now dwell on the interior of the planet," they might say. Or: "We travel between galaxies by a space-time warp." And we can try to understand what they mean by this, and whether it comes from outer space or our own collective unconscious.

It is usually we and not they who portend annihilation. So untrustful of ourselves and unconfident of our potential for saving this world have we become that we call on the outside for help, fully aware that we may bring real doom on our heads, like those frogs of Aesop to whom the gods finally sent a stork.

In recent years, we have seen the first popular UFO backlash. Some observers are actually considering whether the saucers are the craft of a secret military organization on the Earth: Russian, American, or transnational. This is a major premise on which the Air Force opened Project Bluebook, but it had generally been considered right-wing paranoia. It has a new impact coming from one-time "extraterrestrial" advocates like Jacques Vallee (on whom the French scientist in *Close Encounters* was based). Here we leave the optimistic sixties.

Vallee argues that a paramilitary organization could have come into being in the aftermath of World War II. He does not identify the group or their goals, but concludes that their activities are an attempt to brainwash mankind into believing in UFOs. This camouflage is either meant to prepare people for some event on a global scale (which this organization is planning) or to distract general attention from terrestrial to extraterrestrial phenomena in order to disguise the organization's operations by associating them with aliens. Its goal is some particular destiny for humanity. This alarms Vallee because he feels we know little or nothing about these people, and their activities behind the

UFO cover seem manipulative and self-serving. They use, he says, a psychotronic technology, that is, an advanced technological science whose "machines" project mind-altering images that make people think they have seen certain things. With psychotronics, people may report sighting a UFO, being taken aboard, making contact with aliens, and traveling to other planets or star systems—when all these activities are actually thought patterns broadcast from an airborne craft or ground station.[9]

Visitors from outer space could have psychotronic technology also. If such a disguise were used by either aliens or unknown terrestrial groups, UFOs could be mind-waves on a global scale, creating in people the sense that something is happening at the same time that the forces behind the projection are doing something else. It is as though a demonic star-form were projecting a ray from the heavens and creating in its victims another fantasized sky from which come spacecraft carrying aliens; these aliens then take the victims for an imaginary ride. Like the old astral travelers, the kidnapped "go" to planets and stars and visit people there. The images they see are not their own unconscious ones; instead, they are science fiction stories that someone else has written for the occasion and to which chosen contactees are submitted. Following the Freudian laws of thought, the tales and their images will carry something of the person's own personality structure and unconscious needs—but the primary narrative will be manipulated. It will be an outer-space fantasy created either by fellow Earth-beings or by aliens, from unknown motives. Some yogis even claim that the whole life we live is such a fantasy.

Vallee calls the psychotronic masters "messengers of deception." *They* are the UFO phenomenon. There are no extraterrestrials. This same intelligence organization, he claims, is responsible for the bizarre phenomenon of cattle and livestock mutilation. Since the early 1970s, primarily cattle have been surgically disfigured throughout the world. The area most affected has been Colorado and Wyoming. There have been reports, however, from throughout the United States and South America, with hundreds of additional cases in Western Europe. In each incident, a sheep, a cow, or sometimes another creature has had its sexual organs removed. The mutilations have been done with an extremely sharp surgical instrument by intruders who arrived in some sort of flying vehicle. In the most affected areas, local people have become spooked by both the ghoulish phenomenon and its inexplicability. Unusual protective precautions have been taken, guards have been posted, but still the animals are attacked and the intruders escape unseen. Sometimes the cattle are lifted to a height above the ground and then smashed by being dropped. In one case, a cavity inside the sexual organs was packed with sand after mutilation. The people understand that something big is happening, but they are like any primitive population subjected to the activities of an advanced technology. It little matters that they live in the most technological nation in the history of the Earth. They sense their inferiority and lack of control, which is exactly what the mutilators intend, Vallee tells us.[10]

There seems to be no way that any known group could carry out these slaughters. They require not only elaborate airborne machinery ostensibly well out of the range of most occult and Satanic organizations, but also worldwide implementation, which would suggest collaboration on a scale heretofore unimaginable. It is a scheme that any nation would have difficulty carrying out. Some unknown factor, perhaps psychotronic, allows persons or entities to steal in directly under guard, like the invisible spellbinding thieves of mythology, to carry out their deeds. In fact, cattle have been mutilated and deposited right at the heavily guarded gateway to NORAD, the Rocky Mountain missile-defense center. Both the skill of this foray and the choice of target suggest to Vallee a direct military dare or diversionary tactic. But this is because there seems to be no purpose to the cattle mutilations, and one instinctively seeks a purpose. It is too unsettling to think that somehow these events just happen; circumstantial evidence links them to the UFOs in some way. The one mystery engulfs the other. The psychotronic smoke-screen seems the only likely way that daredevils could carry out their brazen acts. But once we accept that possibility, we are almost tempted to suggest that the mutilations themselves could be psychotronic or paranormal physical events. They might also be something else entirely, something we have not yet considered. It is our failure to come up with any other explanation that has lent credence to the paramilitary psychotronic hypothesis. But why should we trust Vallee? Might he not be covering for extraterrestrials by proposing a transnational diversionary tactic in exactly the same way that he claims the mysterious intelligence community is covering its own activities by saucers and livestock disfigurement? Would that not be more in keeping with his earlier work?

Either way, Vallee has rightly pointed out how the mutilations cast a pall over the whole UFO phenomenon. At a time when cults are proclaiming the goodness of our space brethren and some are likening them to the famous Brothers of the Rosy Cross who secretly visited Western Europe during the troubled seventeenth century, the new image of malevolent or prankish surgeons is a shock and a disappointment. Such beings are neither benevolent nor rational. All that distinguishes them from the average canine scavenger is the advanced instruments they use and the scale and whimsy of their operations. Not only are such activities seemingly pointless, they are cruel. What else can we now expect from creatures who cross millions of miles or light-years to come to our planet and, without notifying us of their arrival, disfigure harmless and helpless domestic animals? It is not a reassuring scenario. It is almost easier to blame it on ourselves and leave outer space to more compassionate and intelligent beings. Vallee's choice of an Earth-based operation comes in part from an essential incredulity that this kind of thing makes any sense in extraterrestrial terms. But then, it doesn't make sense in any terms.

Not everyone accepts this pessimistic interpretation. On a number of rural Southwestern communes, members have regularly observed UFOs, and some have claimed communication, either spiritual or person-to-person, with alien beings. They remain uniformly convinced that these beings are well-meaning and wise, and that they are monitoring the Earth for our own good, presiding, like the communes themselves, over the transition of our society from primitive violence to global sharing. The aliens have ostensibly explained their bizarre activity. It is

neither mindless nor pointlessly sadistic, but a scientific operation to detect radioactive pollutants in the areas where the samples are taken, pollutants that might lodge in the genitals. In
fact, the trail of the cattle mutilations reported in Colorado appears to follow the watershed. Thus, the aliens would be check-
ing runoff to see how afflicted the soils are. Other people, however, think that this same operation is being carried out by the
CIA for the same purpose. This explanation still seems incomplete and not a full justification for the behavior.

The communal dwellers are escapees from a media-addicted
society; they find themselves alone under the night sky—and in
the night sky, a new science fiction drama has begun. Or is it
true? The radicals of our own society find their counterparts in
more advanced beings from other worlds, thus legitimizing and
explaining their own existence on the edge of society and at the
edge of history and giving themselves a cosmic image to work
toward in their daily lives. Likewise, the apocalyptic rejection of
nuclear energy becomes associated, through the insoluble mystery of mutilated animals, with the peaceful outer-space brotherhood. The mutilations prove that our nuclear activities are a
profound violation, with long-term consequences of radiation
in the environment. People so much more advanced than we are
seem to think so. One violation calls into play another. The
mutilations and the nuclear activity cancel each other out as two
uncomfortable signals, but with one justifying the other, leaving
someone more intelligent and powerful keeping watch.

But all of this is wild supposition, and though it is interesting
and in some ways appealing, its simplicity is discouraging—as if
the whole phenomenon resolved down to a Hardy Boys mystery. Maybe the hope that something more complex lies behind
it is the hope that we, as incarnated beings, are engaged in a
more complex situation.

There is also the possibility that flying saucers are illusions or
projections of another kind. In the late 1950s, Carl Jung explored the UFO phenomenon and concluded, with some mis-
givings, that the most important thing about the mysterious craft
was not the concrete fact of their existence but the nature of the
human projection onto whatever thing (or non-thing) was there.

Jung did not dismiss a physical source, but he felt that a great number of sightings were individual projections. Others, involving many viewers, were collective hallucinations. He concluded that something was happening in the human psyche that required Unidentified Flying Objects, and he sought their explanation in that. If they should turn out to be metal ships with sentient passengers, we would still have to work out our projection of things seen in the sky, in this instance in the context of real aliens. We would be seeing both the archetype and the actual vistors from another world. But lovers must also resolve the anima and animus archetypes they project upon each other. The man seeks an ancient sea-nymph in himself, and the woman seeks the wise old man inside her; meanwhile, flesh-and-blood beings make a relationship with each other.[11]

There is a general and ancient tradition on Earth of numinous and fantastic events and entities in the firmament. Because the saucers were associated with intelligent beings in an overseer or savior role, Jung related them to the angelic and divine visitations that occurred under older heavens, especially during periods of widespread anxiety and millennial expectations. If seeing sentient-type objects in the sky is a general human activity, set off by internal psychic or external atmospheric phenomena, then peoples of different cultures would explain such sightings in ways reasonable to them. Even before explanation, they would see the things that required seeing, and this would be true whether physical UFOs existed or not. For instance, during periods of sightings elsewhere in the Southwest, Hopi Indians have observed bluestar kachinas in the night air above the mesas.

We expect the aliens now, enough so that we dream of them and our popular literature is filled with them in all guises. Thus, it is no accident that psychic energies are being transformed into UFO visions—from actual superconscious perceptions considered religious in other ages to fragmented subconscious and hysterical hallucinations of people in crazed states. Jung accepts the collective nature of the human unconscious, and he allows that things occurring in one mind can be transferred telepathically to others, or, more commonly, that forms originate simultaneously in all minds, leading to an intimation of flying saucers in this case, an intimation which is then projected onto an unknown phenomenon or into a space where nothing exists but darkness to which it can give form. In terms of the collective unconscious, the contacts with Saturnians, Jovians, or Centaurians share an archetype with the descent of angels in Christian tradition and with the delivery of tablets to the Mormons by some sort of astral beings. Different archetypes lead to mass hysteria about the devil or to sightings of goblins and elves.

Erich von Daniken uses a similar set of arguments to justify the idea that UFOs are outer-space craft perceived by ancient humanity as gods and mythic beings because of their own collective primitivity.[12] In one way, UFOs are modern technological transformations of religious visions to fit our need for psychic relief in an industrial context. In another way, religion itself is a system arising from the misinterpretation of the visitation of the Earth by peoples from outer space throughout history. But this is how deep millennial paradoxes show both their faces at once, even as they contradict each other. The outer-space gods become the magicians and shamans of primitive tribes from whom we inherit the raw methodology of terrestrial vision. Losing that vision in a technological jungle, we project our dilemma and distress outward, but in a technological manner suiting our obsession with a mechanical universe. There we find not the old gods of stars and rivers and plants, but the new gods of a supertechnological cosmos. If no such visitors have ever come here, then the visions are ours alone. But if there have never been such visitors, there is no reason why they might not be coming now or might not still come. And all of this still permits a collective hallucination.

Quasars and pulsars may be similar projections, but scientists seem more willing to accept them as real phenomena which presently lack explanation. No one denies that there are psychological and cognitive factors in the characterizations of these things, but quasars and pulsars still exist. UFOs do not have this purely physical bias. In fact, most scientists consider them products of superstition, delusion, or sheer dishonest reporting. Flying saucers have equal difficulty gaining credence among spiritualists. If the saucers are mechanical spacecraft from other worlds, then they are not visions and are not, per se, of spiritual interest. They are of spiritual consequence only to the degree that the mere existence of alien beings affects our cosmic destiny, or to the degree that the beings who pilot them are spiritually developed or carry authentic prophecy. The zodiac and the astral body have clear occult status. They are traditionary transcendent entities. UFOs may yet be, but they have no such standing now. Ultimately they could turn out to be messengers in an astral or supernal realm, creatures of other dimensions, or energies related to the aura. Wilhelm Reich proposed that they are flashes in the orgone envelope of the Earth, and his adherents have stood in cities atop buildings at night to watch the planet charging itself in the bisexual field around it. But these "phenomena" are still only interpretations in a possible uninvented parapsychology. They have no established spiritual identity.

Because the saucers do not have a firm place in either scientific or spiritual traditions, they necessarily fall in between and exploit the territory between the two. Science cannot accept them as natural phenomena or artificial creations of scientists elsewhere, and the esoteric teaching does not recognize them as divine or astral. But isn't this begging the question? There is, after all, just one creation, and if science is true to its mission, all events that actually happen are finally its responsibility. It may choose to call some things hallucinations or projections, but then it is responsible for an explanation of these. If there are gods or extradimensional forces of any sort, science must find out what these are and place them in its system.

Equally, one cannot reject the spiritual implications of the saucers on the assumption that they are mechanical phenomena. All mechanical entities have a spiritual component, for a spiritual theory demands a coherent universe. The hydrogen of the suns has an inner being, an etheric aspect. Every rock and meteor and atom and subatomic particle must have a vital property, a character set on it by the forces of creation. Or nothing does.

The problem with flying saucers is not their failure to fall into either the spiritual or the physical tradition. It is that they have arisen this late in history, after the religious-scientific division, so they do not have a position already assigned to them. Instead they prey directly on the spiritual-physical split that we have imposed on the present world. That is a most basic feature of their nature. They are no more confusing or uncertain than any other phenomenon in approaching this dichotomy, but they exploit the profound split in our own belief system and thereby receive its full impact. They do not give rise to the split, but the way in which they occur is a symptom of it. They are crude forerunners of a new theory of the universe, and we should consider them with that expectation.

The astronomer Robert Temple has noted that the Dogon people of Africa apparently inherited from their ancestors uncannily precise information about the star Sirius, notably that it has a dark companion circling it every fifty years. Scientists were unable to observe this companion until 1970, so there is a real question about how the Dogon came by this information and whether it is real information or a coincidence between a native myth and a scientific observation. Temple himself pursues the most obvious fantasy. The ancestors of the Dogon were visited by beings from the star system of Sirius sometime around 4500 B.C., and they were taught these facts, which they integrated as mythology, in keeping with their assumption that the visitors were gods. Temple goes on to show that much of the esoteric knowledge of the Egyptians, which forms the basis for parts of the hermetic and magical traditions in the West, has connections with the Sirius material. The ancestors of the Dogon were not the only contactees. Other information, from a visitation in Sumeria, was passed on through Near Eastern mystery cults and continued into the Middle Ages.[13]

Robert Anton Wilson takes this possibility to its limits in his book *Cosmic Trigger.*[14] The occult material of the Sirius connection lodges in the olden mystery cults and continues to the present as a fundamental aspect of the hermetic-Rosicrucian doctrine and the Golden Dawn, and by other paths through alchemy, anthroposophy, and Sufism, so that Crowley, Reich, and Gurdjieff are all modern disciples of the Sirians. The hermetic material is our most fundamental magical instruction. It is concerned directly with higher orders of being, intelligence elsewhere in the universe, ritual contact and influence, awakening humanity from its present troubled sleep, and invoking spirits and controlling events superconsciously and telepathically. Gurdjieff himself wrote the long science fiction tale entitled *All and Everything* (over 1,200 pages in the English translation from a mixture of Armenian and Russian); in the tale, beings from other parts of the universe visit the Earth and attempt to teach terrestrials how to overcome the cosmic difficulties of their locale. It is a spiritual training from outer space, and it combines arrival in a spaceship with incarnation on a world, the two poles of the scientific-spiritual dichotomy.

The Sirians, then, are enlightened visitors. If, hypothetically, their wisdom lies behind Sufism, the Golden Dawn, and alchemy, and also an interstellar capacity (as evidenced by their journey to Earth), then the scientific and magical must have joined into a single force for them and is being transmitted as a unified knowledge to us. The alternative is that primitive societies have embedded the scientific Sirian message in their own native occult systems.

If our esoteric tradition originated in the Sirian star-system, then the Earth forfeits its intrinsic responsibility for generating its own mystical systems. The consequence is the same as the one which follows from von Daniken's chariots of the gods: once we assume the existence of wiser teachers from elsewhere in the remote past, we undermine our own achievements and their indigenous local meanings, and we become addicted to future contact. And if we allow that the Rosicrucian and alchemical message was brought here from another solar system, we must admit that the postindustrial science that will allow interstellar travel in the distant future is very much like the occult sciences we have abandoned. Or perhaps it is a mixture of them and modern technology. Telepathy, synchronicity, and faster-than-light speeds take on new meaning. They challenge contemporary physics, and, at the same time, they invoke the only other major system of thought—the empirical and vitalistic occult with its own sciences of homoeopathy, astrology, alchemy, numerology, and astral travel: the Rosicrucian sciences.

Ultimately, Wilson finds the UFO visitations interesting but not essential. Once we admit the hermetic-technological synthesis, it is no longer necessary to assume that astronauts came here at the dawn of history. The advanced beings in the star system of Sirius could have other ways to send us their knowledge. They could project it in visions. It is not that these messages would surpass the speed of light; they would be irrelevant to it because they would contain information passing instantaneously between sentiences. Thought influencing matter, faster-than-light messages, synchronicity, and parallel universes have all been suggested as resolutions of the contradictions contained in quantum mechanics. If the extremely confusing conditions of quantum theory are to stand as posed, then something else must change. We must give up the pure boundary of the speed of light, or the simple dimensional framework of events in time and space, or the forward flow of time, or the separation of mind and matter. And if quantum theory is not to stand, we have problems at least as great as these. The nature of mind and matter, with or without interstellar travel, and of UFOs, with or without the Sirians, hangs in the balance here.[15]

Wilson also mentions the fairly remarkable experimental results claimed by electronics engineer L. George Lawrence in Oak Grove Park, California, in 1971. Lawrence's study was unconventional to begin with: he was using electronic equipment to study the behavior of plants as receptors of biological signals. Tapping oak trees, cacti, and yuccas, he intended only to pick up signals transmitted across the desert. However, with his device pointed inadvertently at the sky, he received regular pulses that lasted anywhere from a few minutes to hours. Given the precise terms of the experiment as stated by Lawrence, the only conclusion, shocking as it was, was that signals were being sent from out in the galaxy in such a way that they would be received by the preconscious cellular fabric.[16] If these messages reach plants unconsciously, then what could be the effects on human beings, who have so many more cells of such greater complexity? Data from psychotronic civilizations throughout the universe could be pouring into us, and all of human thought could be reconstructed from these signals. We live, then, not in our own cities, but in replicas of those on the other side of the universe.

Lawrence repeated his experiment with plants at the Pisgah

Crater in the Mojave Desert. The crater itself lies in the center of lava beds without any plant life for thirty miles around. Not only did he pick up additional signals, but the signals appeared strongest in the direction of Ursa Major, leading him to wonder if they might not be spillover from the dense star center of the Galaxy.[17]

Lawrence called these signals "an apparent train of interstellar communication signals of unknown origin and destination."[18] They are not the standard radio and electrical signals that man has sought as evidence of intelligent life in the universe. They are biological communications. The inference is not that they are messages aimed at the Earth, but that the universe itself is filled with this kind of "radiation," like a vast unconscious mind-net. The consequences of receiving the signals are unknown. Their purpose is obviously unknown, and no doubt even the meaning and accuracy of the experiment is unknown. Lawrence followed a logical sequence. He made many unconventional assumptions, and his proposition can be attacked from numerous vantages. It is a very leaky boat to set out anywhere in.

But that need not concern us here, for we are working with the images and projections. Experiments with plants yield inexplicable signals. The equipment is aimed at the sky. There are regular pulses with a seeming center of origin. Suddenly we are in a galactic jungle. The wild grasses and dense forests of the Earth are blown not just by the wind and receive not just the photosynthetic sunlight; they are also touched unconsciously by interstellar signals, which reach us too. To cells which are blind and virtually senseless, the sky is a fire of "noise" and "light" and primitive tropism. The stars are fields of living things. Perhaps it is the vegetation of other worlds that is sending out the signals, and perhaps the vegetation of this world broadcasts its own secrets.

The night sky of these signals is violet and green, yellow with sunlight and sugar. It is made up of plants. They are its tissue and its inner connective fabric. The least cosmic of our citizens turn out to have an astral connection.

Under this sky, the saucers are occasional geysers; the fertility of intelligence itself far exceeds them. The pyramids and rock paintings and beating drums of this world become sky events anew. They were already sky events in the sense that their matter originated in the stars, but now they become sky events in a web of sentience linking civilizations and engulfing all provinces of night. It is our unvoiced hope that the peoples of the universe are joined, even though they may never know of each other, and even though they may never come to each other as astronauts; they are engaged in the same cosmic archetypes, local representations of which their lives and artifacts portray. And they are joined by the possibility of unconscious signals among all living things. In fact, plants and animals and cells may compose a vast unconscious field that receives the collective wisdom of the universe through an inner sky—higher centers of being engulfing all the lesser provinces of night. One occultist, Douglas Baker, even proposes, quite apart from Robert Temple's hypothesis, that if the Earth and Sun lie at the heart of a giant cosmic being, then the star system of Sirius is his third eye. It is entirely appropriate that wisdom should flow from the third eye to the heart, and perhaps back from the heart to the third eye. Compared to the night skies of astronomy and astrophysics, this loom is very rich, both harmonic and harmonious. It is the kind of music that Kepler played with his *Harmonice* of creation, and it recalls the Pythagorean unity.

It is also very confusing. Once we open the framework of the universe to this degree, we are everywhere and nowhere. The night sky has vanished. It has turned into a nerve-filled skin, a synapse of the cosmos. The source of our own traditions, or their many sources, become blurred and distorted. Why need the information have come from Sirius? Could it not have come from the unknown vaults of space itself? Could it not have originated somehow within ourselves? If our unconscious mind is merged with the unconscious mind of a cosmic being traced in the sky, how do we tell anymore what is terrestrial and what is extraterrestrial? How do we distinguish between unconscious information and objective external events? How can we distinguish between our own intentions and directions and the general mesh of cosmic entities? The information about the dark companion of Sirius is really minor compared to these problems.

The interstellar brotherhood and the sentient sky are hints of another way of thinking and being. Long before their puzzles can be resolved, they reveal both the extent of our hope and the intricacy of our cosmic paranoia. There are some madmen among us who obviously think that Humpty-Dumpty can be put back together again, and that the universe that lies around us in pieces is a mirage. They would have astrophysics lead back finally to the third eye and the lineage of Hermes Trismegistos. Or they would have the gnostic and hermetic rituals lead eventually to a new galactic science, one that would carry us both into the heavens and the esoteric meaning of the human ceremony. Like astronomers before Copernicus, they would place the throne out among the fixed stars; but unlike the pre-Copernicans, they would do so in full understanding of the atomic nature and mortality of those stars.

Something is meant by all this. It may not be, as Timothy Leary has said, that the Sirian science is a blueprint for life-extension and space-migration, ultimately carrying us to the makers themselves, though he has commented that he fully expects to be alive when the Sun burns itself out in a cinder. It does portend that spacecraft and UFOs are not the crowning revelations in a theory of interstellar civilization. We are driven back into cellular and symbolic material, as we were by creation itself in the making of us, to reach the remotest stars. Or we find that we are already there, lacking only the courage to see ourselves for who we are. We are the aliens we fear. We are the body snatchers, the invaders. We need no visitors to teach us the cosmic truth. We need not travel to reach the ends of space and time.

Our deepest fears are projections of the invasion, and in some way are an evasion of the beauty that arises in us as a condition of being part of the creation. Perhaps now we understand why the extraterrestrials sit over us in judgment and try to save us, and fail in their contact with us, and why this world is a hostile and dark place. Perhaps *we* are the night, the sky, and the rest of it is fields of golden flowers and astral levity, on to eternity.

22

The Pop Star Cult of the Fifties and Sixties

THE LEGACY of World War II was the atom bomb, and those born then and in the eras thereafter lived under the omen of the air-raid sirens. Mounted on lampposts in the cities and on fire stations and barns in the country, they were the Cyclopes of our time, and they screamed for our blood. We were born into postwar prosperity, and our elders demanded gratitude for a bounty neither they nor we understood. They pretended to be giving us a gift for which they slaved all their lives, but they laid false claim to an unknown history, and, in any case, their other oblation was a dearth of meaning, a pathological greed and mistrust. They continue to dismantle the Earth.

The sirens warned us of another holocaust for which the atom bomb was an emblem. For all the times they accidentally went off, we still survived into the sixties. By then it was clear that the threat was fundamental. We had forgotten that the Earth was a planet, so strong had artificial reality become. Collective pollution, overpopulation, and consumption of the world would lead to holocaust too. The threat was so much more serious because it did not rest on any one episode like Eisenhower's shelling of Quemoy or Kennedy's blockade of Cuba. No single confrontation resolved our destiny. It was everything we were. And the nuclear war we seemed to have evaded, against the odds, was happening to us anyway, as radiation leaked into the rivers and the air, and Joan Baez sang *"What have they done to the rain?"*

This was the dark Plutonian half of the era, when a star cult began, like the one that visited the Southeast Indian tribes during the Mississippian Era of the thirteenth century. We had no temple mounds or imported Aztec jewelry, but the candy stores of the nation were filled with colored trading cards of Flash Gordon and the Martian princesses and warlords. Baseball cards came too as totems, figureheads on bright yellow and blue backgrounds, the insignias of dark brown cubs and of orange cardinals on a sprig. They were totem beings, and they generated the full zodiac of baseball statistics. Many young occultists and radical astrologers were trained in the first level of meditation and evocation by these cards and walked their first astral pathways through those blue and orange skies.[1] This was not the legacy of the generation before us, which was prepared only to turn sports figures and pop musicians into industries, convert the star symbols into cash, and join zombie armies which now waged magical war for the planet on both sides of the Iron Curtain. Why else, years later, were the Beatles in Eastern Europe singing *"Back in the USSR"?* The star-cult was our only antidote to planetary invaders who pretended to be our benefactors and our protectors and who enlisted half of our generation in their cause.

The filmmaker Kenneth Anger describes returning to the United States in 1962 after eight years in Europe, and spending the first part of that summer at Coney Island on the beach under the boardwalk. There the kids sat playing their transistor radios; the early rock music was a magical transmission, recalling Jean Cocteau's *Orpheus* and the radio in Death's car on which the poet-hero also listened to the broadcasts of another world.[2] Cocteau's radio was a prophecy of a mutant generation. *"Fools rush in,"* sang Ricky Nelson, and the stars flickered over the sea at the tip of the New World city. Years later, dark berserk warriors were to arise from the shadows of this astral music. The costume angels were kicked out of the heavens, as Richard Alpert warned they would be, before he became Baba Ram Dass. We can enter the wedding party on such a high as a guest, but we *cannot stay there.* Near Pearl Harbor, John Lennon's killer-to-be handed

Kenneth Anger three .38 slugs, marking the end of the ceremony. *"And though I know the danger there,"* sang Ricky Nelson,
"if there's a chance for me, then I don't care."

It is impossible to forget the rocket launchings of the fifties
and sixties against the rich tradition of science fiction that preceded them. Ten, nine, eight, seven, six. . . . For years afterward,
lying awake at night, seeing those spaceships depart the planet.
. . . Ignition, liftoff, *t* minus two seconds—and then fiery separation before the main stage darted past stray clouds through
the blue sky into the night beyond. In that blackness lay everything the world was not. Before the Buddha came to America,
it was our only hope.

In first grade, I had a fantasy saucer in which I went to the
planets of the Solar System and those of other stars. By the time
I was twelve, I had met with imaginary beings all over the universe and had helped found whole civilizations with my friends.
At night, I would see my saucer picking up waves of speed as it
transcended time and space, and with that thrust my mind would
rush forward into images, and finally sleep.

There was a star-cult because we needed a star-cult, and a
star-cult alone would do. We were born into a tremendous heat
and a prophecy. We knew that we were going to be something
different because the world had become absurd. The passion we
felt went beyond anything we could feel the passion for, so we
transformed each other into angels and messengers, and we listened to the interstellar debris.

The signals passed into the night and began their movement
toward the stars. From radio stations in New Orleans and the
American South, they penetrated the Caribbean and gave a
voice to the reggae music of the Rastafarian revival. It didn't
matter what the words said. The intention of the sound was
clear. To the Rastafarians it said: kill the Pope; return to Africa;
Haile Selassie, Emperor of Ethiopia, reigns, an immortal star-
king. It was an astral message twisting slang pop English to its
purposes, and it could as easily have been a Japanese song about
a fisherman or a Zulu chant to a lion.

"Go, go, go Johnny go! Go, go Johnny go!" sang Chuck Berry,
and a billion years from now, again, when alien creatures find

this cut on the Voyager disk somewhere on the other side of the Galaxy, they may be less puzzled than the generation of elders who suspected a danger hidden in the sound and who sought both to choke and exploit it in its infancy. In the end, we returned it to unknown stellar entities.

"I'll build a stairway to heaven," sang Neil Sedaka. *"I'll climb to the highest star."*

The night sky and the astral heavens were both hidden from us, born as we were in the darkness of cities among those who had torn down their own temples. We knew intuitively that *star* and *night* were esoteric words that unlocked secret realms. We knew, in fact, more than those who wrote the songs. When the heavens cried out for their "stars above," and tens of thousands of jukeboxes and radios wailed variants of the word *love,* didn't we understand that our whole civilization was praying for the return of the gods, the return of those powers within us that had brought us into being?

Yes, it is *love which brings us here* and *love which gives us life.*

Yes, we stand, every man and every woman, within the stars.

Who else has survived the incredible galactic and atomic violence to be here for a day of song?

When the old prayers are lost, tribes reinvent offerings out of the rubble and static. The gods are no less attentive.

Bobby Darin called his *"Dream Lover"* from a faraway world. A zodiac figure, like Paul Anka's Venus, she kneeled on the grassy meadow of an unknown science fiction planet beneath eight sun-stars, filling and emptying her pitchers of sacred water, in the Star Card of the tarot, a pelican behind her, awaiting the brief Aquarian era of the sixties. She was Flash Gordon's interstellar daughter.

Del Shannon shrieked: *"I'm a-walkin' in the rain,"* and Frankie Laine *"gambled for love in the moonlight."* *"The Great Pretender"* was invoked by the Platters. Elvis went to *"Heartbreak Hotel,"* as remote as the house of Cepheus. There he dreamed of *"a warmer sun"* in a world long past his own brief life.

The melodies and the dances were otherworldly and exotic. They came out of American-melting-pot/African/folk-European/Oriental/Navajo/Iroquois culture; English ballads merged with Bantu and Hausa chants, Lithuanian folk songs, *"Green-sleeves,"* and *"Danny Boy"*—and the message was global and pancultural. It was as wild as the land itself and the fiery night. We approached a parting more fragrant than body and soul. *"But you must go, and I must stay."*

I can remember leaving a dance at summer camp with feelings of great loneliness—the music of *"Michael, row your boat ashore"* fading in the distance behind me as I walked through fields of high grass with my eyes on the star-filled heavens. I felt both enormous and tiny, and though I thought myself in exile, I also felt utterly liberated, and I sang aloud with Dion and the Belmonts: *"Each night I ask the stars up above: Why must I be a teenager in love?"* The stars and the song together carried an unknown power. It may have been adolescent, but the bigness felt was authentic. All our lives our inner self reaches out for the connection.

The baseball cards changed to tarot cards, and they fell like meteors from an older sky. *"Do you believe in magic?"* the Lovin' Spoonful asked at the cusp of changing times. The Beatles visited India, and they returned with a cosmic instrument. Jimi Hendrix arrived with his songs of the outer Solar System. He traveled faster than sound, and he set his guitar on fire to the gasps of his audience. Other visionaries flocked to the deserts to watch the ancient ceremonies of the Native Americans. The old horned priests went about their business as always. They did not seek new visions; it was all they could do to handle the spirits that were already there. So the new tribes gathered at Woodstock. It was no costume party. The stars were coming to claim their own, as they had with Sufis and Cherokees for millennia. If the magic was in the music, the music was in us.

When the astral prophecy of the sixties made it to Broadway with the nude dancers of *Hair,* the message to the stars could not have been clearer: *"You twinkle above us, we twinkle below."*

And in 1980, in a movie called *Fame,* thirty years after the beginning of the cult, the chorus sang: *"Someday we'll all be stars."* The magicians and astral priests promised likewise.

————

By the late sixties, the star music had disintegrated into acid rock, atomic residue, and things were to get crazier. We had brought something into being that was equal to our passion, and it arrived in a glittering star-suit within the ceremony, by invocation. It told us: this is now outer space.

"How many years?" Bob Dylan had asked before he set out on his aeonic journey to Osiris. An extraterrestrial being lurked outside our world—lover, rescuer, star-dancer, demon, and devil woman. We stared through a thousand veils; we tried every imaginable code. We called, but it never answered. Every song of lover's abandonment told us that: the aliens had come as close as they were going to come, and we could cry our hearts out, and we could die for them, but that law would not be changed. The Stones knew: *"Nobody else's hand will ever do. Nobody else's hand."*

The Big Bopper and Johnny Horton died in the early space missions. David Bowie fell to Earth years later with Valentine Michael Smith and the Spiders from Mars. *"There's a star man / Waiting in the sky,"* he told us. Only our incapacity to meet him keeps him away. But was that star man finally Bowie himself in his synthetic spaceflesh and rock-and-roll-suicide costume? Was it Spock the Vulcan? Juan Matus the sorceror? Baba Ram Dass the Harvard-psychologist-turned-holy-man?

Suzanne held the mirror and her tea and oranges showed the whole intergalactic trade that was now possible. But Leonard Cohen left North America and moved to the Aegean to await the final war, back in darkness. Charles Manson leapt from darkness and bloodied the street altar. How vulnerable we were still: that would not change either. The deaths of Janis Joplin and Jimi Hendrix told us we could not survive on a planet that corrosive, that close to the Sun. The death of John Lennon taught us how fragile a glimmer it always was. We had thought we stood within a lit palace, but it was a momentary phantasm, a message from a distant star magnified by the media to give the sense of a nearby nova, put out by a single quick gust. Those who huddled in the cold in the park in a star memorial now truly feared that all could be lost.

Eldridge Cleaver came home to tell his people there was no Africa, no Cuba, no socialist republic. Abbie Hoffman went into hiding. Porn stores and stage orgies took over the downtown theater strips. And heroin replaced the sacred Indian plants. We had forgotten the Mafia and the Soviet bear. As naked angelic stars, we weren't very good.

And the Beatles, crashing with Hamlet's Mill into Celtic and Germanic star debris, promised: *"There will be an answer. Let it be."*

The American space program faded after the Moon landings, but Ophiel told us to walk down hallways of light and to speak to beings of flame. Posters revealed other worlds with triple stars for suns and spiral nebulae in their heavens, emerald oceans and purple and yellow vines and flowers—the outer galaxies or the insides of atoms and cells. But this was the decorative decay of the cult.

Then the Tibetan Lama Tarthang Tulku sent us into the blue sky, region by region, atom by atom. Space was not outer; it was the actual ground of our existence. "Space is projecting space into space," he wrote.[3]

We talked peace, but the world knew better. We had tried to become anti-macho in putting the deep sirens to rest—but this was the wrong planet. The Pentagon despaired of our standing up to the dark challenge of the eighties. It was time to rearm.

The vision now vanished from the central plaza. The star cult was over, but its children built hidden cities, some of them as small as a room. They bought the sacred hot springs, and lay under real stars in medicinal water, far from the messages. In New Mexico, they sat in rows staring back and forth, men and women, trying to see God in each other. They replaced the rock stars and transformed the cult.

John Lennon set his faith against the rock and roll holocaust, for he was barely a survivor of it. But Dylan stayed a prophet, leaving his family, moving on to the next deadly cult. The stars had led us to another Earth, another plane of this world. Now, all that was left was to return to the roots of art, the roots of human life. Those who remained in the temples would become robots of the negative afterlife. Punk and cold, they proved that men were sorry gods.

———

Who are we to march so boldly from the oath sealed in cell and egg?

What promise have we kept to the dead creatures whose life is now our life?

Why have we come so far through shadows only to betray?

The old songs remain in the night air. Smokey Robinson: *"You've really got a hold on me."* And Sam Cooke, shot dead in a motel: *"What a wonderful world this could be."* Elvis dead on the star cult altar. *"We shall overcome someday,"* but on what planet and when? If not on this planet, will there ever be a planet? Is this our last chance, or as Seth the spirit promised: only the beginning?

A gunman in the night, thinking he was John Lennon, shot himself, shot into the chaos of unfulfilled messages and failed potential. When we are empty, dark forces use us for their ends. *"Oh yes we will find out"*: the Stones.

We stand in darkness in an unknown corner of the Galaxy. And await further messages in the night air.

23

Science Fiction: I: The Origin of Celestial Worlds

THE STELLAR EPIC is as old as our species. The nether worlds and the empyrean sky were discovered by Ice Age shamans and sages stretching from primeval Africa to the islands of the Pacific. Over millions of years of study of the visible heavens and the fact of their own being, they came to an understanding of the invisible truth. Great worlds lay hidden far away, but they impinged on this one through our human nature. We could enter these worlds only after dangerous journeys and in other shapes.

These first philosophers and astronomers are now almost as remote from us as those we invent on the planets of Aldebaran. We inherit their blind collectivity within us and some fragments of their star myths, but that is all.

Science fiction bears the last embers of our former astronomical grandness and of the cosmos that we imaginarily and sympathetically inhabited as we came out of prehuman darkness. It wasn't science fiction then, but it was at least as cosmic as anything that the modern interstellar writers have come up with—the deep shifting cycles of lotus-within-lotus universes we could not know linearly and thus knew radiatively, intuitively. Strangers came then, too, from strange lands, but they were astral strangers, demonoids, daemons, and angelics; they dwelled in cacti and lizards and butterfly-moths and burst suddenly from the Moon and planets onto the Earth, where they initiated our ancestors under the shadow light of the spirit sky, the sky which rose like a village on fire from the bronze sunset.

Neither the Platonic nor the Ptolemaic universes represented the complexity and profundity of this mundus The mediaeval cosmos, which science finally eroded, was not the ancient mythic cosmos. It was a meaningless compromise; it had man in the center for reasons of academic and religious liturgy rather than divination and vision. We did not lose the sacred inner cosmos with Copernicus and Galileo; in a certain sense, they made it possible for us to regain it by laying the basis for star exploration and science fiction. They dismantled a leftover image. The real thing was lost so long ago that neither they nor we have any record of it. Huygens and Herschel rewrote the night sky so that later archaeologists could look simultaneously into our own astronomical past and the imaginary pasts of other planets in other solar systems. When we come to science fiction, it has elements again of tribal Ice Age consciousness. That is why it sparkles with the newness and hope of unknown worlds and at the same time haunts us with the relics and faint intimations of worlds forgotten.

Long before the planets and the stars became places to go to, they visited the Earth in other shapes. We have not inherited the oldest documents detailing these matters in the Stone Age, but we have found tales of similar import among our ancestors and non-Western tribal peoples, tales which are no doubt reflections of the originary stellar fiction. Among the Sherente tribe of Brazil, Venus was a masculine being, Jupiter a woman:

One night [the Jupiter] Star came down from the sky to a young bachelor who had fallen in love with her. The young man hid the star in a gourd, where she was discovered by his brothers. Star told her lover and invited him to accompany her to the sky. Everything was different from its equivalent on earth. Everywhere he saw smoked or roasted human flesh, and when bathing he saw horribly mutilated shapes with open body cavities. He escaped by sliding down the bacaba palm up which he had climbed; and when he got back to earth, he related his adventure. But soon after he died, and his soul went back to Jupiter, and now he is a star beside her in the heavens.[1]

The sense of the sky as a place is incipient in this myth; the preformative and creationary elements of the mythology predominate. In a Winnebago Indian myth cycle, a powerful space-being visits the Earth and impregnates a maiden who dies bearing quadruplets. The firstborn, Manabozho, attacks the one born last, Chokanipok, and, after cutting enormous chunks from his body, scatters them about as flintstones and turns his intestines into "long twining vines." Then, the one born third, Wabassa, flees to the north and is transformed into a shaman rabbit.[2] This is not a story about the objectified heavens as a place. It is an attempt to explain the topography and resources of the Earth in terms of the germinative principle of the sky, from the assumption that the sky, symbolically and enigmatically, contains the terms for the initial appearances of things.

Our own Western tradition has its visitations. The birth of each of the Greek gods is a quasi-stellar event:

> Aphrodite, Goddess of Desire, rose naked from the foam of the sea and, riding on a scallop shell, stepped ashore first on the island of Cytherea; but finding this only a small island, passed on to the Peloponese, and eventually took up residence at Paphos, in Cyprus. . . . Grass and flowers sprang from the soil wherever she trod. . . .
>
> Some hold that she sprang from the foam which gathered about the genitals of Uranus, when Cronus threw them into the sea; others, that Zeus begot her on Dione, daughter either of Oceanus and Tethys the sea-nymph, or of Air and Earth.[3]

The arrival by scallop shell might bear the mark of an extraterrestrial vehicle, but this is clearly not what Aphrodite is about. She represents, in the minds of those who imagined her collectively and over time, the emergence of passions and beauty from the debris of earlier creation, and the original personification of these in sentient creatures who established the present order.

Contemporary science fiction has its episodes of exotic love between aliens and humans, but, in these matters, Aphrodite's visit to Anchises, leading to the birth of Aeneas, is primal and indicative of a revelation we still seek:

So speaking, [Anchises] caught her by the hand. And laughter-loving Aphrodite, with face turned away and love-ly eyes downcast, crept to the well-spread couch which was already laid with soft coverings for the hero; and upon it lay skins of bears and deep-roaring lions which he himself had slain in the high mountains. And when they had gone up upon the well-fitted bed, first Anchises took off her bright jewelry of pins and twisted brooches and earrings and necklaces, and loosed her girdle and stripped off her bright garments and laid them down upon a silver-studded seat. Then by the will of the gods and destiny he lay with her, a mortal man with an immortal goddess, not clearly knowing what he did.

Anchises' first realization of the nature of his lover comes when she awakes him and stands before him by the couch: "Her head reached to the well-hewn roof-tree; from her cheeks shone unearthly beauty such as belongs to rich-crowned Cytherea."[4]

It is no wonder that several contemporary authors, under the spell of science fiction and secular astronomy, have imagined that these visitors were real extraterrestrial beings, perceived by our ancestors as gods. Robert Temple associates the Babylonian fish-tailed Oannes with amphibious beings from the star system of Sirius—beings who, the Dogon say, founded their society: he imagines an intelligent creature "resembling a kind of cross be-tween a man and a dolphin."[5] The literature of our planet abounds with possible spacecraft and extraterrestrial travelers. Von Daniken, Temple, and others have cited references to such things in written and oral tales, in petroglyphs of saucerlike objects, and in inexplicable archaic objects that resemble clocks and computer wheels. Temple relates a Dogon description of an alien descent. The vehicle sounded like large stone blocks being struck in a particular small cave near Lake Debo. "The ark landed on the Fox's dry land and displaced a pile of dust raised by the whirlwind it caused. The violence of the impact roughened the ground."[6] A flame went out from the ark and touched the grass.

Temple finds another "landing" in the Sumerian tale of *Gilgamesh* from the third millennium B.C.: "There appeared stars in the heavens. The host of heaven fell down toward me. I tried to lift it but it was too heavy for me; I tried to move it, but I could not move it."[7]

If extraterrestrials came here, this is how they were received, and their contributions have already been incorporated in our civilization as the deeds of gods and the visions of shamans. That can no longer be changed. The gods exist for other reasons too; and if spacemen were momentarily synchronous with them, this may change aspects of their message, but not their meaning or import: they still speak from within the human psyche. Von Daniken is accurate when he cites "our human past which somehow is bound to become our human future some time or other,"[8] for this is true already in his very assumptions that Thor, Ra, Quetzalcoatl, and Rama were space visitors, not gods; that Ezekiel saw extraterrestrial machines, not divine orbs; that Enkidu was a spaceship in *Gilgamesh* (and that other bizarre monsters were also star vehicles). Our manipulation and redefinition of these events create an awkwardly simplistic relationship between ourselves and the gods. Von Daniken insists that we were bred from such beings and are their children—which makes us gods also. But the universe is so deeply internalized that this claim has no more meaning, even if true, than the profound mystery of DNA itself in the depths of the vast universe.

The World of the Dead was the most visited "planet" of antiquity, and although it was a realm entered through a state of spiritual transformation, it was also a forerunner to the planetary experiences of space-travelers. The Greek description is a familiar one:

> When ghosts descend to Tartarus, the main entrance to which lies in a grove of black poplars beside the Ocean stream, each is supplied by pious relatives with a coin laid under the tongue of its corpse. They are thus able to pay Charon, the miser who ferries them in a crazy boat across the Styx. This hateful river bounds Tartarus on the western

side, and has for its tributaries Acheron, Phlegethon, Cocytus, Aornis, and Lethe. Penniless ghosts must wait forever on the near bank; unless they have evaded Hermes, their conductor, and crept down by a back entrance. . . . A three-headed or, some say, fifty-headed dog named Cerberus guards the opposite shore of Styx, ready to devour living intruders or ghostly fugitives. . . .

The first region of Tartarus contains the cheerless Asphodel Fields, where souls of heroes stray without purpose among the throngs of less distinguished dead that twitter like bats, and where only Orion still has the heart to hunt the ghostly deer.[9]

The kingdom of Osiris, known to the Egyptians, is a different world of the dead. Humanoids there have hawk, jackal, and lion heads. A hare-headed being holds a knife. A hippopotamus goddess and a squat dwarf stand beside each other, bearing knives. Beside them is a ram-headed ghoul. The hawk of Horus, wearing two crowns, is poised on a sepulchral building. The Sun and Moon are replaced by the Eyes of heaven.[10]

The visitor to the Tibetan land of the dead is prepared for fantastic and terrifying creatures:

O nobly-born, from the north [will dawn] the Blue Wolf-Headed Wind-Goddess, waving a pennant in the hand; and the Red Ibex-Headed Woman-Goddess, holding a pointed stake in the hand; and the Black Sow-Headed Sow-Goddess, holding a noose of fangs in the hand; and the Red Crow-Headed Thunderbolt-Goddess, holding an infant corpse in the hand; and the Greenish-Black Elephant-Headed Big-Nosed Goddess, holding in the hand a big corpse and drinking blood from a skull. . . .[11]

This is a world of dull, smoke-colored lights, unabated storms, beasts of prey, deafening sounds, and bands of pursuing monsters. The *Book of the Dead* advises that these specters are the actual consequences of anger, greed, fear, violence, indifference, and other negative emotions and attitudes. It is not that the Bardo realm (into which souls first pass) is merely symbolic; it is that emotions are physical facts that dissolve into inhabited topographies when the corporeal aspect behind an individual disintegrates. These are not biological beasts or geological land-scapes, even though they have an origin in creature existence; they are "psychotronic" representations. Other worlds are de-pendent upon unconscious aspects of our being for their very existence.

Realms of the dead are not the only archaic planets. Fairy tales are filled with Earthlike worlds inhabited by weird and magical creatures. In the Irish accounts, there are trooping fair-ies, changelings, ghosts, leprechauns, giants, demon cats, witch hares, bewitched butter, banshees, and waking dreams. The four-leafed clover captures the suddenness with which this world becomes another. In the Germanic tales of the Brothers Grimm, a prince is entrapped in the body of a frog, a wicked crow is nailed to a palace wall, a flounder grants wishes to a fisherman who throws him back, witches dwell in the centers of deep forests, and Beauty is visited by the Beast. We have not forgotten any of this, and we see it over again in science fiction. The forest is now a remote planet. Mary Shelley later calls the monster back to life beneath flashing stars and with stirrings of odd memories. The tinder box that brings the dogs and the lamp that summons the jinni are now electronic devices. Our destiny still lies in the same unknown hands. Merlin lives backwards, and Arthur draws the sword from the stone. Coyote climbs a thread into the sky and there finds aged spiders sitting in a meadow. While he spends a day in the upper world, a year has passed in the world below.

It is no wonder that time between planets is now dilated and that other worlds are inhabited by knights, princesses, telepathic savages, monstrous intelligent insects, thinking rocks, mer-maids, and disembodied voices. We have known of these "places" from the days of Odysseus and before. They have ex-isted in the uncharted and enigmatic interzone among myth-ological, psychological, and geographical realms. In fact, some of these kingdoms and peoples have been found on the Earth, and some may yet be found on other planets.

The journey of Odysseus was one of the earliest "space" voy-ages. He went into an unknown cosmology which included lotus eaters, the Cyclops, the witch Circê, and the bag full of winds given by Aiolos—living creatures in a leather sack. The shores he visited have been revisited by lost spacefarers of the twentieth century. We cannot reduce those shores to the Aegean, but we can expand the Aegean to the stars.

Then there are the sea journeys of Brendan, a mediaeval Irish monk who was perhaps a Neolithic shaman. He was attacked by a giant spitting fire; he saw a floating crystal column; he came to a place where light passed through the water to the cities beneath. The giant spitting fire could have been a volcano on an island off Iceland. The crystal could have been floating ice. Perhaps Brendan and his crew turned to the south, coasting Vinland, and looked into the transparent coral sea.[12]

The Irish *immrama* and the Norse *Sagas* are the preserved fragments of a vast oral science fiction of the North Atlantic that pervaded Europe from ancient times through the Middle Ages. Men looked to the sea as we now look to the stars, understanding that a mystery lay encompassed there, a mystery of indeterminate size and origin.

The Icelandic seaman Erik the Red sailed to the Americas four times; on one of his voyages, he encountered an aboriginal race, probably Eskimos or Beothuk Indians and named Skraelings ("little people") by the Norsemen. These swarthy, stubby folk looked like trolls. They came in nine skin-boats, whirling their bull-roarers "in the same direction that the sun moves, and they made a noise like flails," according to *The Saga Tale* of A.D. 1005. Freydis, Erik's daughter, suggested an attack upon these puny-seeming beings, but the Skraelings drove back the iron-bearing strangers with slings and arrows and with weapons made of sea-mammal floats which crashed on the ground among the Vikings, giving off horrendous noises.

These were truly blind mediaeval armies in the night. The Norsemen were invaders from the sky; the Skraelings were chthonian beings of darkness. No doubt our species has met itself elsewhere on this planet as strangers, but this is one recorded case that stands for thousands.

When Erik the Red left the Western lands, his ships full of ivory, oil, and hides, he sailed north looking for new worlds. He wintered at an unknown place that he called Eriksholm; the men built homes from driftwood that had been carried by currents from Siberian rivers. At the end of a hard winter, they continued north.

Then Erik came to the end of the world: giant icebergs, half a mile in length, crashed from the face of ice, sending out tidal waves for miles and yet still visible at the distance of Erik's ships, the greatest glacier face on this interglacial Earth. Here Erik looked north into a mirror of continuous blinding daylight, un-inhabitable as the Sun or interstellar space in a way that made Baffinland look like paradise, for Baffinland was at least a con-tinent. Here he floated among the peaks of sunken mountains, the fragments of olden worlds, the glitter so bright that he could not see, where all the languages and landscapes and directions mixed in the polar scramble of atmosphere and solar wind, clos-er to Thor than he had ever been, closer to Middle Earth.[13]

Centuries later, Marco Polo went among the Tartars and to Cathay and visited strange courts. The Portuguese brought Af-ricans, their beads, ostrich egg cups, and wood carvings back from the interior of an adjacent continent whose dimensions were barely gauged. Early sixteenth-century voyagers to the New World returned with coarse-haired red savages who spoke unearthly languages and had freakish customs and beliefs. Were these the lost tribes of Israel? Were they an alternate species? Were they even our human kin? In the late eighteenth century, the returning ships of Captain Cook reported unknown species of plants and animals, exotic kings and chieftains, southern ice, and immense statue heads on Easter Island. Legend, theology, and early anthropology merge here.

We sense the power of the unknown West in Shakespeare's late plays. The tragedies of his kings have ended; the pranksters, fairies, and buffoons of the comedies are put to sea. The Euro-pean theater is shipwrecked on what seems at first a tiny isle but is actually a gateway between aeons and worlds. It is as if Shake-speare knew that only something totally different could follow him. He had enough of Galileo and John Dee in him for that prophecy.

In Ariel and Caliban, he tells us that there are lands on the Earth inhabited by beings who are not like us and who share neither our history nor our Christian tradition. If they work magic, it is by their own native arts.

"This island's mine, by Sycorax my mother," says Caliban.[14] There are not even Egyptians lurking behind his claim. There are only local gods and wilderness. The isle is filled with wild and wondrous sounds and voices.

The Tempest is not itself science fiction, but it is a direct forerunner. Magician and daughter become scientist and daughter a thousand times over, marooned on the planets of other suns. And the handsome spacemen, like the shipwrecked nobles of Shakespeare's play, come to reclaim the lady both from her possessive and powerful father and from the native spirits. The Mirandas of outer space look back at the Earth as a star and say, "O brave new world. . . ."[15]

Some things have never been found: mermaids, winged tribes, Amazon women, the white Christian kingdom of Prester John in Africa, the continent of Atlantis, the antipodes who live upside down, and so on. Their meanings have been transferred to historical episodes, as when the Mormons decided that the American Indians were the lost Hebrew tribes; or they have been assigned to the less glorious things that *have* been found, as when mythical Brazil was abandoned and the name given to a vast tropical wilderness. No Fountain of Youth, no telepathic races, no two-headed humanoids or underwater cities have ever been discovered. Some of these things have been transfused directly into science fiction, and they are found again imaginarily on the planets in that tradition—they and far stranger races and creatures.

It would take the European mind many generations to realize the wonders that were disclosed by early ethnographers and travelers. The Australian Aborigines lived in a dreamtime landscape that was almost supernatural. Their Earth was the bones and blood, genitals and semen, of a collective being of which they were the living members. And they received news of the dead over great distances without visible messages or messengers. They had a science of the interwoven families that challenged any social system elsewhere. The American Indians visited plants in their minds and charmed animals, and if they weren't weird and multicolored by birth, they painted themselves into bizarre spirit-figures and did dances no one had imagined, raising elements of consciousness not yet broached in the West. The actuality of kachinas and medicine men and buffalo dancers and sun-priests was stranger than any fantasy of them. What they failed to do in melodramatic excess they made up for in actually being and in living their lives through as these alien creatures.

Carlos Castaneda is very late for one going out among Indians to seek a fierce and unknown universe. He did not travel to a planet in Andromeda or even to one of the nearer stars like Sirius. He simply crossed the border into Mexico. There he discovered things as incredible and inexplicable as anything science fiction fantasizes for peoples of vastly superior technologies and psychokinetic powers. In the universe of Don Juan, which stretches to the ends of the cosmos, Castaneda is a waif. Because we already suspect that this vital shamanism abounds on our world, and because we intuit such powers vestigially in ourselves (and cannot get at them), we invent corresponding wonders out in interstellar space. Our imagination tries to justify our troubled lives. We set these wonderful planets apart in the heavens so that we might not pollute them with our arrogance and our error, and so that they may outlive us and our Big Bang universe and continue to exist even if we finally fail them in ourselves. The shaman inherits the stars. We must fight for every clump of dirt.

Castaneda describes speaking to animals in unknown languages, entering the psyche of a passing bird, being in two places at the same time, growing new organs in his body, and jumping into a chasm to sure death, only to rematerialize in a marketplace elsewhere. Not only is this the stuff of quasars and black holes, but some people claim that Castaneda has written science fiction disguised dishonestly as ethnography. We do not know.[16]

Even as the myths of Cathay and the Indies have dissipated into anthropology, they have been replaced by a strange new Earth of psychedelic visions, voodoo, faith healing, and ethnoscientific and totemic systems whose complexity rivals that of computers and linguistic philosophy. And the influence of Cathay, Tibet, and India has never been stronger in the West.

An old comic book shows a Martian orchestra with its snouted players. An alien audience attends while they "play" the standard Earth instruments, but intricately colored shapes rise from the openings and blend above them. In other books and magazines, hives of intelligent insectoids go forth in warring ships for a bulbous queen who hatches the generations of her centurions. Beings of mist evaporate into the atmosphere of their planet. Crystal creatures lie sessile across the face of a world, assimilating moisture and accumulating a vast philosophy. Another planet's surface is a giant beast, its tubule sensoria resembling fields of flowers. Runaway planets intersect the Earth's orbit. Some of them are empty; others contain sixteen-eyed pyramid creatures and robots. Giant reptiles ride horselike beasts across unknown plains. The planet of telepaths eludes us. We cannot see its actual shapes, for the inhabitants project only the images they want us to see. They exist, with spider and amoeboid civilizations, at the other end of this Galaxy, or in another galaxy, or not at all. They have their monuments and cities, their "Homers," "Shakespeares," and "daVincis," whatever they are called natively and whatever media and implements they use.

True science fiction began late in our history as a complement to the infinite universe of the astronomers and mathematicians. Imaginary worlds formed in the debris of mythological ones— all located hypothetically among the stars and dimensions of the night sky. Planet zones were generated throughout Newtonian space, and the Darwinian algorithm filled them with life forms.

Ancient myths tell of stellar forces and the supernatural beings who arise in the sky and on other worlds. Even *Genesis* is the tale of the creation of a planet, and the works of Dante and Milton carry this extraterrestrial theme. Aristophanes, Apuleius, Aesop, and Plato are all considered proto–science fiction writers, for they deal with imaginary cities, extraplanetary travel, and talking beasts. The most famous of these writers, in a science fiction context, is Lucian of Samosata, a Syrian Greek stonemason of the second century A.D., who wrote *Verae His-*

toriae (True Stories), which suggest the twentieth-century *Amazing Stories* and *Astounding Science Fiction.* In one of Lucian's stories, a Greek sea vessel is swept to the Moon by waterspouts and winds. There the crew witness preparations for a war with the King of the Sun, who is disputing possession of Jupiter with the Lunar King. A huge double wall is built as protection against the Sun. Finally, both sides agree by treaty to colonize the Morning Star. The Greeks continue on their journey through the Zodiac and visit a city in which talking lamps dwell. Their adventures take them to realms of giants and monsters, cities of gold and gems, and an Isle of Dreams with a dream palace.[17]

This is not really science fiction, nor does it lead to science fiction. Until the secular sky had broken free of the astral heavens, there could be no stellar adventure that was not equally occultism and mythology. Lucian's planets and creatures are simply supernatural Earth realms and spirit beings. However far away they seem to be projected, they portray processes occurring within humanity. Lucian made no attempt to imagine creatures and worlds separate from this system or to use such creatures and worlds to define man in the context of the cosmos. The same is true of Jonathan Swift's *Gulliver's Travels* and other works of the seventeenth and eighteenth centuries. By then, most proto–science fiction books avoid occult and mythological creations, but they still propose other worlds as allegorical and moral extensions of this one—as though the universe were created in our image and reflected only our society.

In his *Billion Year Spree,* a history of science fiction, Brian Aldiss locates the beginning of science fiction in the Gothic novel. Strange worlds were imagined, set in remote unknown lands, with ghosts, giants, castles, sultans, treasures, figures in armor, supernatural beings of mysterious heritage, and villages cut off from humanity where vampires and other shadowy creatures ruled.[18]

Aldiss traces the Gothic novel to Horace Walpole's *The Castle of Otranto,* published in 1765. And where did *Otranto* come from?

"On a June night in 1764, Walpole had a nightmare in which he saw a gigantic hand clad in armour, gripping the bannister of a great staircase. When he woke, he began writing his novel."[19]

Much science fiction also originates in visions, trances, and psychopathic incidents, so the beginning of the genre is as bottomless and untraceable as the stars. Its sources are clouded in our own psychic origin, and they have no clear history.

For Aldiss, science fiction begins with Mary Wollstonecraft Shelley's novel *Frankenstein,* which also has its setting in a dream and was written before the author was twenty, in 1816. Perhaps the monster is her vision of the dark side of her poet husband, but her creature is clearly not a ghost or a golem in the usual sense: he is a "machine" created by a scientist. He ponders his obscure origin and unhappy lot as science fiction creatures will for billions of hypothetical years in the future, and as man will in the context of the science fiction stars. Mary Shelley, suggests Aldiss, gave birth not merely to a monster who lay sleeping just beyond human ken but to all of science fiction.[20] Soon after, Jules Verne created the machinery, and H. G. Wells sent rockets out into the Solar System.

Other modern literary genres, like the Western and the detective story, have *cinema verité* landscapes. The science fiction landscape is decorative and ornate, a feature noted often by critics. It is usually excessive and sloppily written, but it must be the landscape of some thing. Most likely that "thing" is the hidden psyche of science—of astronomy, physics, and also chemistry and biology. Science fiction comes into being with technology and industrialism and probes their unknown and latent meanings. That is why Mary Shelley's robot is the first. The science fiction creature must be artificial and industrial, or it must be discovered (or discover us) on a journey arising from technology. Otherwise, it does not explore this second creation of the universe—the planetology of the sentient species born to the stars.

Science fiction worlds are proposed as other things, so they capture that aspect of ourselves that wishes to propose an Other even as they carry meanings that we no longer have access to in spiritual inquiry and thus have cast into the unknown dimensions of time and space. They may originate in *our* science, but when *its* potential realms are externalized, they seem the products of other, even robot, intelligences. From a stochastic imagination, weird shapes and exotic landscapes emerge. They startle us, for we have succeeded in putting a dark and compelling crack in the mirror of the natural world. We have dressed the imposter so well he could replace us right now, this very next second.

Science fiction also requires the ingredients of the romantic Western novel: adventure in exotic lands, transcendence of social limitations, and the development of a unique personality and soul. "There may be trillions of galaxies, and billions of billions of stars in those, and billions of planets orbiting about those stars," Dr. McCoy tells Captain Kirk during a *Star Trek* episode, "and who knows how many races and individual beings—but only one Kirk in all of that." Without this element of individual human uniqueness, fiction merges with allegory, we no longer care about the individual adventurer and his journeys to lands beyond the sea or other planets, and the trips themselves become collective odysseys, like *Pilgrim's Progress* or Dante's "interplanetary" transits.

Each of us is a unique being, and each alien world and creature is unique and discrete, so there is reason to visit all of them. If they go on forever, then we must go on forever too. They cannot be categorized or generalized. They do not form a zodiac. Or if they do, we will not get to them by praying or meditating. We must approach and enter them in their regional and infinite diversity and experience them as palpable beings, with all their colors, scents, and sounds.

In Poul Anderson's novel *The High Crusade,* we experience the treachery and wonder of the chance cosmic adventure.[21] In 1345, Sir Roger, an English baron, is in the process of raising an army to join King Edward III in France. However, a spaceship lands in his village. Its occupants are five feet tall with blue skin and short tails. Though everyone is frozen with terror at the sight of actual living demons and devils, and exorcism is the first plan, there is no time to weigh alternatives. The invaders shoot fire from a weapon, scorching to death one of the locals. The English soldiers respond without thinking. To their amazement, their arrows penetrate these blue demons. Hundreds of arrows are fired, and three of the demons fall over as easily as popinjays.

Sir Roger is a modern thinker. He has no idea who these invaders are, but he is impressed with their vehicle, and he wants to use it against the French, and then, if successful, against the Infidels in the Holy Land. After taking Jerusalem, he can return heroically to England. He is unfazed by the concern that it is a satanic ship. Enlisting the aid of the crew members still alive, he learns how to operate it. To the objection that they are devils and the ship is cursed, he simply replies that they are sorry devils indeed if they can be killed so easily. Instead, the idea is put forth that they are from a place beyond Cathay, a land which already had elusive precedents in Plutarch, Brendan, and Pytheas.

Sir Roger piles everything into the spacecraft—men, women, children, horses, cows, pigs, chickens. They levitate rapidly. The clouds turn out to be mere mists; the Earth is round, the Moon pocked. The Earth disappears beneath them like a stone "down a great well."

They expect to be taken to France, but their captive pilot has betrayed them and set the ship on automatic controls to return to the home planet, part of an expansionist interplanetary empire that intends to conquer the Earth too.

Sir Roger is undaunted. He imagines that in such an enormous empire there will be great booty, and the creatures themselves do not seem powerful in combat. He succeeds not only in capturing the planet upon landing but in taking over the entire empire. It is his descendants, having organized the many worlds into a feudal kingdom, who meet the first spacemen from Earth.

These English knights in interstellar space who retain their mediaeval world-view and yet conquer a vastly complex civilization are a powerful image of a moment in time and space that transcends the book. Sir Owain's courtship of Lady Catherine beneath strange stars and two moons lies at the center of this image. Are we not always the descendants of peasants and savages, even when we go among the stars? That is the beauty of the single nonallegorical life.

For generations, the offspring of this English army spread their empire, in the course of which they search the suns, right into the center of the Galaxy, for the Earth and the Holy Land. When the first Earthship arrives, they are deeply moved. Their origin in a sacred faraway land was not just a legend. They offer the Earth crew an astrologer to guide them to the court of the King, where they then talk about the results of royal expeditions to promising Sagittarian star clouds.

Science fiction is somewhat of a misnomer. We are actually creating stellar mythology. We are projecting every imaginable aspect of the present world frame into the unknown problematic basis of reality, and we are seeing ourselves reflected back ever more remotely and relativistically, until it might seem that our existence in the universe could be anything at all, even nothing. For lack of a coherent cosmology and a fixed world axis, for lack of the pillar—the mill of the gods and of the old Hamlet—to hold up the frame of the heavens and grind out justice, stars, and sea salt, we have come to hard times, and we have no quadrants or clepsydras with which to realign ourselves or the sky. Adjustments hardly last a year, let alone a generation or an aeon. We tilt cosmogony every which way, and change the dimensions and moral basis likewise, and this has become more acceptable to us than passively waiting for a resolution to our present dilemma. We have come to prefer Shakespeare's pre-modern existential Hamlet to the ancient Scandinavian prince who attempted to keep the constellations in place and on whom the later one was based in the partial and incomplete transmission of Latin Danish history.[22] If we cannot fix a single reality and a coherent universe, we will invent every possible one as a collective contradicting reflection of our present drift. The madness may have once been in the stars, but we have taken it down into our troubled lives. We are the only prophets and the only heroes left; the sky has diluted all other adventures and conquests. Our illusion is that we have escaped the fate of cosmic unity, but we are now that fate, and we alone betray what the cosmos can become.

24

Science Fiction:
II: Self and Cosmos

THE KEY TO SCIENCE FICTION is not the exotic nature of the worlds visited in outer space or the interstellar distances covered. Varieties of planets and creatures can go on forever in these books without our even intuiting a cosmic meaning. The true key to science fiction is the passage of our minds and spirits, and sometimes even our bodies, to other dimensions and realms of consciousness. This may happen on a starship voyage to faraway solar systems and other galaxies, but it also may happen without our ever leaving the Earth. A place is not automatically "cosmic" because a writer tells us it is on another planet. The strange creatures in the Earth's oceans are cosmic, and even the butterflies and grasshoppers in the fields are cosmic. Science fiction does not create the cosmic by astounding us with bizarre machinations; it does not find other worlds only by exaggerating the unearthly.

"There are far too many worlds in this desert alone," the shaman Juan Matus tells Carlos Castaneda, "for us ever to know them all in the pitiably short time of a man's life."[1]

The ordinary novelist must portray the human condition within the terms of a particular century and social milieu. He can imply cosmic forces, but he cannot introduce their raw nature into his books. If he does, they become science fiction. A science fiction writer can move his characters through the stars and can

391

move the stars themselves; he can even have stars think and communicate; he can throw an entire culture into an alien condition. However, we must not be fooled by the landscape. Dostoevsky and Faulkner revealed as much about man's fate among the stars as any science fiction writer; by not bringing the stars into the foreground of their work, they showed their subtle and intricate presence everywhere.

Science fiction writers take the cosmos itself as a figure for our origins and our destiny, a figure writ large and projected out away from us where we seem to see it as a mammoth unity. It is not any particular shape that gives cosmic overtones; it is the fact itself of an eternal enigma in a star-filled night. We cannot evade it or disarm it, so we must enter and reveal it. But mostly science fiction fails. The bigness is corrupting, and the writer ends up with a minor theme ornately decorated with stars, bizarre landscapes, trivial monsters, and other baroque creatures.

One of the most blatant failures of bigness is Olaf Stapledon's tale *Star Maker*. Writing during the gathering clouds of World War II, Stapledon tried to intimate an equivalent horror throughout the universe itself. He moved through planets and stars and galaxies back to the maker of worlds himself. But the unstated shadow of Hitler was actually more alien than the torments of suns, and our own species was more deadly and frightening than a star maker who destroyes whole universes. The local darkness outbid Stapledon. Still, the very scale of the book does invoke a mysterious and unknown bigness.

In the beginning of the *Star Maker*, an individual is induced up into the heavens:

> Rubies lay behind me, amethysts ahead of me. Surrounding the ruby constellations there spread an area of topaz stars, and round the amethyst constellations an area of sapphires. Beside my course, on every side, the colours faded into the normal white of the sky's familiar diamonds. Since I was travelling almost in the plane of the galaxy, the hoop of the Milky Way, white on either hand, was violet ahead of me, red behind.[2]

His speed increases, and the stars and galaxies fly past in a blizzard. Instead of moving outward into an eternity, he approaches the source, the Star Maker himself. This supersentient being puffs out trial universes, observes them in a wink, and then devours them to try again. It is a sterile if grandiose beginning:

> As he lovingly, though critically, reviewed our cosmos in all its infinite diversity and in its brief moment of lucidity, I felt that he was suddenly filled with reverence for the creature that he had made, or that he had ushered out of his own secret depth by a kind of divine self-midwifery. He knew that this creature, though imperfect, though a mere creature, a mere figment of his own creative power, was yet in a manner more real than himself.[3]

But the Starmaker can do nothing to improve the quality of this universe:

> He had seemingly outgrown all desire to save them from the consequences of their finitude and from the cruel impact of the environment. He loved them without pity. For he saw that their distinctive virtue lay in their finitude, their minute particularity, their tortured balance between dullness and lucidity; and that to save them from these would be to annihilate them.[4]

With such a figure for the cosmos itself, Stapledon can arrive only at a kind of astral nihilism.

Charles Dickens touches the secret of our origin and destiny without the stars. In *Great Expectations,* Pip finds out that an escaped convict whom he had met in a graveyard during his childhood stands behind his entire ascension into wealth and noble society, and is, as well, the father of the woman he loves.[5] When he discovers the first truth, he seems to fall from grace entirely, for he had suspected a grander plan. When he learns the second twist, however, he is able to recover his lover from the darkness with which the story is enshrouded, tearing open the curtains of the old house to let daylight into the cobwebs. The story begins with a meeting in the graveyard, seems to forget it, and then returns to it as the turning point of the plot. Science fiction takes this moment and spreads it across universes—which doesn't make it any bigger, but gives us a sense of how big it always was.

There *is* a convict and a graveyard at our beginning, and our very existence throws light through a previously blackened room. This is our inheritance. In a universe of stone and fire, the convict himself is a prince. The rich woman and her daughter are merely a fantasy of better worlds and of how things would be if we had not been born ignorant and poor. We seem not to deserve the cosmos at all, and then we become its salvation. This is the message of science fiction. The ancients knew it as destiny and placed it in the stars by an entirely different method.

Originally, science fiction sought mainly the ulterior worlds, for Western man was still rushing into a strange physical cosmos that was transforming his destiny. We have not yet scratched the surface of that, but we have passed the first threshold of meaning, and it is not going to mean a whole lot more for a long time. We are now moving into the science fiction of reincarnation and mind change, and Hindu and Buddhist images are becoming as common as rocket ships and space-time journeys.

In *Star Trek,* many of the more notable episodes are spiritual or mental, as when Captain Kirk is split into his polarized halves by a transporter malfunction, or when Spock enters alien minds and sees the universe they see—from Hortas of rock and silicon to creatures of sparkling lights. Other beings and intelligences flicker in and out of the universe through which the starship *Enterprise* assiduously travels. They are part of the larger creation. From meetings with them the travelers are changed, and the voyage becomes a cosmic initiation.

"Space: The Final Frontier!" we are told at the beginning of each episode. But it is not space, of course, that is the final frontier. It is ourselves. We are traveling across a layer of the cosmos in an illusion of space and time. The *Star Trek* movie is an epithalamium of man the species and the Creation. An old Earth-made satellite (V'ger) returns from the remote reaches of time and space (which themselves are perhaps only a fragment of the cosmos); now it seeks something more than just data, more than just new planets and vistas. In the end, a man and a woman and the V'ger merge in a metasexual fountain of lights, auras, and atoms, and they clone a new species, just as the dreaming children do in Arthur Clarke's *Childhood's End,* or the transmigrating Hopi ancestors do following the spirit of a great bird.[6] The willowy androgynous-looking beings of *Close Encounters of the Third Kind* may be visitants from outer space, but their manipulation of time and dimension implies that man has come into contact with something new in the cosmos, thus something new in his own nature. The spaceship over Devil's Tower may be pure machinery, but an underlying mantra and cosmic melody are used to make the connection, and the object closely resembles a fully manifested mandala mushrooming into our realm from another space.[7]

In Hindu and Buddhist literature, individuals suddenly awaken to the other lives within them, and this conscious life becomes part of a much longer cosmic journey. In Paramahansa Yogananda's *Autobiography of a Yogi,* the author is summoned by a being who taught him in other lives and who brings those lives back into his consciousness with a touch of the hand. "I remember," he says. Then Babaji, the deathless one, speaks:

> "For more than three decades I have waited for you to return to me.
> "You slipped away and disappeared into the tumultuous waves of the life beyond death. The magic wand of your karma touched you, and you were gone! Though you lost sight of me, never did I lose sight of you! I pursued you over the luminescent astral sea where the glorious angels sail. Through gloom, storm, upheaval, and light I followed you, like a mother bird guarding her young."[8]

Radio telescopes do not reveal the luminescent astral sea, but science fiction tales, looking out through radio telescope images, recreate it.

In the Tibetan novel *Mipam* by Lama Yongden, both Mipam and Dolma are reincarnated century after century until they see each other back at the beginning according to the vows they took then. At the end of the novel, Mipam "remembers." Dolma, the woman he would have married, is returned to the astral sea so that they can complete the episode begun aeons earlier:

> "Because I refused thee the gift of what I possessed of

the Doctrine [he tells her], I remained for centuries unable
to understand it wholly. Be thou delivered from the desire
for vengeance that has brought thee back into this world
for numberless sorrowful incarnations, and may I be delivered from egotism and pride, the primal springs of that
desire.

"Take thy rest for a brief space in the Paradise of the
Great Beatitude, then, having chosen honourable parents
in a neighboring region, and having been born with a male
body, come to me in ten years' time and rejoin me here at
Ngarong to be my pupil and my well-beloved son."9

This is the universe we abandoned, so now our destiny lies in
outer space. Or outer space is our passage through "numberless
sorrowful incarnations" until we return to the source of our
desire, which, according to karmic law, brought all this into
being in the first place, including the vast starry night.

In science fiction itself, the profoundly moral import of karma
is often lost, and the concept is reinvented in terms of a more
random high-technology universe. Karma becomes a corrupt
science of interstellar civilizations that measure the cosmic debt
of creatures bioelectrically and enact cycles of disembodiment
and reembodiment based solely on political power. Tyranny is
extended beyond lifetimes.

In *Lord of Light,* Roger Zelazny creates a world of god-figures
who are merely ruling-class members given divine attributes and
virtual immortality by a science of engrams and mind-transfer.
These decadent nobles have taken on the names and the powers
of the gods and goddesses of the Hindu Vedas. Warring with each
other and changing bodies and sexes, trying to enjoy the
sensual pleasures of eternity, they elevate the few and banish
their renegades to bestial or imperfect bodies. The bulk of mankind remains savage and dispossessed, while these lords—as
Mara, Yama, Vishnu, and Brahma—make beautiful bodies for
themselves, subjugate harems, and accumulate wealth. They
have even forgotten that they are not the actual gods, because
they have been these entities for so long.

In the meantime, Siddhartha, the binder of demons, is banished to the electric field about the Earth, but he is stolen back and reembodied by the rebels, for he seeks to overthrow the old gods and establish a new order. Unwilling at first to reassume his flesh, he eventually develops successful stratagems for the rebellion. The astral and spiritual energies of the Hindu universe cannot be corrupted, for by their karmic measure they determine justice. In this science fiction universe, they are perverted into electricity by biological engineers. In that form, karma can be used, even as computers are used, to measure anything the ruling class desires.[10]

Philip José Farmer has created two imaginary universes in which planetary and biological engineering have become so advanced that beings are kidnapped from their worlds and their bodies, put in new bodies, and whole artificial planets are created by Lords who then rule them as tyrants. In the World of Tiers series, the Lords have each created a planet as his or her private paradise, using synthetic bodies of real beasts, mythological beasts, and beautiful humanoids. However, the Lords have lost touch with their human roots and have become cruel experimenters, warring on each other and trying to destroy each other's worlds simply for amusement because eternity has become tiresome. They delight in trapping each other on their own worlds or invading planets and dislodging the resident Lord, who may be their own father or son or daughter, but from so long ago that it has lost meaning.

In the first novel of the series, *The Maker of Universes,* Farmer creates a cosmos based partly on mythological Greece (including pools of nymphs and naiads), with adjoining regions from modern Germany, the American plains inhabited by Indian tribes, and a South American jungle. All these worlds are placed adjacent to each other on the tiers of one planet, and they are inhabited by reembodied souls stolen from the Earth.[11]

The leading character is Robert Wolff, a discouraged, chubby, middle-aged classics professor who has a nagging wife and is looking for a retirement home in Phoenix. He opens a closet in an unoccupied house, hears a horn, and finds a whole new world:

Sunlight flooded in through an opening. . . . Vegetation that looked something like trees—but no trees of Earth.

Through the branches and fronds he could see a bright
green sky. . . . Six or seven nightmare creatures were gathered at the base of a giant boulder . . . of red quartz-im-
pregnated rock and shaped roughly like a toadstool.

A man in a buckskin breechcloth summons him into this world
with haunting words: "So you finally came!"[12]

When Wolff does not accept the invitation to enter, he is
thrown a horn by the stranger. That night he sneaks back into
the Hohokam Homes Development, and just as guards are closing in on him, he blows the horn and finds himself on the grass
of that other world beneath a moon two and a half times the size
of Earth's moon. Birdcalls fill the air, and orange-yellow fireflies
with ellipsoid wings and 10-foot wingspans dart by. It is more
than just an adventure: his relationship to this place is not arbitrary.

Wolff starts out in this world as a misfit, the one unbeautiful
and "sick" creature in paradise. He can feel sorry for himself
only so long, for, soon enough, paradise turns out to be a deadly
hell. Everyone has been kidnapped into this world and implanted in a body, each from a different epoch and country of the
Earth. Only Wolff seems to have gotten here by some other
means. Over time, the strange world has its influence on him,
and he grows younger, healthier, and stronger. With the woman
Chryseis, whom he meets on the first day, and Kickaha, an
American man in an American Indian body who alone travels
easily between the tiers and cultures of this planet, he sets out
on a mission to reach the top of the tiers, the laboratory and
control room. Alternately harassed and aided by the harpy-eagle
Podarge, at times separated from and at times rejoining Kickaha,
his trickster ally, Wolff is eventually able to storm the great laboratory and free the world—but not before he discovers that he
himself is the Lord who made this world, who imprisoned Chryseis, Podarge, and the rest in their bodies. Driven by a rival Lord
onto the Earth, where he falls victim to amnesia, he in fact lived
a whole second life, begun *in medias res* in Kentucky—his position as a classics professor dimly reflecting his more ancient
and immortal heritage—until the sacred horn was used by Kickaha to summon him, even as Aslan summons the children to
Narnia in the C. S. Lewis novels.

Wolff has taken a journey into the meaning and origin of his own life. As he overcomes the trials and traps, he also confronts his prior ruthlessness and cruelty, his own inner nature, for he is the one who set the traps, who made this world. He returns to the throne as an enlightened Lord, a new being, to replace not only his corrupt successor but also the shallow hedonist that he himself was when he was first immortal.

This is our own dilemma as a race: to get to the bottom of the thing that has made this technology through us, that has made us make this technology and so enslave ourselves by it, and then to transcend it, to return as good kings rather than as the tyrants and despoilers we have been. For Wolff, once the Lord Jadawin, it takes a trip to the Earth in another body, memoryless, to restore humility and to give life back its texture and its meaning.

No doubt there are secret unwritten texts on which the manifest books of science fiction are based. This is their message: "We will be found to be the makers of this whole thing—we who now pretend to be mere impotent and innocent bugs actually project the starry fields to beyond the imagination or powers of even the most Olympian gods. We are the makers of universes. The tyrant we seek to overthrow is ourselves."

Such a discovery will restore our youth and our power, but it will be a terrible reckoning, for we have evaded it so long. It must bring a final unavoidable responsibility for our misdeeds. This is why Farmer's version of serial immortality is so appealing. As banal as his fictional worlds are in some ways, they leave open the eternal hope of finding our place downriver somewhere, or in the next star system, the next incarnation. This is the ultimate promise of the stars: that we will get to the bottom of this somehow, someday, that we will find out—find out in person—who we are. Somewhere, out there for us, is world enough and time. Mipam spends lifetimes searching for the key to a single event. When he is touched by his master, the forgotten knowledge and memory pour through Yogananda's mind.

Man is in exile from something. Mankind has been driven out of the stars, and each individual has lost his or her roots. The race has lost its origin and its destiny. Perhaps all the sentient beings of all the planets are in exile.

Perhaps, then, the universe works as a whole—and as each creature, cell, and particle—to realize itself and bring itself back into unity.

In Piers Anthony's novel *Macroscope,* four people steal an advanced machine from a space station and flee the global military.[13] The machine, the macroscope, is primarily known for its ability to receive a gravitational product of the radioactive decay of objects, and thus make events throughout the Galaxy visible, even those blocked by enclosures or within substances. But it also receives a form of "information rays" that evidently cross the Galaxy and contain instructions from higher civilizations; and, most important of all, it receives an extragalactic ray sent by a supercivilization in an unknown part of the universe, with information exponentially beyond anything in the Milky Way. Unfortunately, this ray merges with a mind-destroying vector, and only one of the four people who now possess the machine, Ivo, can survive its destructive force and draw information from it.

Borrowing technology from this extragalactic ray, the crew reduce themselves to protoplasm to withstand great acceleration. Then they travel rapidly to Neptune, where they reconstruct themselves and establish an Earthlike base and garden on the moon Triton. The Earth, whose armies pursue them, recedes from the rest of the book, and the four are engaged in an extragalactic riddle which also contains the destiny of their planet.

They drive Triton into Neptune, forming a black hole through which they explode into the Milky Way's depths, back through history to before the birth of the Earth and the Solar System. En route, as they pass backwards in time, Ivo visits Phoenicia, and through the macroscope they see their planet covered with jungles and inhabited by dinosaurs. With the temporary aid of Schon, a criminal genius who is jailed for life inside Ivo's personality, they are shown the formation of the Solar System, and they view the Milky Way Galaxy from the outside:

> The pallid white of the stars and nebulae deflowered by Earth's atmosphere existed no more; the colossal fog of interstellar gas and dust had been banished from the vicinity of the observer. The result was a view of the Milky Way

Galaxy as it really existed—ten thousand times as rich as that perceivable from Earth.

Color, yes—but not as any painter could represent, or any atmosphere-blinded eye could fathom. Red in the center where the old lights faded; blue at the fringe where the fierce new lights formed. A spectrum between—but also so much more! Here the visible splay extended beyond the range for which nomenclature existed, and rounded out the hues for which human names did exist. A mighty swirl, a multiple spiral of radiance, wave on wave of tiny bright particles, merged yet discrete. . . .

. . . The great spiral arms, coiling outward from the center, doubled bands of matter beginning as the light of massed stars and terminating as the black of thinning dust. Not flat, not even; the ribbons were twisted, showing now broadside, now edgewise, resembling open mobius strips or the helix of galactic DNA.[14]

Self stands equal to cosmos here.

Eventually, the crew discover that the destructive ray was intentionally attached to the extragalactic information source, and they find the station generating it. There Ivo picks up an instrument like a flute and begins playing it. It brings ultimate reality into being, beyond mind and body. The last vestiges of concrete existence in time and space evaporate, and each of the characters is transported to a place in the stars where physical destiny merges with astrological destiny. Under the influence of this instrument, a person stands instantaneously at the unique spot in the universe where his sign and his being are the same.

The older scientist Groton and his wife find themselves on exotic planets in dangerous situations. Groton discovers that the Destroyer was set in place as a means of protecting the Galaxy from young bellicose cultures that had ravaged it many times by misusing technology from the ray. But he cannot return to Earth. He meets the Horven people, who tell him that his destiny lies outside their astrological charts, for he exists ninety-eight million years in their future. This is essentially what Gorolot the Phoenician had told Ivo: "Either you have never been born, or you come from so far away that you are not truly under any of the signs I know."[15]

The science of astrology in this book measures the basic co-

herent force of the universe. Interstellar civilizations are the
ones that will develop such a science as they naturally seek the
origin of personality and event among the twisted space-time
frameworks of the stars. It is the only system that pinpoints a
concrete event in the entangled cosmic oceans. Without an intrinsic astrological connection, time and space would become
unbundled and flow everywhere; substellar destiny would be
arbitrary.

Ivo and the young woman scientist Afra meet their destinies
at exactly the place where the star music is played. The flute has
made Schon indispensable, and he takes over Ivo and confronts
Afra, who has spurned the Ivo personality behind which he lay
trapped. Schon and Afra then engage in a psychic battle of signs,
with Ivo as the only possible judge; it is a battle between their
absolute planetary aspects, in which they are equal as incarnated
individuals (otherwise Schon would win easily despite Afra's
brilliance).[16] In this contest, the victory goes to the one who is
able to face his or her own true nature. The planets of their birth
are drawn from nature and engulf them. Afra's haughtiness and
fear of her own nature put her way behind, but she wins the
contest under the outer planets, from Saturn on, with the de-
nouement at Pluto, where she forces Schon into confrontation
with the Destroyer itself, which his arrogance cannot handle.
Schon and Ivo finally merge and become a single being. Together with Afra and the macroscope, they return to the Earth,
wondering if it can escape both the Destroyer and its own ter-
ritorial violence. One day it might use the ray to reach beyond
the Galaxy, to meet the people who broadcast the wondrous
message, as their wise and beneficent equals. Then might we
and the immeasurable darkness become one. Thereafter the
whole universe could be crushed in the Big Bang, and somehow
we would have known all there was to know, been all there was
to be. We would have survived.

25

Science Fiction: III: Jesus of Nazareth

THERE ARE TWO WAYS for man to achieve his destiny in the stars: externally, by going out in ships; and internally, through a transformation or transmigration.

Arthur Clarke's *Childhood's End* deals with an internal passage into outer space.[1] In this novel, overlords come from the stars to guide man's evolution into a new phase and to keep him from destroying himself first. The overlords understand the passage beyond, but they themselves are trapped in an evolutionary cul de sac. The Earth people do not know this, and many consider the overlords conquerors and tyrants despite the peaceful regime they initiate. The benevolent guardians can never show themselves, because an earlier appearance so terrified mankind that their shape was preserved in a figure of darkness, the Devil. They fear they will be misunderstood, so they remain hidden during their rule. Outer space adventurers are cut off from exploring the universe, so they feel that the overlords have robbed the human race of its cosmic destiny. But the guardians have turned attention away from external extension to allow for inward expansion.

Under the guidance of the overlords, a generation of children matures without ever becoming adolescents or adults. This is the form of mutation known as neoteny. For instance, anthropologists theorize that man himself is a mutant ape foetus that matured outside of the womb, developing many "advanced" characteristics by suppressing its simian potential. By this measure, we are suppressed apes: simian hair and brawn do not appear, but litheness and intelligence develop in their place. If we became immortal, we might also turn back into foetal apes.

Neoteny has imprinted in the human embryo the sequence of life forms from which man has emerged and so bypassed: ancestors of starfish, frogs, apes, and other unknown animals. Earlier in our evolutionary history, the whole line of bilaterally symmetrical animals, of which we are one branch, emerged from starfish embryos that became sexually mature and gave birth before developing radial symmetry. Later we shared ancestors with lizards and bears. This in itself has been a journey on an interstellar scale—from galactic ash to protozoas to beasts of vision.

In *Childhood's End,* the children develop new capacities. They are able to dream in such a way that their minds pass out of the Solar System, then out of the Galaxy, then into unknown space. This is not internal astral space; it is real stellar geography. The overlords map it: "'I have searched all our records,' said Rashaverak. 'We have no knowledge of such a world, or such a combination of suns. If it existed inside our universe, the astronomers would have detected it, even if it lay beyond the range of our ships.'"[2]

The aliens tell the fathers the truth about their dreaming children: where they go, their predecessors will not be able to follow. Man will go on his transgalactic journey, but not in spaceships or by hallucinogens. He will travel into the impassable stellar infinity through his own quintessence, enveloping not the transportation revolution of the last two centuries but the pre-Cambrian formation of the first terrestrial cells.

In his trilogy, *Out of the Silent Planet, Perelandra,* and *That Hideous Strength,* C. S. Lewis portrays an Earth cut off from the actual events of the Solar System and imprisoned by a renegade creature, a demonic angel made of light. He is more than a malign overlord; he is the actual Devil of whom Terrans have a collective intuitive image in their holy books. This creature desires to take control of all the worlds in the physical cosmos, and the Earth is his throne and fortress. He surrounds himself with a landscape of wars, materialism, and external technology, and he cuts the Terrans off from their heritage in the harmonious sentient cosmos. His ultimate plan calls for the creatures from this world to go out into the universe and subjugate it, planet by planet; he trains them to see only the physical aspect of things so that they will be sufficiently hardened against alien creatures. He robs them of morality and compassion. This is who we are, Lewis is saying. Spaceflight has become necessary to our species, but it will be sterile and self-destructive unless we solve the riddle it is part of.

In the first book, the Devil's plan is disrupted when a corrupt scientist named Weston and his associate kidnap an unsuspecting philologist named Ransom and force him to accompany them on a journey to Mars. The purpose of this expedition is to offer the philologist as a sacrificial victim to the great angelic lord of Mars, Oyarsa.[3]

But Mars is part of the enlightened community of Solar worlds, and Oyarsa is a spiritually advanced being of light who primarily wishes to meet creatures from the imprisoned neighbor world. In the course of the novel, the kidnappers murder many trusting Martian creatures, imagining themselves as frontiersmen opening up new territories and blind to the different zone of creation they have entered. Oyarsa arranges for them to suffer the consequences of their greed and malice, and he initiates Ransom into the order of the Solar System, making him an ally to free the Earth.

In the second volume, Ransom is sent by Oyarsa to the planet Venus (Perelandra) at a time when its beings inhabit the local equivalent of the Garden of Eden. He arrives just before Weston, whose body has now been taken over by the Dark Lord and who has become an Un-Man. "Weston" will proceed to tempt the "Eve" of this world to disobey the commandment of the local lord not to sleep on the fixed land. Ransom must prevent the "original sin" from occurring. The confrontation turns out to be a physical one, since these are flesh-and-blood creatures in a physical cosmos; Ransom must destroy the human vehicle of the Devil in order to save this new world.[4]

In the final volume, Ransom has become an advanced spiritual magus of the Earth, though he bears a serious wound on his heel from his battle with the Un-Man. He collaborates with the lords of the other planets of the Solar System to save this one lost planet of the Sun. The confrontation between forces occurs at a scientific institute that is developing advanced techniques in brain research and human manipulation while occupying and destroying an ancient woods that still bears Druid magical forces. The Dark Lord is physically present at this institute, and he uses experimental parapsychology to gain control of magical forces. But the lords of the other planets arrive to aid Ransom in his battle. The Earth's destiny is restored, and it is returned to the council of the Solar System.[5]

Surely an author could have written such a science fiction romance out of the despair of World War II. But Lewis's despair in the 1940s, and the redemption he sought, was based on far more than one symptomatic war. He saw an Earth that was subject to so-called progressive forces which denied the spirituality of substance and the realm of higher consciousness and revelation. The heavens were a battleground too, of bleak unending meaningless matter.

On his first trip to Mars, Ransom is startled to discover that the nightmare of dark and empty space engendered by modern science is "blasphemous libel." Instead of "the black, cold vacuity, the utter deadness," he finds the universe a great "empyrean ocean of radiance. . . . He felt life pouring into him from it every moment. How indeed should it be otherwise, since out of this ocean the worlds and all their life had come? He had thought it barren: he saw now that it was the womb of worlds, whose blazing and innumerable offspring looked down nightly even upon the earth with so many eyes—and here, with how many more! No; Space was the wrong name. Older thinkers had been wiser when they named it simply the heavens. . . ."[6]

This could be Giordano Bruno speaking, except that the vision takes place on a spaceflight, not by astral projection.

In *Perelandra,* Lewis describes Weston as possessed by a deadly idea:

> It is the idea that humanity, having now sufficiently corrupted the planet where it arose, must at all costs contrive to seed itself over a larger area: that the vast astronomical distances which are God's quarantine regulations, must somehow be overcome. This for a start. But beyond this lies the sweet poison of the false infinite—the wild dream that planet after planet, system after system, in the end galaxy after galaxy, can be forced to sustain, everywhere and for ever, the sort of life which is contained in the loins of our own species—a dream begotten by the hatred of death upon the fear of true immortality. . . .[8]

It is the same fear on which Robert Silverberg bases the immortality quest of *The Book of Skulls:*

> "You have been subtracted from the universe, LuAnn. No, the universe has been subtracted from *you.* Forget what's going to happen to your body now, the worms in your gut, the pretty blue eyes turning to muck, and just think about all you've lost. You've lost it all, sunrise and sunset, the smell of broiling steak, the feel of a cashmere sweater, the touch of my lips that you like so much against your hard little nipples. You've lost the Grand Canyon and Shakespeare and London and Paris and champagne and your big church wedding and Paul McCartney and Peter Fonda and the Mississippi River and the moon and the stars. . . .
>
> "Death may have been good enough for Beethoven and Jesus and President Eisenhower, but, meaning no offense, I'm different. I can't just lie down and go. Why is it all so short? Why does it come so soon? Why can't we drink the universe? Death's been hovering over me all my life."[8]

We imagine countless other blue-green worlds we might still live on: their untouched algae oceans with strands of motley seaweed meters long and wrinkled in the insignia of another DNA; their moist virginal forests covering continents, inhabited by nothing more complicated than soft orange newts; or their tens of thousands of plump fearless birds screeching in one un-

broken column from horizon to horizon across a sea of bearded
flying fish they feed on in an eternal mandala as they drop to
the surface and return. We dream of green fields we could not
explore in a lifetime, rich in exotic clover and fruit, lit by a young
alien sun. So many worlds replace this one in our psyches, so
many second chances lie before us. A soft rain falls in the summer of a different year in a different orbit, a rain so naturally
medicinal it will heal not only us but our whole race, heal us by
gentle voodoo of everything and forever. But these birds may
be our unexamined lives whose calls echo through our deepening coma; the fields may be our precious mortality. We con-
sign them to fantasy and science fiction only after all other paths
and philosophies have failed us.

Our cosmic imperialism is a joke. We are still strangers to our
own planet and to ourselves. We are in no position to conquer
other planets, let alone galaxies, and immortality leads to the
Un-Man or a foetal ape. We cannot force our way into those
green fields by a life-extension narcotic or a starship. Our "meaning" already lies in the cosmos, and our youth is an eternal
return.

The antidote to "the sweet poison of the false infinite" comes
from another dimension of the universe. It is the Great Dance,
which we have met many times in occult literature, but which
appears for the first time in science fiction at the culmination of
Ransom's trip to Perelandra. He sees a loom as complicated as
the universe might actually be:

> It seemed to be woven out of the intertwining undulation
> of many cords or bands of light, leaping over and under
> one another and mutually embraced in arabesques and
> flower-like subtleties. . . . He could see . . . wherever the
> ribbons or serpents of light intersected, minute corpuscles
> of momentary brightness: and he knew somehow that these
> particles were the secular generalities of which history
> tells—peoples, institutions, climates of opinion, civiliza-
> tions, arts, sciences, and the like—ephemeral coruscations
> that piped their short song and vanished. . . . Some of the
> thinner and more delicate cords were beings that we call
> short-lived: flowers and insects, a fruit or a storm of rain,

and once (he thought) a wave of the sea. Others were such things as we also think lasting: crystals, rivers, mountains, or even stars. . . . It did not surprise him then to find that these [universal truths or qualities] and the persons were both cords and both stood together as against the mere atoms of generality which lived and died in the clashing of their streams. . . . The whole solid figure of these enamoured and inter-inanimated circlings was suddenly revealed as the mere superficies of a far vaster pattern in four dimensions, and that figure as the boundary of yet others in other worlds: till suddenly as the movement grew yet swifter, the interweaving yet more ecstatic, the relevance of all to all yet more intense, as dimension was added to dimension and that part of him which could reason and remember was dropped farther and farther behind that part of him which saw, even then, at the very zenith of complexity, complexity was eaten up and faded as a thin white cloud fades into the hard blue burning of the sky, and a simplicity beyond all comprehension, ancient and young as spring, illimitable, pellucid, drew him with cords of infinite desire into its own stillness.[9]

What about the spaceman Jesus Christ, who came to the Earth in the womb of a woman? It is not enough to say that Jesus had the divine spirit in him. So do we all by the same Gnostic prophecy. We are all the sons and daughters of God.

But Jesus was the offspring of an extraterrestrial. He appeared with the Star of Bethlehem. The night sky shined as at the moment of creation:

> Silent night,
> Holy night.
> All is calm.
> All is bright.

And it goes on: a virgin with a holy infant sits huddled beneath the stars. Even on the streets of modern cities, with the stars obliterated, the snow shimmering in headlights, and the glitter and tinsel stars sparkling on Christmas trees, *Silent Night* seems to play as much to the galaxies of eternal time and space as it does to the mortals. We stand outside store windows and min-

iature mangers and are transported into a science fiction landscape—another planet, somewhere else, yet this one.

We don't understand Christmas at all, and our present form
of it is barren. But we do feel something gathering, something
related to the starry sky and to the darkness we cannot probe,
a darkness that still bears a hidden light.

"Tell him to stay away," screamed Herod. "This is my world.
I will not share this kingdom with a star."

His subsequent decision to kill the firstborn in the area
around Nazareth was a massacre of potential invaders, astronauts who at the same time were astrological life forms intro-
ducing Pisces, entering the Earth not by metal ship but from
inside the blood. Star, embryo, and God overlap.

Whether He could have come to this world directly by manifestation or in a ship from another creationary zone is a matter
we shall leave to Gnostic speculation. The Christian mystery
and the transubstantiation are based on the fact that He came
by the womb of our species. He incarnated in the flesh, or an
aspect of Him did. This was called His Son, and, later, the Holy
Ghost.

It is the incarnation that makes Christianity something more
than an extraterrestrial religion carried by a space preacher.
Christ was not like an astronaut who might arrive tomorrow, go
to the United Nations, set up solar energy stations, tap geo-
mantic power sources, and teach telepathic and telekinetic arts.
There are some who no doubt would have preferred this sort of
tour de force. The faithless rabbis, for instance. But this would
have delayed man's ultimate confrontation with his own nature,
his date with himself inside time. Such a being would have come
from outside our biology and history and would have treated
them as manipulatable things rather than as shapes emerging of
their own intrinsic nature. That would have been a denial of the
inner world. Of course, an extraterrestrial Christ may still come.
And he may not. But at least so far, we must earn our own grace.

Christ arises from within our history and biology, and his acts
are those of an Earthborn. He comes as we do, from the egg,
the flesh, the genes, the continuity of tissue from the first cell.
He is shaped of everything which man is, and the fish are too.

His ecstasies, his insights, his tears are expressions of the flesh. Those tears took thousands of millions of years of biological evolution to occur. They do not pity us from some superior position. Christ cries as well for the frog and the mouse, in whose cells the tear ducts were primordially fashioned.

The Son of God is the Son of Man. We are all travelers on a ship braided of the same material; hence, we are all natives of the same place, though our spirit or protoplasm may originate in bean or seed elsewhere. No astronaut, no matter how learned and well-traveled, could come to us from such a cosmic place. He might come from outside our history, but he could not come from outside of time itself, from outside the universe. He might not be human, but he would share in the cosmic biology. We would still have to decide whether to believe in him or not, trust him or not, on the basis of his program and integrity.

The Christian visitation has an impact that UFO magi cannot, for it recapitulates our embryology and history. Christ is tempted by the same passions and apostasies that tempt us. His life is generated by history, and he must merge with history, even as he merged with the egg, transforming it. For us to wish for outer-space rescuers is only an evasion of that history. They cannot forgive us or save us, because they are not us.

From a spiritual viewpoint, our technological culture is just such an invasion from outer space. The machines may stall things for a while, but we still must unfold from within; the machines can have a part in that unfolding, but only a small part. Even if spacemen should come and distract us from the karma of our history and our own nature, it would delay things only a while— a hundred years, a thousand years, a million years; ultimately, we would be faced with the consequences of what we are. Nothing else can speak for us. We cannot seek meaning, for we are the ones who bring meaning itself into being. The delay itself could have any transitional interpretation. We could play with a fleet of new toys, spaceships, lasers, etc., for millennia; but in the end, we would come to the same dilemma of knowing who we are and discovering the nature of our incarnation among stone and fire.

Because karmic law is written into Buddhism and Hinduism

from the beginning, these religions, unlike Christianity, do not require a son of God. The cosmic consequence is already embodied in the flesh. All incarnation is *re*incarnation. Radio astronomy has merely verified, for the educated Oriental cosmologist, the suspicions that he inherited about the night sky and that his ancestors intuited before him—namely, that it is an exact map of the actual and potential universe, of matter and energy, and of the extension of karmic law to the ends of matter and unconsciousness.

The advanced yogi does not need matter or starships to find his way to the ends of time, and he creates his own "black holes" with that other fine material inside him. He can see from before it all to beyond it all, or at least he can see to the limits of all desire, and no other seeing is possible. He sacrifices his life in order to be a mutation, but, like Christ, what he leaves behind cannot be inherited in the cells of his offspring. What he passes into history is far more fragile and far less corruptible.

Frank Herbert's *Dune* trilogy uses the interplay of biochemical and genetic nodes for a major transformation of humanity and civilization from within. Herbert is widely kown as the creator of Arrakis, the desert planet on which his epic takes place. But the severe arid conditions of Arrakis, which trap most of the chemistry of life in gigantic sandworms (up to 400 meters long in the deep desert), also make for a precise balance of ecology and human consciousness, out of which arise the prophets of the trilogy. The planet itself is awesome, and Herbert describes its geology, biochemistry, and meteorology more thoroughly than any other science fiction writer has done for an invented planet. Arrakis is portrayed most vividly in the opening novel, *Dune;*[10] the remaining books, *Dune Messiah*[11] and *Children of Dune,*[12] are tales of mutations, artificial intelligence, and prophecy.

Herbert's precision in constructing his story is like that of the Fremen (or free tribes) of Arrakis, who collect dew in land depressions from light-sensitive ovals and reclaim their own body moisture from stillsuit garments that seal around their bodies and filter out wastes. Nothing is overlooked in the relationship between ecology, mental awareness, and genetics. Paranormal thought is nurtured in carefully layered generations of inbred adepts and the delicate chemistry of the sandworms and the Dune planet itself.

The sandworms of Arrakis excrete a spice, Melange, which is used throughout the inhabited planets of the Guild as a life-extension drug, a tool for high-speed interstellar navigation, and an accurate prophetic hallucinogen. Without its powers for "seeing" through space, the pilots could not travel between worlds, and the Guild would collapse. Melange is also addictive, so its value is high, and the planet where it is uniquely produced is subjugated to its economics. Guild interest is in keeping Arrakis both militarily secure and fecund for worms.

The planet is inhabited by Fremen, who are the descendants of a very ancient religious schism group of Zensunni wanderers. They have adapted culturally (and probably biologically) to the planet. Their numbers are far greater than is suspected elsewhere, and their collective survival on the desert includes an intimate and religious relationship with the sandworms, which they call Shai-Hulud. The Guild, the royal houses, and their trained soldiers consider the worms ravaging killers without exception—the most dangerous big creatures known. But the Fremen have learned, secretly, how to ride them, and an attack by worm-mounted Fremen on the city of off-planet powers and imported soldier-adepts changes the power balance in the confederacy and brings on a new millennium. It also transforms Fremen culture and weakens the water-wise rituals. This attack is directed by the prophet of *Dune* and *Dune Messiah*, Paul Atreides, who has taken on the name of an Arrakis-adapted kangaroo mouse, Muad'Dib.

Paul's mother, Lady Jessica, is a trained Bene Gesserit adept. She has studied at a very old school of martial, psychic, and logical training, which almost exclusively initiates women students. Paul's father, Duke Leto Atreides, has been granted Arrakis as his base planet, and Paul moves there with his family at the age of fifteen.

But he should never have been born at all, for Lady Jessica also participated in a Bene Gesserit breeding program that was

aimed at combining certain traits over generations with the physical and mental training, and through genes passed in a line from
women to women. Ultimately, this line would produce a male
Bene Gesserit, the Kwisatz Haderach, who would have the capacity for seeing through space and time into the *unknown,* for
which no amount of training and impeccable behavior could
prepare one. Kwisatz Haderach means "Shortening of the Way";
it is a genetic solution to a philosophical issue that underlies all
social and political systems. Although the Bene Gesserit program is directed toward such a being in the future, he is also a
divine mythology, and no adept should have the arrogance to
attempt to give birth to him. Much of *Dune* itself concerns
whether Paul Atreides is or is not this long-sought being. By
the end of the book, his powers transcend even the prophecy,
so judgment is impossible; the reality is more powerful than the
myth. Since the philosophical solution lies deeper than the social
system and the political web, Muad'Dib's revolution changes the
cosmos. But he could not have accomplished his revolution
without becoming one of the Fremen. His ascension is simultaneously within the Fremen spiritual tradition (which calls for
an outsider as messiah) and the Bene Gesserit spiritual tradition
(which calls for an unwelcome male), so it is blasphemy to either
and works toward destroying both systems while fulfilling their
prophecies.

The Reverend Mother is a Bene Gesserit prophet and leader
who has swallowed and converted a poison by means of her
penetrating awareness and her control of normally unconscious
inner-body processes. Not only is the poison neutralized as a
threat to her life, but the act of transformation brings on an
illumination which raises her to a higher level of awareness and
initiation. She gains a true insight into primal levels of nature
and history. The Fremen conduct the Reverend Mother ritual
by using the "Water of Life," which is, in Herbert's words, "that
liquid exhalation of a sandworm produced at the moment of its
death from drowning which is changed within the body of a
Reverend Mother to become . . . an 'awareness spectrum' narcotic."[13]

Paul undergoes this life-threatening ritual too, and emerges with a particular prophetic vision. His insight into space and time is partly genetic, partly Bene Gesserit, and partly Melange. Alia, Paul's sister, who is an embryo at the time of Jessica's initiation, gains the power prenatally. However, it overwhelms her, and in the latter two novels she is taken over by the dark side of her ancestry, concealed from her in the secrecy of the breeding program. Paul's children, Leto and Ghanima, but primarily Leto, the boy, gain the power over space and time from birth. They are the "children of Dune," and they surpass their father's prophecy and institute the full new millennium.

Paul's vision is fully realized when he is blinded in an attack in *Dune Messiah:*

> "They've blinded my body, but not my vision. . . . I live in an apocalyptic dream. My steps fit into it so precisely that I fear most of all I will grow bored reliving the thing so exactly. . . .
>
> "I am in the world beyond this world here. For me, they are the same. I need no hand to guide me. I see every movement all around me. . . . I have no eyes, yet I see."[14]

By the end of the novel, though, Paul abandons his position so that his children may survive, and he disappears into the desert. He is thought to have died and is eulogized, but he returns transformed as the blind prohpet of the third book.

It is through Leto that the full implications of the illumination are explored. Seeing through time and space is not as unambiguously insightful as might be thought. There are many possible universes, and there are things which are not seen. What is clear is that there is no external messiah in *Dune;* Herbert builds through direct process only, in his specific mixture of ecological constraints, genetic message, and the untapped powers of extrasensory mind.

Leto realizes that he has inside him the memory of the generations leading up to him—the immediate ones more vividly, the remote ones through training and, ultimately, by aid of Melange. "Memory" goes equally into the future; in fact, it is the same thing. "There is no difference between one hundred thousand years and a heartbeat," Leto tells Jessica. "No difference.

That is the first fact about Time. And the second fact: the entire universe with all of its Time is within me."[15]

He makes the point even more poignantly in his memoirs:

"The life of a single human, as the life of a family or an entire people, persists as memory. . . . In this persistent memory they store more and more experiences in a sub-liminal reservoir. Humankind hopes to call upon this material if it is needed for a changing universe. But much that is stored can be lost in that chance play of accident we call 'fate.' . . . The species can forget! This is the special value of the Kwisatz Haderach which the Bene Gesserits never suspected: the Kwisatz Haderach cannot forget."[16]

After ingesting the spice, he reaches the exact point at which his father turned back. Through the presently framed cellular fabric of himself, as through a window, he sees the whole cosmos in all directions:

This was what his grandmother and the Sisterhood sought! He knew it. His awareness flowed on a new, higher level. He felt the past carried in his cells, in his memories, in the archetypes which haunted his assumptions, in the myths which hemmed him, in his languages and their prehistoric detritus. It was all of the shapes out of his human and nonhuman past, all of the lives which he now commanded, all integrated in him at last. And he felt himelf as a thing caught up in the ebb and flow of nucleotides. Against the backdrop of infinity he was a protozoan creature in which birth and death were virtually simultaneous, but he was both infinite and protozoan, a creature of molecular memories.[17]

Leto had located the node from which the future could be shaped. There was no turning back. Muad'Dib had seen a linear universe through his prescience, but his attempt to guide the reins of its future motion distorted the seeing. Instead of charging the future with certainty, he projected his own uncertainty and thus amplifed disorder. Leto does not have that problem:

. . . [He] held the multi-thread reins, balanced in his own vision-lighted view of time as multilinear and multilooped.

He was the sighted man in the universe of the blind. . . .
A thought as yet undreamed in the farthest future could
reflect upon the *now* and move his hand.[18]

Herbert is also interested in personality, memory, and identity. When do we cease being ourselves? When do we terminate?
If another being has our entire memory grafted onto him, is he
us? Can we and he go our separate ways from that moment as
different entities? And what is it we try to preserve when the
animal inside us struggles with every last breath and wit for life?

The *Dune* cycle and other Herbert books are filled with varieties of clones, transplanted brains, cyborgs, and artificial intelligences. In *Dune Messiah,* there is the ghola Hayt, made from
the cells of the body of Duncan Idaho, who died while defending
Muad'Dib. This ghola, created in deep chemical tanks by the
Tleilaxu, the inhabitants of a renegade planet, is bestowed upon
Muad'Dib as a gift by the Guild. The ghola presents a complex
danger, for it freely acknowledges that its purpose is to destroy
Paul, and thus that its makers do not fear his knowing this. It is
a decoy, but it is also a haunting likeness of Idaho. The trap goes
beyond being a simple political plot against Paul's power. The
ghola is a Tleilaxu invention, bearing designs that no one can
know, not even the thing itself. To destroy it is as dangerous as
to accept it, in a game where every move covers a series of
paradoxes and countermoves. And then there is Hayt himself,
made of Idaho, and seeking his identity: "Duncan . . . , Duncan
. . . ," Paul wonders. "Where was Idaho in this shaped-to-mea-
sure flesh? It wasn't flesh, . . . it was a shroud in fleshly shape!
Idaho lay dead forever on the floor of an Arrakeen cavern."[19]

The ghola gets flashes of imagery, brief unretainable memories of another life. "Aren't you curious?" Alia asks him. "Of
course. Curiosity urges me forward, but I move against a heavy
reluctance. I think: 'What if I'm not the one they believe me
to be?'"[20]

Our own perceptions are much dimmer, but we live a life in
the flesh made of ancient cellular blueprints too. What if . . . we
are not? What then? And whose memory is it, in the cells, in
the psyche, that sustains all this from the beginning? Who will
get our memory? What holds it all to itself?

"I think," says the ghola, "what a joy it is to be alive, and I wonder if I'll ever leap inward to the root of this flesh and know myself as once I was. The root is there. Whether any act of mine can find it, that remains tangled in the future. But all things a man can do are mine. Any act of mine may do it."[21]

Later he tells Paul: "When the Tleilaxu first awakened me, I had visions. I was restless, lonely . . . , not really knowing I was lonely. Not then. My visions revealed nothing! The Tleilaxu told me it was an intrusion of the flesh which men and gholas all suffer, a sickness, no more."[22]

"I was there," the ghola dwarf Bijaz tells him. "I was there when they put your dead flesh into the tank and I was there when they removed it, alive and ready for training."[23]

So Hayt should have no claim to the original, no claim to the life of which he is just a clone. Yet, at the turning point of the book, when the whole future lies in the balance, Hayt reclaims the dead life:

> A sensation of living two lives simultaneously spread through his awareness: Hayt/Idaho/Hayt/Idaho. . . . He became a motionless chain of relative existence, singular, alone. Old memories flooded his mind. He marked them, adjusted them to new understandings, made a beginning at the integration of a new awareness.[24]

With terrible pain that wants to refuse it all, sleep forever, with delicious ecstasy that wishes to swallow again and again, as many times as possible, the bright and haunting images stored forever in the cells, Hayt embraces Idaho—and the sand that flowed through Idaho's hands, the songs that passed from his lips, the memories that he had at all times of other times, the overwhelming passion to encompass them all, and his own.

And on a night in 1969, hundreds of commune-dwellers gathered in a mountain meadow, close to the New Mexico stars, and sat among the crickets in darkness. They were joined, in time and space, by comrades in the deserts of eastern Oregon, by others on a mountain in India, and by still others who climbed to the sacred hot springs of Lake County, California, the realm of Orion and earth water tinted by Sirius. Together they sang: "Thank God / For the light within us."

At first this might have been a sacral cliché. But they shared the moment with each other and no one else—except those on other worlds around other stars with whom they might have imagined they were sharing it to do honor to the whole of creation, and with the crickets and grasses in their own night. It was better than our electric insistence that we are here. For once, in this century in the West, we were serious and sincere before the cosmos. We didn't need an answer. Of course, we are not alone.

Each time they sang those words, the light within them was different, weighed slightly differently, felt in tenderness as the thing they were projecting out into space.

In the distant resonance, in their cells, the sounds of the cities called them back to a shattered civilization in which their lives began and would end, and the Everly Brothers sang: "I can make you mine, kiss your lips of wine / Any time, night or day."

Whose lips? Whose wine? Which light? When?

It is foolhardy to say that the whole creation is inside us. The stars are there all right, and without their vast sparkling cataclysm, nothing would happen. But it's also clear—imaginary or not—that a spirit, a light, is inside us. From ceaseless angles of being, we look out to see it reflected back—from the lake at dusk, from the streaks of clouds on the horizon, from the distant meadows on the mountainside, and from each other's faces. It is reflected through us, our memories, and the billions of flowers in the fields.

We are the marriage of vision and light. We bring the inner and outer lights together, or we see the one light passing from our center into the heart of the cosmos.

And this light stands out regardless of the Soviet bear's claw which smacks millions of souls into line, and notwithstanding the deadening materialism of the Western world, and despite all the dictators of the Orient and the Tropics.

The light must finally penetrate even cold granite stone, billions of meters deep. Factory workers in Poland, Japanese monks, West Virginia miners, migrants in the desert—it is all they have. We are all made in ancient hives of infinitesimal shimmers of that light. We don't have to know why or how. We are dense enough that we can't get at its source, that it can't pass through us all the time; but when it does, in moments of grief or joy, the old songs play, and the singers of our beginning sing with us; we know then how we are alive.

There is much yet to be done. Every echo tells us that, and every whisper tells us that too. We must act for ourselves, and we must act for the speechless animals. They stand before the ceremony, and they will stand before it, motionless, forever. The manifold design has entrusted us with this single moiré—a warble of blue sky, a throbbing of organdy and loam, and a clarity so lucid and final nothing can be seen through it but itself. We are creatures entangled in a primitive oil. We are dancers to the muffled drum. Fuzziness and nausea mark the limits equally of mind and matter. We struggle to recover and retain the dwindling past, and, in the same gesture, we grasp toward the unshaped future. We are surrounded by lords, avatars, yogis, aliens, science fiction heroes, clones, and memories of memories—diamonds reflecting through us, and a faint aura of sandalwood and brine. But we are the heroes of this masque, just as we are the singers of this song. For having come so far through flesh and cells in darkness, for being the mysterious stranger and the one whom the mysterious stranger affrights, we stand on this enchanted evening bathed in a richness even the gods cannot imagine—and with no other clue in the darkness. Something in us wants the Christ and Boddhisattva functions to be fulfilled. Something in us wants the aliens to come, to merge with us. Something in us wants to get back every memory, every thing we have lost, every thing that was put together ever and once to make us. It *is* a sickness, but it is a wonder and a gift too. And though nothing yet in this century has worked out, we still expect to survive intact, and to deliver the torch to those who will revive us in some other place in some other way. That is the garden of childhood we come from and return to, beyond the stars, and beyond the figments and mirages of space and time.

Notes

NOTE ON *Io* AND NORTH ATLANTIC BOOKS: These materials are edited and published by the author of this volume. The journal and publishing company have been located in many different areas since the first publication of the journal in 1964. Each specific title and issue of the journal is listed in the Notes at the site of its original publication. However, *Io* and North Atlantic Books are currently located at 635 Amador Street, Richmond, California 94805.

Preface

1. Michel Foucault, *Les Mots et Les Choses* (Paris: Editions Gallimard, 1966); excerpt entitled "The Writing of Things," translated by William Christian, in *Io,* No. 5 (*Doctrine of Signatures*), Ann Arbor, Mich., 1968, p. 20.
2. Ibid.
3. Ibid., pp. 20–21.

CHAPTER 1
The Night Sky

SOME MATERIAL IN THIS CHAPTER has been rewritten from previous books by the author. These are cited along with other references.

1. Claude Lévi-Strauss, *The Raw and the Cooked,* translated from the French by John and Doreen Weightman (New York: Harper and Row, 1969), pp. 232–233. The chapter in which these pages occur, "Double Inverted Canon," is one of the most thorough descriptions of a particular system of mytho-astronomy and ethnoastronomy in the anthropological literature. Lévi-Strauss explores the intricate interre-

lationship between a series of constellations and other stellar events and various systems of taxonomy, social structure, and etiology among a number of South American Indian bands and tribes.

2. *Io,* No. 6 (*Ethnoastronomy Issue*), Ann Arbor, Mich., 1969, pp. 58–68. This includes the following reprints: Alice C. Fletcher, "Star Cult Among the Pawnee" (1902); Ralph N. Buckstaff, "Stars and Constellations of a Pawnee Sky Map" (1927); and Alice C. Fletcher, "Pawnee Star Lore [excerpts]" (1904).

3. This is printed on the wall by the entrance to the Morrison Planetarium, Golden Gate Park, San Francisco.

4. Richard Grossinger, *The Planet with Blue Skies,* unpublished notes.

5. Richard Grossinger, *The Long Body of the Dream* (Plainfield, Vermont: North Atlantic Books, 1974), p. 20.

6. Richard Grossinger, *The Slag of Creation* (Plainfield, Vermont: North Atlantic Books: 1975), pp. 232–233 (the lightning bugs).

7. This has been said on a number of occasions by the poet Charles Olson.

8. Richard Grossinger, *The Provinces* (Plainfield, Vermont: North Atlantic Books, 1975), p. 122 (ellixis alleghensis of light and astral birthstone).

9. An earlier version of the section on death appeared in *The Difficulties,* Volume 1, No. 1, edited by Tom Beckett (Kent, Ohio: Viscerally Press, 1980), pp. 17–20.

10. A 1974 movie by the American director Arthur Penn.

11. *The Tibetan Book of the Dead,* translated and edited by W. Y. Evans-Wentz (Oxford, England: Oxford University Press: 1960), back of the dedication page.

12. "Hang Me, Oh Hang Me," traditional folk ballad popularized by Dave Van Ronk.

13. This was quoted by Baba Ram Dass in a public talk, 1980.

14. Robert Kelly, "Re: The Occult", *Io,* No. 6 (*Ethnoastronomy Issue*), Ann Arbor, Mich., 1969, p. 107.

15. Ibid.

16. D. H. Lawrence, *The Rainbow* [1915] (New York: Random House, 1943), p. 42.

17. Parts of the Orion section came from Richard Grossinger, *The Planet with Blue Skies,* unpublished notes. The closing three paragraphs (preceding Andromeda) are rewritten from a longer untitled piece which appeared in *Handbook,* No. 2: *Silence,* edited by Susan Mernit and Rochelle Ratner, New York, 1978. Much of the factual information

on the cross-cultural mythology of Orion comes from Richard Hinckley Allen, *Star Names: Their Lore and Meaning* [1899] (New York, Dover Books, 1973), pp. 303–320.

18. Johann Heinrich Lambert, *The System of the World,* translated from the French by James Jacque (1800); excerpted in *Theories of the Universe: From Babylonian Myth to Modern Science,* edited by Milton K. Munitz (Glencoe, Ill.: The Free Press, 1957), p. 251.

19. Stephen Fulder, *The Root of Being: Ginseng and the Pharmacology of Harmony* (London: Hutchison, 1980).

20. Andromeda is the furthest object visible to the naked eye except for another galaxy, M-33, in Triangulum, fainter yet, but visible to some on a dark, clear night.

CHAPTER 2
The Creation

THE BASIC ASTRONOMICAL SOURCE for this chapter was Steven Weinberg, *The First Three Minutes: A Modern View of the Origin of the Universe* (New York: Basic Books, 1977); and the basic mythological source was *Primal Myths: Creating the World,* edited by Barbara C. Sproul (New York: Harper and Row, 1979).

1. Fred Hoyle, *The Nature of the Universe* (New York: Harper and Bros., 1950); excerpted in *Theories of the Universe: From Babylonian Myth to Modern Science,* edited by Milton K. Munitz (Glencoe, Ill.: The Free Press, 1957), p. 426.

2. Munitz, *Theories of the Universe,* p. 428.

3. Kip S. Thorne, "Gravitational Collapse," *Scientific American,* 217:5 (November 1967), 97.

4. John Milton, *Paradise Lost* (1667), Book II, line 1052; reprinted in *John Milton: Complete Poems and Major Prose,* edited by Merritt Y. Hughes (New York: Odyssey Press, 1957), p. 257.

5. Aleister Crowley (The Master Therion), *Magick in Theory and Practice* (New York: Castle Books, no date), p. xiv.

6. Hesiod, *Theogony,* translated from the Greek by Charles Olson, in his poem "Maximus from Dogtown—I," *Maximus Poems IV, V, VI* (London and New York: Cape Goliard/Grossman, 1968), p. 2.

7. Edward H. Schafer, *Pacing the Void: T'ang Approaches to the Stars* (Berkeley: University of California Press, 1977), p. 28.

8. Ibid., p. 27.

9. Paracelsus, *The Hermetic and Alchemical Writings of Paracelsus the Great,* translated from the Latin by A. E. Waite (London: James Elliott, 1894), Volume 1, p. 307; excerpted in *Alchemy: pre-Egyptian Legacy, Millennial Promise (Io,* No. 26), edited by Richard Grossinger (Richmond, Calif.: North Atlantic Books, 1979), p. 15.

10. Wilhelm Reich, *Ether, God, and Devil—Cosmic Superimposition,* translated from the German by Therese Pol (New York: Farrar, Straus and Giroux, 1972).

11. Maria Leach, *The Beginning* (New York: Funk and Wagnalls, 1956); excerpted in *Primal Myths: Creating the World,* edited by Barbara C. Sproul (New York: Harper and Row, 1979), p. 44.

12. E. W. Nelson, *The Eskimo About Bering Strait,* 18th Annual Report of the Bureau of American Ethnology (Washington, D.C., 1899); excerpted in Sproul, *Primal Myths,* p. 221.

13. F. H. Cushing, *Outlines of Zuni Creation Myths,* Thirteenth Annual Report of the Bureau of American Ethnology (Washington, D.C., 1896); excerpted in Sproul, *Primal Myths,* pp. 284–286.

14. *The Popul Vuh,* translated from the Mayan into Spanish by Adrián Recinos, English translation from the Spanish by Deli Goetz and Sylvanus G. Morley (Norman, Oklahoma: University of Oklahoma Press, 1950); excerpted in Sproul, *Primal Myths,* p. 288.

15. T. G. H. Strehlow, *Aranda Traditions* (Melbourne: University of Melbourne Press, 1947); excerpted in Sproul, *Primal Myths,* p. 321.

16. Teuira Henry, *Ancient Tahiti,* Bernice P. Bishop Museum Bulletin, No. 48 (Honolulu: Bishop Museum Press, 1928); excerpted in Sproul, *Primal Myths,* p. 350.

17. *The Nihongi,* translated from the Japanese by W. G. Alston (London: Allen and Unwin, 1956); excerpted in Sproul, *Primal Myths,* p. 212.

18. A. E. Waite, *The Holy Kabbalah* (New Hyde Park, N.Y.: University Books, 1960).

19. Edward Dorn, *Some Business Recently Transacted in the White World* (West Newbury, Mass.: Frontier Press, 1971), p. 82.

CHAPTER 3
Occult Astronomy

1. *The Celestial Elder's Canon of the Spirit Lights (An Ancient Chinese Book of Interior Astrology)*, translated by Nathan Sivin, *Io*, No. 4 (*Alchemy Issue*, enlarged edition), Plainfield, Vermont, 1973, p. 234.

2. Ibid.

3. Ibid.

4. Gerald S. Hawkins, *Stonehenge Decoded* (New York: Dell, 1965).

5. Alexander Marshack, *The Roots of Civilization: The Cognitive Beginnings of Man's First Art, Symbol and Notation* (New York: McGraw-Hill, 1972).

6. Hugh A. Moran and David H. Kelley, *The Alphabet and the Ancient Calendar Signs* (Palo Alto, Calif.: Daily Press, 1969), p. xvii.

7. Ophiel, *The Art and Practice of Astral Projection* (St. Paul, Minn.: The Gnostic Institute, 1961).

8. Julia Lorusso and Joel Glick, *Healing Stoned: The Therapeutic Use of Gems and Minerals* (Albuquerque, N.M.: Brotherhood of Life, 1976).

9. Rudolf Steiner, *The Spiritual Guidance of Man and of Mankind* (Dornach, Germany: Rudolf Steiner Press, 1911); quoted and translated from the German in John Meeks, "Johannes Kepler and the Philosophical Defence of Astrology," *Io*, No. 27 (*Star Rhythms: Readings in a Living Astrology*), edited by William Lonsdale (Richmond, Calif.: North Atlantic Books, 1979), p. 73.

10. Johannes Kepler, *Tertius interveniens;* quoted in Arthur Koestler, *The Sleepwalkers: A History of Man's Changing Vision of the Universe* (New York: Grosset and Dunlap, 1959), p. 244.

11. Hermes Trismegistus, *The Divine Pymander and Other Writings*, translated by John D. Chambers (1882); republished by Samuel Weiser, Inc., New York, 1972.

12. Ibid., p. 5.

13. Ibid., p. 8.

14. Ibid., p. 25.

15. Hua-jui fui-jen, "Kung tz'u"; quoted in Edward H. Schafer, *Pacing the Void* (Berkeley: University of California Press, 1977), p. 38.

16. Rodney Collin, *The Theory of Celestial Influence* (London: Stuart and Watkins, 1954), pp. 72–73.

17. Ibid., p. 77.

18. Pierre Teilhard de Chardin, *The Phenomenon of Man,* translated from the French by Bernard Wall (New York: Harper and Row, 1959).

19. Ibid., p. 73.

20. Ibid.

21. P. D. Ouspensky, *In Search of the Miraculous: Fragments of an Unknown Teaching* (New York: Harcourt, Brace and World, 1949).

22. Frances A. Yates, *Giordano Bruno and the Hermetic Tradition* (Chicago: University of Chicago Press, 1964), p. 57.

23. Henry Cornelius Agrippa, "Astronomical Geomancy" (1655); reprinted in *Io,* No. 5 (*Doctrine of Signatures*), Ann Arbor, Mich., 1968, pp. 56–60.

24. Carl Sagan, "Interview," conducted by Richard Grossinger (January 23, 1972), *Io,* No. 14 (*Earth Geography Booklet,* No. 3: *Imago Mundi*), Cape Elizabeth, Maine, 1972, pp. 374–386.

25. Ibid., p. 384.

CHAPTER 4
Star Myth

THIS CHAPTER IS DONE in the spirit of *Hamlet's Mill* (Boston: Gambit, 1969) and is dedicated to the authors of that work, Giorgio de Santillana and Hertha von Dechend.

1. Edward Kelly, "The Theatre of Terrestrial Astronomy" (ca. 1590); reprinted in *Alchemy: pre-Egyptian Legacy, Millennial Promise* (*Io,* No. 26), edited by Richard Grossinger (Richmond, Calif.: North Atlantic Books, 1979), pp. 56–68.

2. Dante Alighieri, *The Divine Comedy,* Cantica I: *Hell* (1314), translated from the Italian by Dorothy Sayers (Baltimore: Penguin Books, 1949), p. 71 (Canto I, lines 2 and 3).

3. Giorgio de Santillana and Hertha von Dechend, *Hamlet's Mill: An Essay on Myth and the Frame of Time* (Boston: Gambit, 1969), pp. 204 and 337.

4. Ibid., pp. 275–277 and 313–315.

5. Alfred North Whitehead, *Process and Reality* (Toronto: Macmillan, 1929).

6. De Santillana and von Dechend, *Hamlet's Mill,* p. 48.

7. Ibid.

8. Ibid.

9. Ibid., p. 343.

10. Whitehead, *Process and Reality.*

11. Robert K. G. Temple, *The Sirius Mystery* (New York: St. Martin's Press, 1976), pp. 58–59.

12. Frances A. Yates, *Giordano Bruno and the Hermetic Tradition* (Chicago: University of Chicago Press, 1964), pp. 367–370.

13. Carl L. Becker, *The Heavenly City of the Eighteenth-Century Philosopher* (New Haven: Yale University Press, 1932), p. 129.

14. Ibid., p. 45.

15. Isaac Bashevis Singer, *The Family Moskat,* translated from the Yiddish by A. H. Gross (New York: Knopf, 1950), p. 594.

16. Ibid.

17. Isaac Bashevis Singer, *Shosha,* translated from the Yiddish by Joseph Singer (New York: Fawcett, 1978), pp. 129–130.

18. De Santillana and von Dechend, *Hamlet's Mill,* p. 5.

19. Ibid., pp. 5–6.

20. Ibid., p. 6.

21. Ibid., pp. 41–42, 63, 156, 166, 173, 220, 249, 251–252, and 291–292.

22. Michael Collins, *Carrying the Fire: An Astronaut's Journey* (New York: Farrar, Straus, and Giroux, 1974), p. 472.

23. Charles Olson, *The Maximus Poems, Volume Three* (New York: Grossman, 1975), p. 39.

24. Denis Diderot, *Oeuvres,* Volume 18 (1765); quoted in Becker, *The Heavenly City,* p. 147.

25. George Bernard Shaw, *Back to Methuselah* (New York: Brentano's, 1921), p. xlvi.

CHAPTER 5

Ancient Astronomy

1. Kjell Akerblom, *Astronomy and Navigation in Polynesia and Micronesia: A Survey,* Ethnographic Museum of Stockholm Monograph Series, No. 14 (Stockholm, 1968), p. 18.

2. Ibid., p. 24.

3. Ibid., pp. 24–25.

4. Ibid., p. 27.

5. Ibid., pp. 104 and 114.

6. Eldon Best, *The Astronomical Knowledge of the Maori, Genuine and Empirical: Including Data Concerning Their Systems of Astrogeny,*

Astrolatry, and Natural Astrology, with Notes on Certain Other Natural Phenomena, Dominion Museum Monographs, No. 3 (Wellington, New Zealand, 1922).

7. Ibid., p. 6.

8. Akerblom, *Astronomy and Navigation,* p. 13.

9. Edwin Krupp, ed., *In Search of Ancient Astronomy* (Garden City, N.Y.: Doubleday, 1977), p. 187.

10. Ibid., p. 191.

11. Ibid., pp. 149, 156, and 159.

12. Henry Wright, Department of Anthropology, University of Michigan, personal communication, 1969.

13. A. T. Olmstead, *History of the Persian Empire* (Chicago: University of Chicago Press, 1948), p. 200.

14. Ibid., p. 202.

15. Ibid., p. 452.

16. Ibid., pp. 453–456.

17. Philip Wheelwright, ed., *The Presocratics* (Indianapolis: Odyssey Press, 1966), pp. 44–52.

18. Ibid., p. 57.

19. Ibid., p. 59.

20. Ibid., p. 58.

21. Ibid., pp. 69–89.

22. Ibid., pp. 27–28.

23. Ibid., pp. 182–199.

24. Werner Heisenberg, *Physics and Beyond,* translated from the German by Arnold J. Pomerans (New York: Harper and Row, 1971), p. 241.

25. Lucretius, *The Nature of the Universe,* translated from the Latin by R. E. Latham (Baltimore: Penguin Books, 1951); excerpted in *Theories of the Universe: From Babylonian Myth to Modern Science,* edited by Milton K. Munitz (Glencoe, Ill.: The Free Press, 1957), p. 55.

26. Ibid., pp. 44 and 53.

27. Ibid., p. 45.

28. Quoted here from Wheelwright, *The Presocratics,* p. 162.

29. Ibid., p. 160.

30. Plato, *Timaeus,* translated from the Greek by H. D. P. Lee (Baltimore: Penguin Books, 1965).

31. F. M. Cornford, ed. and trans., *Plato's Cosmology: The Timaeus of Plato* (New York: Humanities Press, 1937); excerpted in Munitz, *Theories of the Universe,* p. 79.

32. Plato, *Timaeus,* pp. 45 and 47.

33. Aristotle, *On the Heavens,* translated from the Greek by W. K. C. Guthrie (Cambridge, Mass.: Harvard University Press, 1939).

34. Elias Bickerman and Morton Smith, *The Ancient History of Western Civilization* (New York: Harper and Row, 1976), p. 143.

35. A remark made by Robert Kelly in private conversation, ca. 1966.

36. Arthur Koestler, *The Sleepwalkers: A History of Man's Changing Vision of the Universe* (New York: Grosset and Dunlap, 1959), pp. 49–50.

37. Rudolf Thiel, *And There Was Light: The Discovery of the Universe,* translated from the German by Richard and Clara Winston (New York: Knopf, 1957).

38. Michael Collins, *Carrying the Fire: An Astronaut's Journey* (New York: Farrar, Straus and Giroux, 1974), p. 472.

39. Thiel, *And There Was Light.*

40. Ibid., p. 50.

41. J. L. E. Dreyer, *A History of the Planetary Systems from Thales to Kepler* (Cambridge, England: Cambridge University Press, 1905); excerpted in Munitz, *Theories of the Universe,* pp. 120–124.

42. Dante Alighieri, *Paradise,* translated from the Italian by Dorothy Sayers and Barbara Reynolds (Baltimore: Penguin Books, 1962).

CHAPTER 6

The History of Western Astronomy: The Sun in the Center

THE BULK OF THE BIOGRAPHICAL MATERIAL on Copernicus comes from Arthur Koestler, *The Sleepwalkers: A History of Man's Changing Vision of the Universe* (New York: Grosset and Dunlap, 1959).

1. Nicolaus Copernicus; quoted in Koestler, *The Sleepwalkers,* p. 202.

2. Nicolaus Copernicus, *De Revolutionibus* (1543), translated from the Latin by John F. Dobson and Selig Brodetsky, in *Occasional Notes of the Royal Astronomical Society* (London, 1947); excerpted in *Theories of the Universe: From Babylonian Myth to Modern Science,* edited by Milton K. Munitz (Glencoe, Ill.: The Free Press, 1957), pp. 158 and 162.

3. Ibid., p. 169.

4. Frances A. Yates, *Giordano Bruno and the Hermetic Tradition* (Chicago: University of Chicago Press, 1964).

5. Ibid.

6. Giordano Bruno; quoted in Rudolf Thiel, *And There Was Light: The Discovery of the Universe,* translated from the German by Richard and Clara Winston (New York: Knopf, 1957), p. 112.

7. Ibid., p. 112.

8. Giordano Bruno; quoted in Yates, *Giordano Bruno,* p. 244.

9. Ibid., p. 256.

10. Robert Kelly, "The Alchemist"; reprinted in *Alchemy: pre-Egyptian Legacy, Millennial Promise (Io,* No. 26), edited by Richard Grossinger (Richmond, Calif.: North Atlantic Books, 1979), p. 130.

11. Giordano Bruno; quoted in Thiel, *And There Was Light,* p. 113.

12. Cyrus Gordon, *Before Columbus: Links Between the Old World and Ancient America* (New York: Crown, 1971).

13. Carl O. Sauer, *Northern Mists* (Berkeley, Calif.: Turtle Island Foundation, 1968).

14. Ibid.

15. Ibid.

16. Ibid.

17. Frances A. Yates, *Theatre of the World* (Chicago: University of Chicago Press, 1969).

18. Ibid.

CHAPTER 7

The History of Western Astronomy: The Planets

THE BULK OF THE BIOGRAPHICAL MATERIAL on Kepler and Galileo comes from Arthur Koestler, *The Sleepwalkers: A History of Man's Changing Vision of the Universe* (New York: Grosset and Dunlap, 1959).

1. Johannes Kepler, Letter to Michael Maestlin; quoted in Koestler, *The Sleepwalkers,* pp. 261–262.

2. Johannes Kepler, *Harmonice Mundi* (1619); quoted in Koestler, *The Sleepwalkers,* p. 262.

3. "Unerringly impelling this dead, impregnable, uninjurable wall, and this most buoyant thing within; there swims behind it all a mass of tremendous life, only to be adequately estimated as piled wood is— by the cord; and all obedient to one volition, as the smallest insect."

(Herman Melville, *Moby Dick* (1851) [New York: New American Library, 1961], p. 327).

4. Johannes Kepler, *Mysterium Cosmographicum;* quoted in Rudolf Thiel, *And There Was Light,* translated from the German by Richard and Clara Winston (New York: Knopf, 1957), p. 116.

5. Johannes Kepler, Letter to Herwart von Hohenburg; quoted in Koestler, *The Sleepwalkers,* p. 304.

6. Johannes Kepler, *Astronomia Nova* (1609); quoted in Koestler, *The Sleepwalkers,* p. 332.

7. Johannes Kepler, *Harmonice Mundi* (1619); quoted in Thiel, *And There Was Light,* p. 295.

8. Galileo Galilei, *Sidereus Nuncius* (1610); quoted in Koestler, *The Sleepwalkers,* p. 365.

9. Johannes Kepler; quoted in Koestler, *The Sleepwalkers,* p. 367.

10. "The whole of this visible world is only an imperceptible fleck in the ample bosom of nature. No idea of ours can approach it. . . . Let man think of himself as one who has strayed into this out-of-the-way corner of nature, and, from this narrow prison in which he finds himself lodged—I mean the universe—let him learn to estimate at their just value the earth, kingdoms, cities, and himself. What is a man, in the midst of infinity?" (Blaise Pascal, *Pensées sur la Religion* (1647); quoted in Arthur O. Lovejoy, *The Great Chain of Being* [Cambridge, Mass.: Harvard University Press, 1936], p. 127.)

11. John Milton, *Paradise Lost* (1667), Book II, lines 891–893; in *John Milton: Complete Poems and Major Prose,* edited by Merritt Y. Hughes (New York: Odyssey Press, 1957), p. 253.

12. Galileo Galilei, *Dialogue Concerning the Two Chief World Systems* (1632), translated from the Latin by Stillman Drake (Berkeley: University of California Press, 1953); quoted in Koestler, *The Sleepwalkers,* p. 474.

CHAPTER 8

The History of Western Astronomy: The Gravitational Field

1. Arthur Koestler, *The Sleepwalkers: A History of Man's Changing Vision of the Universe* (New York: Grosset and Dunlap, 1959).

2. Isaac Newton, "Four Letters to Richard Bentley" (1692); reprinted in *Theories of the Universe: From Babylonian Myth to Modern*

Science, edited by Milton K. Munitz (Glencoe, Ill.: The Free Press, 1957), p. 212.

3. Ibid., p. 210.

4. Isaac Newton, *Philosophiae Naturalis Principia Mathematica* (1687), translated from the Latin by Andrew Motte (Berkeley: University of California Press, 1946); reprinted in Munitz, *Theories of the Universe,* p. 209.

5. Isaac Newton; quoted in A. Pannekoek, *A History of Astronomy* (London: Allen and Unwin, 1961), pp. 264–265.

6. Steven Weinberg, *The First Three Minutes: A Modern View of the Origin of the Universe* (New York: Basic Books, 1977), p. 149.

7. Bertrand Russell, source unavailable.

8. Isaac Newton; quoted in Pannekoek, *A History of Astronomy,* p. 273.

9. Ibid., p. 274.

10. Ibid.

11. William Blake, *Jerusalem* (1804–1820); excerpted in *The Portable Blake,* edited by Alfred Kazin (New York: Viking Press, 1946), p. 463.

12. William Blake, *The Four Zoas* (1797); excerpted in Kazin, *The Portable Blake,* p. 379.

13. Percy Bysshe Shelley, "Adonais: An Elegy on the Death of John Keats" (1821), in *Selected Poems,* edited by Edmund Blundin (London and Glasgow: Collins, 1954), pp. 441, 443, and 449.

14. Edgar Allan Poe, "Eureka" (1848), in *The Works of Edgar Allen Poe,* Volume 9 (New York: Funk and Wagnalls, 1904), p. 41.

15. Rudolf Thiel, *And There Was Light: The Discovery of the Universe,* translated from the German by Richard and Clara Winston (New York: Knopf, 1957).

16. Pierre Simon Laplace; quoted in Thiel, *And There Was Light.*

CHAPTER 9

The History of Western Astronomy: The Stars

GENERAL INFORMATION IN THIS CHAPTER comes from Rudolf Thiel, *And There Was Light,* translated from the German by Richard and Clara Winston (New York: Knopf, 1957); A. Pannekoek, *A History of Astronomy* (London: Allen and Unwin, 1961); Richard Berendzen, Richard Hart, and Daniel Seeley, *Man Discovers the Galaxies* (New

York: Science History Publications, 1976); William Graves Hoyt, *Planets X and Pluto* (Tucson: University of Arizona Press, 1980); and A. F. O'D. Alexander, *The Planet Uranus: A History of Observation, Theory, and Discovery* (New York: American Elsevier, 1965).

1. Christian Huygens; quoted in Thiel, *And There Was Light,* p. 177.

2. Walter H. Hesse, *Our Evolving Universe* (Encino, Calif.: Dickenson, 1977), pp. 68–69.

3. Christian Huygens, *Cosmotheoros* (English translation, 1698); excerpted in *Theories of the Universe: From Babylonian Myth to Modern Science,* edited by Milton K. Munitz (Glencoe, Ill.: The Free Press, 1957), p. 222.

4. Thomas Wright, *An Original Theory or New Hypothesis of the Universe* (1750); reprinted in Munitz, *Theories of the Universe,* p. 230.

5. Ibid., p. 225.

6. Immanuel Kant, *Universal Natural History and Theory of the Heavens* (1755), translated from the German by W. Hastie (Glasgow, 1900); excerpted in Munitz, *Theories of the Universe,* p. 232.

7. Ibid., p. 238.

8. Ibid., p. 243.

9. Ibid., p. 237.

10. William Herschel; quoted in Pannekoek, *A History of Astronomy,* p. 317.

11. Ibid., p. 318.

12. William Herschel; quoted in Berendzen et al., *Man Discovers the Galaxies,* p. 313.

13. William Herschel; quoted in Alexander, *The Planet Uranus,* p. 52.

14. Sir Joseph Banks; quoted in Hoyt, *Planets X and Pluto,* p. 21.

15. William Herschel; quoted in Alexander, *The Planet Uranus,* p. 59.

16. William Herschel; quoted in Thiel, *And There Was Light,* p. 237.

17. Ibid., p. 233.

18. George Adams, *Astronomical and Geographical Essays,* 5th edition, corrected and enlarged by William Jones (London: W. and S. Jones, 1803), pp. 7–9.

19. H. Wilhelm Olbers; quoted in Thiel, *And There Was Light,* p. 250.

20. Journalistic account; quoted in Thiel, *And There Was Light,* p. 272.

21. Johann Galle; quoted in Hoyt, *Planets X and Pluto,* p. 53.

22. Sir John Herschel; quoted in Berendzen et al., *Man Discovers the Galaxies,* p, 184.

23. Henry Norris Russell; quoted in Hoyt, *Planets X and Pluto,* pp. 231–232.

24. Theodore Enslin, in *Io,* No. 5 (*Doctrine of Signatures*), edited by Richard Grossinger (Ann Arbor, Mich., 1968, p. 4).

CHAPTER 10

The History of Western Astronomy: The Elements

GENERAL INFORMATION IN THIS CHAPTER comes from Rudolf Thiel, *And There Was Light,* translated from the German by Richard and Clara Winston (New York: Knopf, 1957); A. Pannekoek, *A History of Astronomy* (London: Allen and Unwin, 1961); Richard Berendzen, Richard Hart, and Daniel Seeley, *Man Discovers the Galaxies* (New York: Science History Publications, 1976); Bentley Glass, Owsei Temkin, and William L. Straus, Jr., eds., *Forerunners of Darwin* (1745–1859) (Baltimore: Johns Hopkins University Press, 1959); and Otto Struve and Velta Zebergs, *Astronomy of the Twentieth Century* (New York: Macmillan, 1962).

1. Joseph Addison, *Spectator,* No. 519; quoted in *The Great Chain of Being,* by Arthur O. Lovejoy (Cambridge, Mass.: Harvard University Press, 1936), p. 239.

2. D. H. Lawrence, *The Rainbow* [1915] (New York: Random House, 1943), pp. 416–417.

3. George Ellery Hale; quoted in Struve and Zebergs, *Astronomy of the Twentieth Century,* p. 121.

4. Ibid., p. 122.

5. Agnes Clerke; quoted in Struve and Zebergs, *Astronomy of the Twentieth Century,* p. 435.

6. Rodney Collin, *The Theory of Celestial Influence* (London: Stuart and Watkins, 1954), p. 38.

7. This subject is the basis of a long essay by the author entitled "Melville's Whale," which appears in *Io,* No. 22 (*An Olson-Melville Sourcebook,* Volume 1: *The New Found Land, or North America*), edited by Richard Grossinger (Plainfield, Vermont, 1976), pp. 97–152.

8. In a letter about *Moby Dick* to Nathaniel Hawthorne, Melville wrote: "By visible truth we mean the apprehension of the absolute condition of present things."

9. Herman Melville, *Moby Dick* [1851] (New York: New American Library, 1961), p. 360.

10. Ibid., p. 302.

CHAPTER 11

The History of Western Astronomy: The Space-Time Continuum

GENERAL INFORMATION IN THIS CHAPTER comes from Rudolf Thiel, *And There Was Light,* translated from the German by Richard and Clara Winston (New York: Knopf, 1957); Richard Berendzen, Richard Hart, and Daniel Seeley, *Man Discovers the Galaxies* (New York: Science History Publications, 1976); and Otto Struve and Velta Zebergs, *Astronomy of the Twentieth Century* (New York: Macmillan, 1962).

1. Sigmund Freud, *The Interpretation of Dreams,* translated from the German by James Strachey (New York: Avon Books, 1965), p. 313.

2. Ibid., p. 651.

3. Herman Melville, *Pierre or, The Ambiguities* [1852] (New York: New American Library, 1964); quoted in Paul Metcalf, *Genoa: A Telling of Wonders* (Highland, North Carolina: The Nantahala Foundation, 1965), p. 107.

4. Harlow Shapley; quoted in Berendzen et al., *Man Discovers the Galaxies,* p. 183.

5. Albert Einstein, *Relativity: The Special and General Theory,* translated from the German by R. W. Lawson (New York: Peter Smith, 1920); excerpted in *Theories of the Universe: From Babylonian Myth to Modern Science,* edited by Milton K. Munitz (Glencoe, Ill.: The Free Press, 1957), p. 275.

6. Philippe Le Corbeiller, "The Curvature of Space," in *The New Astronomy,* compiled by the editors of *Scientific American* (New York: Simon and Schuster, 1954), pp. 49–65.

CHAPTER 12

The History of Western Astronomy: The Atom

GENERAL INFORMATION IN THIS CHAPTER comes from Steven Weinberg, *The First Three Minutes: A Modern View of the Origin of the Universe* (New York: Basic Books, 1977); Werner Heisenberg, *Across the Frontiers,* translated from the German by Peter Heath (New York: Harper and Row, 1971); Banesh Hoffman, *The Strange Story of the Quantum* (New York: Dover Books, 1947); and Nigel Calder, *The Key to the Universe* (Baltimore: Penguin Books, 1978).

1. Niels Bohr, *Atomic Physics and the Description of Nature* (Cambridge, England: Cambridge University Press, 1934), p. 57.

2. Gell-Mann took this phrase from Joyce's *Finnegan's Wake* (1939).

3. Gary Snyder, "The Manichaeans," in *The Back Country* (New York: New Directions, 1960); reprinted in *Inside Outer Space: New Poems of the Space Age,* edited by Robert Vas Dias (Garden City, N.Y.: Doubleday, 1970), p. 291.

4. Edward Dorn, "This is the way I hear the Momentum," in *Io,* No. 6 (*Ethnoastronomy Issue*), edited by Richard Grossinger (Ann Arbor, Mich., 1969), p. 109.

5. Ibid., p. 110.

6. Émile Durkheim, *Suicide* (1897), translated by J. Spaulding and G. Simpson (New York: The Free Press, 1938).

7. P. D. Ouspensky, *In Search of the Miraculous: Fragments of an Unknown Teaching* (New York: Harcourt, Brace and World, 1949).

8. Steven Weinberg, *The First Three Minutes,* p. 154.

9. Morris Edward Opler, "Myths and Tales of the Jicarilla Apache Indians," *Memoirs of the American Folklore Society,* Volume 31 (New York, 1938), pp. 133–134.

10. Weinberg, *The First Three Minutes,* pp. 154–155.

11. Samuel Beckett, *Murphy* (New York: Grove Press, 1957), p. 1.

12. Samuel Beckett, *Waiting for Godot* (New York: Grove Press, 1954), p. 51.

13. Ibid.

CHAPTER 13

The History of Western Astronomy: Quasars, Pulsars, and Black Holes

GENERAL INFORMATION IN THIS CHAPTER comes from Richard Berendzen, Richard Hart, and Daniel Seeley, *Man Discovers the Galaxies* (New York: Science History Publications, 1976); Otto Struve and Velta Zebergs, *Astronomy of the Twentieth Century* (New York: Macmillan, 1962); *The New Astronomy*, compiled by the editors of *Scientific American* (New York: Simon and Schuster, 1954); Nigel Calder, *Violent Universe* (New York: Viking Press, 1969); and Walter Sullivan, *Black Holes: The Edge of Space, The End of Time* (Garden City, N.Y.: Doubleday, 1979).

1. The physicist Werner Heisenberg wrote: "In a darkened world no longer illuminated by light of [the] center, the 'unum, bonum, verum' . . . are scarcely more than despairing attempts to make Hell a more agreeable place to live in. This must be particularly emphasized against those who think that by spreading the civilization of science and technology even to the uttermost ends of the earth, they can furnish all the essential preconditions for a golden age. One cannot escape the Devil so easily as that." (*Across the Frontiers,* translated from the German by Peter Heath [New York: Harper and Row, 1971], p. 132.)

2. Johannes Hevelius; quoted in Richard Hinckley Allen, *Star Names: Their Lore and Meaning* [1899] (New York: Dover Books, 1963), p. 473.

3. Richard Grossinger, *The Unfinished Business of Doctor Hermes* (Plainfield, Vermont: North Atlantic Books, 1976), pp. 128–129.

4. James Bogan, "Rhapsody for McCoy Tyner," unpublished poem.

5. William H. Press; quoted in Sullivan, *Black Holes,* p. 202.

6. From the 1962 movie *Dr. Strangelove* by the American director Stanley Kubrick.

CHAPTER 14

Language, Mind,
and Astrophysics

1. John Wheeler; transcribed from verbal remarks at a conference in *The Nature of Time,* edited by Thomas Gold (Ithaca, N.Y.: Cornell University Press, 1967), p. 234.

2. R. Buckminster Fuller, "Vision 65 Summary Lecture," in *The American Scholar,* 35:2 (Spring 1966), 215.

3. Benjamin Lee Whorf, *Language, Thought, and Reality* (Cambridge, Mass.: M.I.T. Press, 1956), pp. 52–55.

4. Alexander Stephen, *Hopi Journal* (1892); excerpted in *Io,* No. 3 (Winter, 1966–1967), edited by Richard Grossinger (Ann Arbor, Mich.), pp. 39–40.

5. Whorf, *Language, Thought, and Reality,* p. 55.

6. C. S. Lewis, *Out of the Silent Planet* (New York: Macmillan, 1965), pp. 43–44.

7. Whorf, *Language, Thought, and Reality,* pp. 55–56.

8. Ibid., pp. 58–60.

9. Claude Lévi-Strauss, *The Savage Mind,* translation from the French anonymous (Chicago: University of Chicago Press, 1966), p. 59.

10. Claude Lévi-Strauss, *From Honey to Ashes,* translated from the French by John and Doreen Weightman (New York: Harper and Row, 1973), pp. 288–290.

11. Jane Roberts, *Seth Speaks: The Eternal Validity of the Soul* (Englewood Cliffs, N.J.: Prentice-Hall, 1972), p. 12.

12. Charles Stein, transcript of a discussion with Richard Grossinger, in *Alchemy: pre-Egyptian Legacy, Millennial Promise (Io,* No. 26), edited by Richard Grossinger (Richmond, Calif., 1979), pp. 220–221.

13. Wilhelm Reich, *Ether, God and Devil—Cosmic Superimposition,* translated from the German by Therese Pol (New York: Farrar, Straus and Giroux, 1972).

14. D. H. Lawrence, *The Rainbow* [1915] (New York: Random House, 1943), p. 303.

15. Robert Duncan, *The H. D. Book,* Part 2, Chapter 3, in *Io,* No. 6 (*Ethnoastronomy Issue*), edited by Richard Grossinger (Ann Arbor, Mich., 1969), p. 127.

16. Richard Grossinger, "The Star Invasion Dream," in *The Unfin-*

ished *Business of Doctor Hermes* (Plainfield, Vermont: North Atlantic Books, 1976), pp. 60–62.

CHAPTER 15
Astrology

1. For a full description and discussion of millennial science, see Richard Grossinger, "Alchemy: pre-Egyptian Legacy, Millennial Promise," in *Io*, No. 26 (*Alchemy: pre-Egyptian Legacy, Millennial Promise*), edited by Richard Grossinger (Richmond, Calif.: North Atlantic Books, 1979), pp. 177–253.

2. I am grateful to Dr. Paul Lee of the Platonic Academy in Santa Cruz, California, for an account of this episode.

3. Marc Edmund Jones, *Horary Astrology* (Berkeley, Calif.: Shambhala, 1971), p. 25.

4. Carl G. Jung, *The Interpretation of Nature and Psyche*, translated from the German by R. F. C. Hull, in *Psyche and Symbol* (Garden City, N.Y.: Doubleday, 1958).

5. C. S. Lewis, *Perelandra* (New York: Mamillan, 1965), pp. 147–148.

6. Dane Rudhyar, *The Astrology of Personality* (Garden City, N.Y.: Doubleday, 1963).

7. Michael Gauquelin, *The Cosmic Clocks: From Astrology to a Modern Science* (Chicago: Henry Regnery, 1967), p. 131.

8. Ibid.

9. I am indebted to William Lonsdale and his astrological talks in 1977 in Plainfield, Vermont, for many of the images of the zodiac. These talks have been collected in a book currently at press with the working title *The Signs of the Zodiac in the Late Twentieth Century* (Richmond, Calif.: North Atlantic Books, 1981).

10. William Sampson, *The Zodiac: A Life Epitome* [1928] (New York: ASI Publishers, 1975), p. 13.

11. Ibid.; this image is developed on pp. 245–249.

12. Ibid., pp. 360–361.

13. For the original version of this discussion, see Richard Grossinger, *The Unfinished Business of Doctor Hermes* (Plainfield, Vermont: North Atlantic Books, 1976), pp. 120–121.

14. Quoted here from Edward H. Schafer, *Pacing the Void: T'ang Approaches to the Stars* (Berkeley: University of California Press, 1977).

CHAPTER 16

The Planets: The Solar System

IN CHAPTERS 16–20, my two main sources for general information are Alan E. Nourse, *Nine Planets: Astronomy for the Space Age* (New York: Harper and Row, 1960), and Wernher von Braun and Frederick I. Ordway, *New Worlds: Discoveries from Our Solar System* (Garden City, N.Y.: Doubleday, 1979). I would also like to thank Ken Wilson of the Morrison Planetarium in San Francisco for his close reading of these chapters.

1. William Graves Hoyt, *Planets X and Pluto* (Tucson: University of Arizona Press, 1980), pp. 161–162.

2. Ibid., p. 162.

3. Alex Haley, *Roots* (Garden City, N.Y.: Doubleday, 1976).

4. Johannes Kepler, *Somnium, Sive Astronomia Lunaris* (1630), translated from the Latin by Patricia Frueh Kirkwood, in *Kepler's Dream,* edited by John Lear (Berkeley: University of California Press, 1965).

5. Johannes Kepler, *Somnium, Sive Astronomia Lunaris* (1630), translated by Ludwig Gunther; quoted in Arthur Koestler, *The Sleepwalkers: A History of Man's Changing Vision of the Universe* (New York: Grosset and Dunlap, 1959), p. 417.

6. Lear, *Kepler's Dream,* pp. 155–157; also, for an earlier version of this passage, see Richard Grossinger, *The Continents* (Los Angeles: Black Sparrow Press, 1973), pp. 49–52.

7. Richard Grossinger, *The Slag of Creation* (Plainfield, Vermont: North Atlantic Books, 1975), p. 219.

CHAPTER 17

The Planets: Mercury and Venus

1. Rudolf Hauschka, *The Nature of Substance,* translated from the German by Mary T. Richards and Marjorie Spock (London: Stuart and Watkins, 1966).

2. Svante Arrhenius, *The Destiny of the Stars* (1918); quoted in Patrick Moore, *The Planet Venus* (New York: Macmillan, 1957), pp. 108–109.

3. C. S. Lewis, *Perelandra* (New York: Macmillan, 1965), pp. 37–38.

4. I. S. Shklovskii and Carl Sagan, *Intelligent Life in the Universe* (New York: Dell, 1966), pp. 467–468.

5. Immanuel Velikovsky, *Worlds in Collision* (New York: Dell, 1965).

6. No source or citation is listed on this pamphlet.

CHAPTER 18

The Planets:
The Moon, the Earth, and Mars

1. Rudolf Hauschka, *The Nature of Substance*, translated from the German by Mary T. Richards and Marjorie Spock (London: Stuart and Watkins, 1966), pp. 193–195.

2. William Faulkner, *Absalom, Absalom!* (New York: Random House, 1936).

3. P. D. Ouspensky, *In Search of the Miraculous* (New York: Harcourt, Brace, and World, 1949). Ouspensky quotes Gurdjieff as saying the following: "The intelligence of the sun is divine. But the earth can become the same; only, of course, it is not guaranteed and the earth may die having attained nothing" (p. 25). "The process of the growth and the warming of the moon is connected with life and death on the earth. Everything living sets free at its death a certain amount of the energy that has 'animated' it; this energy, or the 'souls' of everything living—plants, animals, people—is attracted to the moon as though by a huge electromagnet, and brings to it the warmth and the life upon which its growth depends, that is, the growth of the ray of creation. In the economy of the universe, nothing is lost, and a certain energy having finished its work on one plane goes to another" (p. 85).

4. Carlos Castaneda, *Journey to Ixtlan* (New York: Simon and Schuster, 1972), p. 114.

5. G. I. Gurdjieff; quoted in Ouspensky, *In Search of the Miraculous*.

6. Richard Grossinger, *The Windy Passage from Nostalgia* (Plainfield, Vermont: North Atlantic Books, 1974), p. 67.

7. Rudolf Thiel, *And There Was Light*, translated from the German by Richard and Clara Winston (New York: Knopf, 1957), p. 64.

8. Lucretius, *The Nature of the Universe*, translated from the Latin by R. E. Latham (Baltimore: Penguin Books, 1951); quoted here from *Theories of the Universe: From Babylonian Myth to Modern Science*, edited by Milton K. Munitz (Glencoe, Ill.: The Free Press, 1957), p. 45.

9. Percival Lowell; quoted in Otto Struve and Velta Zebergs, *Astronomy of the Twentieth Century* (New York: Macmillan, 1962), pp. 143–144.

10. Father Athanasius Kircher; quoted in Thiel, *And There Was Light,* pp. 60–61.

11. Edgar Rice Burroughs, *A Princess of Mars* [1912] (New York: Ballantine Books, 1963), p. 60.

12. Quoted here from Hadley Cantril, *The Invasion from Mars: A Study in the Psychology of Panic* (Princeton, N.J.: Princeton University Press, 1940), p. 141.

CHAPTER 19

The Planets: Jupiter and Its Moons

1. Richard Grossinger, *Solar Journal: Oecological Sections* (Los Angeles: Black Sparrow Press, 1970), p. 34.

2. Ibid., pp. 34–35.

3. Ibid., pp. 35–36.

4. I. S. Shklovskii and Carl Sagan, *Intelligent Life in the Universe* (New York: Dell, 1966), pp. 471–473. For a further discussion of the moral implications of the Dyson sphere, see Gary Snyder, "Interview," conducted by Richard Grossinger and David Wilk (November 9, 1971), in *Io,* No. 25 (*Ecology and Consciousness*), edited by Richard Grossinger (Richmond, Calif., 1978), pp. 152–154.

5. Arthur C. Clarke, "A Meeting with Medusa," in *Jupiter,* edited by Carol Pohl and Frederik Pohl (New York: Ballantine Books, 1973), pp. 252 and 254.

6. Fred Haddock, "Interview" (1968), conducted by Richard Grossinger, in *Io,* No. 6 (*Ethnoastronomy Issue*), edited by Richard Grossinger (Ann Arbor, Mich., 1968), pp. 43–46.

7. Much of the new information on the Jovian moons comes from Rick Gore, "What Voyager Saw: Jupiter's Dazzling Realm," *National Geographic,* 157:1 (January 1980), 2–29. (In an interesting footnote to the images of the Jovian moons, the parapsychologist Jule Eisenbud has shown me a "photograph" generated by the psychic photographer Ted Serios on July 3, 1965. It is a virtual replica of the Voyager 2 photograph of Ganymede taken from a range of 1,200,000 km. more than a decade later. It was "shot" by Serios in the same series as a

number of Martian landscape replicas. Even assuming these photographs are "authentic" in some sense, a parapsychologist must ask: Is it foreknowledge of the broadcast image; or is it far sight of the moon itself? If it is neither of these things, then what do we have? "A shot through a knothole," wrote someone at the Jet Propulsion Laboratory in Pasadena familiar with Serios's work.)

8. Jonathan Eberhart, "Io: Charting the Fire," *Science News,* 117:16 (April 19, 1980), 251–252.

9. Haddock, "Interview."

10. Arthur C. Clarke, 2001: *A Space Odyssey* (New York: New American Library, 1968).

11. Rudolf Hauschka, *The Nature of Substance,* translated from the German by Mary T. Richards and Marjorie Spock (London: Stuart and Watkins, 1966), pp. 167–169.

CHAPTER 20

The Planets: Saturn, Uranus, Neptune, Pluto, and Their Moons

1. Galileo Galilei; quoted in Wernher von Braun and Frederick I. Ordway, *New Worlds: Discoveries from Our Solar System* (Garden City, N.Y.: Doubleday, 1979), p. 246.

2. Christian Huygens; quoted in von Braun and Ordway, *New Worlds,* p. 246.

3. James Maxwell; quoted in von Braun and Ordway, *New Worlds,* p. 247.

4. Quoted in the *San Francisco Chronicle* (Nov. 13, 1980), p. 1.

5. Ibid.

6. Quoted in the *San Francisco Chronicle* (late November 1980, date unavailable).

7. Rudolf Hauschka, *The Nature of Substance,* translated from the German by Mary T. Richards and Marjorie Spock (London: Stuart and Watkins, 1966), pp. 170–174.

8. Piers Anthony, *Macroscope* (New York: Avon Books, 1969), pp. 182–183.

9. Gerrit Lansing, "The Neptunian Character," in *Io,* No. 16 (*Earth Geography Booklet,* No. 4: *Anima Mundi*), edited by Richard Grossinger (Plainfield, Vermont, 1973), pp. 6–7.

10. Percival Lowell; quoted in William Graves Hoyt, *Planets X and Pluto* (Tucson: University of Arizona Press, 1980), p. 141.

11. Vesto Slipher; quoted in Hoyt, *Planets X and Pluto,* p. 179.

12. Clyde Tombaugh; quoted in Hoyt, *Planets X and Pluto,* p. 188.

13. Dale Cruikshank, Carl Pilcher, and David Morrison; quoted in Hoyt, *Planets X and Pluto,* p. 245.

14. Fritz Brunhübner, "Pluto" (1934); reprinted in *Io,* No. 14 (*Earth Geography Booklet,* No. 3: *Imago Mundi*), edited by Richard Grossinger (Plainfield, Vermont, 1972), pp. 281–290.

15. Oskar Seyffert, *A Dictionary of Classical Antiques* (New York: Meridian Books, 1956), p. 263.

16. Brunhübner, "Pluto."

17. Ibid.

18. James Hillman, *The Dream and the Underworld* (New York: Harper and Row, 1979), pp. 27–28.

CHAPTER 21

Flying Saucers
and Extraterrestial Life

1. Mel Noel, "UFO Lecture" (1966), *Io,* No. 4 (*Alchemy Issue*), edited by Richard Grossinger (Ann Arbor, Mich., 1967), p. 111.

2. Ibid., p. 114.

3. Lt. Col. Wendelle C. Stevens, ed., *UFO . . . Contact from the Pleiades,* Volume 1 (Phoenix, Arizona: Genesis III Productions, 1979), no page numbers.

4. The actor portraying the radical journalist Hunter Thompson says this at the end of the 1980 American film *Where the Buffalo Roam.*

5. A film made in 1977 by the American director Steven Spielberg.

6. Stevens, *UFO.*

7. Jack Finney, *The Invasion of the Body Snatchers* (New York: Dell, 1954).

8. A film made in 1977 by the American director George Lucas.

9. Jacques Vallee, *Messengers of Deception: UFO Contacts and Cults* (Berkeley, Calif.: And/Or Press, 1979).

10. Ibid.

11. Carl G. Jung, *Flying Saucers: A Modern Myth of Things Seen in the Sky,* translated from the German by R. F. C. Hull, in *Civilization in Transition* (New York: Pantheon Books, 1964), pp. 307–433.

12. Erich von Daniken, *Chariots of the Gods?* (New York: Bantam Books, 1970).

13. Robert K. G. Temple, *The Sirius Mystery* (New York: St. Martin's Press, 1976).

14. Robert Anton Wilson, *Cosmic Trigger* (Berkeley, Calif.: And/Or Press, 1977).

15. Ibid.

16. Peter Tompkins and Christopher Bird, *The Secret Life of Plants* (New York: Harper and Row, 1973), pp. 46–48.

17. Ibid., p. 49.

18. Ibid., p. 50.

CHAPTER 22

The Pop Star Cult
of the Fifties and Sixties

1. See Rob Brezsny, "Qabalistic Sex*Magic for Shortstops and Second Basemen," in *Baseball I Gave You All the Best Years of My Life,* edited by Kevin Kerrane and Richard Grossinger (Richmond, Calif.: North Atlantic Books, 1978), pp. 381–390.

2. Kenneth Anger, "Interview," conducted by *Spider Magazine* (1965); reprinted in *Io,* No. 12 (*Earth Geography Booklet,* No. 1: *Economics, Technology, and Celestial Influence*), edited by Richard Grossinger (Cape Elizabeth, Maine, 1972), pp. 24–25.

3. Tarthang Tulku, *Time, Space, and Knowledge* (Emeryville, Calif.: Dharma Publishing, 1977), p. 10.

CHAPTER 23

Science Fiction:
The Origin of Celestial Worlds

1. Claude Lévi-Strauss, *The Raw and the Cooked,* translated from the French by John and Doreen Weightman (New York: Harper and Row, 1969), p. 168.

2. Ellen Russell Emerson, *Indian Myths or Legends, Traditions, and Symbols of the Aborigines of America, Compared with Those of Other Countries Including Hindostan, Egypt, Persia, Assyria, and China* [1884] (Minneapolis: Ross and Haines, 1965), p. 337.

3. Robert Graves, *The Greek Myths* (Baltimore: Penguin Books, 1955), Volume 1, p. 49.

4. Hesiod, *The Homeric Hymns and Homerica,* translated from the Greek by H. G. Evelyn-White (Cambridge, Mass.: Harvard University Press, 1914), pp. 417–419.

5. Robert K. G. Temple, *The Sirius Mystery* (New York: St. Martin's Press, 1976), p. 207.

6. Ibid., pp. 211–212.

7. *The Gilgamesh Epic,* translated from the Sumerian by Alexander Heidel; quoted in Temple, *The Sirius Mystery,* p. 92.

8. Eric von Daniken; quoted in Temple, *The Sirius Mystery,* back cover.

9. Graves, *The Greek Myths,* Volume 1, pp. 120–121.

10. *The Egyptian Book of the Dead,* translated by E. A. Wallis Budge (New Hyde Park, N.Y.: University Books, 1960), pp. 268–278.

11. *The Tibetan Book of the Dead,* translated and edited by W. Y. Evans-Wentz (Oxford, England: Oxford University Press, 1960), pp. 145 and 162.

12. Geoffrey Ashe, *Land to the West: A Search for Irish and Other Pre-Viking Discoverers of America* (New York: Viking Press, 1962), pp. 73–143.

13. For the original version of this passage, see Richard Grossinger, *The Continents* (Los Angeles: Black Sparrow Press, 1973), pp. 102–104.

14. William Shakespeare, *The Tempest* (ca. 1609), Act I, Scene ii, line 331, in *The Complete Works of William Shakespeare,* edited by William Aldiss Wright (Garden City, N.Y.: Doubleday, 1936), p. 1304.

15. Ibid., Act V, Scene i, lines 181–182, p. 1322.

16. See Carlos Castaneda, *The Teachings of Don Juan: A Yaqui Way of Knowledge* (Berkeley: University of California Press, 1969); *A Separate Reality* (New York: Simon and Schuster, 1971); and *Journey to Ixtlan* (New York: Simon and Schuster, 1972).

17. Lucian's story is retold by Brian W. Aldiss, in *Billion Year Spree* (Garden City, N.Y.: Doubleday, 1973), pp. 58–59.

18. Aldiss, *Billion Year Spree.*

19. Ibid., p. 16.

20. Ibid., pp. 20–30.

21. Poul Anderson, *The High Crusade* (Garden City, N.Y.: Doubleday, 1960).

22. Giorgio de Santillana and Hertha von Dechend, *Hamlet's Mill: An Essay on Myth and the Frame of Time* (Boston: Gambit, 1969), pp. 86–87.

CHAPTER 24
Science Fiction:
Self and Cosmos

1. Carlos Castaneda, *A Separate Reality* (New York: Simon and Schuster, 1971), indirect quote.
2. Olaf Stapledon, *Star Maker* [1937] (New York: Dover Books, 1968), p. 262.
3. Ibid., pp. 424–425.
4. Ibid., p. 424.
5. Charles Dickens, *Great Expectations* [1861] (New York: Dodd, Mead, 1947).
6. *Star Trek,* a television series made during the 1960s, and a movie made in 1980 by the American producer Gene Rodenberry.
7. A film made in 1977 by the American director Steven Spielberg.
8. Paramahansa Yogananda, *Autobiography of a Yogi* (Los Angeles: Self Realization Fellowship, 1946), p. 316.
9. Lama Yongden, *Mipam: A Tibetan Novel* [1938] (San Francisco: Mudra, 1971), pp. 324–325.
10. Roger Zelazny, *Lord of Light* (New York: Avon Books, 1967).
11. Philip José Farmer, *The Maker of Universes* (New York: Ace Books, 1965).
12. Ibid., pp. 8–9.
13. Piers Anthony, *Macroscope* (New York: Avon Books, 1969).
14. Ibid., p. 324.
15. Ibid, p. 309.
16. Ibid., pp. 437–480.

CHAPTER 25
Science Fiction:
Jesus of Nazareth

1. Arthur C. Clarke, *Childhood's End* (New York: Ballantine Books, 1953).
2. Clarke, *Childhood's End,* p. 170.
3. C. S. Lewis, *Out of the Silent Planet* (New York: Macmillan, 1965).
4. C. S. Lewis, *Perelandra* (New York: Macmillan, 1965).

5. C. S. Lewis, *That Hideous Strength* (New York: Macmillan, 1965).

6. Lewis, *Out of the Silent Planet*, p. 32.

7. Lewis, *Perelandra*, pp. 81–82.

8. Robert Silverberg, *The Book of Skulls* (New York: Berkley, 1972), pp. 25–27.

9. Lewis, *Perelandra*, pp. 218–219.

10. Frank Herbert, *Dune* (New York: Berkley, 1965).

11. Frank Herbert, *Dune Messiah* (New York: Berkley, 1969).

12. Frank Herbert, *Children of Dune* (New York: Berkley, 1976).

13. Herbert, *Dune*, pp. 532–533.

14. Herbert, *Dune Messiah*, pp. 187–188.

15. Herbert, *Children of Dune*, p. 199.

16. Ibid., p. 119.

17. Ibid., p. 271.

18. Ibid., pp. 345–346.

19. Herbert, *Dune Messiah*, p. 78.

20. Ibid., p. 114.

21. Ibid., pp. 123–124.

22. Ibid., p. 129.

23. Ibid., p. 206.

24. Ibid., p. 237.

Bibliography

Adams, George. *Astronomical and Geographical Essays.* 5th edition. Corrected and enlarged by William Jones. London: W. and S. Jones, 1803.

Agrippa, Henry Cornelius. "Astronomical Geomancy" (1655). Reprinted in *Io,* No. 5 (*Doctrine of Signatures*), edited by Richard Grossinger. Ann Arbor, Mich., 1969.

Akerblom, Kjell. *Astronomy and Navigation in Polynesia and Micronesia: A Survey.* Ethnographic Museum of Stockholm Monograph Series, No. 14. Stockholm, 1968.

Aldiss, Brian W. *Billion Year Spree.* Garden City, N.Y.: Doubleday, 1973.

Alexander, A. F. O'D. *The Planet Uranus: A History of Observation, Theory, and Discovery.* New York: American Elsevier, 1965.

Allen, Richard Hinckley. *Star Names: Their Lore and Meaning* (1899). New York: Dover Books, 1963.

Anderson, Poul. *The High Crusade.* Garden City, N.Y.: Doubleday, 1960.

Anger, Kenneth. "Interview," conducted by *Spider Magazine* (1965). Reprinted in *Io,* No. 12 (*Earth Geography Booklet,* No. 1: *Economics, Technology, and Celestial Influence*), edited by Richard Grossinger. Cape Elizabeth, Maine, 1972.

Anthony, Piers. *Macroscope.* New York: Avon Books, 1969.

Aristotle. *On the Heavens.* Translated from the Greek by W. K. C. Guthrie. Cambridge, Mass.: Harvard University Press, 1939.

Ashe, Geoffrey. *Land to the West: A Search for Irish and Other Pre-Viking Discoverers of America.* New York: Viking Press, 1962.

Becker, Carl L. *The Heavenly City of the Eighteenth-Century Philosopher.* New Haven: Yale University Press, 1932.

Beckett, Samuel. *Murphy.* New York: Grove Press, 1957.

––––––. *Waiting for Godot.* New York: Grove Press, 1954.

Berendzen, Richard, Richard Hart, and Daniel Seeley. *Man Discovers the Galaxies.* New York: Science History Publications, 1976.

Best, Eldon. *The Astronomical Knowledge of the Maori, Genuine and Empirical: Including Data Concerning Their Systems of Astrogeny, Astrolatry, and Natural Astrology, with Notes on Certain Other Natural Phenomena.* Dominion Museum Monographs, No. 3. Wellington, New Zealand, 1922.

Bickerman, Elias, and Morton Smith. *The Ancient History of Western Civilization.* New York: Harper and Row, 1976.

Blake, William. *The Four Zoas* (1797) and *Jerusalem* (1804–1820). In *The Portable Blake,* edited by Alfred Kazin. New York: Viking Press, 1946.

Bogan, James. "Rhapsody for McCoy Tyner." Unpublished poem.

Bohr, Niels. *Atomic Physics and the Description of Nature.* Cambridge, England: Cambridge University Press, 1934.

Brezsny, Rob. "Qabalistic Sex*Magic for Shortstops and Second Basemen," In *Baseball I Gave You All the Best Years of My Life,* edited by Kevin Kerrane and Richard Grossinger. Richmond, Calif.: North Atlantic Books, 1978.

Brunhübner, Fritz. "Pluto" (1934). Reprinted in *Io,* No. 14 (*Earth Geography Booklet,* No. 3: *Imago Mundi*), edited by Richard Grossinger. Plainfield, Vermont, 1972.

Buckstaff, Ralph N. "Stars and Constellations of a Pawnee Sky Map" (1927). Reprinted in *Io,* No. 6 (*Ethnoastronomy Issue*), edited by Richard Grossinger. Ann Arbor, Mich., 1969.

Burroughs, Edgar Rice. *A Princess of Mars* (1912). New York: Ballantine Books, 1963.

Calder, Nigel. *The Key to the Universe.* Baltimore: Penguin Books, 1978.

———. *Violent Universe.* New York: Viking Press, 1969.

Cantril, Hadley. *The Invasion from Mars: A Study in the Psychology of Panic.* Princeton, N.J.: Princeton University Press, 1940.

Castaneda, Carlos. *Journey to Ixtlan.* New York: Simon and Schuster, 1972.

———. *A Separate Reality.* New York: Simon and Schuster, 1971.

———. *The Teachings of Don Juan: A Yaqui Way of Knowledge.* Berkeley: University of California Press, 1969.

The Celestial Elder's Canon of the Spirit Lights (An Ancient Chinese Book of Interior Astrology). Translated by Nathan Sivin. In *Io,* No. 4 (*Alchemy Issue,* enlarged edition), edited by Richard Grossinger. Plainfield, Vermont, 1973.

Clarke, Arthur C. *Childhood's End.* New York: Ballantine Books, 1953.

————. "A Meeting with Medusa." In *Jupiter,* edited by Carol Pohl and Frederik Pohl. New York: Ballantine Books, 1973.

————. *2001: A Space Odyssey.* New York: New American Library, 1968.

Collin, Rodney. *The Theory of Celestial Influence.* London: Stuart and Watkins, 1954.

Collins, Michael. *Carrying the Fire: An Astronaut's Journey.* New York: Farrar, Straus and Giroux, 1974.

Copernicus, Nicolaus. *De Revolutionibus* (1543). Translated from the Latin by John F. Dobson and Selig Brodetsky. In *Occasional Notes of the Royal Astronomical Society.* London, 1947.

Cornford, F. M., ed. and trans. *Plato's Cosmology: The Timaeus of Plato.* New York: Humanities Press, 1937.

Crowley, Aleister. *Magick in Theory and Practice.* New York: Castle Books, no date.

Cusanus, Nicolas. *Of Learned Ignorance* (1440). Translated from the Latin by Fr. Germain Heron. New Haven: Yale University Press, 1954.

Cushing, F. H. *Outlines of Zuni Creation Myths.* Thirteenth Annual Report of the Bureau of American Ethnology. Washington, D.C., 1896.

Dante Alighieri. *Hell.* Translated from the Italian by Dorothy Sayers. Baltimore: Penguin Books, 1949.

————. *Paradise.* Translated from the Italian by Dorothy Sayers and Barbara Reynolds. Baltimore: Penguin Books, 1962.

Davidson, Martin. *The Stars and the Mind.* London: Watts, 1947.

de Santillana, Giorgio, and Hertha von Dechend. *Hamlet's Mill: An Essay on Myth and the Frame of Time.* Boston: Gambit, 1969.

Dickens, Charles. *Great Expectations* (1861). New York: Dodd, Mead, 1947.

Dorn, Edward. *Some Business Recently Transacted in the White World.* West Newbury, Mass.: Frontier Press, 1971.

————. "This is the way I hear the Momentum." In *Io,* No. 6 (*Ethnoastronomy Issue*), edited by Richard Grossinger. Ann Arbor, Mich., 1969.

Dreyer, J. L. E. *A History of the Planetary Systems from Thales to Kepler.* Cambridge, England: Cambridge University Press, 1905.

Duncan, Robert. *The H.D. Book* (Part 2, Chapter 3). In *Io,* No. 6 (*Ethnoastronomy Issue*), edited by Richard Grossinger. Ann Arbor, Mich., 1969.

Durkheim, Émile. *Suicide* (1897). Translated by J. Spaulding and G. Simpson. New York: The Free Press, 1938.

Eberhart, Jonathan. "Io: Charting the Fire." *Science News,* 117:16 (April 19, 1980), 251–254.

Eddington, A. S. *The Expanding Universe.* Cambridge, England: Cambridge University Press, 1933.

The Egyptian Book of the Dead. Translated by E. A. Wallis Budge. New Hyde Park, N.Y.: University Books, 1960.

Einstein, Albert. *Relativity: The Special and General Theory.* Translated from the German by R. W. Lawson. New York: Peter Smith, 1920.

Emerson, Ellen Russell. *Indian Myths or Legends, Traditions, and Symbols of the Aborigines of America, Compared with Those of Other Countries Including Hindostan, Egypt, Persia, Assyria, and China* (1884). Minneapolis, Minn.: Ross and Haines, 1965.

Enslin, Theodore. "Note." In *Io,* No. 6 (*Ethnoastronomy Issue*), edited by Richard Grossinger. Ann Arbor, Mich., 1969.

Farmer, Philip José. *The Maker of Universes.* New York: Ace Books, 1965.

Faulkner, William. *Absalom, Absalom!* New York: Random House, 1936.

Finney, Jack. *The Invasion of the Body Snatchers.* New York: Dell, 1954.

Fletcher, Alice C. "Pawnee Star Lore" (1904) and "Star Cult Among the Pawnee" (1902). Reprinted in *Io,* No. 6 (*Ethnoastronomy Issue*), edited by Richard Grossinger. Ann Arbor, Mich., 1969.

Freud, Sigmund. *The Interpretation of Dreams* (1900). Translated from the German by James Strachey. New York: Avon Books, 1965.

Fulder, Stephen. *The Root of Being: Ginseng and the Pharmacology of Harmony.* London: Hutchison, 1980.

Fuller, R. Buckminster. "Vision 65 Summary Lecture." *The American Scholar,* 35:2 (Spring 1966), 206–218.

Galileo Galilei. *Dialogue Concerning the Two Chief World Systems— Ptolemaic and Copernican* (1632). Translated from the Latin by Stillman Drake. Berkeley: University of California Press, 1953.

Gauquelin, Michel. *The Cosmic Clocks: From Astrology to a Modern Science.* Chicago: Henry Regnery, 1967.

Glass, Bentley, Owsei Temkin, and William L. Straus, Jr., eds. *Forerunners of Darwin (1745–1859).* Baltimore: Johns Hopkins University Press, 1959.

Gold, Thomas, ed. *The Nature of Time.* Ithaca, N.Y.: Cornell University Press, 1967.

Gordon, Cyrus. *Before Columbus: Links Between the Old World and Ancient America.* New York: Crown, 1971.

Gore, Rick. "What Voyager Saw: Jupiter's Dazzling Realm." *National Geographic,* 157:1 (January 1980), 2–29.

Graves, Robert. *The Greek Myths.* Volume 1. Baltimore: Penguin Books, 1955.

Grossinger, Richard. *The Continents.* Los Angeles: Black Sparrow Press, 1973.

———. *The Long Body of the Dream.* Plainfield, Vermont: North Atlantic Books, 1974.

———. *Planet Medicine: From Stone-Age Shamanism to Post-Industrial Healing.* Garden City, N.Y.: Doubleday, 1980.

———. *The Planet with Blue Skies,* unpublished manuscript.

———. *The Provinces.* Plainfield, Vermont: North Atlantic Books, 1975.

———. *The Slag of Creation.* Plainfield, Vermont: North Atlantic Books, 1975.

———. *Solar Journal: Oecological Sections.* Los Angeles: Black Sparrow Press, 1970.

———. *The Unfinished Business of Doctor Hermes.* Plainfield, Vermont: North Atlantic Books, 1976.

———. *The Windy Passage from Nostalgia.* Plainfield, Vermont: North Atlantic Books, 1974.

———, ed. *Alchemy Issue (Io,* No. 4, enlarged edition). Plainfield, Vermont, 1973.

———, ed. *Alchemy: pre-Egyptian Legacy, Millennial Promise (Io,* No. 26). Richmond, Calif.: North Atlantic Books, 1979.

———, ed. *Doctrine of Signatures (Io,* No. 5). Ann Arbor, Mich., 1968.

———, ed. *Earth Geography Booklet,* No. 1 *(Io,* No. 12: *Economics, Technology, and Celestial Influence).* Cape Elizabeth, Maine, 1972.

———, ed. *Earth Geography Booklet,* No. 3 *(Io,* No. 14: *Imago Mundi).* Plainfield, Vermont, 1972.

———, ed. *Earth Geography Booklet,* No. 4 *(Io,* No. 16: *Anima Mundi).* Plainfield, Vermont, 1973.

———, ed. *Ecology and Consciousness (Io,* No. 25). Richmond, Calif.: North Atlantic Books, 1978.

———, ed. *Ethnoastronomy Issue (Io,* No. 6). Ann Arbor, Mich., 1969.

———, ed. *An Olson-Melville Sourcebook.* Volume 1 *(Io,* No. 22: *The New Found Land, or North America).* Plainfield, Vermont, 1976.

Haddock, Fred T. "Interview" (1968), conducted by Richard Grossinger. In *Io,* No. 6 *(Ethnoastronomy Issue),* edited by Richard Grossinger. Ann Arbor, Mich., 1969.

Haley, Alex. *Roots.* Garden City, N.Y.: Doubleday, 1976.

Hauschka, Rudolf. *The Nature of Substance.* Translated from the Ger-

man by Mary T. Richards and Marjorie Spock. London: Stuart and
Watkins, 1966.

Hawkins, Gerald S. *Stonehenge Decoded*. New York: Dell, 1965.

Heisenberg, Werner. *Across the Frontiers*. Translated from the German
by Peter Heath. New York: Harper and Row, 1971.

———. *Physics and Beyond*. Translated from the German by Arnold
J. Pomerans. New York: Harper and Row, 1971.

Henry, Teuira. *Ancient Tahiti*. Bernice P. Bishop Museum Bulletin,
No, 48. Honolulu: Bishop Museum Press, 1928.

Herbert, Frank. *Children of Dune*. New York: Berkley, 1976.

———. *Dune*. New York: Berkley, 1965.

———. *Dune Messiah*. New York: Berkley, 1969.

Hermes Trismegistus. *The Divine Pymander and Other Writings*. Translated by John D. Chambers (1882). New York: Samuel Weiser, 1972.

Hesiod. *The Homeric Hymns and Homerica*. Translated from the Greek
by H. G. Evelyn-White. Cambridge, Mass.: Harvard University
Press, 1914.

———. *Theogony*. Translated from the Greek by Charles Olson. In
Maximus Poems IV, V, VI, by Charles Olson. London and New York:
Cape Goliard/Grossman, 1968.

Hesse, Walter H. *Our Evolving Universe*. Encino, Calif.: Dickenson,
1977.

Hillman, James. *The Dream and the Underworld*. New York: Harper
and Row, 1979.

Hoffman, Banesh. *The Strange Story of the Quantum*. New York: Dover Books, 1947.

Hoyle, Fred. *The Nature of the Universe*. New York: Harper and Bros.,
1950.

Hoyt, William Graves. *Planets X and Pluto*. Tucson: University of
Arizona Press, 1980.

Hubble, Edwin. *The Realm of the Nebulae*. New Haven: Yale University Press, 1936.

Johnson, Francis R. *Astronomical Thought in Renaissance England*.
Baltimore: Johns Hopkins University Press, 1937.

Jones, Marc Edmund. *Horary Astrology*. Berkeley, Calif.: Shambhala,
1971.

Jung, Carl G. *Flying Saucers: A Modern Myth of Things Seen in the
Skies*. Translated from the German by R. F. C. Hull. In *Civilization
in Transition*. New York: Pantheon Books, 1964.

———. *The Interpretation of Nature and Psyche*. Translated from the
German by R. F. C. Hull. In *Psyche and Symbol*. Garden City, N.Y.:
Doubleday, 1958.

Kant, Immanuel. *Universal Natural History and Theory of the Heavens* (1755). Translated from the German by W. Hastie (1900). Glasgow, 1900.

Kelly, Edward. "The Theatre of Terrestrial Astronomy" (ca. 1590). Reprinted in *Io,* No. 26 (*Alchemy: pre-Egyptian Legacy, Millennial Promise*), edited by Richard Grossinger. Richmond, Calif.: North Atlantic Books, 1979.

Kelly, Robert. "The Alchemist" (1961). Reprinted in *Io,* No. 26 (*Alchemy: pre-Egyptian Legacy, Millennial Promise*), edited by Richard Grossinger. Richmond, Calif.: North Atlantic Books, 1979.

———. "Re: The Occult" (1963). Reprinted in *Io,* No. 6 (*Ethnoastronomy Issue*), edited by Richard Grossinger. Ann Arbor, Mich., 1969.

Kepler, Johannes. *Somnium, Sive Astronomia Lunaris* (1630). Translated from the Latin by Patricia Frueh Kirkwood. In *Kepler's Dream,* edited by John Lear. Berkeley: University of California Press, 1965.

Kerrane, Kevin, and Richard Grossinger, eds. *Baseball I Gave You All the Best Years of My Life* (*Io,* No. 24). Richmond, Calif.: North Atlantic Books, 1978.

Koestler, Arthur. *The Sleepwalkers: A History of Man's Changing Vision of the Universe.* New York: Grosset and Dunlap, 1959.

Krupp, Edwin, ed. *In Search of Ancient Astronomy.* Garden City, N.Y.: Doubleday, 1977.

Lansing, Gerrit. "The Neptunian Character" (1963). Reprinted in *Io,* No. 16 (*Earth Geography Booklet, No. 4: Anima Mundi*), edited by Richard Grossinger. Plainfield, Vermont, 1973.

Lawrence, D. H. *The Rainbow* (1915). New York: Random House, 1943.

Leach, Maria. *The Beginning.* New York: Funk and Wagnalls, 1956.

Le Corbeiller, Phillipe. "The Curvature of Space." In *The New Astronomy,* compiled by the editors of *Scientific American.* New York: Simon and Schuster, 1954.

Lévi-Strauss, Claude. *From Honey to Ashes.* Translated from the French by John and Doreen Weightman. New York: Harper and Row, 1973.

———. *The Raw and the Cooked.* Translated from the French by John and Doreen Weightman. New York: Harper and Row, 1969.

———. *The Savage Mind.* Translation from the French anonymous. Chicago: University of Chicago Press, 1966.

Lewis, C. S. *Out of the Silent Planet.* New York: Macmillan, 1965.

———. *Perelandra.* New York: Macmillan, 1965.

———. *That Hideous Strength.* New York: Macmillan, 1965.

Lonsdale, William. *The Signs of the Zodiac in the Late Twentieth Century*. Richmond, Calif.: North Atlantic Books, 1981.

———, ed. *Star Rhythms* (*Io,* No. 27). Richmond, Calif.: North Atlantic Books, 1979.

Lorusso, Julia, and Joel Glick. *Healing Stoned: The Therapeutic Use of Gems and Minerals*. Albuquerque, New Mexico: Brotherhood of Life, 1976.

Lovejoy, Arthur O. *The Great Chain of Being*. Cambridge, Mass.: Harvard University Press, 1936.

Lucretius. *The Nature of the Universe*. Translated from the Latin by R. E. Latham. Baltimore: Penguin Books, 1951.

Marshack, Alexander. *The Roots of Civilization: The Cognitive Beginnings of Man's First Art, Symbol and Notation*. New York: McGraw-Hill, 1972.

Meeks, John. "Johannes Kepler and the Philosophical Defence of Astrology." In *Io,* No. 27 (*Star Rhythms*), edited by William Lonsdale. Richmond, Calif.: North Atlantic Books, 1979.

Melville, Herman. *Moby Dick* (1851). New York: New American Library, 1961.

———. *Pierre or, The Ambiguities* (1852). New York: New American Library, 1964.

Metcalf, Paul. *Genoa: A Telling of Wonders*. Highland, North Carolina: The Nantahala Foundation, 1965.

Milton, John. *Paradise Lost* (1667). In *John Milton: Complete Poems and Major Prose,* edited by Merritt Y. Hughes. New York: Odyssey Press, 1957.

Moore, Patrick. *The Planet Venus*. New York: Macmillan, 1957.

Moran, Hugh A., and David H. Kelley. *The Alphabet and the Ancient Calendar Signs*. Palo Alto, Calif.: Daily Press, 1969.

Munitz, Milton K, ed. *Theories of the Universe: From Babylonian Myth to Modern Science*. Glencoe, Ill.: The Free Press, 1957.

Nelson, E. W. *The Eskimo About Bering Strait*. 18th Annual Report of the Bureau of American Ethnology. Washington, D.C., 1899.

The New Astronomy. Compiled by the editors of *Scientific American*. New York: Simon and Schuster, 1954.

Newton, Isaac. *Philosophiae Naturalis Principia Mathematica* (1687). Translated from the Latin by Andrew Motte. Berkeley: University of California Press, 1946.

The Nihongi. Translated from the Japanese by W. G. Alston. London: Allen and Unwin, 1956.

Noel, Mel. "UFO Lecture"(1966). In *Io,* No. 4 (*Alchemy Issue,* enlarged edition), edited by Richard Grossinger. Plainfield, Vermont, 1973.

Nourse, Alan E. *Nine Planets: Astronomy for the Space Age.* New York: Harper and Row, 1960.

Olmstead, A. T. *History of the Persian Empire.* Chicago: University of Chicago Press, 1948.

Olson, Charles. *Maximus Poems IV, V, VI.* London and New York: Cape Goliard/Grossman, 1968.

————. *The Maximus Poems, Volume 3.* New York: Grossman, 1975.

Ophiel. *The Art and Practice of Astral Projection.* St. Paul, Minn.: The Gnostic Institute, 1961.

Opler, Morris Edward. "Myths and Tales of the Jicarilla Apache Indians." *Memoirs of the American Folklore Institute,* Volume 31. New York, 1938.

Ouspensky, P. D. *In Search of the Miraculous: Fragments of an Unknown Teaching.* New York: Harcourt, Brace and World, 1949.

Pannekoek, A. *A History of Astronomy.* London: Allen and Unwin, 1961.

Paracelsus. *The Hermetic and Alchemical Writings of Paracelsus the Great.* Translated from the Latin by A. E. Waite. London: James Elliott, 1894.

Plato. *Timaeus.* Translated from the Greek by H. D. P. Lee. Baltimore: Penguin Books, 1965.

Poe, Edgar Allen. "Eureka." In *The Works of Edgar Allen Poe,* Volume 9. New York: Funk and Wagnalls, 1904.

The Popul Vuh. Translated from the Mayan into Spanish by Adrián Recinos. English translation from the Spanish by Deli Goetz and Sylvanus G. Morley. Norman, Oklahoma: University of Oklahoma Press, 1950.

Ptolemy. *The Almagest.* Translated from the Greek by R. C. Taliaferro. Chicago: Encyclopedia Britannica, 1952.

Reich, Wilhelm. *Ether, God and Devil—Cosmic Superimposition.* Translated from the German by Therese Pol. New York: Farrar, Straus and Giroux, 1972.

Roberts, Jane. *Seth Speaks: The Eternal Validity of the Soul.* Englewood Cliffs, N.J.: Prentice-Hall, 1972.

Rudhyar, Dane. *The Astrology of Personality.* Garden City, N.Y.: Doubleday, 1963.

Sagan, Carl. "Interview," conducted by Richard Grossinger (January 23, 1972). In *Io,* No. 14 (*Earth Geography Booklet,* No. 3: *Imago Mundi*), edited by Richard Grossinger. Plainfield, Vermont, 1972.

Sampson, William. *The Zodiac: A Life Epitome* (1928). New York: ASI Publishers, 1975.

Sauer, Carl O. *The Early Spanish Main.* Berkeley: University of California Press, 1966.

————. *Northern Mists.* Berkeley, Calif.; Turtle Island Foundation, 1968.

Schafer, Edward H. *Pacing the Void: T'ang Approaches to the Stars.* Berkeley: University of California Press, 1977.

Seyffert, Oskar. *A Dictionary of Classical Antiques.* New York: Meridian Books, 1956.

Shakespeare, William. *The Tempest* (ca. 1609). In *The Complete Works of William Shakespeare,* edited by William Aldiss Wright. Garden City, N.Y.: Doubleday, 1936.

Shaw, George Bernard. *Back to Methuselah.* New York: Brentano's, 1921.

Shelley, Percy Bysse. "Adonais: An Elegy on the Death of John Keats" (1821). In *Selected Poems,* edited by Edmund Blunden. London and Glasgow: Collins, 1954.

Shklovskii, I. S., and Carl Sagan. *Intelligent Life in the Universe.* New York: Dell, 1966.

Silverberg, Robert. *The Book of Skulls.* New York: Berkley, 1972.

Singer, Dorothea Waley. *Giordano Bruno: His Life and Thought with an Annotated Translation of His Work, On the Infinite Universe and Worlds.* New York: Abelard-Schuman, 1950.

Singer, Isaac Bashevis. *The Family Moskat.* Translated from the Yiddish by A. H. Gross. New York: Knopf, 1950.

————. *Shosha.* Translated from the Yiddish by Joseph Singer. New York: Fawcett, 1978.

Snyder, Gary. *The Back Country.* New York: New Directions, 1960.

————. "Interview," conducted by Richard Grossinger and David Wilk (November 9, 1971). In *Io,* No. 25 (*Ecology and Consciousness*), edited by Richard Grossinger. Richmond, Calif.: North Atlantic Books, 1978.

Sproul, Barbara C. *Primal Myths: Creating the World.* New York: Harper and Row, 1979.

Stapledon, Olaf. *Star Maker* (1937). New York: Dover Books, 1968.

Stephen, Alexander. *Hopi Journal* (1892). Excerpted in *Io,* No. 3 (Winter 1966–1967), edited by Richard Grossinger. Ann Arbor, Mich.

Stevens, Lt. Col. Wendelle C., ed. *UFO . . . Contact from the Pleiades.* Phoenix, Arizona: Genesis III Productions, 1979.

Strehlow, T. G. H. *Aranda Traditions.* Melbourne: University of Melbourne Press, 1947.

Struve, Otto, and Velta Zebergs. *Astronomy of the Twentieth Century.* New York: Macmillan, 1962.

Sullivan, Walter. *Black Holes: The Edge of Space, The End of Time.* Garden City, N.Y.: Doubleday, 1979.

Tarthang Tulku. *Time, Space, and Knowledge.* Emeryville, Calif.: Dharma Pulishing, 1977.

Teilhard de Chardin, Pierre. *The Phenomenon of Man.* Translated from the French by Bernard Wall. New York: Harper and Row, 1959.

Temple, Robert K. G. *The Sirius Mystery.* New York: St. Martin's Press, 1976.

Thiel, Rudolf. *And There Was Light: The Discovery of the Universe.* Translated from the German by Richard and Clara Winston. New York: Knopf, 1957.

Thorne, Kip S. "Gravitational Collapse." *Scientific American,* 217:5 (November 1967), 88–98.

The Tibetan Book of the Dead. Translated and edited by W. Y. Evans-Wentz. Oxford, Engand: Oxford Univerity Press,1960.

Tompkins, Peter, and Christopher Bird. *The Secret Life of Plants.* New York: Harper and Row, 1973.

Vallee, Jacques. *Messengers of Deception: UFO Contacts and Cults.* Berkeley, Calif.: And/Or Press, 1979.

Vas Dias, Robert, ed. *Inside Outer Space: New Poems of the Space Age.* Garden City, N.Y.: Doubleday, 1970.

Velikovsky, Immanuel. *Worlds in Collision.* New York: Dell, 1965.

von Braun, Wernher, and Frederick I. Ordway. *New Worlds: Discoveries from Our Solar System.* Garden City, N.Y.: Doubleday, 1979.

von Daniken, Erich. *Chariots of the Gods?* New York: Bantam Books, 1970.

Waite, A. E. *The Holy Kabbalah.* New Hyde Park, N.Y.: University Books, 1960.

Weinberg, Steven. *The First Three Minutes: A Modern View of the Origin of the Universe.* New York: Basic Books, 1977.

Wheelwright, Philip, ed. *The Presocratics.* Indianapolis: Odyssey Press, 1966.

Whitehead, Alfred North. *Process and Reality.* Toronto: Macmillan, 1929.

Whorf, Benjamin Lee. *Language, Thought, and Reality.* Cambridge, Mass.: M.I.T. Press, 1956.

Wilson, Robert Anton. *Cosmic Trigger.* Berkeley, Calif.: And/Or Press, 1977.

Yates, Frances A. *Giordano Bruno and the Hermetic Tradition.* Chicago: University of Chicago Press, 1964.

————. *Theatre of the World.* Chicago: University of Chicago Press, 1969.

Yogananda, Paramahansa. *Autobiography of a Yogi.* Los Angeles: Self-Realization Fellowship, 1946.

Yongden, Lama. *Mipam: A Tibetan Novel* (1938). San Francisco: Mudra, 1971.

Zelazny, Roger. *Lord of Light.* New York: Avon Books, 1967.

Index